GROWING PAINS
IN
LATIN AMERICA

GROWING PAINS
IN
LATIN AMERICA

An Economic Growth Framework as Applied to Brazil, Colombia, Costa Rica, Mexico, and Peru

Liliana Rojas-Suarez

Editor

CENTER FOR GLOBAL DEVELOPMENT
Washington, D.C.

Growing Pains in Latin America: An Economic Growth Framework
as Applied to Brazil, Colombia, Costa Rica, Mexico, and Peru
may be ordered from:
BROOKINGS INSTITUTION PRESS
c/o HFS, P.O. Box 50370, Baltimore, MD 21211-4370
Tel.: 800/537-5487; 410/516-6956; Fax: 410/516-6998; Internet: www.brookings.edu

Library of Congress Cataloging-in-Publication data
Growing pains in Latin America : an economic growth framework as applied to Brazil,
Colombia, Costa Rica, Mexico, and Peru / Liliana Rojas-Suarez, editor.
    p.   cm.
Includes bibliographical references and index.
ISBN 978-1-933286-31-0 (pbk. : alk. paper)
1. Latin America—Economic policy. 2. Latin America—Economic conditions.
I. Rojas-Suarez, Liliana. II. Title.
HC125.G69 2009
338.98—dc22   2009015007

9 8 7 6 5 4 3 2 1

The paper used in this publication meets minimum requirements of the
American National Standard for Information Sciences—Permanence of Paper
for Printed Library Materials: ANSI Z39.48-1992.

Typeset in Adobe Garamond

Composition by Circle Graphics
Columbia, Maryland

Printed by Versa Press
East Peoria, Illinois

Center
for Global
Development

The Center for Global Development is an independent, nonprofit policy research organization dedicated to reducing global poverty and inequality and to making globalization work for the poor. Through a combination of research and strategic outreach, the Center actively engages policymakers and the public to influence the policies of the United States, other rich countries, and such institutions as the World Bank, the IMF, and the World Trade Organization to improve the economic and social development prospects in poor countries. The Center's Board of Directors bears overall responsibility for the Center and includes distinguished leaders of nongovernmental organizations, former officials, business executives, and some of the world's leading scholars of development. The Center receives advice on its research and policy programs from the Board and from an Advisory Group that comprises respected development specialists and advocates.

The Center's president works with the Board, the Advisory Group, and the Center's senior staff in setting the research and program priorities and approves all formal publications. The Center is supported by an initial significant financial contribution from Edward W. Scott Jr. and by funding from philanthropic foundations and other organizations.

Contents

Preface

At the Center for Global Development, we aim to generate ideas and policy recommendations that will improve the well-being of the majority of the poor and near poor in the developing world. Of all regions, Latin America stands out for the variety of development models its governments have implemented over the last half century, often inspired by the region's leading thinkers and often following deep economic crises that reversed short-term advances in income growth and poverty alleviation. This varied experience—and the lessons it offers to policymakers in Latin America and to rich-world development institutions—are therefore of particular interest to us at the Center.

In this book, Liliana Rojas-Suarez and other close students of Latin American economies ask key questions: Why, despite the impressive macroeconomic and other reforms of the last two decades, have most countries in the region been unable to generate higher growth on a sustained basis? What can individual countries do to help reforms deliver growth and a better distribution of its benefits? How should policymakers respond to the increasing discontent among large segments of the population with the results of market-based reforms?

This book stands firmly in the spirit of the development policy approach most recently propounded in the 2008 report of the Spence Commission on Growth: every country needs to forge its own practical approaches by adhering to just a few principles. Policymakers should eschew any universal model and instead adapt and continuously adjust policies to their own country's circumstances. *Growing Pains in Latin America* also complements an earlier CGD book on Latin America, *Fair Growth*, in which my coauthors and I suggest a set of tools from which policymakers can pick and choose depending on country conditions. The emphasis on fairness as a fundamental objective in *Fair Growth* is reinforced in this new book, which argues that growth cannot be sustained if its gains are not broadly shared by the population.

To address country-specific questions while benefiting from lessons at the regional level, Liliana Rojas-Suarez with Simon Johnson (an MIT professor and a member of CGD's advisory group) organized a task force including the region's top scholars and economic policy practitioners to consider the impact of policy reforms on growth, poverty, and inequality. The group developed a region-specific framework, building on three characteristics that distinguish Latin America from other regions: It is the most democratic, it is the most financially open (more so than East Asia, which is more open on trade), and it has the greatest economic and social inequality. This framework is then applied in case studies of Brazil, Colombia, Costa Rica, Mexico, and Peru.

The resulting country-specific recommendations are a good example of the kind of work reflected in the Center's tag line: independent research and practical ideas for global prosperity. The book provides proposals that, while innovative and challenging, are also doable. Their practicality reflects broad consultation in each country with private sector representatives, academicians and other analysts, and the highest-level policymakers.

The book's applied analytical framework will interest not only policymakers in Latin America but also development policy experts in the rich world, including the bilateral aid agencies (especially those in the United States, Canada, and Spain, which take special interest in Latin America) and in multilateral financial institutions (particularly the World Bank, the International Monetary Fund, and the Inter-American Development Bank). Policy advisors in these institutions face the challenge to strike an appropriate balance between consistency, on the one hand, and the need to adapt to country circumstances, on the other.

The framework sets forth five necessary foundations for sustainable growth: secure property rights, sufficiently equal opportunities for broad segments of the population, sufficient economic and political competition, macroeconomic stability, and broad sharing among the population of the benefits from growth. By identifying which of these foundations needs to be strengthened in a specific country, policymakers can craft country-specific approaches to alleviate the most critical constraints. For example, Mexico is particularly constrained by inadequate economic competition in key sectors, such as telecommunications. Enhancing the powers and autonomy of the Federal Competition Commission, creating specialized courts in competition and regulatory cases, and other efforts to improve an adequate implementation of antimonopoly laws are therefore important. Peru faces challenges in the broad sharing of the benefits of growth. Deep reforms of the state and the political system are essential so that legislation can be passed, and policies executed, that will reach the poor, especially in the rural areas. Colombia, on the other hand, has an activist judicial system that intervenes excessively in granting social benefits to the population, to the point that the government faces unremitting fiscal pressures. To help support macro-economic stability, a key policy recommendation in Colombia involves creating incentives for the Constitutional Court to curtail its ability to tamper with economic matters.

While the analyses and recommendations differ significantly from country to country, they build on a common framework, and the reader will find some important commonalities. For example, there is an emphasis in all case studies on the political logic of incremental reform. Even when a major revamping is seen as essential, the studies call for pilot efforts designed to build constituencies that will support reform. Another common thread is the attention given to institutional strengthening, from reform of congresses, political parties, and electoral processes to the overhaul of judiciary systems and of mechanisms and institutions that determine competition policies.

I hope that this brief introduction will whet the reader's appetite to dig into the rest of this important book and that the framework and the case studies it contains will provide the basis for lively and informed policy discussions—and better policy design—in Latin America itself and in the rich-world development institutions that aim to support Latin America's drive to overcome its growing pains and enter a period of sustained, and shared, growth.

We are grateful to the Open Society Institute, the Tinker Foundation, and the Andean Finance Corporation, whose support helped make this book possible.

Nancy Birdsall
President
Center for Global Development

Washington, D.C.
May 2009

Acknowledgments

Thorais book is the result of the collective efforts of many people, and I am grateful to all of them. I would first like to acknowledge the members of the CGD Task Force for their hard work in developing the analytical framework that is presented in chapter 2: Mauricio Cárdenas, Javier Corrales, José de Gregorio, Augusto de la Torre, Eduardo Lora, Carmen Pagés, Ernesto Stein, Kurt Weyland, and Jeromin Zettelmeyer. My special gratitude goes to Simon Johnson who was my cochair in this endeavor and a continuous source of ideas, enthusiasm, and leadership.

I am also deeply grateful to all of the authors of the case studies presented in chapters 3 to 7. They were all willing to apply the CGD framework to their own country experiences, organize discussion seminars, and write more drafts than they care to remember. Their contributions are the heart and soul of this book.

Many commentators and discussants contributed significantly to improve the quality of this project. At different stages, the book benefited from comments and suggestions by Mauricio Cárdenas, Miguel Castilla, Eduardo Fernandez Arias, Francis Fukuyama, David Holiday, Eduardo Lora, Nora Lustig, Guillermo Perry, Nancy Truitt, George Vickers, John Williamson, and participants in workshops organized by the Economic Commission for Latin America and the Caribbean in Santiago, the Universidad Pacífico in Lima, the

Fundaçao Getúlio Vargas in Rio de Janeiro, the Costa Rican Investment Promotion Agency in San José, El Colegio de México, and the Centro de Investigación y Docencia Económica in México City.

I owe my gratitude to many CGD colleagues. Leda Basombrío, Carlos Gallardo, Verónica Gonzales, Emily Paul, and Sebastián Sotelo provided insightful research assistant support. As always, our communications team played an integral role in helping to bring this project to conclusion. Thank you very much to Lawrence MacDonald, Heather Haines, and John Osterman for their invaluable support. With his usual proficiency, Michael Treadway brilliantly edited the entire manuscript.

This book would not have seen the light of day without the support of the Open Society Institute, the Tinker Foundation, and the Andean Finance Corporation. Their intellectual engagement throughout this research project is greatly appreciated. Thanks are also due to El Fondo de Cultura Económica, a most prestigious editorial house in Latin America. Thanks to the Fondo's endorsement, the Spanish version of this book is already in the process of being published.

Finally, my deep thanks to Nancy Birdsall for her continuous support of this project, her comments and suggestions throughout the endeavor, and her deep belief that Latin America can indeed rise to its potential.

1

Introduction: A New Approach to Growth in Latin America

LILIANA ROJAS-SUAREZ

Before the eruption of the severe global economic and financial crisis in the third quarter of 2008, *all* of the countries of Latin America had been experiencing positive rates of economic growth for five consecutive years. Five years of continuous growth, with no economic or financial crisis, might sound unimpressive in a global context where even a deep crisis in East Asia in the late 1990s produced only a relatively short pause in an otherwise sustained path of rapid growth. But for Latin America, long known as the world's most economically and financially volatile region,[1] five consecutive years of generalized positive growth was an achievement not seen since the 1970s.

Although recent growth in GDP has indeed been high by the region's standards over the last three decades, growth in income per capita has not been suffi-

The author would like to acknowledge the very helpful comments and suggestions of Nancy Birdsall, Mauricio Cárdenas, Augusto de la Torre, Francis Fukuyama, Eduardo Lora, and participants in workshops organized by the Economic Commission for Latin America and the Caribbean, the Universidad Pacífico in Lima, the Fundação Getúlio Vargas in Rio de Janeiro, the Costa Rican Investment Promotion Agency in San Jose, and El Colegio de México and the Centro de Investigación y Docencia Económica in Mexico City. The excellent research assistance and valuable comments of Leda Basombrio were essential contributions. The errors that remain are, of course, the author's sole responsibility.

1. See, for example, Hausmann and Gavin (1996), Caballero (2001), and Guidotti, Rojas-Suarez, and Zahler (2004).

Table 1. *Income per Capita in Latin America Relative to the Most Developed Countries, 1975–2005*
Percent[a]

Country	1975	1980	1985	1990	1995	2000	2005
Argentina	−36.0	−40.1	−55.0	−63.5	−55.2	−58.0	−58.8
Bolivia	−85.2	−87.2	−90.4	−91.5	−91.1	−91.7	−91.9
Brazil	−68.3	−65.8	−70.3	−73.3	−72.4	−75.0	−75.7
Chile	−79.7	−76.4	−79.0	−76.1	−68.3	−68.3	−65.3
Colombia	−76.0	−75.6	−77.4	−76.8	−75.3	−79.4	−78.9
Costa Rica	−67.3	−67.6	−74.0	−73.9	−71.2	−71.6	−70.6
Dominican Republic	−78.6	−78.5	−80.6	−81.9	−80.5	−76.9	−76.3
Ecuador	−82.5	−82.8	−85.2	−86.6	−86.8	na	−87.5
El Salvador	−73.3	−78.9	−83.8	−85.0	−82.6	−84.0	−84.8
Guatemala	−80.6	−80.0	−84.6	−85.9	−85.2	−85.9	−86.8
Honduras	−85.8	−85.1	−87.3	−88.6	−88.8	−90.0	−90.1
Mexico	−63.0	−59.9	−63.7	−68.0	−69.9	−68.1	−69.0
Nicaragua	−65.6	−79.1	−82.7	−88.4	−89.3	−89.2	−89.4
Panama	−73.4	−75.4	−75.9	−81.2	−78.8	−79.0	−78.0
Paraguay	−81.7	−76.8	−80.0	−81.5	−81.4	−85.8	−86.6
Peru	−69.6	−73.8	−78.2	−84.1	−81.9	−83.6	−82.6
Uruguay	−64.5	−62.1	−72.1	−70.8	−67.4	−69.5	−71.2
Venezuela	−58.0	−64.9	−73.3	−76.0	−75.7	−80.0	−80.9

Sources: United Nations Development Program and World Bank, *World Development Indicators 2007*.
a. Values are expressed as the percentage deviation of the indicated country's income per capita from average income per capita (in current dollars at purchasing power parity) among countries in the top decile on a social subindex of the Human Development Index (see footnote 5 in the text).
na = not available.

ciently rapid to reduce Latin America's income gap relative to other world regions.[2] Indeed, with a few exceptions, the gaps are widening not only relative to the most advanced economies, but also with respect to other emerging market economies at similar levels of social development.[3] Table 1 traces the evolution of this gap for individual Latin American countries relative to the world's most advanced economies in terms of social development (for example, on indicators of health and education). Table 2 does the same relative to countries whose social

2. See Birdsall et al. (2008) for an estimation of the gap in income per capita between developing regions and the countries of the Organization for Economic Cooperation and Development (OECD). Taking a long-term view, Pritchett (1997) established that the income gap between rich and poor countries widened significantly in the last century.
3. See Edwards (2007) for a historical analysis of economic growth in Latin America and a comparison with other emerging economies. The papers in Edwards et al. (2007) present analyses of economic growth from a historical perspective for a number of Latin American countries.

Table 2. *Income per Capita in Latin America Relative to Countries with Similar Social Development, 1975–2005*
Percent[a]

Country	1975	1980	1985	1990	1995	2000	2005
Argentina	18.4	5.1	−16.0	−36.3	−28.0	−34.1	−37.2
Bolivia	−6.5	−11.0	−27.6	−35.0	−34.2	−38.2	−44.2
Brazil	−32.6	−17.8	−3.0	3.8	15.3	18.1	15.4
Chile	−19.4	−8.2	−14.2	−5.9	6.1	7.5	12.7
Colombia	−29.3	−14.5	2.0	37.7	−5.9	−12.6	−18.6
Costa Rica	−39.5	−43.1	−51.5	−54.5	−53.6	−55.5	−55.2
Dominican Republic	−36.7	−24.6	−12.5	7.1	−25.5	−2.2	−8.4
Ecuador	−48.5	−39.7	−32.9	−20.3	−49.6	n.a.	−51.6
El Salvador	−43.1	−49.3	−47.1	−41.8	−27.2	−24.5	−27.8
Guatemala	22.9	38.9	16.0	7.4	9.7	4.8	−9.5
Honduras	−10.4	3.6	−3.8	−13.3	−17.0	−25.7	−32.0
Mexico	46.4	55.5	48.5	26.1	0.9	8.3	0.7
Nicaragua	−26.9	−49.8	−43.7	−54.9	−55.2	−48.9	−49.5
Panama	5.4	−4.4	−1.6	−26.0	−29.1	−28.8	−28.8
Paraguay	−27.6	−10.0	−18.3	−27.1	−37.7	−51.8	−56.5
Peru	−10.1	−8.2	−1.5	−6.0	−31.1	−30.6	−32.7
Uruguay	−34.2	−33.5	−48.0	−49.1	−47.6	−52.2	−56.2
Venezuela	66.3	36.4	9.0	−5.6	−18.6	−32.2	−37.9

Sources: United Nations Development Program and World Bank, *World Development Indicators, 2007*.
a. Values are expressed as the percentage deviation of the indicated country's income per capita from average income per capita (in current dollars at purchasing power parity) among a group of countries in the same decile on the social subindex of the Human Development Index as the indicated country (see footnote 5 in the text).
n.a. = not available.

development, as defined by the social components of the Human Development Index (HDI), is similar to that in Latin America.[4]

With the exception of Chile (and a slight improvement in the Dominican Republic), the last three decades have seen the gap in income per capita widen in all Latin American countries relative to the most advanced economies (the numbers in table 1 are increasingly negative). Some countries (such as Bolivia,

4. The HDI has three components, the first relating to health, the second to education, and the third to income. To group countries by level of social development, here we construct a social subindex formed by the first two components (equally weighted). The economies in the advanced group are those in the top decile of the constructed social subindex. Countries are categorized as having a similar degree of social development if they belong to the same decile of the social subindex (calculated for every year reported in table 2). In both tables, each number indicates the percentage difference between the indicated country's income per capita and the average income per capita of the relevant group of countries. Thus, a negative number implies that that country's income per capita is below the average income of the relevant comparator.

Ecuador, Honduras, and Nicaragua) have seen a steady deterioration in relative income per capita, while in others (such as Argentina, Brazil, Colombia, El Salvador, and Uruguay) some improvement took place in the early to mid-1990s but was later reversed. Of all the countries considered, Nicaragua's income per capita relative to that in advanced countries has deteriorated the most (by 24 percentage points) over the entire period, closely followed by Argentina and Venezuela (almost 23 percentage points in each).

A similar result emerges when we compare the Latin American countries with their peers in terms of social development. By 2005 only Chile and Brazil had achieved incomes per capita above the corresponding average for this group of countries. A closer look at individual countries reveals even more disappointing results. For example, Mexico, which by the mid-1970s had an income per capita well above the average for its peers, has been steadily losing ground ever since, so that by 2005 it had fallen back close to the average. Even more dramatic are the cases of Argentina, Guatemala, Panama, and Venezuela. In all these countries income per capita relative to their peers' average has declined significantly, from an above-average position in 1975 to a sharply below-average position by 2005.

The deep international financial crisis taking place at this writing raises increasing concerns about the sustainability of even the modest recent gains. Views differ on the relative ability of Latin America to weather the current crisis. Some analysts remain optimistic, arguing that the reforms and policy decisions of the last decade and a half in many countries in the region will help them absorb the adverse shock without drastic disruptions. These analysts recognize that Latin America will not be insulated from the global crisis and that the region's growth is almost certain to slow significantly, but they argue that the reforms and policies of the 1990s and early 2000s,[5] especially those that contributed to improved macroeconomic indicators—better fiscal positions, lower external debt, and large accumulations of foreign exchange reserves—will spare most countries in the region from a major crisis in their own economies.[6]

Other analysts paint a more skeptical picture. Without denying the benefits of the reform efforts, they argue that when properly measured to control for cyclical fluctuations (such as a temporary increase in fiscal revenue in many countries, due to temporary increases in commodity prices), fiscal stances in the region are not particularly strong on a permanent, "structural" basis. Indeed, the argument is that

---

5. Improved financial regulatory and supervisory frameworks, freer trade arrangements, and improvements in macroeconomic management are cited as key reforms.

6. Not even the most optimistic analysts, however, saw all countries in the same favorable position as of late 2008. For example, the majority of experts (optimistic and otherwise) viewed the weak fundamentals in Venezuela as self-generated problems that had been building long before the current international crisis.

in many countries, fiscal vulnerabilities to external shocks in the period 2003–07 remained practically as large as in the 1990s.[7] In this view the possibility of a serious crisis in some Latin American countries cannot be ruled out.[8] Despite these diverging views, experts find common ground in recognizing the enormous differences among countries in the region. For example, even analysts with opposite points of view regarding Latin America's prospects as a region praise Chile's domestic growth capacity as well as its ability to face sudden adverse external shocks. At the other extreme, a large majority of analysts do not find Venezuela's current economic, social, and political conditions to be conducive to sustainable growth.

This book tackles a complex issue that looks far beyond the current crisis: What can Latin American countries do to accelerate economic growth while ensuring its sustainability? The issue is complex because many countries in the region have already undertaken a significant number of reforms and policies in a variety of areas, yet positive results, in terms of rapid and sustained economic growth, have remained for the most part elusive. An additional, and perhaps more important, complexity arises from the fact that large segments of the population, deeply discontented with the results of market-based policies, are unwilling to support additional efforts at reform. As will become evident throughout the book, "inaction," "paralysis," and "impasse" are terms frequently used to describe the current state of problems facing a number of countries in the region.

A large and growing literature, briefly discussed below, already examines both the theory of growth acceleration and the diagnostics of growth in developing countries; there are, in addition, a host of empirical studies of Latin America as a whole and of specific countries.[9] What, then, does this book add to the discussion? In a nutshell, this book's major contribution is twofold. First, it approaches the subject matter by developing a straightforward and simple analytical framework *especially designed for Latin America.* Second, and related to the first, it uses this framework to advance specific policy recommendations for a

7. Among supporters of this view are Izquierdo, Ottonello, and Talvi (2008).

8. Supporters of this view argue that the favorable external environment that Latin America faced from 2003 through mid-2008—unprecedentedly high export prices, rapid growth in the global economy, and benign financial conditions—explain the lion's share of the region's improved economic performance during that period. These external conditions led to an "endogenous" increase in fiscal revenue and thus to an improvement in reported fiscal balances. However, as the external environment deteriorates, fiscal revenue will decrease, exposing the underlying fiscal vulnerabilities. These vulnerabilities are viewed as particularly important in those countries where increases in fiscal expenditure (financed by temporary increases in revenue) focused mostly on current rather than investment spending. Some of the case studies in this book raise this issue as a serious problem that weakened the foundations for growth.

9. See, for example, Birdsall et al. (2008), where the emphasis is on policies to achieve growth and improved equity in Latin America.

sample of countries on how to proceed with the reform process, taking into account the *specific local conditions (economic, social, and political) that character-ize those countries.*

The book is the collective effort of many authors, all of them experts in the eco-nomics and politics of growth in Latin America. Some of them participated in the Task Force that constructed the book's analytical framework, which is summa-rized below and fully presented in chapter 2. Although simple and intuitive, the framework is capable of dealing with the many ingredients that shape the process of economic growth in the region: from the macroeconomic stance to the quality of political institutions; from productivity to income inequality; from advances in democracy to popular resistance to further reform. Most important, the frame-work specifically avoids applying a straitjacket to the region's problems: the partic-ularities and uniqueness of each country are highlighted wherever the framework is applied.

A second group of experts formed teams to apply the framework to each of five countries in the region: Brazil, Colombia, Costa Rica, Mexico, and Peru. Large and small, and representing various parts of the region, these five countries clearly illustrate both the commonalities and the sharp differences within Latin America. The resulting analyses are presented in chapters 3 through 7. In each chapter the emphasis is on specific recommendations for policy actions that are *doable,* in both the economic and the political sense.

The rest of this introductory chapter has four sections. The first discusses some essential economic and political characteristics that distinguish Latin Amer-ica from other world regions and that had to be taken into account in construct-ing the analytical framework. The next section walks the reader through the main elements of the analytical framework, emphasizing the differences between it and other approaches in the literature. The third section summarizes the most impor-tant results obtained from applying the framework to the five countries listed above. The chapter concludes with some final thoughts about the relevance of the lessons from the country studies for other countries and the region as a whole.

What Is Different about Latin America? Some Key Stylized Facts

In creating an analytical framework tailored specifically to Latin America, we con-sidered it important to identify some key features that distinguish the region from other developing areas of the world. Of course, Latin America shares many com-mon features with the rest of the developing world, and countries within Latin America differ significantly among themselves, but three particular features are shared by most countries in the region. The first is of an economic nature: Latin America is the most financially open of the world's developing regions. The sec-ond is political: Latin America is also the world's most democratic developing region. The third encompasses both the economic and the social arenas: Latin

America is also the world region with the greatest economic and social inequality. This section will explore all three of these features and the constraints they impose on achieving sustained growth.

Latin America Is the World's Most Financially Open Developing Region

Using data from the Annual Reports on Exchange Arrangements and Exchange Restrictions published by the International Monetary Fund, a recent study (Chinn and Ito, 2007) constructed an annual index of financial openness for 181 countries.[10] Table 3 presents regional averages of Chinn and Ito's index covering the period 1970–2006. Like the country-specific indices on which they are based, the regional indices take higher values the more open the region is to cross-border capital transactions.

Two things are worth noting about the indices for Latin America. The first is that since the mid-1990s, the region as a whole has embarked on a continuous process of liberalization of the capital account: the financial openness index has steadily increased. The second, perhaps more important, is that except for the industrial countries (the "high-income" group in the table), Latin America is the most financially open region in the world. By 2006 Latin America's index of financial openness was more than double that of the Middle East and North Africa and triple that of Eastern Europe and Central Asia. All other regions lagged significantly behind. Moreover, this trend in the regional index is quite representative of the situation in most individual countries in Latin America.[11] With the exception of Argentina, Honduras, and Venezuela, all of the Latin American countries have increased the openness of their capital accounts since the mid-1990s.[12]

Why might a highly open capital account deserve special consideration when designing an analytical framework for understanding economic growth in the region? To answer this question it is important to recall that the *impetus* toward capital account liberalization in Latin America started in the late 1980s and early

10. The study used principal components methodology to construct the index from the first standardized principal component of the following variables: the presence of multiple exchange rates, restrictions on current account transactions, restrictions on capital account transactions (in turn divided into thirteen categories reflecting restrictions on different types of financial instruments, activities, and financial entities), and requirements that exporters surrender the foreign exchange proceeds of their exports. Given the methodology used, the index lacks a predefined range of values.

11. The median index among Latin American countries is even higher than the regional average in all years since 1995. Using the median rather than the average does not, however, change the ranking of regions on the financial openness measure.

12. By 1995 Argentina had one of the most open capital accounts of the region (as did Peru). However, following the eruption of that country's financial crisis in the early 2000s, a number of restrictions were imposed on cross-border transactions. By 2006 Argentina had become the most financially closed country in the region.

Table 3. *Financial Openness Indices by World Region, 1970–2006*[a]

Region	1970	1975	1980	1985	1990	1995	2000	2005	2006
East Asia and Pacific	-0.44	-0.41	-0.32	0.01	-0.05	0.32	-0.17	-0.10	-0.13
Eastern Europe and Central Asia	-1.13	-1.13	-1.80	-1.46	-0.78	-0.09	-0.30	0.36	0.46
High-income countries	0.21	0.30	0.61	0.85	1.08	1.73	1.70	1.85	1.85
Latin America and Caribbean	0.13	-0.06	-0.13	-0.96	-0.78	0.17	0.66	1.06	1.03
Latin America	0.21	-0.01	0.07	-1.09	-0.82	0.36	1.09	1.58	1.54
Caribbean	-0.22	-0.36	-1.35	-0.71	-0.71	-0.17	-0.13	0.12	0.11
Middle East and North Africa	-1.03	-0.78	-0.47	-0.35	-0.38	0.06	0.33	0.51	0.60
South Asia	-1.05	-1.23	-1.24	-1.00	-1.00	-0.16	-0.47	-0.42	-0.42
Sub-Saharan Africa	-0.93	-0.63	-0.90	-0.83	-0.86	-0.55	-0.52	-0.47	-0.53

Source: Chinn and Ito (2007).

a. A higher value indicates greater openness of the capital account.

1990s, when, in an attempt to end the region's "paralysis" following the 1982 debt crisis, the Brady Plan first allowed for the *securitization* of governments' external liabilities (beginning with Mexico in 1989). Since then, a highly liquid market for international bonds and other securities issued by Latin American countries and other emerging markets has developed, displacing unsecuritized bank lending as a major source of portfolio flows to the region.[13] Two basic differences between international bank loans and international bonds are central for understanding the importance of international securitization for the achievement of sustained growth in Latin America.[14] The first is that a well-developed secondary market exists for international bonds, but not for unsecuritized bank loans. The second is that, in contrast to the institutions now well established for negotiations involving internationally active banks, concerted arrangements among bondholders to deal with collective action problems in cases of sovereign default are still in the early stages. (The inclusion of collective action clauses in recent bond issues by a number of emerging market countries is a step in the right direction.) Together, the existence of this well-developed secondary market for international bonds and the absence of pre-established arrangements for default on those bonds imply that any news affecting investors' perceptions of a country's capacity or willingness to service its debt is reflected immediately in bond prices. A key measure here is the spread between the yield on bonds issued by a given country and the yield on U.S. Treasury bonds of corresponding maturity. If both bonds are denominated in U.S. dollars (or in euros, as some recent bond issues have been), both are free of exchange rate risk, and the spread between them can be considered a measure of country or default risk.

When investors' perceptions of risk deteriorate significantly for a given country, the yield and the spread on that country's external debt increase sharply, raising the country's financing costs and severely limiting the availability of external sources of finance. Because an increase in spreads constitutes a market signal of an increase in country risk, it quickly translates into higher domestic interest rates.[15] Since the financial system in most Latin American countries is dominated by

---

13. This process started with the emergence of the Brady bonds. We explicitly emphasize here the process of international securitization rather than the more general process of financial integration. Although the latter is often the focus when describing the depth of countries' participation in a wide variety of cross-border flows as well as structural processes (such as the role of foreign banks in the region), countries in the region increasingly resort to the international bond market, rather than more traditional loans from international banks, to meet their financing needs.

14. I previously presented this argument in Rojas-Suarez (2003) to explain the importance of international securitization for the conduct of monetary policy in Latin America.

15. For evidence on how country risk affects domestic interest rates in Latin America, see Rojas-Suarez and Sotelo (2007).

short-term instruments, domestic interest rates at all maturities are affected, with adverse implications for investment and economic growth.[16]

This transmission mechanism from international to domestic interest rates is reinforced by two additional characteristics of the region's economies. The first is that national saving rates remain very low, and local financial markets remain underdeveloped. Indeed, a recent study by Gutierrez (2007) shows that the average national saving rate for the region has remained at the low (20 to 23 percent) levels observed in the 1960s and 1970s. In this context, domestic sources of finance are very limited and thus cannot offset the severe curtailment of external financing that often follows a deterioration in investors' perceptions of creditworthiness.[17] Thus, in countries with "freer" capital accounts, domestic interest rates are likely to be strongly influenced by international perceptions of country creditworthiness.

The second characteristic is that in sharp contrast to its financial openness, most of Latin America (with the notable exception of most of the Central American countries) remains relatively closed in terms of trade flows, and exports remain highly concentrated in commodities.[18] Although the situation has improved in recent years, standard indicators of trade openness, such as the simple ratio of

---

16. In addition, the experience in Latin America shows that, to a large extent, private debt can be considered a contingent liability of the government. Historically, when the private sector has encountered severe difficulties, governments have often "absorbed" its liabilities into the public sector accounts. Thus, it is difficult in practice for investors to distinguish between government risk and private sector risk. In this context, adverse shocks increase the perceived risk of liabilities issued by *both* the public and the private sector. This, of course, pushes interest rates up.

17. At any point in time, a country's given stock of debt (both domestic and external) becomes riskier if the country's capacity to roll over maturing debt decreases sharply. If, following a sudden adverse shock, increased perceptions of default lead to an increase in spreads and a severe reduction in market access, the country's overall capacity to service its existing obligations decreases. Domestic interest rates increase as domestic holders of the country's liabilities perceive the deterioration of borrowers' capacity to meet payments. Notice that this transmission mechanism from default risk to domestic interest rates operates even if the country has a flexible exchange rate system. The reason is that even a large depreciation of the currency cannot generate external resources quickly enough to offset a sharp decrease in the availability of foreign sources of finance. This problem, of course, is greater, the larger the stock of debt and the shorter the maturity structure. It is precisely the recognition of limited capacity of domestic financial and capital markets, in the context of an open capital account, that has encouraged a number of governments in recent years to accumulate large stocks of international reserves and to buy back expensive external debt and issue new debt at better terms (lower rates and longer maturities).

18. Some extreme examples of commodity concentration are Ecuador and Venezuela; on the other hand, countries like Brazil, Costa Rica, El Salvador, and Mexico are diversifying significantly into manufacturing exports, which now exceed 50 percent of all goods exports in those countries. A critical problem associated with the lack of trade diversification is the high volatility that characterizes commodity prices. The events of 2007–08 provide the most recent example. After dramatically increasing during 2007 and the first half of 2008, prices of a number of commodities exported by the region fell sharply in the second half of 2008. At this writing, it is still too early to assess whether the region will face a significant adverse terms of trade shock, compounding the adverse effects of the capital account shock associated with the U.S.-led global financial crisis.

exports plus imports to GDP, show that the region has a long way to go to reach the level of openness of East Asia and the industrial countries.[19] This characteristic implies that export flows have very limited scope to mitigate the lack of financing resulting from a severe adverse shock to the capital account, even if that shock is accompanied by a significant depreciation of local currencies.

The message, therefore, is clear: to maximize the growth benefits from access to international capital markets, liberalized capital accounts need to be accompanied by macroeconomic stability *at all times*. Any deviation will quickly result in reduced perceptions of the country's creditworthiness, a wider spread on the country's external debt, and higher domestic interest rates, to the detriment of investment and growth.

Increased access to international capital markets is by no means a panacea, however; it also brings potential risks. As the current international financial crisis has demonstrated, sudden reversals of capital inflows *not related to local developments* can dramatically affect countries' growth prospects. Self-insurance policies, such as the accumulation of foreign exchange reserves and fiscal stabilization funds that build up resources during economic booms to be used in harder times, need to be important components of a strong macroeconomic agenda.

In spite of the current deep uncertainties in the international capital markets, there are no indications that Latin America will cease to be the world's most financially open developing region any time in the foreseeable future.[20] As mentioned above, very low national saving rates imply that most countries in the region need external sources of funding to finance growth, and this need will remain in place long after the current turmoil ends.[21] Hence countries in the region simply cannot

19. Of course, the region has made important progress in reducing tariffs and (in some countries) nontariff restrictions, and these policies help explain the sustained improvement in the region's trade openness in the last two decades. The point advanced here, however, is that Latin America needs a large, dynamic, competitive, and diversified export sector to help offset the severe impact on growth from a deterioration in investors' perceptions of countries' creditworthiness. This is also the reason why we prefer the simple ratio of exports plus imports to GDP as the appropriate indicator of trade openness, rather than other more sophisticated indicators such as that advanced by Sachs and Warner (1995) and updated by Wacziarg and Horn Welch (2003). Those indicators do not include some key factors that restrict trade openness, such as the lack of adequate infrastructure and bureaucratic customs arrangements (see Birdsall and Rojas-Suarez 2004).

20. In recent years external government liabilities of a number of countries in Latin America have achieved investment grade ratings by international credit rating agencies. Some other governments have placed the achievement of investment grade among their top priorities. Moreover, a number of countries in the region depend on inflows from foreign direct investment, and this type of flow is quite sensitive to the extent to which cross-border flows (including transfers of dividend payments) are free of encumbrances. In this context it is safe to state that open capital accounts are "here to stay" in most countries in the region.

21. Most studies of the relationship between saving and growth conclude that sustained growth is needed for saving rates to increase (although some others, such as Gutierrez, 2007, find an ambiguous causality). Thus, increasing saving rates in Latin America is a long-term process. In the short and the medium term, savings from abroad, in the form of foreign direct investment and portfolio flows, are perceived by policymakers in many countries in the region as an engine of growth.

afford important deviations from macroeconomic stability (including the establishment of self-insurance policies to deal with the vagaries of international capital markets) if they are to achieve sustained growth. Add to this the region's
repeated experience with hyperinflation and financial crises in the 1980s and
1990s, and it becomes apparent that Latin America has less room for macroeconomic *mistakes* than most other regions.[22]

Latin America Is the Developing World's Most Democratic Region

The indices of the strength of democratic institutions often used in country comparisons differ in their definition and measurement of democracy. Some indices
adopt a relatively narrow concept, focusing on the rights of citizens to vote freely
in fair elections between competing parties; others define democracy more broadly,
to include indicators of the degree of "participation" and the development of a
"political culture," where citizens actively and freely take part in public debate, elect
representatives, and join political parties. Two of the best known indices of democracy are those of Freedom House and the Economist Intelligence Unit (EIU); the
latter is the broadest measure of democracy among those that cover the majority of
countries in the world.[23]

Despite their differences in definition and measurement, Latin America stands
out on both these measures as the most democratic region in the developing
world. Table 4 presents regional averages of two indices from Freedom House's
democracy survey: the index of civil liberties and the index of political rights.[24]
The former is a narrow index that concentrates on the freedom and rights of
expression, belief, and association of individuals, as well as on respect for the rule
of law. The latter is a broader index that seeks to measure the quality of the electoral process, the strength of political pluralism and participation, and the ability
of the government to implement democratically based decisions. Both indices
range from 0 to 7, where a lower number indicates fewer or smaller obstacles to
democracy. Data for both indices are available for the period 1973–2008.

Both indices show that democracy has improved significantly in Latin America from the 1970s to the present, and that as of 2008 Latin America enjoyed the

22. Although this volume does not focus on the issue of volatility (which would require an entire
book in itself), macroeconomic stability (broadly defined to include self-insurance policies) is essential to contain the high volatility of economic and financial indicators that have characterized the
region and that have been shown to be detrimental to growth. Indeed, unless countries have adequate
macroeconomic and self-insurance policies, freer capital markets can lead to higher economic and
financial volatility.

23. In addition, the United Nations Development Program (UNDP) has an "Electoral Democracy Index," but it is constructed for Latin America only and therefore does not allow for regional
comparisons. Also, the index has been calculated only until 2002. In any case, the results for individual countries on the UNDP index are similar to those of the other indices considered here.

24. The regional averages are simple averages. The classification of countries by region follows
the World Bank's *World Development Indicators*.

Table 4. *Political and Civil Rights Indices by World Region, 1973–2008*[a]

Region	1973	1975	1980	1985	1990	1995	2000	2005	2008
Political rights[b]									
East Asia and Pacific	5.2	5.3	4.8	4.5	4.3	3.7	3.9	3.6	4.0
Eastern Europe and Central Asia	6.0	5.9	5.9	6.0	4.0	4.0	3.8	3.8	3.7
High-income countries	2.9	2.7	2.5	2.2	2.1	1.9	1.9	1.8	1.8
Latin America and Caribbean	4.1	4.4	3.8	3.0	2.5	2.7	2.3	2.3	2.2
Latin America	4.1	4.4	3.9	2.9	2.4	2.9	2.3	2.3	2.3
Caribbean	4.3	4.6	3.6	3.2	2.7	2.4	2.3	2.4	2.2
Middle East and North Africa	5.8	5.8	5.4	5.4	5.7	5.8	5.8	5.9	5.8
South Asia	3.3	3.9	4.4	4.3	4.8	4.6	4.6	4.6	4.9
Sub-Saharan Africa	5.8	5.9	5.5	5.9	5.6	4.6	4.5	4.3	4.3
Civil liberties[c]									
East Asia and Pacific	4.9	4.8	4.6	4.7	4.4	4.0	3.8	3.5	3.5
Eastern Europe and Central Asia	6.0	5.9	5.5	6.0	3.9	4.2	4.0	3.4	3.3
High-income countries	2.8	2.6	2.4	2.5	2.1	2.1	2.1	1.8	1.7
Latin America and Caribbean	3.5	4.0	3.7	3.2	2.9	3.0	2.7	2.7	2.6
Latin America	3.3	3.7	3.8	3.2	2.9	3.3	2.8	2.6	2.6
Caribbean	4.3	5.2	3.7	3.4	2.7	2.6	2.5	2.7	2.5
Middle East and North Africa	5.5	5.5	5.4	5.6	5.2	5.9	5.5	5.2	5.2
South Asia	3.9	4.0	4.3	4.8	4.8	5.3	4.8	4.5	4.4
Sub-Saharan Africa	5.3	5.2	5.5	5.8	5.1	4.6	4.4	4.0	4.0

Source: Freedom House.

a. Each index ranges from 0 to 7, where 7 indicates the greatest weakness.

b. Component indices measure the strength of the electoral process, political pluralism, and participation, and the functioning of government.

c. Component indices measure the strength of freedom of expression and belief, associational and organizational rights, rule of law, and personal autonomy and individual rights.

highest average level of democracy of any developing region.[25] Of course, the central reason behind the improvement is the abandonment of military regimes in Latin America. Whereas in the 1970s twelve of the eighteen Latin American countries had a military government, there has been none in the region since 1991.[26] Other indices, such as the new EIU Index of Democracy, first estimated for 2006, confirm this result and provide additional information about the *depth* of democracy. For example, although the region as a whole ranks high for the quality of its electoral processes, the extent of political participation and the development of a political culture are still very low. As stated by Kekic (2007) of the EIU, a democratic political culture requires not only a politically engaged citizenry, but also the willingness of losing parties to accept the judgment of the voters and allow the peaceful transfer of power. The EIU gives very low ratings on political culture to Bolivia, Ecuador, and Nicaragua.

A similar result is obtained by the Polity IV Index, which assesses in a single index both the quality of democracy and the autocratic authority of governments.[27] Once again, Latin America as a whole stands out as the most democratic region in the developing world. By this index, Ecuador and Venezuela had the lowest scores in the region in 2007, and Costa Rica and Uruguay the highest. The differences in scores indicate that not all democracies are alike in Latin America— a fact that will become evident in the country analyses presented in chapters 3 through 7.

Like its financial openness, Latin America's overall improvement on these indicators of democracy needs to be taken into account when designing an analytical framework linking policy reforms and growth. Some economic reforms might not be sustainable, even if they deliver growth, if a significant proportion of voters do not share in the benefits of that growth or in other reform outcomes. A disgruntled population can use its newly acquired voice to express its dissatisfaction through the electoral process, the legislature, and other forums. As has been widely documented (see, for example, Birdsall, de la Torre, and Menezes, 2008), there is an important (and in some countries increasing) risk of a backlash against "markets" and, by association, against the market-based policies and reforms imple-

25. Over the last thirty years, Latin America and South Asia have traded places in terms of the degree of democracy. In the 1970s South Asia was the most democratic region in the developing world, according to the Freedom House political rights index, but democracy has been weakening in almost every country in this region since then, and South Asia is now the second-least democratic region of the developing world, after the Middle East and North Africa.

26. General Augusto Pinochet led the last military government in Latin America, that of Chile, which ended in 1991.

27. The Polity Index (an index of the Polity Project; www.systemicpeace.org/polity/polity4.htm) consists of six measures that document key qualities of executive recruitment, constraints on executive authority, and political competition. It also documents changes in the institutionalized qualities of governing authorities.

mented in the region since the early 1990s. Chapter 2 discusses the relationship between democracy and the reform process in more detail.[28]

Indeed, results for 2007 from Latinobarómetro, a well-known regional survey of public opinion, indicate that about half of Latin Americans are dissatisfied with the "workings of the market system."[29] As figure 1 shows, public support for free markets has been declining since the late 1990s. Dissatisfied citizens want greater government intervention in economic activities and increased social protections. The declining trend in the number of "market supporters" is consistent with the fact that over the last few years, several "leftist" presidential candidates have scored victories over candidates more openly supportive of market-based policies.[30]

As of this writing, the deep financial and economic crisis in the United States and other industrial countries is exacerbating concerns about a potential backlash against market-based reforms and policies in Latin America. Although the crisis has appropriately underscored the need for major changes in the global financial regulatory and supervisory framework, a number of politicians (and some analysts) around the world are using the opportunity presented by the crisis to fulminate against markets in general. Thus, rather than advancing proposals on how to improve the functioning of markets through adequate regulation and counter-cyclical policies, these critics often focus solely on increased restrictions on the scope of market activity.

Given the global economic slowdown that is accompanying the financial crisis, Latin America is likely to face, over the next few years, a significant deterioration of the international environment in which it operates, affecting both financial and trade flows. The result may be a sharp reduction in economic growth in the region, a rise in unemployment, and thus the potential for even further popular discontent with market-based reform. This discontent runs the risk of inducing not only an abandonment of the future reform agenda, but even a reversal of policies and reforms already in place that have helped generate growth. Under these circumstances, time is of the essence, to allow the gains from growth—however modest—to be shared more broadly among the population. These considerations

28. Przeworski, Alvarez, and Cheibub (2000) is an important reference in the literature on the relationship between democracy and development.

29. Corporación Latinobarómetro (2007).

30. Three of the five countries where Latinobarómetro finds increased support for democracy— Bolivia, Ecuador, and Nicaragua—are precisely the countries that the EIU index classifies as least democratic (together with Venezuela). This apparent paradox can be resolved by noting that the low score obtained by these three countries on the EIU index is due to very low levels of "political culture" (as described in the text). However, the current presidents of Bolivia, Ecuador, and Nicaragua represent constituencies that have previously felt excluded from government, which explains the improved support for a democratic system highlighted by the Latinobarómetro survey.

Figure 1. *Popular Support for the Market Economy in Latin America*

Percent[a]

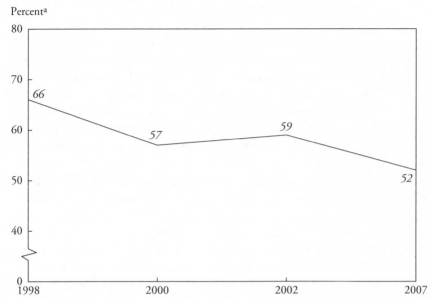

Source: Latinobarómetro.

a. Percent of individuals surveyed who said they "support" or "strongly support" the functioning of markets in their country.

therefore need to be an essential ingredient in any framework dealing with the linkage between reform and growth in Latin America.

Latin America Has the World's Most Unequal Distribution of Income

As figure 4 in chapter 2 shows, since the 1960s Latin America has persistently had one of the most unequal distributions of income of all world regions. By 2005 it had taken first place away from Sub-Saharan Africa on income inequality as measured by the Gini coefficient.

The causes of this inequality, and the reasons why it has persisted as a deep, structural phenomenon, are subjects of an ongoing academic debate. Explanations run from historical institutional arrangements at the country level; to ethnic, structural, and cultural diversity; to the socioeconomic characteristics of ancestors at the household level.[31] Many authors have also extensively analyzed the relationship between income inequality and economic growth in developing

31. Some important references on the causes of persistent inequality are Alesina et al. (2003), Fearon (2003), and Putterman and Weil (2008).

countries,[32] identifying the channels through which inequality might adversely affect growth.[33] As Birdsall (2007) concluded in a recent review of the literature, the evidence suggests that inequality above some level is likely to reduce growth. This finding by itself should be a matter of concern for policymakers in Latin America, given its highly unequal income distribution.[34]

There are also a number of reasons why high income inequality, together with inequality of land ownership and education, might act to deter the implementation of pro-growth *reforms and policies.* A prominent study in the Latin American context is that by Birdsall et al. (2008). These issues will be developed further in chapter 2. Suffice it to emphasize here that, among all regions in the developing world, *Latin America has the unique combination of being the most democratic and the most unequal.* Together these two characteristics affect the policymaking process, influence policy options, and contribute to explaining the results presented in figure 1. No analytical framework aimed at achieving sustainable growth in Latin America can ignore these characteristics.

The Analytical Framework

This section briefly explains the main elements of this study's analytical framework, described further in chapter 2, and the differences between it and alternative methodologies used to analyze the linkages between policy reforms and growth. What sets the analytical framework presented in this book apart from others in the literature is that it incorporates the three features, discussed above, that distinguish Latin America from its developing peers: its greater financial openness, its greater strength of democratic institutions, and its greater inequality. This framework is called the CGD Framework in later chapters.

Although the framework as designed is Latin America–specific, that does not imply that it does not build on previous analysis. Indeed, it is important to recognize its most important commonality with other contributions to the literature, namely, the search for "foundations for economic growth." As in a number of

32. Some literature reviews include Birdsall (2007) and World Bank (2006).

33. For example, Birdsall (2007) concludes from a review of the literature that high inequality affects growth in developing countries through three channels: through the interaction of inequality with imperfect markets for capital and information; by discouraging the evolution of economic and political institutions consistent with accountable governments (which in turn allow for an adequate investment climate); and by undermining the civic and social life that sustains effective collective decision making. An example of the last channel is the correlation observed between income inequality and criminal violence (see, for example, Fajnzylber, Lederman, and Loayza, 2002).

34. Citing a study by Cornia, Addison, and Kiiski (2004), Birdsall cautiously (because of serious measurement problems) identifies a Gini coefficient of 0.45 as a threshold level. As the Gini coefficient increases, the effect of income distribution on growth is reportedly more negative. As figure 4 in chapter 2 shows, the regional income Gini coefficient for Latin America has fluctuated around 0.5.

other analyses, the fundamental question asked here is the following: What are the main foundations that encourage the accumulation of physical and human capital as well as improvements in productivity—the three factors that lead to economic growth?[35]

Researchers have tried to answer this question using several different approaches.[36] For example, the identification of growth foundations is at the core of the recent literature on *institutions.* Following North (1991), institutions can be broadly defined as the set of formal rules and informal conventions that shape incentives for economic and social behavior. In this literature, pro-growth institutions are those that ensure an adequate structure of rewards for those who provide labor and capital; that secure property rights and contract enforcement for all economic agents; that promote competition as a means of providing incentives for productivity growth; and that allow for relatively equal access to economic opportunity.[37] From a policy perspective, the question is then how to achieve such outcomes. As noted by Zettelmeyer (2006), a number of analysts as well as multilateral organizations have answered this question by promoting what are now known as "second generation" reforms, so called because they complement the reforms encompassed in the earlier "Washington consensus" (Williamson, 1990) by addressing the deep constraints to growth more directly. An example of this type of reform is reform of the judicial system, whose inefficiencies and lack of independence from political pressures in many countries undermine respect for the rule of law, the enforcement of contracts, and the protection of property rights. At the empirical level, indicators of the "quality of institutions" are being used to assess the impact of institutions on economic growth.[38] Quite often the analysis takes the form of cross-country regressions of the type pioneered by Barro (1991).[39]

More recently, the approach developed by Hausmann, Rodrik, and Velasco (2005) addresses the issue of growth foundations by arguing that countries need to identify the *single most important binding constraint* on economic growth and then focus on removing it. These authors argue that the presence of multiple distortions in an economy makes it very difficult, if not impossible, to identify and avoid the unintended adverse consequences of a reform agenda covering a variety

---

35. José De Gregorio, a member of the Task Force that produced the analytical framework, poses the question in this precise form in De Gregorio (2005).

36. A good survey of the literature on reforms and growth as applied to Latin America is contained in Zettelmeyer (2006).

37. See, for example, Acemoglu, Johnson, and Robinson (2005) and Easterly and Levine (2003).

38. Commonly used indicators of institutional quality are the governance indicators constructed by Kaufmann, Kraay, and Mastruzzi (2008), the measures of economic freedom developed by the Cato Institute and the Heritage Foundation, and the measures of political institutional quality from the Polity IV database by Marshall and Jaggers (2007).

39. See, for example, De Gregorio and Lee (2003) and Blyde and Fernandez-Arias (2004).

of economic areas: reforming one area might worsen existing distortions in other areas. The authors ground their alternative framework in economic first principles, arguing that capital accumulation and entrepreneurship are the basic *foundations* for economic growth. Thus, insufficient investment, and therefore low economic activity, can be explained by either financing costs that are too high or private returns to investment that are too low. From these two *potential* restrictions on growth, the authors build a "decision tree" for policymakers.

For example, if the problem is a high cost of finance, it could be due to either insufficient access to international capital markets or insufficient local sources of finance. If the latter is the obstacle, it may be because of either low domestic saving or problems with intermediating saving, and so on. This process of *branching down the decision tree* continues until policymakers are satisfied that the truly binding constraint has been identified. In the authors' view, this simple approach will facilitate getting the right *diagnosis* of impediments for growth, from which the appropriate recommendations for policy reform will logically follow.[40]

The Hausmann-Rodrik-Velasco approach is appealing in its simplicity and for explicitly recognizing that policy and reform recommendations need to take into account that different countries face different circumstances. However, a major criticism is that in most countries, constraints are present at every fork of the decision tree. In other words, there may be not one or a few but *many* binding constraints, with no particular reason (at least at the theoretical level) to prioritize any over the others. This leaves policymakers with little basis for choosing among a large set of possible policy actions.[41] In contrast, as will be discussed below, the framework in this book and its application to a number of countries show the intricacies, interrelations, and complementarities of a large number of constraints (political, social, and economic) that Latin American countries face simultaneously. Moreover, from the recommendations developed in chapters 3 through 7, the reader will find that dealing with identified constraints entails a policy and reform agenda that is multidimensional and layered.

The quest for sound analysis of the foundations of growth and an associated reform strategy that is adequate to individual countries' circumstances is far

---

40. In the authors' view, because the resulting list of policy and reform recommendations to deal with the binding constraint will be relatively short and focused, it will also be relatively simple to trace the potential effects of those reforms in other areas of the economy, thus minimizing unintended adverse consequences.

41. In their assessment of the Hausmann-Rodrik-Velasco framework (as applied by World Bank economists in twelve pilot studies), Leipziger and Zagha (2006) could not reach definitive conclusions. In their view the growth diagnostics approach, while providing a framework for formulating hypotheses on growth constraints, "provides neither the hypotheses nor the empirical tools for testing them" (Leipziger and Zagha, 2006, p. 2).

from over. In 2008 the Commission on Growth and Development (2008) published its "Growth Report," also known as the Spence Report after the commission's chairman Michael Spence. The focus of the report was on learning from successful growth experiences, defined as episodes where countries grew at an average annual rate of 7 percent or more over at least a twenty-five-year period. From an analysis of thirteen such experiences, the report identified a number of policy and reform *ingredients* that appeared to be necessary for sustained growth; among these was significant public investment in infrastructure, health, and education. But the report refrained from offering either a recipe based on the identified ingredients or a specific growth strategy applicable to all countries. In the authors' view, the right combination of ingredients—as well as their timing, sequencing, and quantities—varies so much across countries that it should be left in the hands of skilled and experienced leaders and policymakers in each country.

In this context of an already large amount of work on growth and reform, how does the framework in this book deal with the identification of growth foundations in Latin America, and with the empirical design of policies and reforms to impact those foundations? In brief, the framework is developed in four *building blocks.* The first is to identify the foundations for growth that apply in Latin America, taking into account the particular features that distinguish Latin America from other developing regions. This is perhaps the most important difference of the present framework from others aimed at linking reform and growth. The second building block is to ask, based on the existing literature on reform in Latin America, whether alternative reforms and policies have the potential to affect (positively or negatively) the identified foundations. The third building block is to develop a taxonomy of the types of obstacles—economic, social, or political—that specific countries might face that can prevent reforms from having a *positive* impact on one or several of the foundations. The last building block, of a completely empirical nature, is to address those obstacles, either head on or by finding legitimate ways to work around them.[42]

Since the framework is fully developed in chapter 2, it is unnecessary to describe it in detail here. However, it will be useful to discuss briefly how the foundations for growth in Latin America were identified. As stated above, the identification process was guided by Latin America's unique status as the most financially open, most democratic, and at the same time most unequal region of the developing world.

---

42. In contrast to the Hausmann-Rodrik-Velasco approach, the framework in this book does not try to identify one or two *binding obstacles.* Instead, as will be seen below, the empirical search is for "weak growth foundations" and the policies and reforms that can strengthen them. As can be seen from the empirical studies in this book, the obstacles to effective implementation of policies and reforms can truly be multidimensional.

Latin America's greater financial openness reflects past decisions on the part of policymakers in the region to let market forces, through the behavior of the international capital markets, assess the performance of their economies. Recognizing that growth and development require external sources of finance, policymakers throughout Latin America pay considerable attention to international *market signals.* One such signal is the Global Emerging Market Bond Index (EMBI Global) spread, which is broadly used as a measurement of investors' perceptions of risk in individual countries. That is why, with a few exceptions (most notably Argentina and Venezuela), the trend in Latin America since the mid-1990s has been toward removing capital controls and obstacles to foreign direct investment in a number of economic sectors (including, quite prominently, the banking sector). Even in the midst of the international financial crisis taking place at this writing, there is no indication that the vast majority of Latin American countries are considering reimposing restrictions on cross-border financial transactions.

These circumstances imply that, in general, the policy choice has been for market-based growth. This has allowed the international capital markets to play a significant role in assessing the appropriateness of policies and reforms, rewarding the implementation of policies and reforms that strengthen the functioning of the markets while penalizing those that constrain it. The first three foundations for growth in Latin America, therefore, generate incentives for the adequate functioning and behavior of markets and market participants. These three foundations, which are in line with those proposed by supporters of the *institutional approach,* are

- *secure property rights* for the majority of the population, so that individuals and firms can benefit from their investments;
- *sufficiently equal opportunities* for broad segments of the society, which essentially means lowering barriers to entry to individuals and firms without political connections or great wealth—in other words, *leveling the playing field* for market-based interactions; and
- *sufficient economic and political competition,* to avoid capture of the state by powerful elites.

As we have seen, however, liberalization of capital accounts and exposure to international capital markets also mean that for growth to be sustainable, macroeconomic stability is a must. Achieving such stability requires the implementation of self-insurance policies by both the fiscal (stabilization funds and active debt management strategies) and the monetary authorities (accumulation of reserves) to deal with the vagaries of the international capital markets. As discussed above, in Latin America, with its combination of high financial openness, limited trade openness, underdeveloped local financial markets, and low national saving rates, capital inflows are likely to reverse course at the first sign of economic instability. Add to this the region's long history of economic and financial crisis (including periods of hyperinflation and the total collapse of banking systems), and the need for the fourth growth foundation becomes clear:

- *macroeconomic stability,* to ensure that sufficient public funds are allocated to pro-growth reform efforts and that the reform process will not be interrupted to deal with macroeconomic crises.

In other words, in Latin America macroeconomic stability is more than just a policy objective; it becomes a foundation that is needed for any other policy or reform to deliver growth. Recognizing the crucial need to maintain macroeconomic stability if growth in the region is to be sustained, for purposes of the framework the Task Force *upgraded* macroeconomic stability from a policy goal to a foundation for growth.

Latin America's unique status as both the most democratic and the most unequal region in the developing world formed the basis for the inclusion of a fifth and last foundation in the growth framework. As discussed above, these two features have together played a key role in slowing or distorting countries' market-based reform agendas (and at times stopping them altogether).

How does one reconcile the need for well-functioning markets with the discontent of large segments of the population with the workings of the market system? Clearly, this clash between what the region needs and what many of its people seem to want threatens sustained growth. To resolve this conflict, the fifth foundation for sustained growth in Latin America calls for

- *broad sharing among the population of the benefits from growth,* to ensure that market-based reforms and policies conducive to growth are sustainable.

As will be discussed below, the experiences of several Latin American countries show that this foundation has often remained weak during the implementation of pro-growth reform agendas. Birdsall et al. (2008) also emphasize this point and therefore recommend, as part of their *toolkit to promote fair growth* in Latin America, the implementation of well-designed programs to reach the poor and the middle class.

The five foundations cannot be prioritized; all must be built simultaneously. Without the first three, there cannot be market-based growth, but without the last two, no acceleration of growth can be sustainable. The rest of the framework builds on these foundations to guide policymakers in assessing the strengths and weaknesses of the foundations in their individual countries and in identifying policies and reforms that can fortify these foundations. At the same time, the framework stresses that the local conditions specific to each country—economic, social, and political—are essential to determine whether reforms and policies are needed to directly affect a certain foundation or foundations, or to deal with obstacles that prevent reforms from *reaching* the foundations in the first place.

Everything else that the reader needs to know about the framework is developed in chapter 2. The next section discusses some of the results achieved when the framework was actually applied to a sample of five Latin American countries.

Applying the Framework: What Did We Learn?

The analyses and results from applying the framework to Brazil, Colombia, Costa Rica, Mexico, and Peru are the subject of chapters 3 through 7. As the reader will discover, the studies provide a wealth of knowledge for understanding the linkages between reforms and growth in each country. In applying the framework, the chapters' authors not only identified the local constraints that had prevented reforms from being implemented or from being effective, but also explained *how* these constraints came to be.

Throughout their analyses, the authors deal with a number of fascinating and intriguing questions, such as the following: Why, in Brazil, despite great advances in reducing inflation, improving the fiscal stance, and reducing the external debt, does macroeconomic stability remain one of the *weakest* foundations for growth? Why, in Peru, where the constitution gives considerable formal authority to Congress, do legislators very often choose *not* to legislate or even to deliberate on major policy issues? How, in Costa Rica, did it come to pass that a road that everybody agrees is needed, and that faces no financing constraints, still has not been built? The answers to these and many other questions contribute significantly to our understanding of the dynamic of the reform process and the reasons for its successes and failures in each country.

Most important, each case study provides very specific policy recommendations intended to answer the following question: how to proceed with a reform agenda conducive to sustainable growth? Each case study is thus truly unique. The variety of reforms that the authors have chosen to focus on, in the context of the framework, is as large as it is rich. The detailed recommendations that they present are equally rich and varied.

Thus, rather than summarizing the findings of each case study, which would fail to do justice to the authors' efforts, the rest of this section discusses some of the key issues that the authors tackle when applying the analytical framework to their countries. All of the studies base their analysis in the reform period that started in Latin America in the early 1990s and that, at different paces and intensities, continues today.

Have Reforms Been Able to Strengthen the Growth Foundations?

With the analytical framework as their guide, each of the country studies distinguishes between the foundations that reforms *aimed* to strengthen and those that were *actually* strengthened (or weakened). Of course, the policymakers in charge of the design and implementation of reforms did not have in mind the foundations-based framework utilized in this book, but it is not hard to identify intentions and outcomes ex post.

All the country studies assessed that, albeit with different intensities, the reform process of the 1990s aimed at *directly* strengthening two of the growth founda-tions: macroeconomic stability and economic competition. This is not surprising, because these two foundations coincide with some of the central recommenda-tions of the Washington consensus, which most countries in the region embraced in the 1990s following either a period of deep crisis (Brazil, Mexico, and Peru) or a period of very slow growth (Colombia).[43]

Strengthening the broad sharing of the benefits from growth was also an important policy objective in two countries in the sample, Colombia and Brazil, but for different reasons. In Colombia, efforts to contain the drug cartels and to facilitate a peace agreement with the country's guerilla movements led to the writ-ing of a new constitution in 1991. Under that constitution, expenditure on health and education was significantly expanded, and the population was granted increased access to the judicial system and the political process. Thus, broadening the beneficiaries of the growth process was seen as a means of restoring peace in an unsettled domestic security situation. Brazil likewise enacted a new constitution, in 1988, but for the purpose of solidifying democracy and ending twenty years of fiscal centralism. Under the new constitution a large number of public expenditure items were created or expanded, to encourage a broader sharing of the benefits from growth. Particularly important were the creation of an unemployment insurance system and the generation of income transfers through social assistance programs.[44]

Although a number of countries aimed at *leveling the playing field* for market participants (the equality of opportunities foundation) through reforms that lib-eralized markets (trade and financial reforms, for example), improving property rights was not a direct policy objective. In some cases (the pension reforms in Colombia and Peru, for example) reform did contribute to enhancing property rights ex post, but this was not a central objective.

Objectives and outcomes, however, differed significantly across countries. In some cases the reforms indeed contributed to enhancing some of the growth foun-

---

43. Costa Rica did not experience a crisis in the late 1980s or the 1990s. Having recovered from the 1982 debt crisis that plagued the entire region, the country saw a decent pace of growth in the early 1990s, but with high inflation and a large public debt. Extensive government intervention in eco-nomic activity, including a state monopoly on banking, was perceived as generating important ineffi-ciencies that constrained the activities of the private sector, and therefore as an obstacle to growth.

44. In an effort to improve the sharing of growth benefits, in recent years an increasing number of countries in the region have been implementing targeted antipoverty programs, such as conditional cash transfers, which allow poor families to receive a certain amount of money under a "social con-tract," in which the beneficiaries agree to send their children to school regularly or to bring them to health centers. Two well-known programs of this kind are the Oportunidades program in Mexico and Bolsa Familia in Brazil.

dations; in others, however, attempts to enhance a foundation either missed the goal or had the undesirable effect of weakening other foundations. A few examples will illustrate these outcomes, focusing first on the positive ones.

EXAMPLES THAT IMPROVED THE GROWTH FOUNDATIONS

All of the case studies identified foundations that were actually strengthened following reform. With the exception of the study on Mexico, all the studies also agreed that economic (but not necessarily political) competition had improved, albeit to different degrees in different countries. This success is largely attributed to important advances in trade and financial liberalization, as well as the establishment of adequate regulatory and supervisory authorities.[45] In the case of Brazil, a number of regulations limiting entry and competition, such as widespread price controls, were eliminated, and a new competition law and revamped antitrust agencies were put in place. As the study of Costa Rica emphasizes, trade liberalization there has shifted the country's comparative advantage from land to human capital, so that there is now strong competition for human resources, to the benefit of workers. In some countries, such as Brazil, Colombia, and Peru, privatization involving the breakup of public monopolies was also assessed as contributing to improved competition. In contrast, certain privatizations, discussed below and in the chapters on Costa Rica and Mexico, were perceived more as a problem than as a solution.

Most of the studies also agreed that the financial, trade, and regulatory reforms had contributed to *leveling the playing field,* thus improving the equal opportunities foundation. The study of Costa Rica is vocal in underlining the positive effects of trade openness and diversification on equalizing and improving opportunities. For example, underqualified workers—notably women in the textile sector—have found employment in manufacturing, where before they had access only to lower-productivity jobs. Meanwhile professionals in some fields have been able to find private sector jobs where in the past only public sector jobs were available to them, and entrepreneurs have found external sources of finance willing to take risks that the local financial markets would not have taken. A number of other reforms were also assessed as having effectively contributed to equalizing opportunities. For example, in Brazil, minimum age requirements and a new rule for calculating benefits (the *fator previdenciário*) made eligibility for pensions more similar for poor and rich workers.

Although all the case studies pointed to improved macroeconomic indicators, one of the most interesting findings is that only the study on Peru strongly asserted that the reform process has indeed strengthened the *macroeconomic stability*

---

45. In the Mexican case, it is recognized that the trade reform successfully contributed to economic competition. However, these gains are assessed as being largely offset by important deficiencies in the privatization process.

Table 5. *Indices of Central Bank Autonomy by World Region, 2003*[a]

Region	Economic autonomy	Political autonomy	Overall
East Asia and Pacific	0.60	0.41	0.51
Eastern Europe and Central Asia	0.73	0.80	0.76
High-income countries	0.73	0.56	0.64
Middle East and North Africa	0.64	0.35	0.49
South Asia	0.58	0.32	0.45
Sub-Saharan Africa	0.58	0.31	0.44
Latin America	0.83	0.47	0.65
Brazil	0.75	0.50	0.63
Colombia	0.88	0.13	0.50
Costa Rica	0.88	0.50	0.69
Mexico	0.75	0.63	0.69
Peru	1.00	0.38	0.69

Source: Arnone et al. (2007).

a. Each index ranges from 0 to 1, where 1 indicates maximum autonomy.

foundation. This conclusion is based not only on current macroeconomic indicators, but also on the overall economic and political infrastructure that supports the sustainability of adequate macroeconomic policies. Unlike in some other countries in the region, high inflation in Peru is tolerated neither by the population nor by the monetary authorities nor by the politicians. And even though President Alberto Fujimori's government was tainted by one of the most serious corruption scandals in all of Latin America, the main thrust of the macroeconomic reforms undertaken during his presidency has been maintained and solidified. One indicator of Peru's increased strength in conducting sound macroeconomic policies is the capacity of the central bank to freely pursue monetary policy. As table 5 shows, Peru's central bank today has the greatest economic autonomy among the countries in the sample. However, it does not rate as highly in terms of political independence, since the tenure of its governor coincides with that of the president, and the governor is designated by the executive branch. Nonetheless, Peru's overall score on central bank autonomy is above both the Latin American average and that of all other developing regions except Eastern Europe.

As mentioned above, strengthening property rights was not perceived as an objective of most reform efforts, and indeed, indicators of the strength of this growth foundation do not paint an encouraging picture for Latin America as a whole. As shown in table 6, which reports regional averages on the Gwartney and Lawson (2008) index of legal structure and security of property rights, by 2006 Latin America, together with South Asia and Sub-Saharan Africa, stood out as one of the developing regions with the weakest property rights. Among countries in the sample, Costa Rica recorded the highest value on this index. This is consistent

Table 6. *Index of Legal Structure and Security of Property Rights by World Region, 1970–2006*[a]

Region	1970	1975	1980	1985	1990	1995	2000	2005	2006
East Asia and Pacific	5.19	4.20	4.99	5.08	5.10	5.12	4.70	5.31	5.26
Eastern Europe and Central Asia	4.38	2.78	5.57	5.65	6.11	5.62	5.70	5.57	5.58
High-income countries	7.56	5.87	6.77	6.79	7.17	7.70	7.90	7.92	7.67
Middle East and North Africa	3.42	3.55	2.79	3.89	3.61	5.52	5.87	6.34	6.05
South Asia	3.13	1.96	3.71	3.58	2.96	4.95	4.61	4.91	4.49
Sub-Saharan Africa	5.08	4.31	4.23	4.20	4.23	4.67	4.55	4.44	4.24
Latin America	3.39	3.26	4.38	3.98	4.60	5.06	4.52	5.04	4.87
Brazil	6.16	5.40	5.86	5.72	6.19	5.76	5.35	5.22	5.19
Colombia	2.82	3.33	3.98	3.40	3.41	2.85	3.53	5.03	4.49
Costa Rica	na	na	5.21	5.25	5.46	5.80	6.87	6.91	6.79
Mexico	4.69	4.09	6.29	5.38	6.76	5.30	4.25	5.68	5.45
Peru	1.36	1.15	3.77	2.23	2.93	4.76	3.94	5.06	5.00

Source: Gwartney and Lawson (2008).

a. The index ranges from 0 to 10, where 10 indicates the highest level of legal structure and security.

with the assessment by the authors of the country study that Costa Rica's institutional framework is strong and has actually been getting stronger since the beginning of the reform efforts of the 1990s. Especially strong are those institutions, related to the country's trade agreements, that helped to consolidate the guarantees against undue uncompensated expropriation that the constitution grants to both local firms and foreigners. In Peru, despite some important setbacks associated with both corruption and inefficiency of the legal and judicial systems, the broad indicator of security of property rights has improved over time; however, it remains quite low. Mexico and Brazil are cases of particular concern; by 2006 the property rights indicator in both countries was well below its level of 1990. Colombia's deficiencies in this area are also apparent: that country reports the lowest value on this indicator among the countries in the sample. As will be discussed below, weaknesses in this foundation are an important reason why the authors of most of the case studies include proposals to reform the judiciary system among their recommendations.

When Unintended or Undesirable Results Happen: Examples of Weakened Foundations

Together the analyses in the case studies provide a comprehensive explanation of why some foundations for growth were weakened rather than strengthened during the reform process. There are several possible reasons for this outcome. First, a given foundation may simply have been disregarded during the reform process, despite factors signaling its deterioration over time; these can be described as "missing foundations." Second, a reform attempting to strengthen a foundation may have failed to deliver and instead weakened the foundation. Third, reforms aimed at strengthening one foundation may have had the *unintended consequence* of weakening other foundations. Each of the case studies presents vivid discussions of all three plausible explanations. This subsection briefly describes some examples:

• In Peru, the broad sharing of the benefits from growth was the *missing foundation* during the reform process of the 1990s and early 2000s. At the national level, poverty rates have started to decrease significantly only since 2004, but to a large extent this success can be attributed to the economic boom brought on by high commodity prices. Moreover, the recent reduction in poverty rates has not been sufficiently inclusive. As the authors of the Peru chapter—Eduardo Morón, Juan Francisco Castro, and Cynthia Sanborn— show, although economic growth has reduced income inequality on a national basis, urban-rural disparities are widening: the incidence of poverty in Peru's urban areas declined from 37 percent in 2004 to 26 percent in 2007, but that in rural areas declined only from 70 percent to 65 percent in the same period. More worrisome is the authors' view that the reduction in poverty cannot be attributed to particular past reform efforts; this leaves poverty and inequality highly vulnerable to future developments in the economic cycle. Especially in the context of the current global crisis, Peru's gains in poverty reduction run the risk of being reversed. Not surprisingly, the authors focus their recommendations on reforms that aim directly at broadening the benefits from growth on a *permanent basis.*

• Improving the efficiency and allocation of resources, thereby strengthening the foundation for *economic competition,* was an explicit aim of Mexico's extensive privatization program of the 1980s and 1990s. Although some analysts have praised the program's overall benefits (see Chong and López-de-Silanes, 2005), major problems were associated with certain key privatizations. As Gerardo Esquivel and Fausto Hernández-Trillo discuss in their chapter, the privatization of the public telephone company Telmex (Teléfonos Mexicanos) was implemented without an appropriate institutional framework and resulted in predatory behavior and the use of monopoly power. The National Highways Concession Program of the 1990s also failed to meet expectations, and the Mexican government had to embark on an extremely costly road recovery program. Since the large losses associated with the highway bailouts were socialized, this reform also had a negative impact on the broad sharing of the benefits of growth foundation. Both these cases provide clear examples of reforms that aimed at but failed to strengthen growth foundations.

• The study of the Brazilian experience by Armando Castelar Pinheiro, Regis Bonelli, and Samuel de Abreu Pessôa reveals a number of reforms that actually weakened the macroeconomic stability foundation in that country. The interplay between democratization and Brazil's highly unequal income distribution resulted in increased demand by large segments of the population for policies and reforms to redirect government expenditures toward the poor. However, the ability of current beneficiaries to veto cuts in existing expenditures, in the context of a fragmented party system, resulted in an overall increase in current government expenditure and transfers, rather than a redistribution of a constant level of expenditure. A major challenge for policymakers ever since Brazil's democratization has been how to finance increased government expenditure. At first, inflation provided the financing source. When the eruption of hyperinflation—and the subsequent policies to correct the problem—in the late 1980s made apparent the unsustainability of this strategy, the government instead relied on expanding the net public debt. When the Russian crisis of the late 1990s spread to other emerging markets, including Brazil, exposing the extreme economic fragilities associated with high external debt ratios, the Brazilian government turned to raising existing taxes and creating new ones; many of these were quite distortionary, especially for financial intermediation. By 2007 the total tax burden had reached 37 percent of GDP, 12 percentage points higher than the average during 1968–86. However, the increase in public consumption was so large that even higher taxes were not enough, and public investment, particularly in infrastructure, was severely curtailed.

Overall public investment declined from an average of 8 percent of GDP in 1968–78 to a meager 2.7 percent by 2003–05. A growth decomposition exercise included in the Brazil chapter reveals, not surprisingly, that physical capital accumulation has been negative over the last decade.[46] Thus, since the early 1990s, even as Brazil has implemented policies and reforms, such as price stability and flexible exchange rates, designed to strengthen the macroeconomic stability foundation, electoral incentives have led politicians to implement a poorly conceived structure of public spending, greatly skewed toward current expenditures at the expense of public investment. This type of expenditure policy, combined with an extremely high tax burden on investment and financial intermediation and a large public debt (both for the purpose of financing public consumption), has kept Brazil's macroeconomic stability foundation quite fragile.

• Another example of a weakened foundation in Brazil is the lack of protection of *property rights* in spite of reforms of the judiciary and the legal system. Once again, in the context of a highly unequal income distribution in a society where democratization has given greater voice to the disenfranchised, there are strong political incentives to overlook the law as a way to attenuate income disparities. For example, it has become accepted practice for supposedly landless peasants to trespass on rural land, and for supposedly homeless families to trespass on urban land. The desire to reduce the country's stark income inequality also motivates judges to bias their contract enforcement decisions to favor the poorer party. This weakened enforcement of the law is a serious constraint on the property rights foundation (as reflected in the low value of the index in table 6) and a severe obstacle to productive private investment.

• The case of Colombia presents some clear examples of reforms that strengthened some growth foundations while weakening others. Policies and reforms aimed at broadening the beneficiaries of growth through fiscal decentralization, the enhancement of social expenditures, and improved access to the judicial system resulted in deep-rooted fiscal costs that have at least partly offset the benefits of other policies aimed at strengthening macroeconomic stability. As Roberto Steiner, Irene Clavijo, and Natalia Salazar observe in their chapter on Colombia, a key part of the problem is that the 1990 constitution commits the nation to building a *welfare state,* a provision somewhat at odds with the market-oriented reforms being introduced at the same time. The constitution also granted the Constitutional Court very broad powers, and the result has been a very activist

---

46. Growth decomposition exercises were conducted for all case studies, and the results are shown in the individual chapters. A particular characteristic of Brazil is that economic growth in the last decade can be mostly explained by a recovery of total factor productivity from the sharp decline during the "lost decade" that followed the debt crisis of 1982. Accumulation of human capital decelerated in the most recent decade while physical capital actually contracted.

judicial system. For example, the court has intervened in the determination of public sector wages, has allowed citizens to claim health benefits far beyond those provided for under the health care law, and has extended to *all* pensioners benefits that were supposed to compensate only some retirees whose pensions had not been fully adjusted for inflation. All these interventions have imposed large fiscal costs on the government—the cost of the pension decision alone has been estimated at 12.5 percent of GDP. Clearly, the court has taken the notion of equality too far, and its decisions have severely affected the government's ability to undertake prudent fiscal management and have even compromised financial sector stability. Another, truly frightening example involves the 1998 crisis affecting the country's mortgage banks. To provide support to low-income borrowers, the government forced banks to temporarily accept properties returned by debtors in exchange for the complete write-off of their mortgage. Basing its decision on an overly broad concept of equality, the Constitutional Court extended this benefit to *all debtors.*

• In some ways the case of Costa Rica contrasts with that of Colombia. The reform of the Costa Rican public sector sought to *reduce* the role of the state-centered system in order to improve macroeconomic stability and enhance economic competition through increased private sector involvement. But the implementation of this reform actually weakened political competition and the broad sharing of the benefits of growth. How did this happen? As Jorge Cornick and Alberto Trejos explain in their chapter on Costa Rica, the public sector was downsized without any clear definition of priorities among different government entities and programs; instead, budgetary restrictions were imposed across the whole of the public sector, and public servants were encouraged to leave. The best, the youngest, and the brightest did just that. For those who stayed, the pride of working as a public servant was dramatically curtailed as they were hit by a triple whammy: first, the perception became widespread that they were the "low-quality" workers in the economy; second, budget allocations for many projects were sharply reduced; and third, a complicated system of checks and balances intended to control corruption instead tended to criminalize even honest mistakes, complicating interactions between the private sector and the government. Checks and balances are certainly essential to the appropriate functioning of any government, but the systems put in place in Costa Rica were poorly designed, generating serious obstacles to the execution of projects. Unfortunately, the government branches most affected were those most important to the broader sharing of the benefits of growth: education, public infrastructure, and social assistance. The weakening of this key growth foundation contributed to the solidification of an antireform political party. In the context of a legislative system where any congressman can delay, and ultimately stop, the approval of a bill by recourse to the Supreme Court, the antireform party, although small, has been able to block the passage of needed reforms. Legislative paralysis thus goes hand in hand with ineffective political competition—a negative outcome for an important growth foundation.

The Proposals

The examples presented above provide just a flavor of the issues and problems discussed in the country chapters in this book. As the reader can easily infer, the discussions in all the chapters provide fertile ground for advancing policy recommendations, and the authors took this task to heart. Keeping within the parameters of the book's analytical framework, all the recommendations aim at enhancing the identified growth foundations. Once again, to avoid repetition, the rest of this section briefly summarizes some of the most important proposals. Also, given the variety of areas tackled in the proposals, the focus here is on a common theme in all chapters: the area of institutional strengthening. Another common theme is the recognition that the implementation of recommendations requires delicate political economy balancing acts.

• How to *better share the benefits from growth* in Peru? In addition to proposals to reform the education system (what the authors identify as a missing reform), Morón and his coauthors suggest that deep reforms of the state and the political system are essential so that legislation can be passed, and policies executed, that will reach the poor, especially in the country's rural areas. An important component of the diagnosis with respect to reform of the state is that lack of *implementation capacity*—reflected in a shortage of professional civil servants—constrains the process of fiscal and political decentralization, which in turn delays and even prevents the execution of much-needed projects, especially in infrastructure and the delivery of social services. Recommendations include introducing a merit-based career path for new public servants; programming budgetary expansions in a results-based format; and consolidating small geographic units into fewer, larger ones. As the authors emphasize, in the face of managerial constraints it would be easier to distribute public resources and monitor their utilization if the focus were on seven to ten macroregional governments rather than on the twenty-five existing regions. For this purpose, the authors encourage the creation of a pilot macroregion as a way of demonstrating the potential benefits of consolidation.

• Although Peru's existing political parties are weak and fragmented, reform of the political system is more easily said than done, because politicians face few incentives to modify the existing structure once elected. Contributing to the problem is the fact that parties revolve around personalities rather than programs or ideology and have few roots in society. Party weakness, in turn, translates into members of Congress lacking technical capacities or political incentives to hold government accountable and to appropriately represent their constituencies. Morón and his coauthors offer several recommendations to strengthen the party system, from enhancing the electoral authority, to strengthening the monitoring of compliance with the existing party law, to building a well-endowed congressional research service available to all members. But because the Congress lacks incentives for internal discipline, external vigilance of its activities is the indispensable force for change. In this regard a central recommendation is to enhance the capacity of nongovernmental research and advocacy organizations of different orientations, and of the independent media, to monitor public agencies, try to hold politicians accountable, and educate the general public so as to improve the quality of citizen demands.

• Reforming *competition policy* is one of the central recommendations in the chapter on Mexico. Although a law was passed in 2006 enhancing the powers of the Federal Competition Commission (FCC), the judicial and legal systems continue to be major obstacles. Through a number of judicial protection mechanisms (called *amparos*), decisions by the FCC can be delayed for prolonged periods. Moreover, legal deficiencies have limited the collection of fines in cases where monopoly practices have been detected. Thus, among their specific recommendations, Esquivel and Hernández-Trillo call for full autonomy (including financial autonomy) for the FCC, to allow it to avoid capture by other government agencies, and for the creation of specialized courts in competition and regulatory cases (similar to Chile's Tribunal for the Defense of Free Competition). These measures aim at improving transparency and accountability on the part of those in charge of implementing the antimonopoly laws, thereby generating incentives to avoid unnecessary delays in executing the law.

• Reforms of the judicial system are also proposed in the Brazil case study, in this case to secure *property rights,* which the authors assess as extremely weak, with contracts constantly breached and rulings delayed by politically motivated judges. Among the authors' specific proposals are the following: adopt performance indicators as a criterion for promoting judges, replacing the current practice of promotion by seniority (one proposed indicator is the percentage of a judge's decisions that are confirmed on appeal); impose discipline on the executive (by far the leading litigator in judicial proceedings in Brazil) in its use of appeals for the purpose of delaying expenditure; index judicially imposed obligations and debt to the SELIC (the policy-determined interest rate) so as to reduce financial incentives to delay final court rulings; and raise public awareness of the consequences of poor judicial performance for economic development and social equity.

• A key recommendation of Steiner and his coauthors is to curtail the ability of Colombia's Constitutional Court to tamper with economic matters in general and with *macroeconomic stability* in particular. As mentioned above, an extreme interpretation of the concept of "fairness" has resulted in excessive judicial activism, to the detriment of macroeconomic stability. Recognizing that the court is a tremendously popular institution, and one that contributes to social cohesion, the Colombian team advances three recommendations aimed at providing incentives for the court to encourage the strengthening of all of the growth foundations. The first is to reduce the politicization of court magistrates by allowing them to run for a second term, after a cool-off period of perhaps five years has elapsed; this would replace the current system under which magistrates may not be reelected but face practically no restrictions on their involvement elsewhere in politics after completion of their tenure. The second recommendation is to seek a consensual definition by all powers of what constitutes an adequate health care plan and other social services, so that judges cannot decree the provision of services beyond what is in the agreed plans. To make this consensual agreement sustainable, the definitions in the plans should be enhanced as the country achieves higher levels of development (which would also need to be defined). The third recommendation would implement a process by which the Constitutional Court reviews laws as soon as they are approved. If a law were then overturned on procedural grounds, this would happen before it becomes operational.

• Finally, the authors of the Costa Rica chapter view as central a reform of that country's legislative system that would enhance *all* of the growth foundations, but particularly the *broad sharing of the benefits of growth.* Congressional rules that used to work adequately in a two-party system have proved ineffective, leading to reform paralysis in the current context where a minority antireform party forms part of the political landscape. Some of the legislative reforms the authors propose to deal with these obstacles include the following: setting a deadline by which the Congress must vote on proposed laws; granting the executive limited power to declare certain bills urgent, to shorten the decision time (a practice followed in Chile); creating alternative ways for representatives to put forward their positions, place them on the record, and propose amendments, without causing the long delays to which the current procedures are subject; and requiring a quorum only for votes and not for debate. Citing the success of the CAFTA referendum in late 2007, Cornick and Trejos stress the advantages of such referenda: a vote happens on a fixed date without the possibility of filibustering, and the results are binding and widely viewed as legitimate. Recognizing the high costs of this second-best (or third-best?) alternative for passing growth-enhancing reforms, the authors propose that consideration of this mechanism take place at the same time that national elections occur.

Some Concluding Remarks

It is hoped that this introductory chapter has increased readers' appetite to get immersed in the complex, sometimes intriguing, sometimes disturbing, but always fascinating interactive process of reform and growth that started in Latin America in the late 1980s and early 1990s and continues to evolve today. In the chapters that follow, the reader will find well-thought-out—and thought-provoking—answers to a number of important questions: Why did two similar reforms generate very different outcomes in different countries? How did political interests interact with the technical design of reforms in individual countries? Why, given the current state of development of Latin American countries, is it neither useful nor practical to advance recommendations at a very general level? Most important, what should be done to enhance the foundations for sustained growth? Although the detailed and specific reform agendas proposed in the individual case studies can at times be daunting, the reader will be left with a feeling of optimism, as the solutions proposed are not only well conceived but doable. Indeed, in keeping with the analytical framework that has guided this book, the recommendations focus on finding solutions to deal with existing obstacles—directly when possible, and with second-best policies and incentives when necessary.

Although the specific recommendations for reforms and policies differ substantially from country to country, two commonalities in the *process of implementing reforms* emerge from all the country studies. The first is an emphasis on incremental reform. Even in those cases where a major revamping is recommended (for example, in competition policy in Mexico, or the reform of the state in Peru), the proposals are not for "big bang" reforms. Instead the authors call for "pilot projects," designed to build constituencies that will support and endorse further change and reform, and to enhance the ability of the media and nongovernmental organizations to educate public opinion and monitor the government's and politicians' actions. The second commonality, related to the first, is the need for enhanced communication between governments and civil societies, focusing on persuasion and collaboration rather than the top-down imposition of policies and reforms. To return to where this introduction started, the emphasis on reform through *agreement and negotiation* rather than by decree is fully consistent with the reality of Latin America today as the most financially open, most democratic, but also most unequal region in the developing world. Under these conditions, the way to move forward with reform, while at the same time preventing (and in some cases containing) a backlash against market-oriented reforms and possible civil unrest, is to encourage much greater collaboration between governments and civil societies than was perceived as necessary in the early days of reform.

References

Acemoglu, Daron, Simon Johnson, and James A. Robinson. 2005. "Institutions as a Fundamental Cause of Long-Run Growth." In Philippe Aghion and Steven N. Durlauf, eds., *Handbook of Economic Growth,* Vol. 1A. Amsterdam: Elsevier.

Alesina, Alberto, Arnaud Devleeschauwer, William Easterly, Sergio Kurlat, and Romain Wacziarg. 2003. "Fractionalization." *Journal of Economic Growth* 8, no. 2 (June): 155–94.

Arnone, Marco, Bernard J. Laurens, Jean-François Segalotto, and Martin Sommer. 2007. "Central Bank Autonomy: Lessons from Global Trends." IMF Working Paper WP/07/88. Washington: International Monetary Fund (July)

Barro, Robert. 1991. "Economic Growth in a Cross Section of Countries." *Quarterly Journal of Economics* 106, no. 2. (May): 407–43

Birdsall, Nancy. 2007. "Income Distribution: Effects on Growth and Development." Working Paper 118. Washington: Center for Global Development (April).

Birdsall, Nancy, and Liliana Rojas-Suarez. 2004. "Regionalism for Financing Development: The Unexploited Potential." In Nancy Birdsall and Liliana Rojas-Suarez, eds., *Financing Development: The Power of Regionalism*. Washington: Center for Global Development (September).

Birdsall, Nancy, Augusto de la Torre, and Rachel Menezes. 2008. *Fair Growth: Economic Policies for Latin America's Poor and Middle-Income Majority*. Washington: Center for Global Development and Inter-American Dialogue.

Blyde, Juan S., and Eduardo Fernandez-Arias. 2004. "Why Does Latin America Grow More Slowly?" Economic and Social Studies Series RE1-04-016. Washington: Inter-American Development Bank.

Caballero, Ricardo. 2001. "Macroeconomic Volatility in Reformed Latin America." Inter-American Development Bank, Washington (January).

Chinn, Menzie D., and Hiro Ito. 2007. "A New Measure of Financial Openness." University of Wisconsin (May)

Chong, Alberto, and Florencio López-de-Silanes, 2005. "Privatization in Mexico." In *Privatization in Latin America: Myths and Reality*. Stanford University Press and Inter-American Development Bank.

Commission on Growth and Development. 2008. *The Growth Report: Strategies for Sustained Growth and Inclusive Development*. Washington: World Bank.

Cornia, Giovanni Andrea, Tony Addison, and Sampsa Kiiski. 2004. "Income Distribution Changes and Their Impact in the Post-Second World War Period." In Giovanni Andrea Cornia, ed., *Inequality, Growth and Poverty in an Era of Liberalization and Globalization*. Oxford University Press.

Corporación Latinobarómetro. 2007. *Informe Latinobarómetro 2007* (November). www.latino barometro.org.

De Gregorio, José. 2005. "Sustained Growth in Latin America." Economic Policy Papers 13. Santiago: Central Bank of Chile (May).

De Gregorio, José, and Jong-Wha Lee. 2003. "Growth and Adjustment in East Asia and Latin America." Working Paper 245. Santiago: Central Bank of Chile.

Easterly, William, and Ross Levine. 2003. "Tropics, Germs and Crops: The Role of Endowments in Economic Development." *Journal of Monetary Economics* 50, no. 1: 3–39.

Edwards, Sebastian. 2007. "Crises and Growth: A Latin American Perspective." Working Paper 13019. Cambridge, Mass.: National Bureau of Economic Research (April).

Edwards, Sebastian, Gerardo Esquivel, and Graciela Marquez, eds. 2007. *The Decline of Latin American Economies: Growth, Institutions and Crises*. University of Chicago Press.

Fajnzylber, Pablo, Daniel Lederman, and Norman Loayza. 2002. "Inequality and Violent Crime." *Journal of Law and Economics* 45, no. 1 (April): 1–40.

Fearon, James D. 2003. "Ethnic Structure and Cultural Diversity by Country." *Journal of Economic Growth* 8, no. 2 (June): 195–222.

Guidotti, Pablo, Liliana Rojas-Suarez, and Roberto Zahler. 2004. "Designing Financial Regulatory Policies that Work for Latin America: The Role of Markets and Institutions: Views from the Latin American Shadow Financial Regulatory Committee." *Journal of Financial Stability* 1, no. 2 (December): 199–228.

Gutierrez, Mario. 2007. "Savings in Latin America after the Mid 1990s: Determinants, Constraints and Policies." Serie Macroeconomía del Desarrollo 57. Santiago, Chile: CEPAL (January)

Gwartney, James, and Robert Lawson. 2008. *Economic Freedom of the World: 2008 Annual Report*. www.freetheworld.org.

Hausmann, Ricardo, and Michael Gavin. 1996. "Securing Stability and Growth in a Shock-Prone Region: The Policy Challenge for Latin America." Working Paper 315. Washington: Inter-American Development Bank (January).

Hausmann, Ricardo, Dani Rodrik, and Andrés Velasco. 2005. "Growth Diagnostics." Harvard University.

Izquierdo, A., P. Ottonello, and E. Talvi. 2008. "If Latin America Were Chile: A Comment on Structural Fiscal Balances and Public Debt." Inter-American Development Bank, Washington.

Kaufmann, Daniel, Aart Kray, and Massimo Mastruzzi. 2008. "World Wide Governance Indicators." World Bank, Washington (June).

Kekic, Laza. 2007. "The Economist Intelligence Unit's Index of Democracy." In *The World in 2007*. London: The Economist.

Leipziger, Danny, and Roberto Zagha. 2006. "Getting out of the Rut: Applying Growth Diagnostics at the World Bank." *Finance and Development* 43, no. 1 (March): 16–17.

Marshall, Monty, and Keith Jaggers. 2007. "Polity IV Data Set" (www.systemicpeace.org/polity/polity4.htm).

North, Douglas. 1991. "Institutions." *Journal of Economic Perspectives* 5, no. 1: 97–112.

Pritchett, Lant. 1997. "Divergence, Big Time." *Journal of Economic Perspectives* 11, no. 3: 3–17.

Przeworski, Adam, Michael E. Alvarez, and Jose Antonio Cheibub. 2000. *Democracy and Development: Political Institutions and Well-Being in the World, 1950–1990*. Cambridge University Press.

Putterman, Louis, and David N. Weil. 2008. "Post-1500 Population Flows and the Long Run Determinants of Economic Growth and Inequality." Working Paper 14448. Cambridge, Mass.: National Bureau of Economic Research.

Rojas-Suarez, Liliana. 2003. "Monetary Policy and Exchange Rates: Guiding Principles for a Sustainable Regime." In Pedro-Pablo Kuczynski and John Williamson, eds., *After the Washington Consensus: Restarting Growth and Reforms in Latin America*. Washington: Institute for International Economics (March).

Rojas-Suarez, Liliana, and Sebastian Sotelo. 2007. "The Burden of Debt: An Exploration of Interest Rate Behavior in Latin America." *Contemporary Economic Policy* 25, no. 3 (July): 387–414.

Sachs, Jeffrey, and Andrew Warner. 1995. "Economic Reform and the Process of Global Integration." *Brookings Papers on Economic Activity*, no. 1: 1–118.

Wacziarg, Romain, and Karen Horn Welch. 2003. "Trade Liberalization and Growth: New Evidence." Working Paper 10152. Cambridge, Mass.: National Bureau of Economic Research (November).

Williamson, John. 1990. "What Washington Means by Policy Reform." Chapter 2 in John Williamson, ed., *Latin American Adjustment: How Much Has Happened?* Washington: Institute for International Economics.

World Bank. 2006. *World Development Report 2006: Equity and Development*. Washington.

Zettelmeyer, Jeromin. 2006. "Growth and Reforms in Latin America: A Survey of Facts and Arguments." IMF Working Paper WP/06/210. Washington: International Monetary Fund (September).

2

Helping Reforms Deliver Growth in Latin America: A Framework for Analysis

CGD TASK FORCE

Growth in Latin America: The Facts

From at least the early 1950s through the 1970s, much of Latin America experienced a remarkable stretch of relatively rapid economic growth.[1] This growth was impressive but ultimately proved unsustainable. Under the weight of government debt and associated problems, and in the face of a significant adverse global shock, growth declined sharply throughout Latin America in the 1980s. The early 1990s brought recovery, but this was quickly interrupted by the economic and financial crises that plagued the region during the second half of that decade and the early 2000s. From 2004 to 2007, growth rates increased significantly. However, as discussed in chapter 1, in the context of the global financial crisis that started in 2008, many Latin American countries are once again experiencing a serious economic slowdown.

Income per capita is the standard measure of how overall economic performance affects people. Figure 1, taken from Zettelmeyer (2006), traces the logarithm of income per capita in a number of Latin American countries from 1960 to 2005.

The CGD Task Force was chaired by Simon Johnson and Liliana Rojas-Suárez. The Task Force members were Mauricio Cárdenas, Javier Corrales, José De Gregorio, Augusto de la Torre, Eduardo Lora, Carmen Pages, Ernesto Stein, Kurt Weyland, and Jeromin Zettelmeyer.

1. The data are less reliable before the 1950s, making it impossible to say exactly when this growth phase began. The 1930s were a period of global depression, which encompassed most of Latin America also. The long growth period likely started sometime in the 1940s.

Figure 1. *Income per Capita and Structural Breaks in Selected Latin American Countries, 1960–2006*[a]

Logarithm of income per capita

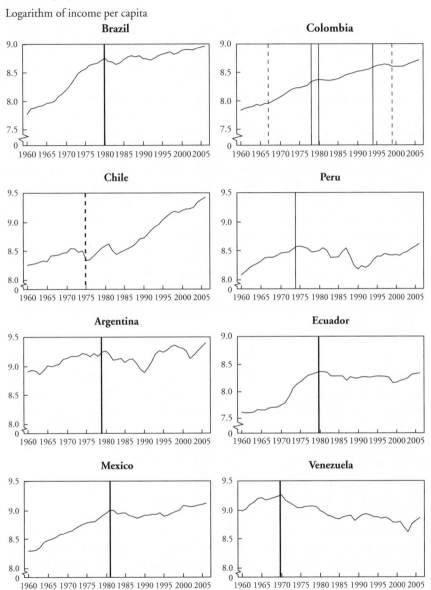

Source: Zettelmeyer (2006).

a. Solid vertical lines indicate downward structural breaks in the series, and dashed vertical lines upward breaks, both with a probability $p < 0.10$ (thick lines) or $p < 0.25$ (thin lines).

Dashed vertical lines indicate the beginnings of growth accelerations—periods when growth rates were significantly higher than in the previous period—and solid lines, periods of deceleration.[2] These graphs present a vivid picture, which statistical analysis confirms: although the details vary from country to country, income growth per capita in Latin America clearly accelerated in the 1960s and 1970s and then decelerated in the 1980s and 1990s.[3] It remains to be seen whether a new and statistically significant period of growth acceleration can be identified in some countries in at least some part of the 2000s. As the discussion in chapter 1 indicates, with the exception of Chile (and a slight improvement in the Dominican Republic), the last three decades have seen the gap in income per capita widen in all Latin American countries relative to the most advanced economies.

Of course, decelerations of growth and even outright economic crises are far from uncommon around the world (see Berg et al., 2006, and Jones and Olken, 2005). Recent decades have seen sharp slowdowns of various kinds in places as disparate as the former Soviet bloc and East Asia. In most of these cases one observes, first, a period of confusion and disorganization, often followed by the adoption of reforms that seek to address what are perceived to be the underlying problems—excessive state control of the economy or weak corporate governance, for example. The details of the reform packages vary, of course, according to what is politically feasible or regarded as a priority, but the desire to reform is a nearly universal feature.

Latin America is no exception to this pattern, and the lags observed in the region between the crises of the early 1980s and the attempted reforms of the late 1980s and 1990s were completely within the range of experience elsewhere. But two other characteristics typify most of the reform initiatives in Latin America: economic growth remained volatile after the reforms were implemented, and any gains from growth were not shared by large segments of the population. These continuing problems spurred calls in a number of countries, not for more reform, but rather for the undoing of some of the reforms that had been achieved.[4]

Reform remains controversial in Eastern Europe and East Asia, but in both regions, most countries have found their way onto strong growth paths in the past decade. In contrast, Latin America has seen lower average growth rates and higher volatility of growth than any developing region except Sub-Saharan Africa. It is important not to exaggerate the differences between Latin America and the more successful developing regions, but a gap does appear to be opening up between

2. The solid and dashed lines represent structural breaks in the time series. The procedure used to identify such breaks is performed in stages, one break at a time, and is based on the work of Bai and Perron (1998, 2003); the specifics of the procedure can be found in Berg et al. (2006).

3. However, as Berg et al. (2006) note, the high volatility of output in the region makes it difficult in some countries to identify the decelerations in the 1980s and the accelerations in the 1990s.

4. The important exception is Chile, which launched its reforms even before the regionwide crisis of the 1980s but intensified its efforts soon after.

these regions of similar income per capita and comparable economic potential (see chapter 1).

With so many Latin Americans experiencing such a meager payoff from reform, patience with reform is wearing thin among important social groups. And if reform should falter, the risk is real that Latin America will fall further behind. However, reports of a generalized political backlash against the market economy and market-oriented reform should be taken with caution. As box 1 shows, one of the important differences among countries in Latin America is in the composition of the main political actors. Although a turn toward the left has been seen in some countries, there are nevertheless important differences in ideology and governance between, for example, the current government of Venezuela and that of Uruguay. Meanwhile Chile's government coalition seems, until recently at least, to have been ably accommodating social demands, and the latest elections in Peru are a signal of the urgent need to start incorporating those demands in the political agenda. These are but a few examples of the extent to which the political scene varies dramatically from country to country, whether in terms of the ideological leanings of government leaders, or of the extent to which wide sectors of the population have been included in the debate, or of the main demands being debated.

Where Did All the Reform Go? Factors Breaking the Link between Reform and Growth

The effort at reform in Latin America has been genuine, and it has been long-lived, stretching from the 1980s through the 1990s and continuing into the present decade, although with different timing in different countries. Figure 2 shows how countries have performed in terms of the best available single indicator of structural reform across the region, that of Lora (2001). The index reflects advances in five types of reform: trade, financial, privatization, tax, and labor reform. Although the index leaves out a number of other reforms that have been and are being implemented in many countries—reform of the social sectors and of institutions in particular—it does show that the pace of change was rapid in the 1990s but slowed significantly in the 2000s.[5] As suggested by Lora (2007), reform of the state, in its multiple institutional facets, has been proceeding since the 1980s in a number of countries, but slowly; also, in contrast to the more traditional reforms, reforms of the state have tended to be implemented piecemeal rather than bundled.[6]

---

5. Lora and Panizza (2002) suggest that the pace of reform was at its most rapid between 1989 and 1994, with Chile again an exception. For an analysis of the early period of reforms, see Edwards (1995).

6. In Lora's (2007) view the unbundling of institutional reforms reflects the attempt of governments to exploit political opportunities for reform whenever they become available, in the expectation that the process would continue.

Box 1. *A Rereading of the Politics of Market Reform in the 2000s: Things Are Not That Bad*

The anti-market forces that have gained political ground across South America since 1998 are far more heterogeneous than meets the eye. Indeed, these forces agglomerate several quite different *varieties of discontent* with the market. Some are clearly inimical to market reform, whereas others represent political demands that could be accommodated by "reforming the reforms" rather than reversing them.

The various leftist movements that have come to power since the late 1990s include, in different proportions, all of the following distinct, but not mutually exclusive, species:

• *Anti-establishment revolutionaries.* This is the old radical left that has never liked the status quo. Their main slogan, "*¡Que se vayan todos!*" became the vox populi during the 1999 constitutional assembly in Venezuela, the 2001 financial crisis in Argentina, and the 2003 crisis in Bolivia.

• *Rent seekers:* These are the old protectionists prominent among business and labor groups, and the patronage-seeking politicians who lost ground with the reforms of the 1990s and are looking for an opportunity to regain control of the state. Their slogan is "Down with globalization and FTAs!" An example is the opposition in 2006–07 in Costa Rica to CAFTA (the Central American Free Trade Agreement), where a popular referendum was needed in late 2007 to ratify the agreement into law.

• *Nationalists:* This group opposed the foreign policy of many Latin American countries, launched in the 1990s, of close realignment with the United States, in the pursuit of free trade and aggressive drug interdiction, and with the International Monetary Fund, because of its perceived micromanagement of national legislation and strict conditionalities. Since 2001, following the 9/11 terrorist attacks and the Argentine financial crisis, both the United States and the IMF appear to these groups—whose slogan is "Down with imperialism!"—to have become far more hard-line.

• *Pro-transparency forces:* These groups wish to see more institutional transparency in the conduct of government affairs: more participation in budget decisions, less corruption, more accountability for decision-makers, better-functioning courts, greater transparency in party and campaign finance, and so on. Their slogan is "Down with corruption!"

• *Pro-access forces:* These groups want more access to the market, through lower prices for privatized services, lower interest rates, and expanded credit opportunities for low-income groups. They advocate dismantling the oligopolies that were created or allowed to survive in the 1990s, making tax systems less onerous on consumers, and expanding the number of well-paying private sector jobs. Their slogan is "Down with inequity!"

• *Big spenders:* These groups want to spend more on old-fashioned progressive policies, such as social services (education and health in particular) and infrastructure and energy development. Their slogan is "We need to invest in our future!"

• *Identity promoters:* The focus of these groups is on ending the system of de facto ethnic apartheid that still prevails in many countries, especially in the Andes, and giving these long-neglected ethnic minorities greater political representation and power. Their slogan is "Multiculturalism starts at home!"

(continued)

Box 1. *A Rereading of the Politics of Market Reform in the 2000s: Things Are Not That Bad (continued)*

The story of the 2000s is one of struggle *among* these various market discontents, at least as much as between them and the pro-market forces. Once in office, leftist leaders have confronted serious internal conflicts among these various forces that got them elected. These different factions have disagreed not just about what to do about markets (the first three groups versus the last four), but also about which other priorities to pursue (the last four groups among themselves).

The main reason for this dissension is that many of these forms of discontent are incompatible with one another. Clearly, the first two groups, and to a lesser extent the third, are the most serious enemies of market reform. But it is not clear that the others are completely adverse to market reform. Rather, they present demands that are more supplementary to than incompatible with market forces. This means that their demands could in principle be met while, simultaneously, market reforms are being pursued—compromise with these groups need not derail the reform agenda.

Figure 2 also shows the extent of variation across countries in terms of the timing, speed, and depth of reform. Chile was clearly among the first countries to pursue market-oriented reforms, so that by 1985 it was already ahead of the pack. Argentina and Peru, in contrast, started their reforms much later and in a much different fashion: the steep increase in the index in these countries in the late 1980s and early 1990s is a good illustration of what has come to be known as "shock therapy," whereas Chile, and later Brazil, followed a much more gradual approach. Venezuela and Peru are examples of countries that did not follow through with reform: starting from much the same, mostly unreformed position, Venezuela has lagged behind Peru and remains among the least aggressively reforming countries.

As a first step toward building an analytical framework for assessing the preconditions for successful reform, we identify here two possible general explanations for why the reforms implemented in Latin America have not produced unambiguously sustainable growth in income per capita. The first is that some of the reforms were not aimed at improving growth in income directly and immediately, but had other objectives instead. The second is that the reforms *did* attempt to generate growth but were thwarted by one or more obstacles, which may have taken different forms in different countries.

Not All Reforms Were Pro-Growth . . .

It is certainly the case that some of Latin America's reforms were not really aimed at accelerating growth of "measured" income per capita, at least in the short or the medium term, but instead were intended to improve living standards directly, by

Figure 2. *Index of Structural Reform in Selected Latin American Countries, 1985–99*[a]

1.0 = maximum reform

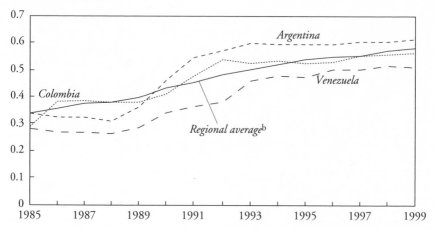

1.0 = maximum reform

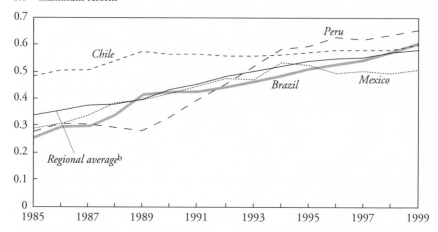

Source: Lora (2001).

a. Index is an unweighted average of five subindices measuring the extent of trade, financial, tax, privatization, and labor reform.

b. Excludes Dominican Republic, Honduras, and Nicaragua.

improving the delivery of public services. And in fact, housing, health, and other social indicators did improve during the 1990s in the region as a whole, even in some countries where growth stagnated, and have continued to improve in the 2000s (box 2 and figure 3). These are impressive achievements, and they help explain why many Latin American countries show convergence toward industrial country levels in terms of social indicators despite failure to converge in terms of

Box 2. *Progress under Alternative Measures of Poverty: The Example of Colombia*

Measures of poverty according to *unsatisfied basic needs* (UBN) can give results that are very different from measures based on income, such as the standard poverty line. UBN-based poverty measures take into account the availability to households of both physical capital, such as access to public utilities and the quality of the dwelling, and human capital, in particular the educational attainment of the household head.

Colombia's recent experience is an interesting case in point. The UBN index considers five criteria for poverty: an inadequate dwelling, insufficient basic public utilities, excessive number of persons per room, school inattendance, and economic dependence. If one of these criteria is met, the household is considered to be in poverty; if two or more are met, the household is considered to be in misery or extreme poverty. The table below shows that by the UBN index, Colombia has seen a spectacular reduction in both poverty and extreme poverty in the last thirty years, much greater than when poverty is defined according to income.

Other measures of structural poverty refer to the general health of the population. In particular, low infant mortality rates reflect adequate levels of nutrition as well as access to health care. In Colombia, the number of infants who die before the end of their first year fell from 77 per 1,000 in 1960 to 17 per 1,000 in 2006. In Latin America and the Caribbean as a whole for the same period, this indicator fell by a similar amount, from 75 per 1,000 to 20 per 1,000. The same is true for life expectancy. In sum, Colombia has witnessed great progress against poverty in terms of physical conditions, and much more progress by this measure than when measured in terms of income.

Colombia: Poverty as Measured by Unsatisfied Basic Needs, Selected Years
Percent of all households

Unsatisfied basic need (UBN)	1973	1985	1993	2005
Inadequate dwelling	31.2	13.8	11.6	10.4
Insufficient basic public utilities	30.3	21.8	10.5	7.4
Excessive number of persons per room	34.3	19.4	15.4	11.1
School inattendance	31.0	11.5	8.0	3.6
Economic dependence	29.0	15.9	12.8	11.2
Households in poverty (one UBN)	70.2	54.4	35.8	27.7
Households in extreme poverty (two or more UBNs)	44.9	22.8	14.9	10.6

Source: Departamento Nacional de Estadistica de Colombia.

Figure 3. *Infant Mortality by World Region, 1960–2006*

Deaths per 1,000 live births[a]

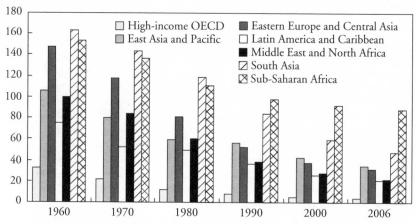

Source: World Bank, *World Development Indicators 2008.*
a. During the first year of life.

income per capita.[7] However, this phenomenon has been going on for at least forty years, and the extent to which the improvement in social indicators can be attributed to the reforms of recent decades (as opposed to general global trends, driven by improvements in technology and means of service delivery) remains controversial.[8]

. . . And Even the Reforms That Were Pro-Growth Faced Serious Obstacles

In general, however, the reforms that have been implemented since the 1980s crises *were* intended to promote income growth. When they failed, that failure can be attributed to one or more of three possible reasons. First, it could be that the reforms pursued were of second-order importance for growth given the region's unique circumstances: they might have worked in other parts of the world, but something about their nature prevented them from having a pro-growth impact in Latin America, or at least in some Latin American countries. In other words, the reforms were *not relevant* to the region.

7. Statements about convergence should be treated with care. "Convergence" is not invariant to nonlinear transformations, for example in the relationship between infant mortality and life expectancy. Here we mean, rather loosely, that the absolute gap with developed countries with respect to health and other social indicators has been reduced in the past twenty years, but the gap with respect to income per capita has not.

8. Even when there is clear evidence that reform improved public services (for example, the privatization of water supply in Argentina; see Galiani, Gertler, and Schargrodsky, 2005), this does not seem to have impressed the public. In some countries the population opposes specific reforms, and in a few these reforms are now even being undone.

Second, the reforms might have been pro-growth in a first-order sense, but were not properly implemented or were incomplete. They may have suffered from important problems of technical design, including problems of reform sequencing and lack of complementary reforms, or the design and implementation stages may have failed to take into account the particular features of Latin American countries, including institutional and political obstacles. This implies that certain binding constraints were evident before the reform started, but were not addressed, and therefore that figure 2 does not tell the whole story.

Third, the reforms may have been of first-order importance for growth, and they may have been adequately implemented, at least initially, but other, unanticipated problems may have emerged during (and perhaps even because of) the reform process. These could include not only domestic events but also external shocks, such as a sudden reversal of capital inflows resulting from a drying up of global liquidity.

The possibility that pro-growth reforms in Latin America faced fatal obstacles to their implementation raises the question of whether certain key structural characteristics of Latin American societies impede the successful implementation of reform. We focus here on two such characteristics and raise the following question: What can be expected in terms of reform from societies that share the combination of a *democratic political regime* and a *highly unequal income distribution?*

Nearly all the Latin American countries (Costa Rica is an exception) are young democracies—some might call them "forever young," given their frequent lapses from full democracy since independence in the nineteenth century. In the 1980s and 1990s a total of twenty-four countries in the region became democratic (Converse and Kapstein, 2006). Might this relative inexperience with democracy somehow interrelate with the region's sharply skewed income distribution to affect the outcome of reform? Recent literature on political economy helps to provide an answer. For example, Acemoglu and Robinson (2006) argue that in young democracies, the demand for income redistribution increases significantly as the poor acquire voting rights. To the extent that these demands remain unsatisfied, inequality might act as an obstacle to the implementation of pro-growth reforms. Others have also argued for a negative relationship between inequality and pro-growth reforms on the grounds that high and persistent inequality has an effect on the selection of reforms to be undertaken and on the institutions on which their implementation depends. For instance, Engerman and Sokoloff (2002) have documented that certain initial endowments have caused countries to end up with very unequal distributions of wealth, human capital, and political power; this inequality, in turn, has hindered the development of institutions that encourage economic activity, as the elite classes have tended to use public resources to perpetuate the existing distribution of income. Rodrik (1996) advances some alternative explanations for the negative relationship between inequality and

Figure 4. *Income Gini Coefficients by World Region, 1960–2005*

100 = most unequal

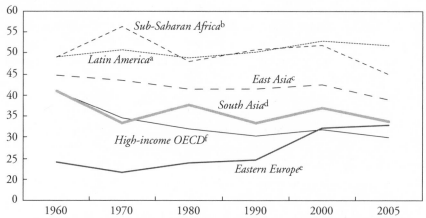

Sources: World Institute for Economics Development Research, World Income Inequality Database, version 2a; World Bank, *World Development Indicators.*

a. Argentina, Bolivia, Brazil, Chile, Colombia, Costa Rica, Ecuador, El Salvador, Guatemala, Honduras, Mexico, Nicaragua, Panama, Peru, Uruguay, Venezuela.

b. Kenya, Côte d'Ivoire, Nigeria, South Africa, Tanzania, Zambia.

c. Hong Kong, Indonesia, Malaysia, Philippines, Singapore, South Korea, Thailand.

d. Bangladesh, India, Pakistan, Sri Lanka.

e. Bulgaria, Czech Republic, Estonia, Hungary, Latvia, Lithuania, Poland, Romania.

f. Australia, Belgium, Canada, Denmark, Finland, France, Germany, Ireland, Italy, Japan, Luxembourg, Netherlands, Norway, Portugal, Spain, Sweden, Switzerland, United Kingdom, United States.

pro-growth reform. First, in a highly unequal setting like that in Latin America, governments may face more pressure from powerful interest groups to make policy decisions that benefit those groups. Second, and alternatively, when inequality is high, governments may feel forced to undertake redistributive policies rather than policies that will maximize overall income and growth. Rodrik also discusses the importance of having a well-educated labor force for reforms to work.

Latin America is a region of great inequality in a variety of dimensions. Figure 4 traces income inequality for different world regions since the 1960s, as measured by the Gini coefficient. Throughout the period, together with Sub-Saharan Africa, Latin America has been one of the two most unequal regions in the world, and the gap, especially between Latin America and the high-income countries and emerging Asia, has been widening.

Data on inequality of land ownership and schooling, although sparse, also depict Latin America as "first among unequals." Behrman, Birdsall, and Pettersson (2008) report, for the five countries in their sample (Argentina, Bolivia, Brazil, Paraguay, and Uruguay), a Gini coefficient for land ownership of over 0.75 in the

Table 1. *Selected Indicators of Financial Access by World Region*[a]

Region	Branches per 100,000 population	ATMs per 100,000 population	Loan accounts per 1,000 population	Deposit accounts per 1,000 population
Latin America	8.2	13.9	77.9	411.5
East Asia	8.8	16.7	329.0	302.1
Industrial countries	35.9	67.2	451.0	975.6
World	8.4	16.6	80.6	312.9

Source: Beck, Demirgüç-Kunt, and Martinez Peria (2006).

a. Data are unweighted medians of the countries in the region as of 2004 or the most recent year for which data are available.

decade of the 1980s.[9] For a larger sample of Latin American countries, the schooling Gini averaged 0.46, compared with 0.29 and 0.39 for the high-income countries and East Asia, respectively, in the early to mid-1980s. Access to education remained highly unequal in Latin America in 2000: in that year the schooling Gini in the region was 0.42, compared with 0.35 for East Asia and 0.26 for the high-income countries. (Unfortunately, data on land distribution do not allow for comparisons in the most recent decades.)

Access to financial services in Latin America is also very unequal. Standard indicators of financial access in the region are usually below those of industrial countries, and some (especially the number of loan accounts per person) are significantly below those in East Asia as well (table 1). This is yet another manifestation of how large numbers of Latin Americans are not sharing the benefits of reform and the market system.

Differences in access to financial services *within* Latin America are also striking. Chile is an outlier in the region in terms of loans extended: its figure of 417 loan accounts per 1,000 population is even comparable with some industrial countries. Chile and Trinidad and Tobago also have many more ATMs per person (an average of 22.3 per 100,000 population) than countries like Honduras and Nicaragua (where the average is 3.1 per 100,000), but here even Chile's figure is well short of industrial country levels. The figures for deposit accounts display much less variation.

How do all these aspects of inequality in Latin America affect the reform process? Behrman et al. (2008) provide statistical support for a negative relationship between one form of inequality (education inequality) and the pursuit of reform (figure 5). Examining various indicators of advances in financial sector reform, they find consistently that longer-run inequalities in schooling are nega-

9. The paper by Behrman et al. was prepared as background material for this project.

Figure 5. *Financial Reforms and Schooling Inequality*

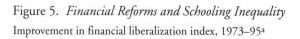
Improvement in financial liberalization index, 1973–95[a]

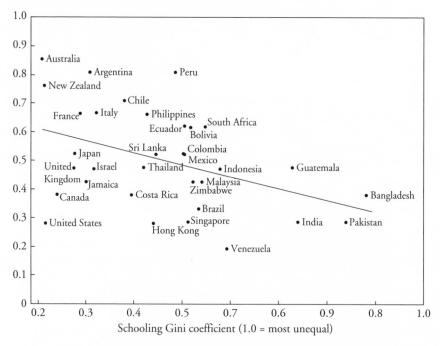

Sources: Abiad and Mody (2003); Thomas, Wang, and Fan (2001); authors' calculations.

tively related to an index of financial liberalization, in terms of both the level of liberalization achieved and the change over time.[10] (Box 3 briefly describes their methodology and presents the results of their analysis.) They also find support for the argument that structural inequality in the prereform period (as measured by schooling inequality) is associated with less reform during the 1990s, in terms of both the final level achieved and the advance each country made.

Thus, both theoretical arguments and empirical evidence support the proposition that inequality has had a negative effect on the reform process in Latin America—perhaps even on those reforms that were correctly conceived in technical terms. Unequal distribution of income, assets, education, and financial access may have restrained the advance of reform in the region and, perhaps more critically, may increase the potential for backlash against reform. The practical importance of this finding is that, in a setting like Latin America, reform efforts

10. Figure 5 also provides evidence for the argument that Latin American countries are very different from each other, and have been for decades. In the 1970s Argentina, Brazil, and Jamaica were clearly distinguished by their more equal access to education, whereas Guatemala was notorious for its lack of equality.

Box 3. *Statistical Estimation of the Relationship between Inequality and Reform*

Behrman et al. (2008) examine statistically what determines whether a country chooses to undertake reform. Following Abiad and Mody (2003), they hypothesize that "structural reform" (specifically, financial sector reform) occurs in response to some combination of external and internal shocks, combined with longstanding structural factors and the potential feedback from learning, if the reform appears to be successful—for example, in triggering more rapid growth. Relevant developments conducive to reform in the case of Latin America might be the apparent failure of the import substitution model, pressure from international institutions for structural reform, the increasing worldwide trend toward trade and financial liberalization, or a severe bank crisis.

These hypotheses are tested in a panel regression using data from thirty-seven developing and developed countries over the period 1975 to 2000 (divided into five-year periods), in which financial reform, measured as the level of a financial liberalization index, is the dependent variable. Schooling inequality is treated as a structural factor determining reform: the authors regard schooling inequality as a measure of long-term inequality, which changes only slowly. The other regressors are growth in real GDP per capita, average years of schooling, a dummy variable for the occurrence of a banking crisis, U.S. interest rates, a measure of the reform gap (measured as the difference between the country's actual level on the financial reform index and its potential level, estimated as the maximum value of the index), an index of the quality of institutions, and a dummy variable for the existence of an IMF program in the country.

The table below displays the main results of the study. The finding that schooling inequality is negatively related to financial reform, and significant in all specifications in which it is included, is consistent with the authors' hypothesis that schooling inequality is an important structural factor determining reform. These results also hold for different measures of financial reform, including the change in the financial liberalization index between 1973 and 1995.

Regressions of Financial Liberalization Index on Schooling Inequality and Other Variables[a]

Independent variable	Regression				
	1	*2*	*3*	*4*	*5*
Reform gap	−0.705***	−0.718***	−0.724***	−0.545***	−0.528***
	(0.073)	(0.074)	(0.074)	(0.089)	(0.094)
Schooling Gini	−1.150***	−1.201***	−1.214***		0.384
	(0.28)	(0.27)	(0.27)		(0.39)
Growth in GDP	−0.0102**	−0.0113**	−0.0113**	−0.00968*	−0.00949*
per capita in	(0.0052)	(0.0054)	(0.0054)	(0.0051)	(0.0052)
previous year					
Freedom House	−0.00990	−0.00883	−0.00724	0.00320	0.00437
index[b]	(0.013)	(0.013)	(0.013)	(0.012)	(0.012)
Federal funds	−0.0120**	−0.0109*	−0.0111*	−0.0122**	−0.0122**
rate	(0.0057)	(0.0058)	(0.0058)	(0.0055)	(0.0055)

(continued)

Regressions of Financial Liberalization Index on Schooling Inequality and Other Variables[a]
(continued)

Independent variable	Regression				
	1	*2*	*3*	*4*	*5*
Dummy for presence of IMF program in previous period	0.0129 (0.037)	0.0127 (0.037)	0.0122 (0.036)	0.0128 (0.033)	0.0138 (0.033)
Dummy for bank crisis in previous period		−0.0374 (0.031)	−0.128 (0.090)	−0.197** (0.085)	−0.204** (0.087)
Dummy for bank crisis in previous period × schooling Gini			0.217 (0.19)	0.345* (0.18)	0.361** (0.18)
Average years of schooling, persons 15 and older				0.135*** (0.022)	0.160*** (0.036)
R^2	0.68	0.68	0.68	0.72	0.73

Source: Behrman et al. (2008), using data from the following sources: schooling Gini coefficient, Thomas, Wang, and Fan (2001); growth in real GDP per capita (period average in constant 2000 US dollars), World Bank, *World Development Indicators 2005;* Freedom House index (average of political rights and civil liberties, equally weighted), *Freedom in the World 2006;* Federal funds rate, Federal Reserve; IMF program dummy, IMF, "History of Lending Arrangements," various years; bank crisis dummy, Bordo et al. (2001, p. 55); average years of schooling of the adult population, Barro and Lee (2000).

a. The dependent variable is the level of the financial liberalization index described in the source. The sample in all regressions consists of 182 observations from 37 countries. Asterisks indicate statistical significance at the *10 percent, **5 percent, or ***1 percent level. Robust standard errors are in parentheses.

b. A higher score indicates lower institutional quality. The index is calculated as the average of the political rights and the civil liberties indices of the Freedom House Index.

need to take inequality into account in the design of reform. In this regard, the book by Birdsall, de la Torre, and Menezes (2008) develops what the authors call an "equity toolkit" for Latin America: a full set of policy recommendations that will promote growth while enhancing equity. A number of these recommendations are validated for various countries in the later chapters in this volume.

Finally, a note of caution. Identifying inequality (especially education inequality) as a constraint on reform does not imply that it is only the poor and the less educated who resist reform. Inequality is just one of the constraints (others are discussed below) that have prevented reforms from delivering sustainable growth and raising income per capita. It is therefore not surprising to find that there are no significant differences in discontent with the *outcome* of reforms across groups with different amounts of education. Data from Latinobarómetro support this contention.[11]

A Proposed Framework for Analyzing Reforms and Growth in Latin America

The discussion thus far makes clear the need to explore in a systematic way the particular factors that have either supported or obstructed the implementation of pro-growth reforms or made them more or less effective. This section develops a framework for analyzing the relationship between reforms and growth in the region. Chapter 1 discussed the differences between alternative approaches and the one presented here. The objective is to construct a framework that will allow researchers and policymakers to do the following:

• identify mechanisms through which alternative reforms can (or cannot) deliver sustained growth in Latin American countries

• understand the factors specific to Latin America that generate issues for appropriate design, problems for implementation, and other local constraints—political, social, or institutional—that affect how reforms can deliver growth

• derive at least some preliminary conclusions about why certain reforms in the past did not lead to growth, in order to advance feasible policy recommendations for the future

• focus attention on the political economy of inequality and access in the reform process, and

• most important, serve as an instrument for further assessments of the reform process in individual countries and for cross-country comparisons.

Pulling together the evidence and analytical discussion in the first two sections of this chapter, the framework is formed by four blocks, each one answering one of the following questions:

• What are the foundations for growth—the first-order underlying issues—in Latin America?

---

11. We are indebted to Pedro Dal Bo for arguments explaining the lack of support for reform among the more educated segments of the population. Data from Latinobarómetro (www.latino-barómetro.org) show that in some countries, such as Bolivia, Colombia, El Salvador, Nicaragua, and Peru, the more educated are even slightly less enthusiastic about the results of privatization than the less educated. However, these rankings vary from year to year and should therefore be viewed with caution.

• How, at the analytical level, can individual reforms impact the foundations for growth?

• What local features of the economy and society in individual countries act as potential constraints and obstacles, breaking the link from reforms to growth?

• How can these constraints and obstacles be addressed, either head on or by finding legitimate ways to work around them? Are there alternative reforms that can more effectively address the same purpose? Are there any private sector arrangements that can serve to reduce, contain, or appropriately get past these obstacles?

The rest of this section develops each of these four blocks. The third and fourth blocks explicitly recognize that countries in the region differ significantly one from another in terms of economic and social development as well as political features. Some of these differences are evident from the earlier discussion. A central point behind the conceptual framework is that major differences between countries imply that reforms will act differently and result in different outcomes in different countries—hence regional generalizations have limited usefulness. To exemplify the application of the framework to individual reforms and countries, the discussion makes reference to the existing literature on reform in the region.

What Are the Foundations for Growth in Latin America?

As discussed in chapter 1, this framework identifies economic growth with *market-based* growth. Although this definition by no means precludes a sensible role for government (and indeed, government interventions to deal with market imperfections are encouraged), the Task Force acknowledged that the Latin American experience with government-led growth has been disappointing and that such a model is not advisable for the region. Moreover, in the context of an open capital account (the type of regime chosen by most countries in the region since the late 1980s), the adequate functioning of a market economy is a necessary condition for the sustainability of growth gains (see chapter 1 for further discussion).

The Task Force identified five foundations for market-based growth in Latin America. The first three are essential for the appropriate functioning of any market economy. The last two are more specifically a concern in Latin America. By recognizing the region's specific features and its long history of economic, social, and political crises, the foundations try to capture the essential need for economic stability and social inclusion for growth to be sustained. The five foundations are

• Secure *property rights* for the population, so that people can expect to benefit from their investments and cannot be unexpectedly expropriated by the state or by the politically powerful.

• Sufficiently *equal opportunities* for broad segments of the society, so as to level the playing field in market-based interactions. Broadly speaking, this means lowering barriers to entry into business to people without political connections or large stocks of wealth. This is distinct from the first foundation: a person might have secure property rights but no way to access new market opportunities, for example because regulatory requirements create a high fixed cost of doing business, or because ordinary citizens cannot raise capital through bank loans or in other ways. Problems with this foundation are apparent in Latin America, where, as discussed above, lack of access has been an important manifestation of inequality, which in turn constrains pro-growth reform.

• Sufficient *economic and political competition* to avoid capture of the state by elites of one kind or another. This is distinct from the first two foundations, because even if ordinary people have secure property rights and meaningful opportunities, the considerable resources of the state might still be funneled toward a relatively few favored individuals or companies. Recent research on a wide range of countries indicates that political connections of various kinds remain important and a major brake on development.

• Latin America's frequent economic and financial crises during the 1980s and since have often resulted in sharp recessions and in the need for fiscal adjustment to restore macroeconomic balance. These adjustments, in turn, have required drastic cuts in social expenditure and in vital infrastructure spending, with adverse consequences for the poor and for long-term growth. Although the major economies in the world can sometimes get away with maintaining large macroeconomic imbalances for prolonged periods (the United States being a current example), the characteristics and history of Latin America imply that investors will tend to flee at the first sign of trouble, deepening the financial difficulties and exacerbating the crisis. Thus, *macroeconomic stability* is a key foundation for sustained growth in Latin America, necessary to ensure that sufficient public funds are allocated to pro-growth reform efforts and, conversely, that the reform process does not have to be interrupted to deal with macroeconomic imbalances.

• Given the recent history in Latin America of discontent with the outcome of reform (box 1) and disillusion with various alternative development models, a fifth foundation for growth is the need for *broad sharing of the benefits of growth* among the population. Realistically, only a minority of the population will ever want to make the kind of productive investments for which the first three foundations are of primary importance—in all societies, most people work as employees or in small-scale independent activities, or are outside the labor force, living as pensioners or students or other dependents. Yet these people, too, need to benefit from reform if there is not to be a serious political backlash against it—and this is true whether reform succeeds or fails in restoring economic growth. If GDP per capita grows but most people see no increase in their real income, they may become opponents of reform, and their opposition may lead to consequences that undermine the sustainability of growth.

The importance of this last foundation cannot be overstressed. As discussed above, important segments of the population in a number of Latin American countries today are voting for redistributive policies. Taking these demands into account is essential for long-term growth.

Before leaving this subsection, an important clarification is needed. Although the framework emphasizes the central role of the identified foundations in achieving sustained growth in Latin America, the Task Force fully acknowledges that there can be episodes where growth is ignited without improvement in any of the foundations. For example, a sharp improvement in the terms of trade can spark growth—indeed, this has happened several times in the region, including during 2003–08. The Task Force maintains, however, that for such growth accelerations to be sustainable, the foundations for growth identified above need to improve.

How Do Reforms Impact the Foundations for Growth?

Every reform affects economic growth differently. Therefore any analysis of the potential for reform to have an impact on the foundations for growth requires a list of reforms to be considered. However, the list of all the reforms that have been or might someday be implemented in Latin America is certain to be both long and varied, and each of these reforms will cover a number of different issues and activities and thus can be disaggregated further.

The Task Force strongly believes that the task of identifying which particular reforms are needed to strengthen the growth foundations in a given country should be left up to the country itself. In the chapters that follow, experts from five countries in the region each choose a set of reforms to analyze for their country. These reforms will, of course, include some that have already been implemented and some that have not but that are considered essential for the future. The Task Force makes no presumption about what reforms are best for what countries, and it certainly does not presume that a common set of policies is right for all countries in the region. However, to illustrate the workings of the framework, we offer the following, necessarily incomplete, classification:

• reforms that directly improve the workings of the market: trade, financial, labor, pension, privatization, and land titling (these include adequate regulation, including consumer protection and antidumping arrangements)

• reforms oriented toward the provision of social services: education, health, and the social safety net

• reforms of economic and financial infrastructure: central bank independence, decentralization, tax collection, budgetary institutions, customs, registries, regulatory agencies, and supervisory authorities

Table 2. *Potential Impact of Reforms on the Foundations for Growth:*
An Illustrative Example[a]

Reform	Property rights	Equal opportunity	Competition	Macroeconomic stability	Broad sharing of growth benefits
Trade		✓	✓✓	?	?
Financial	✓	✓	✓	✓✓	✓
Labor	✓	✓✓			✓
Pension	✓	✓✓		✓✓	?
Privatization with regulation[b]	✓	✓		✓	✓
Budgetary institutions		✓	✓	✓✓	✓
Education[c]		✓		✓	✓✓
Decentralization	?	?			✓✓
Tax reform	?	✓	✓	✓	✓
Judiciary	✓✓	✓	✓	✓	✓
Electoral process		✓	✓	✓	✓
Legislative	✓	✓	✓	✓	✓
Anticorruption	✓	✓	✓	✓	✓

a. One checkmark indicates a positive potential impact of the indicated reform on the indicated foundation, two checkmarks a strong positive impact, a question mark an uncertain or mixed impact, and a blank cell no impact.

b. The table illustrates the potential impact of telecommunications privatization; privatization of other state enterprises might have somewhat different impacts.

c. Reform of other social services (for example, health care) would likely have similar impacts.

• reform of political institutions: the judicial system, the legislature, and electoral processes; and

• reform of governance institutions: measures to control corruption and improve the rule of law.

Table 2 lists several of the main types of reform and indicates which of the foundations each type has the *potential* to affect. This is, of course, just an overall summary assessment. The matching of reforms with foundations is derived from a review of the literature on the effects of individual reforms on growth, but it should be taken only as illustrative and not representing every case and circumstance. A blank cell means that the indicated reform does not affect the indicated growth foundation; a single checkmark indicates a positive impact of the reform on the growth foundation, and two checkmarks mean a very strong positive effect. A question mark implies that the direction of the impact of the reform on the foundation depends on other factors; the reform could even have a negative effect. A good example is trade reform. Reform that opens the country further to international trade should promote *equal opportunity,* by lowering barriers to entry in the affected sectors, and it should strongly enhance economic *competition* in those sectors. But if trade reform is implemented without adequate mechanisms to compensate the losers, it could have a negative impact on the *broad sharing of the benefits of growth*.[12]

The most important conclusion to be drawn from table 2 is that, according to the literature, a wide range of reforms have the *potential* to positively impact at least some, and in some cases most, of the foundations for growth. A key issue, therefore, is to assess whether each reform, when and where it has been applied, has delivered on its potential. Most important is whether those reforms that had the potential to impact the "broad sharing" foundation actually did so, because, as stressed above, this foundation is central to the sustainability of growth in Latin America.[13]

What Might Prevent Reforms from Delivering Growth?

A reform might fail to reach its potential for a number of reasons, and therefore it is important to analyze the various obstacles to reform and the constraints to which various reforms are subject. We leave open the possibility that a particular reform might not have had a significant *direct* impact on growth, but did facilitate the implementation of other reforms that were clearly pro-growth, thus promoting growth *indirectly*. Argentina's reform of education in 1991–99 is a clear example. By bringing together two political actors from different political factions within the ruling party (the Justicialist Party) at the time, this reform allowed the passage of other reforms that more directly promoted growth in the mid-1990s (see Corrales, 2004).

What factors might act as obstacles to the success of a reform that has the potential to enhance, directly or indirectly, the foundations for growth? The list is long. Some of these factors are universal, threatening successful reform anywhere in the world. However, as we will see next, others are associated with the particular features of Latin American countries (which can differ from country to country). Following the discussion above, we can identify the following sets of obstacles:

• *Problems of relevance.* A reform may be inappropriate for a country, either because the country is not ready for it or because the country's particular features make the reform undesirable. For example, Rojas-Suárez (2002, 2008) argues that implementation of the bank capital requirements proposed by the Basel Com-

---

12. The impact of trade liberalization on the growth foundations is complex, since the effects on relative wages over time might create new losers as the process evolves. Compensation policy therefore needs to be designed in a dynamic fashion and not limited to addressing the initial effects of trade liberalization.

13. See Birdsall and Londoño (1997) for evidence.

mittee on Bank Supervision (the so-called Basel II requirements) would be inappropriate for the Latin American region because, among other reasons, the risk assessment techniques proposed in Basel II would tend to intensify the procyclicality of bank credit. This would increase the fragility of the countries' financial systems rather than reduce it as intended by Basel II.

• *Problems of design.* A reform may fail to properly align incentives with desired outcomes. In other words, even if the reform is intended to have a positive impact on one or several of the growth foundations, it might not create the correct incentives for this to occur. This could happen for a number of reasons:

• *Technical inadequacies.* The list of examples is quite long. A good illustration is the case of pension reform in Bolivia. This reform replaced an antiquated, overly generous pay-as-you-go system with a very ungenerous, fully funded system, creating a strong incentive for workers (who could choose between the two systems) to retire under the old system. The huge fiscal expenditure that resulted had a negative effect on the macroeconomic stability foundation. Peru's pension reform provides another example: here increasing coverage was not made part of the reform, which thus missed an opportunity to impact another foundation, the broader sharing of the benefits of growth (see Morón, 2006).

• *Lack of needed sequencing.* The experience with trade reform in several Latin American countries provides examples of this common design problem. In most of these countries (Chile being a notable exception), the capital account was liberalized simultaneously with the current account. In a context of fixed exchange rates, this lack of proper sequencing resulted in a real appreciation, which eroded the potential gains from trade.[14] Another classic example of inadequate sequencing in the region, first identified by Díaz-Alejandro (1985), is the liberalization of financial markets *before* an appropriate supervisory framework is put in place. A number of authors identify this problem as an important factor explaining the eruption of banking crises in Latin America in the 1980s and 1990s (see, for example, Hausmann and Rojas-Suarez, 1996).

• *Lack of complementary reforms.* This is another common problem in many countries in Latin America. A good example here is the need for adequate budgetary institutions to complement decentralization. As discussed in Wiesner (2003) and Tanzi (1995), a number of decentralization efforts in the region during the 1990s generated only limited growth gains and instead contributed to fiscal instability.

• *Lack of adequate adaptation.* Sometimes a reform that has worked elsewhere (typically in industrial countries) has failed in Latin America because it

---

14. See, for example, Devlin, Ffrench-Davis, and Griffith-Jones (1995).

was not properly adapted to the particular features of Latin American economies. For example, the bank capital requirements suggested by the Basel Committee call for banks to hold capital equivalent to at least 8 percent of assets. This requirement usually works well in industrial countries, but the recommended ratio might prove too low for the more risky financial environments of Latin American countries.

• *Obstacles from local conditions.* Even if a reform is correctly designed, at least initially, features of the local environment may pose barriers to its appropriate implementation or its effectiveness. These obstacles include

   • *Institutional constraints.* For example, privatization might fail to deliver growth if the agency in charge of regulating the privatized entities lacks sufficient power to promote and protect competition. Torero, Schroth, and Pasco-Font (2004) note that the privatization of telecommunications in Peru brought about important improvements for consumers in terms of coverage, quality, and price of the services. However, the telecommunications regulatory agency still lacks authority over the licensing of operators or their rights to use spectrum, as well as capacity to exercise merger control. These tools are essential to promoting competition in the sector, and their absence undermines the competition foundation.

   • *Adverse political dynamics, including lack of legitimacy of the reform.* This constraint relates to the demands of different segments of the population as these express themselves through political interest groups. As was stated in box 1, some of these demands are consistent with pro-growth reform. Others, however—most notably those calling for expropriation and trade protection—clearly run counter to strengthening the foundations of growth. For example, domestic protectionist interests in Brazil mobilized themselves more effectively than did the pro-liberalization forces and succeeded in preventing trade reform (see Abreu, 2004). Expropriation directly violates the property rights foundation, and protectionism undermines both competition and equal opportunity.

   • *Insufficient implementation capacity.* In many Latin American countries the public sector has too few personnel with the skills, especially management skills, needed to implement reform effectively. Decentralization is one of the reforms most affected by this obstacle, because subnational governments are even more prone than the central government to such skill shortages.[15]

   • *Inequality of income, assets, and education.* Inequality was identified above as both an important constraint on implementing pro-growth reform or its components and a threat to the effectiveness of reform once implemented. An

---

15. As discussed by Daughters and Harper (2007), lack of implementation capacity is one of the major obstacles to successful decentralization in many Latin American countries.

example relevant to a number of countries in the region is the constraint on effective bank supervision, and therefore on macroeconomic stability, derived from the concentration of wealth. The concentration of assets in the hands of a relatively few very wealthy individuals makes it easier for banks to engage in lending to insiders.[16]

These obstacles are not always independent of each other, but rather can interact. In some cases problems of design can reflect insufficient analysis or even bad advice, whereas in others the implementation of a poorly designed policy can be the result of capture by particular political interests, or of institutional deficiencies.

How Can Constraints and Obstacles Be Overcome? Are There Alternative Initiatives?

Once the constraints and obstacles to reform have been identified, the question then becomes what to do about them. This is the core of the analysis presented in the next five chapters. Just to provide a flavor of what is to come, here we provide a few very succinct examples of proposals already found in the literature. Some are of general relevance, while others apply to individual country experiences.

DEALING WITH PROBLEMS OF DESIGN

• To hedge against external shocks in economies with liberalized trade systems, commodity exports can be taxed during boom periods and the proceeds used to finance a special fund to counter excessive volatility and to finance incentives for local export diversification and innovation. The copper stabilization fund in Chile is considered a successful tool in this regard.[17]

• Since the specific recommendations of the Basel Committee for Banking Supervision are considered inappropriate for Latin America, at least in the short run, some have suggested that countries in the region implement ex ante loan-loss provisions,[18] as a mechanism to improve the quality of the banking system, and rely more on this supervisory tool than on capital requirements (Rojas-Suárez, 2002, 2008).

• To reap the potential gains from decentralization, countries can design clear rules within the transfer system, with special emphasis on how the funds are distributed among different regional and local governments.[19]

---

16. See De Juan (1996).

17. Because economic stability is considered essential for decreasing poverty and inequality, Birdsall et al. (2008) also include stabilization funds in their equity toolkit.

18. Ex ante loan-loss provisions require that provisioning increase in good times. In bad times, when nonperforming loans increase, the accumulated funds can be used to offset the weakening of bank capital.

19. Daughters and Harper (2007) assess the quality of the transfer systems and other achievements in the decentralization efforts of fourteen Latin American countries.

• To help deepen domestic capital markets so that they play a more central role in raising investment and economic growth, pension funds can be allowed to broaden their investment base. One way to do this is through innovative financial instruments that cater to the investment needs of Latin America, in a manner compatible with investors' demand for adequate returns and the safety of their investments. For this purpose a variety of new instruments have been proposed by the Latin American Shadow Financial Regulatory Committee (2005).

• Countries should not mimic the usual tax mix of industrial countries, but instead take into account the importance of the informal sector. As an example, Artana (2004) proposes a specific tax structure for the case of the Dominican Republic.

• The proper design of a fiscal budgetary institution requires introducing transparency rules at the same time that fiscal rules are introduced. Filc and Scartascini (2004) summarize progress at the country level in designing procedures and practices according to which fiscal budgets are drafted, discussed, and implemented in the region.

DEALING WITH OBSTACLES ARISING FROM LOCAL CONDITIONS

When confronted with an institutional or political constraint, the first-best solution is obviously to remove the constraint. But this might not be feasible in the short run. Hence, the following recommendations fall in the category of *second-best arrangements:*

• Countries can organize a process aimed at constructing a private-public sector alliance to develop a consensus about long-term strategies that would result in both private and public welfare gains. Examples are public-private partnerships for deepening financial systems, and strategies to support the private sector in overcoming obstacles for improved competitiveness.

• To overcome the constraints imposed by an inadequate judicial system on bank credit to small firms, countries can collect and disseminate information through private credit bureaus. These and other proposals to improve access to financial services in Latin America are contained in Secretaría General Iberoamericana (2006).

• To reduce social exclusion from pension funds in Peru, the government could introduce noncontributory pensions for older workers in extreme poverty. Although this would increase government spending, it should be considered as a preemptive measure to bolster the political sustainability of the pension reform (see Morón, 2006).

• To stimulate societal demand for education reform, evaluation results can be used in a transparent way both for teacher selection and for determining acceptance to universities. In addition, to minimize bureaucratic resistance to producing, analyzing, and disseminating school tests, a dedicated unit could be created for that purpose that is independent of the ministry of education (see Corrales, 2004).

• International tax agreements can help overcome political resistance to changes in the status quo. As Artana (2004) notes, in the Dominican Republic, trade liberalization under CAFTA (the Central American Free Trade Agreement) created an important fiscal loss that everyone involved (political parties, various business organizations) knew needed to be repaired.

• In Brazil, to reduce the incentives for politicians to use the courts as a tool to advance their political interests, increased use could be made of the ADC (Ação Declaratória de Constitucionalidade, or Direct Action of Constitutionality), which allows the Supreme Court to declare the constitutionality of normative laws and acts, with binding effect over the lower courts (see Sousa, 2007).

Some Lessons from the Framework

The following parting thoughts summarize what the Task Force learned, in the process of designing the framework described in this chapter, about the linkages between reforms and growth in Latin American countries:

• A most important conclusion is that the framework can indeed be a powerful tool for designing and implementing pro-growth reforms. As the following chapters will show, the application of the framework to specific country experiences yields a systematic identification of constraints and obstacles that have prevented reforms from maximizing their growth potential. The chapters show that the framework helped in generating country-specific recommendations to overcome these problems.

• In setting the stage for developing the framework, the Task Force concluded that many social demands that could be read as opposing reforms could instead be seen as complementary to market-led growth (box 1). For example, pro-access and pro-transparency movements call for less inequity and less corruption, both of which positively affect long-term growth. The strength of these demands varies from country to country and needs to be taken into account when designing reforms. After all, some reforms, especially those dealing with institutions (such as judicial reform), may find fertile ground for their appropriate implementation in countries with pro-growth social demands.

• The existing literature and the discussion in the following chapters show that most of the reforms of the 1990s had the *potential* to positively affect the foundations for growth. However, in many cases the reforms as actually implemented only weakly addressed the first-order problems that undermine growth in Latin American countries. In particular, as Birdsall et al. (2008) emphasize, the extreme inequality and widespread poverty in many of these countries, both of which are associated with educational shortfalls and the concentration of resources in the hands of a few, received too little emphasis—the "broad sharing" foundation, essential for growth in Latin America, was not properly addressed. To put this in the language of property rights: the problem was not how to improve average property rights or even marginal property rights, but rather how to improve the property rights, broadly construed, of people living on the fringes of society.

• Instead, in most countries in the region, the emphasis was on designing and implementing reforms that had proved effective in societies with much greater access and less poverty and inequality, such as in Western Europe and East Asia. In those societies, pushing for better functioning of the state, or even just lowering inflation and opening the economy to trade, created meaningful opportunities (and higher real wages) for a broad cross section of society. In contrast, when such reforms were implemented in Latin America, the relatively well educated and people with significant initial resources gained, but the rest of society experienced little or no increase in real earnings (although they did see some real improvement in access to health care, clean water, and decent housing). In other words, social indicators converged, but incomes did not. This disparity of outcomes explains much of the emerging reform fatigue and the potential (and in some places actual) backlash against reform.

• The underlying issues of inequality and poverty were not effectively addressed, not because policymakers were unaware of the issues, but rather because these are very hard problems given Latin America's existing power structures and economic and political institutions. These problems *can* be addressed, but the past fifty years have shown that progress on these fundamental issues is difficult. It remains so today, although, as stated above, support for improving equity is perhaps stronger than in the past. Countries are trying to improve equity in different ways. In some, expropriation and unilateral repudiation of contracts are likely to undermine property rights and make growth less likely, and a return to greater state control of the economy is unlikely to produce sustainable growth. In other countries, however, the potential for organized, market-based efforts for broadening opportunities has started to develop.

• Some lessons from other emerging markets can be encouraging for Latin America. Growth per se does not necessarily lead to better institutions. But growth of the kind seen in parts of Asia has generally created the kind of constituencies that favor further reform. Institutional change has come about, in large part, because broad-based homegrown groups have flourished, and because they have demanded better protection, greater access, and other institutional improvements, which in turn feed back to sustain growth.

• As the country case studies in the next five chapters will show, problems of design sometimes weakened the capacity of reforms to affect the foundations for growth. These problems reflected a combination of technical inadequacies, sequencing problems, and lack of necessary complementary reforms. But the Task Force believes that the more important problems facing reform had to do with institutional and political obstacles. In some cases the main problem was political capture of some key institutions; in others, the force of certain special interests was

the stumbling block; in still others, extreme inequality emerged as a major obstacle. Lack of capacity to carry through the needed actions also seems to have played
a crucial role.

• The country studies will also show the importance of complementarity
between reforms. For example, many reforms failed to realize their growth potential partly because of deficiencies in the judicial system.

• Although the Task Force emphasizes the importance of country-level differences for the design and implementation of policies, it is necessary to continue examining lessons from other parts of the world for their relevance to
Latin America. One such lesson is that emerging Asia has made substantial
progress since 1960 using a strategy of promoting manufactured exports to create new constituencies for further reform. The middle-income countries that
have acceded to the European Union—such as Portugal and Spain in the
1980s—have made similar progress starting from higher levels of income than
those in Asia, and thus their experience may prove more relevant to Latin
America.

References

Abiad, Abdul, and Ashoka Mody. 2003. "Financial Reform: What Shakes It? What Shapes It?"
  IMF Working Paper WP/03/70. Washington: International Monetary Fund.
Abreu, Marcelo de Paiva. 2004. "Trade Liberalization and the Political Economy of Protection
  in Brazil since 1987." Special Initiative on Trade and Integration, INTAL-ITD Working
  Paper. Washington: Inter-American Development Bank.
Acemoglu, Daron, and James Robinson. 2006. *Economic Origins of Democracy and Dictatorship*.
  Cambridge University Press.
Artana, Daniel. 2004. "República Dominicana: Análisis del Proyecto de Reforma Tributaria."
  Chemonics-AID (July).
Bai, Jushan, and Pierre Perron. 1998. "Estimating and Testing Linear Models with Multiple
  Structural Changes." *Econometrica* 66, no. 1 (January): 47–78.
———. 2003. "Computation and Analysis of Multiple Structural Change Models." *Journal of
  Applied Econometrics* 18: 1–22.
Barro, Robert J., and Jong-Wha Lee. 2000. "International Data on Educational Attainment:
  Updates and Implications." CID Working Paper 42. Cambridge, Mass.: Center for International
  Development at Harvard University.
Beck, Thorsten, Asli Demirgüç-Kunt, and Maria Soledad Martinez Peria. 2006. "Reaching
  Out: Access to and Use of Banking Services across Countries." Policy Research Working
  Paper WPS3754. Washington: World Bank (October).
Behrman, Jere, Nancy Birdsall, and Gunilla Pettersson. 2008. "Schooling Inequality and Finan-
  cial Reform in Latin America." Center for Global Development, Washington.
Berg, Andrew, Jonathan D. Ostry, Marcos Souto, and Jeromin Zettelmeyer. 2006. "Estimat-
  ing Multiple Structural Breaks on GDP Growth Series." International Monetary Fund,
  Washington.
Birdsall, Nancy, and Juan Luis Londoño. 1997. "Asset Inequality Matters: An Assessment of
  the World Bank's Approach to Poverty Reduction." *American Economic Review Papers and
  Proceedings* 87, no. 2: 32–37.

Birdsall, Nancy, Augusto de la Torre, and Rachel Menezes. 2008. *Fair Growth: Economic Policies for Latin America's Poor and Middle-Income Majority.* Washington: Center for Global Development and Inter-American Dialogue.

Bordo, Michael, Barry Eichengreen, Daniella Klingebiel, and Maria Soledad Martinez-Peria. 2001. "Is the Crisis Problem Growing More Severe?" *Economic Policy* 32: 51–82.

Converse, Nathan, and Ethan Kapstein. 2006. "The Economics of Young Democracies: Policies and Performance." Working Paper 85. Washington: Center for Global Development (March).

Corrales, Javier. 2004. "Multiple Preferences, Variable Strengths: The Politics of Education Reform in Argentina." In Joan Nelson and Robert Kaufman, eds., *Crucial Needs, Weak Incentives: Social Sector Reform, Democratization, and Globalization in Latin America.* Woodrow Wilson Center Press and Johns Hopkins University Press.

Daughters, Robert, and Leslie Harper. 2007. "Fiscal and Political Decentralization Reforms." In Eduardo Lora, ed., *The State of State Reform in Latin America.* Inter-American Development Bank and Stanford University Press.

De Juan, Aristóbulo. 1996. "The Roots of Banking Crises: Microeconomic Issues and Supervision and Regulation." In Ricardo Hausmann and Liliana Rojas-Suarez, eds., *Banking Crises in Latin America.* Washington: Inter-American Development Bank.

Devlin, Robert, Ricardo Ffrench-Davis, and Stephanie Griffith-Jones. 1995. "Surges in Capital Flows and Development: An Overview of Policy Issues." In R. Ffrench Davis and S. Griffith-Jones, eds., *Coping with Capital Surges: The Return of Finance to Latin America.* Boulder, Colo.: Lynne Rienner Publishers.

Díaz-Alejandro, Carlos. 1985. "Good-Bye Financial Repression, Hello Financial Crash." *Journal of Development Economics* 19, nos. 1–2 (September–October): 1–24.

Edwards, Sebastian. 1995. *Crisis and Reform in Latin America: From Despair to Hope.* Oxford University Press.

Engerman, Stanley L., and Kenneth L. Sokoloff. 2002. "Factor Endowments, Inequality and Paths of Development among New World Economies." Working Paper 9259. Cambridge, Mass.: National Bureau of Economic Research.

Filc, Gabriel, and Carlos Scartascini. 2004. "Budget Institutions and Fiscal Outcomes: Ten Years of Inquiry on Fiscal Matters at the Research Department." Inter-American Development Bank, Washington.

Galiani, Sebastián, Paul Gertler, and Ernesto Schargrodsky. 2005. "Water for Life: The Impact of the Privatization of Water Services on Child Mortality." *Journal of Political Economy* 113, no. 1: 83–120.

Hausmann, Ricardo, and Liliana Rojas-Suárez, eds. 1996. *Banking Crises in Latin America.* Washington: Inter-American Development Bank.

Jones, Benjamin, and Benjamin Olken. 2005. "The Anatomy of Start-Stop Growth." Working Paper 11753. Cambridge, Mass.: National Bureau of Economic Research.

Latin American Shadow Financial Regulatory Committee. 2005. "Putting Pension Funds to Work in Latin America: New Financial Instruments to Help Deepen Financial Markets." Statement no. 13 (July 14).

Lora, Eduardo. 2001. "Structural Reforms in Latin America: What Has Been Reformed and How to Measure It." IADB Research Department Working Paper 466. Washington: Inter-American Development Bank.

———. 2007. *The State of State Reform in Latin America.* Inter-American Development Bank and Stanford University Press.

Lora, Eduardo, and Ugo Panizza. 2002. "Structural Reforms in Latin America under Scrutiny." IADB Research Department Working Paper 470. Washington: Inter-American Development Bank.

Morón, Eduardo. 2006. "La Reforma Previsional Pendiente en el Perú." Universidad del Pacífico.

Rodrik, Dani. 1996. "Understanding Economic Policy Reform." *Journal of Economic Literature* 34, no. 1: 9–41.

Rojas-Suárez, Liliana. 2002. "Can International Capital Standards Strengthen the Soundness of Banks in Emerging Markets?" *Capco Institute Journal of Financial Transformation* (July): 51–63.

———. 2008. "Domestic Financial Regulations in Developing Countries: Can They Effectively Limit the Impact of Capital Account Volatility"? In Joseph Stiglitz and J. A. Ocampo, eds., *Capital Market Liberalization and Development.* Oxford University Press.

Secretaría General Iberoamericana (SEGIB). 2006. "La Extensión del Crédito y los Servicios Financieros: Obstáculos, Propuestas y Buenas Prácticas." Madrid (September).

Sousa, Mariana. 2007. "A Brief Overview of Judicial Reform in Latin America: Objectives, Challenges and Accomplishments." In Eduardo Lora, ed., *The State of State Reform in Latin America.* Inter-American Development Bank and Stanford University Press.

Tanzi, Vito. 1995. "Fiscal Federalism and Decentralization: A Review of Some Efficiency and Macroeconomic Aspects." In Michael Bruno and Boris Pleskovic, eds., *Annual World Bank Conference on Development Economics.* Washington: World Bank.

Thomas, Vinod, Yan Wang, and Xibo Fan. 2001. "Measuring Education Inequality: Gini Coefficients of Education for 140 Countries, 1960–2000." *Journal of Education Planning and Administration* 17, no. 1: 5–33.

Torero, Máximo, Enrique Schroth, and Alberto Pasco-Font. 2004. "The Impact of Telecommunications Privatization in Peru on the Welfare of Urban Consumers." *Economía* 4: 91.

Wiesner, E. 2003. *Fiscal Federalism in Latin America: From Entitlements to Markets.* Washington: Inter-American Development Bank.

Zettelmeyer, Jeromin. 2006. "Growth and Reforms in Latin America: A Survey of Facts and Arguments." IMF Working Paper WP/06/210. Washington: International Monetary Fund (September).

3

Pro- and Anti-Market Reforms in Democratic Brazil

ARMANDO CASTELAR PINHEIRO, REGIS BONELLI, AND SAMUEL DE ABREU PESSÔA

This chapter is motivated by a riddle: why, after implementing so many reforms over the last quarter century, has Brazil fared so poorly at accelerating economic growth? There are two possible answers. The first is that the reforms were well chosen and well targeted but faced serious obstacles in meeting the growth objective. They may have been poorly implemented or incomplete, perhaps because of problems of design (poor sequencing or lack of complementary reforms, for instance), or because they were sidetracked by problems not initially foreseen or that emerged during, or were even caused by, the reform process itself. This explanation fits the facts in Brazil's case: the process of market-oriented reform did face implementation problems, for example in the regulation of infrastructure, and it does remain incomplete in several areas, from education to judicial reform.

The other explanation hinges on the reforms themselves: although pursued forcefully, they may have targeted the wrong foundations, failing to address those that were actually constraining growth. This may have occurred, for instance, if the reforms were selected to foster goals other than accelerating growth. This description, too, fits the Brazilian case, not so much because the reforms as a whole

We thank Liliana Rojas-Suarez, John Williamson, José De Gregorio, and other participants at CGD's "Helping Reforms Deliver Growth in Latin America" workshop for helpful comments on an earlier version of this paper. A longer version of this paper including a technical annex and a list of acronyms is available on CGD's website, www.cgdev.org.

aimed at the wrong foundations, but rather because several of the reforms were more concerned with distribution than with growth, while others did seek to foster growth but did not do so in a market-oriented way. More important, the reforms that pursued these other goals were not neutral with respect to growth but actually compromised the foundations for growth. In short, even as policymakers were, with one hand, fighting inflation, opening the economy, eliminating restrictions on business practices, and privatizing, with the other hand they were actively pursuing what we call anti-market reforms: changes in legal norms and policies that discouraged investment and productivity growth. These reforms seriously weakened the link between market-oriented reform and growth. As a result, the reforms as a whole, while reducing the burden of regulation, at the same time enhanced the role of the state in directly allocating resources, by expanding public expenditure, and weakened property rights.

One can point to several examples of this parallel reform agenda. The 1988 constitution sought to enhance political competition and equality of opportunity, but it also contained some clearly nationalist and statist provisions: it established public monopolies in telecommunications, oil, and the distribution of natural gas; created barriers to foreign ownership in mining and electricity; and reduced contract flexibility in labor markets. In addition, the stabilization plans of the 1980s and 1990s relied on price freezes that breached financial contracts and, in the case of the 1990 plan, blatantly disregarded property rights. More recently, a large primary fiscal surplus contributed to stabilizing the public debt-GDP ratio, but it coexisted with a huge expansion in taxes and current expenditure. Income transfer programs helped spread the benefits of growth, but these were structured in such a way that they discouraged participation in the social security system. A more independent judiciary increased protection against arbitrary government decisions, but, by pursuing distributive goals rather than imposing the rule of law, judges have often weakened contract and property rights.

We regard the expansion in public expenditure, the change in its composition (a decline in public investment and a rise in current outlays), and the concomitant increase in the tax burden as the most harmful of Brazil's anti-market reforms, because of the consequences for macroeconomic stability. Looking forward, priority should be given to a fiscal reform aimed at reducing current expenditure and the tax burden, while creating the fiscal space needed for an increase in public infrastructure investment. Implementation of such a reform will require overcoming political barriers of various sorts. Part of the rise in current public spending stemmed from new obligations enshrined in the 1988 constitution or created in the following years, which were perceived as necessary for securing citizenship rights and the stability of democratic institutions. The new constitution also ended twenty years of fiscal centralism, eventually causing a major expansion in state and municipal revenue and fiscal spending that will be hard to reverse, given that political support for spending reduction is weak.

This chapter discusses the Brazilian reform riddle and identifies the reforms that we see as having the greatest potential to enhance future growth, while highlighting the role of politics in explaining past outcomes and shaping the new reform program. We begin by reviewing the main stylized facts of Brazil's recent growth performance. We then discuss the recent history of reforms, the way they affected the foundations for growth, and the issues of reform selection and incompleteness. Next, taking a more forward-looking approach, we analyze the reforms that we believe have the greatest promise of positively impacting the foundations for growth in Brazil. The chapter ends with some brief concluding remarks.

Some Stylized Facts on Growth and Inclusion in Brazil

Growth and Productivity

After five decades of strong performance, Brazil's GDP growth rate plunged in the early 1980s; in the quarter century since then, average growth rates have yet to return to their previous levels. Figure 1 shows that since the late 1980s, long-term real GDP growth (as measured by a ten-year moving average) has stayed around 2.5 percent a year, roughly a third of its 1950–80 average. With population continuing to grow rapidly, growth in income per capita has been just a little over

Figure 1. *Growth of GDP, 1948–2007*

Percent a year

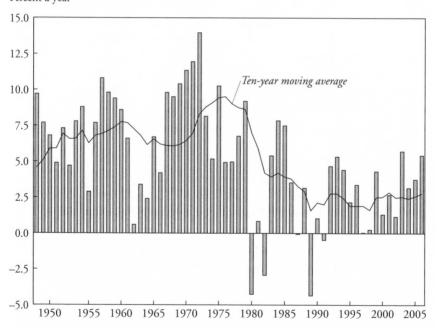

Sources: Instituto de Pesquisa Econômia Aplicada (www.ipeadata.gov.br) and authors' calculations (2006 and 2007 data are based on quarterly GDP estimates).

1 percent a year. Having outperformed most other Latin American countries from the 1950s through the 1970s, Brazil has been performing below average since then. In particular, Brazil has been comparatively unsuccessful in exploiting the exceptionally favorable external conditions—including strong demand for certain commodities produced by Brazil, as well as low international interest rates—that characterized the mid-2000s.

This comparison highlights the contrasts among three main subperiods since 1950. The first, from 1950 to 1980, was marked by rapid output growth, with Brazil outpacing other countries in the region, which nonetheless also did well. The second, from 1981 to 1994, combined a sharp deceleration in growth with poor performance on other macroeconomic indicators, particularly inflation, which was very high. This subperiod was also marked by a less favorable external environment, which led to a contraction in growth throughout the region, with few exceptions. The most recent subperiod, 1995–2007, encompasses the post-stabilization years, which were marked by low inflation and a more open and less regulated economy, not only in Brazil but also in most other Latin American countries.

The mediocre economic record in this last period suggests that either the structural reforms implemented in the 1990s had only a limited impact on GDP growth, or other factors hampered their effect. What might have hindered Brazil's growth? Apparently not a lack of demand. Indeed, whenever economic activity has accelerated in recent years, price pressures forced a deceleration in the following years, suggesting that the economy had been operating at close to full capacity. This would imply that Brazil's inability to grow more rapidly has been due to supply constraints. Which of these were most critical? We examine this question by applying a supply-side, Solow-type decomposition to GDP growth in each of the three subperiods, assuming a Cobb-Douglas function:

$$y_t = A_t k_t^{\alpha} H_t^{1-\alpha}$$

$$H_t = \exp\left[\phi(h_t)\right] = \exp\left[\frac{\eta}{1-\psi} h_t^{1-\psi}\right],$$

where y_t, k_t, A_t, and h_t are, respectively, GDP per worker, the capital-labor ratio, total factor productivity (TFP), and average labor force schooling at time t. (See the longer version of this chapter on the CGD website for more detail on the decomposition.)

Table 1 shows that the rapid GDP growth of 1951–80 reflected a combination of rising employment and a substantial increase in labor productivity. In turn, roughly two-thirds of the latter was generated by the increment in the economy's capital-labor ratio, with almost all the remainder stemming from TFP growth. Remarkably, human capital accumulation contributed virtually nothing to the expansion of output during this high-growth period. Most of the growth

Table 1. *Brazil: Accounting for Growth, 1951–2006*
Percent change per year (annual averages)

Item	1951–80	1981–94	1995–2006
GDP[a]	7.1	1.9	2.6
Employment	3.0	2.1	2.1
GDP per worker	4.1	−0.2	0.5
Contributions to change in GDP per worker			
Capital per worker	2.6	0.5	−0.9
Human capital	0.1	0.8	0.7
Total factor productivity	1.4	−1.5	0.7

Sources: Authors' calculations using data from Instituto de Pesquisa Econômica Aplicada (www.ipea data.gov.br) and Instituto Brasileiro de Geografia e Estatística.

a. Calculated as the average log change in GDP, which produces slightly lower growth rates than taking the geometric mean.

slowdown in the "lost decade" that followed resulted from a decline in labor productivity growth, which actually turned negative, with a smaller part coming from slower employment growth. The contraction in GDP per worker, in turn, was the result of TFP growth turning negative and the capital-labor ratio rising at a much slower pace, effects that were partly compensated for by an expansion in human capital. Finally, the rise in GDP growth in the poststabilization period was due entirely to faster growth in labor productivity, which in turn is fully explained by the recovery in TFP growth. Indeed, the acceleration in GDP growth would have been even larger had the capital-labor ratio not contracted sharply. Meanwhile the contribution of human capital accumulation, rather than continuing to accelerate, saw a marginal decline from the previous subperiod.

How does Brazil's growth decomposition compare with that of other countries? To answer this question we repeated the above exercise using international GDP, investment, and labor force data. (Again, the online version of this chapter has more detail.) The growth decomposition was performed for country groups in order to benchmark the numbers for Brazil. We divided the countries in our sample into six control groups and considered separately the two most recent "economic miracle" countries, China and India. All comparisons point to the conclusion that reform had a positive impact on growth, but that this impact was unevenly concentrated on bringing TFP growth back from the negative rates observed during the "lost decade," with comparatively smaller gains in rates of physical and human capital accumulation.

Did Growth Become More Inclusive?

A problem with the above analysis is that the observed increase in income since 1994 may have been so unevenly distributed that some population segments experienced significant income gains, at least compared with the average, and others none. Determining whether this is in fact the case becomes especially important given that some reforms in Brazil aimed not at accelerating growth, but precisely at improving the income distribution or reducing poverty. Thus an important question is whether growth in the postreform period, although slow, was at least more equitable than before.

The prereform period can fairly be characterized as anti-poor: from 1960 to 1990 the share of total income accruing to the poorest half of the population declined by 6 percentage points, while the share going to the richest 20 percent increased by 11 percentage points (Barros and Mendonça, 1995). In the years that followed, however, growth was clearly pro-poor: the share of the poorest half in total income rose from 11.5 percent in 1990 to 14.0 percent in 2005. Meanwhile the proportion of households living in poverty dropped from 36 percent to 23 percent, and the Gini coefficient, a standard measure of inequality, fell from 0.61 to 0.57.

Growth also became more inclusive over time, being especially pro-poor in 2001–05, even though household income per capita grew by only 2.5 percent a year. This highlights the fact that greater inclusiveness resulted mainly from the improvement in income distribution, as revealed by the decline in the Gini coefficient from 0.60 to 0.57. Depending on the indicator adopted, between 70 and 90 percent of the reduction in poverty can be attributed to improvement in the income distribution. Barros et al. (2007) analyze the factors responsible for this drop in inequality and conclude that it resulted in equal measure from increases in labor and in nonlabor income. This contrasts with the finding of Kakwani, Neri, and Son (2006) of a large increase in nonlabor income, with the rise in labor income playing a subsidiary role.[1]

A problem with the above results is that changes in the income per capita of different groups in society may have been measured incorrectly. The poor and the nonpoor have different consumption baskets, and therefore using a single consumer price index to deflate changes in nominal income for all households may bias the results. This problem becomes particularly important following the kind of reforms adopted in Brazil, notably trade liberalization, which not only expanded access to a broader set of goods but also produced large swings in relative prices, including those of foodstuffs. Carvalho Filho and Chamon (2006) try to account for this by looking directly at household food expenditure in the 1990s: they find that this category of spending fell at all income levels. Assuming that the share of food in total expenditure varies according to Engel's Law, they conclude that the increase in mean household income must have been much larger than that recorded by the national household surveys and the national accounts. The over-

1. This difference stems in part from the fact that Barros et al. used the Gini coefficient, which attributes greater weight to the middle of the distribution than the social welfare function used by Kakwani et al., which "mixes" the Gini and Theil indices.

statement of consumer price inflation and the consequent underestimation of income growth resulted from the introduction of new products in the consumption basket and from the substitution effect stemming from relative price changes and were particularly strong for the lower income deciles.[2]

However, there are reasons for concern looking forward. For one thing, as noted by Carvalho Filho and Chamon (2006), the gains stemming from relative price changes are one-time gains that will not be repeated. For another, reform does not seem to have increased Brazil's historically low elasticity of poverty with respect to average income: Ferreira, Leite, and Ravallion (2007) estimate this elasticity to be 1.09, about half the value obtained in the literature for the average developing country. Our own results, summarized in table 2, confirm that finding. We added data for 2005 and 2006 to Ferreira et al.'s dataset and estimated the following equation with household data:

$$\ln \frac{H_t}{H_{t-1}} = \beta_0 + \beta_1 \ln \frac{y_t}{y_{t-1}} + \beta_2 \ln \frac{G_t}{G_{t-1}} + \varepsilon_t,$$ (1)

where H_t is the share of the poor in total population, y_t is average family income, and G_t is the Gini coefficient. The estimated coefficient on average family income is somewhat lower than 1 in absolute value, and that on the Gini is about 2. A dummy for the period 1994–2006, interacted with $\ln(y_t/y_{t-1})$, yielded insignificant results, which we interpret to mean that, despite recent improvements, there is no statistically significant evidence of an increase in Brazil's growth elasticity of poverty.

A final reason for concern is that social spending in Brazil, although high, is mostly neutral in distributive terms. Thus, although the income distribution has improved since the mid-1990s, the large rise in current public spending explains a comparatively limited share of this gain, and that only recently, when better-targeted programs were implemented. One reason is that the new spending added to rather than substituted for already existing programs, so that public subsidies to well-off families, notably through the social security system, were kept in place and in some cases even increased. Although monetary transfers other than pensions account for an important share of gross income among households in the bottom quintile of the household income distribution, they account for a relatively small part of total public social spending.

The other main reason why growth in public spending contributed relatively little to improving the income distribution is that it was financed mainly by an

---

2. This result is not surprising when one considers more closely the specific changes introduced in the 1990s. Reforms in this period focused on disassembling much of the policy apparatus inherited from the postwar era, one important feature of which was a strong anti-poor bias, partly stemming from adverse relative prices. In this way, the observed welfare gain over the 1990s can be interpreted as partly the result of the unwinding of previous noninclusive policies.

Table 2. *Estimates of the Growth Elasticity of Poverty in Brazil*

Independent variable	Ordinary least squares estimates			Instrumental variables estimates		
	1	*2*	*3*	*4*	*5*	*6*
Constant (β_0)	−0.005	0.005	0.003	−0.004	0.001	0.001
	(0.009)	(0.005)	(0.006)	(0.009)	(0.003)	(0.003)
Average family income (β_1)	−0.73	−0.94	−0.85	−0.85	−0.88	−0.86
	(0.08)	(0.04)	(0.04)	(0.15)	(0.05)	(0.06)
Gini coefficient (β_2)		1.94	1.97		2.00	1.96
		(0.04)	(0.18)		(0.20)	(0.20)
Dummy for 1994–2006			−0.03			−0.07
			(0.07)			(0.12)
R^2	0.80	1.00	0.98	0.78	0.98	0.98
Adjusted R^2	0.79	0.99	0.97	0.77	0.97	0.97
Standard error of the regression	0.04	0.02	0.01	0.04	0.01	0.01

Source: Authors' regressions using data from the Pesquisa Nacional por Amostra de Domicilios (PNAD).
a. The dependent variable is the change in the percent share of the poor in the total population. Numbers in parentheses are standard errors.

increase in indirect taxes, which are especially regressive. Although all families were burdened by the significant rise in taxes, the poor were affected disproportionately. Families with monthly incomes of up to twice the minimum monthly salary saw their tax burden increase by 21 percent between 1996 and 2004, compared with an 8 percent rise for families earning more than thirty times the minimum salary. Because higher indirect taxes are mostly levied at the production stage and passed along in the distribution chain, they are not visible in the price charged to consumers, and so their size goes largely unnoticed.

At the end of the day, the overall program of taxes and transfers has done very little to change the income distribution. Unlike in Europe, the Gini coefficient in Brazil is roughly the same before and after taxes and monetary transfers. However, there is an important asymmetry between the visibility of benefits, such as the Bolsa Família program (a family stipend program for the poor, enlarged under its present name in 2003), and that of their financing. And this, perhaps more than the results themselves, makes this process of expanding the state popular among voters.

What Has Worked, What Hasn't, and Why

Have Reforms Addressed the Foundations for Growth?

When Brazil started its reform process, most of the foundations for market-based growth identified in the CGD framework (see chapter 2 of this volume) were badly compromised: inflation was high, the fiscal accounts were in shambles, human capital was modest and highly concentrated, and widespread discretionary state intervention meant that property rights were not secured against administrative expropriation, but rather helped ensure the appropriation of rents by elite groups, from civil servants to large industrial firms. Reforms have tried and partly succeeded in putting these foundations right. The focus has been on fostering the first two of the foundations in the CGD framework, *political and economic competition* and *macroeconomic stability*. It is easy to see why.

Brazil became a military dictatorship in 1964, and a return to democracy was on the agenda from the mid-1970s onward; this process accelerated with the enactment of the amnesty law in 1979. The political reforms of the 1980s involved the transfer of power back to civilians. In 1985 Congress elected a civilian president, in 1988 it enacted a new constitution, and in late 1989 a new president was elected by popular vote. Reforms in the rules governing the creation of political parties, the adoption of the new constitution, changes in electoral rules, and the strengthening of the judiciary were all critical to allowing fair and broad participation in political affairs.

Brazil entered the 1980s with very high inflation, which would only begin to subside in 1994, and serious disequilibria in its fiscal accounts, including a large public debt, which remains a problem to this day. Several reforms focused on curbing the expansion of public expenditure and liabilities, and others on raising revenue. Financial reform was critical to limiting the ability of state and municipal governments to finance their expenses through their own banks, to be rescued ultimately by the national treasury; pension reforms, both through the *fator previdenciário* (a new pension adjustment formula) and the establishment of a minimum retirement age for civil servants, sought to limit the expansion of pension expenditure; changes in fiscal and budgetary institutions, such as the creation of two new senior vice ministries (the Secretariat for the Control of State Enterprises and the National Treasury Secretariat), the end of the "monetary budget," and the enactment of the Fiscal Responsibility Law, to name a few, helped to limit the expansion of public spending and increase its transparency. In the financial sector, several reforms in the wake of the banking crisis of the second half of the 1990s made the financial system more robust against macroeconomic shocks. Tax reform allowed for a major rise in public revenue. Proceeds from the privatization of state enterprises were used to redeem public debt. Trade liberalization made aggregate supply more flexible, facilitating management of the business cycle and keeping the prices of tradable goods in check, notably after the launching of the Real Plan (a wide-ranging macroeconomic stabilization program) in 1994.

One of the main aims of the reform process was to increase competition in the economy, in an effort to boost productivity and enhance consumer welfare. The previous economic model had been based on widespread state intervention—

which encompassed a tight control of supply through high entry barriers—and the transfer of rents to producers (at the expense of consumers), to foster investment and compensate for lower competitiveness. The idea behind the reforms was to reduce entry barriers, state intervention, and producer rents. Trade liberalization brought a significant decline in tariffs and the end of various nontariff barriers. Several regulations limiting entry and competition, such as widespread price controls, were discontinued, and a new competition law and revamped antitrust agencies were put in place. Privatization was also guided by the goals of creating a competitive environment for the privatized firms and eliminating public monopolies.

The other growth foundations received less emphasis but were not forgotten. The importance of the third pillar in the CGD framework, *securing property rights,* has been generally acknowledged, even if more rhetorically than in practice. The return to democracy and the creation of an independent judiciary were aimed at protecting private individuals and firms against public expropriation. Measures against corruption and several changes in regulation, notably in infrastructure and finance, were likewise aimed at protecting the rights of citizens, investors, creditors, and shareholders against expropriation, both public and private.

A greater emphasis on basic education was the most important of several measures that addressed the fourth pillar, *equalizing opportunities.* Other important reforms included a move toward free universal health care. Administrative reform fostered the adoption of public examinations as the main criterion for entry to the civil service. Financial reform stimulated the birth of microcredit operations, and changes in the regulation of the use of collateral expanded the access of poorer consumers to credit. Minimum age requirements and the *fator previdenciário* made the criteria for eligibility to pensions more similar for poor and rich workers. Measures to curtail corruption also helped equalize opportunities.

Income transfers through social assistance programs were the main instruments used to encourage a *broader sharing of the benefits of growth*—the final pillar in the CGD framework. The constitution created an unemployment insurance system and made rural workers eligible for public pension benefits, even if they had contributed virtually nothing to the pension system in the past.[3] Several other transfer programs were later created to benefit the poor, some of them tied to requirements concerning school attendance and health care; these programs were later consolidated in the Bolsa Família program. A large increase in enrollment in basic and higher education was also important, as it contributed to lowering the skill premiums that foster inequality. Other reforms that led indirectly to a broader sharing of the benefits of growth include the lowering of inflation and the

---

3. In the early 1990s the Lei Orgânica da Assistência Social (LOAS) established a similar income transfer program for people aged 65 and above and the disabled, provided they lived in households where income per capita was below one-fourth the minimum monthly salary.

relative price changes caused by trade liberalization, which benefited the poor disproportionately.

Pragmatism and Anti-Market Reforms

As a rule, the reforms just described were not ideologically driven, but rather were adopted as a means of fostering private investment and TFP growth. This was perceived as the only way to reverse the growth slowdown that had begun in the early 1980s, in a context in which the state lacked the fiscal resources to lead this process itself as it had in 1950–80. These "pragmatic reforms" amounted to a broad but incoherent and uncoordinated reform process (Pinheiro, Bonelli, and Schneider, 2007). The individual reforms were largely disconnected one from another and pursued multiple and sometimes conflicting goals. While some were market-oriented, others enhanced the role of the state or conspired to curb market-based growth. Pragmatism also proved to be a weak impetus for reform: several reforms were abandoned midway when the problems they sought to solve fell off the priority list. The end result is that Brazil pursued many reforms but was left with *insufficient improvement in the overall envelope of foundations,* as several reforms were only partly implemented, or were sidetracked into pursuing other objectives, or tended to strengthen one foundation while weakening others.

In particular, although the reform process was supposedly market oriented, it left as its legacy a much larger state: public consumption nearly doubled as a share of GDP, from an average of 10.9 percent in 1951–80 to 20.0 percent in 1995–2005, causing public saving and investment to fall substantially. In 1991–2005 the primary (noninterest) expenses of the federal government rose by 8 percent of GDP. Pension expenditure accounted for the bulk of this rise, jumping from 4 percent of GDP in 1991 to 9 percent in 2005. Pension spending by state and municipal governments also rose sharply. Meanwhile capital outlays by the federal government declined by half, reaching a mere 0.6 percent of GDP in 2006.

In the initial years after the adoption of the new constitution, governments financed their growing current expenditure by letting inflation accelerate, counting on a reverse Tanzi effect (since revenue was better indexed to inflation than was expenditure)[4] and augmented revenue from seignorage. Indeed, revenue from the "inflation tax" averaged 1.5 percent of GDP in 1989–94, twice as much as the average for 1951–80. When inflation came down after 1994, the government expanded the (net) public debt instead, which ended 2006 at 45 percent of GDP, after peaking at 52 percent of GDP in 2003, up from 31 percent a decade earlier. High interest rates kept government bonds attractive, but they also reduced GDP growth by discouraging private investment and financial intermediation,

---

4. The Tanzi effect refers to a decline in the real value of tax revenue in an environment of high inflation.

in addition to feeding back into higher public spending through increased interest payments.

When borrowing was no longer feasible, governments turned to raising taxes. The federal government, in particular, boosted its tax proceeds by creating new taxes and raising rates on social contributions (this revenue is not shared with state and municipal governments). These efforts had three important effects. First, they counterbalanced the decentralization promoted by the constitution and, indeed, brought about some recentralization. Second, as no compensating tax reduction occurred in the states and municipalities, the total tax burden rose to new highs: from a relatively stable 25 percent in 1968–86, the tax share of GDP rose to 31 percent in 1995–2002, 33 percent in 2003–05, and 37 percent in 2007. Third, the complexity of the tax system also increased. The number of separate taxes increased over time, and so did their rates. Some are applied cumulatively, some share the same tax base, and others have rates that vary regionally. The end result is a complex, unstable, costly, and regressive tax system that is difficult to monitor. Among other things, the system greatly distorts relative prices, increases transaction costs, fosters movement to the informal sector, discourages financial intermediation, encourages rent seeking, shifts resources into tax planning, and concentrates income.

The surge in public consumption was so large that notwithstanding the rise in debt and taxes, it could only be accommodated through a significant decline in capital expenditure: total public investment, which includes investment by federal state-owned enterprises, dropped from 7.9 percent of GDP in 1968–78 to 2.7 percent in 2003–05.[5] Infrastructure was especially hard hit, with public investment in this area (again including state-owned enterprises) declining by about 4 percent of GDP between 1971–80 and 2001–03, which was not compensated by a rise in private outlays. One consequence has been a deterioration in infrastructure capital, with negative effects on productivity growth and income distribution.

Thus, Brazil's failure to achieve a greater acceleration of growth in the post-reform period resulted from a combination of reform failures: some reforms did not go far enough, others were not implemented at all, and still others actually compromised rather than strengthened the foundations for growth. Table 3 provides a scorecard of the positive and negative influences of these various reforms on the five foundations discussed above. To summarize:

• Democratization has fostered political competition, a broader sharing of the benefits of growth, and more equal opportunity. Compared with most of the 1951–80 period, however, it has reduced the security of property rights, despite greater protection against administrative expropriation, and indirectly weakened

---

5. Reclassifications resulting from privatization account for about 1 percent of GDP.

Table 3. *Brazil: Actual Impact of Reforms on the Growth Foundations*

Reform	Period	Property rights	Equal opportunities	Competition	Broad sharing of growth benefits	Macro-economic stability
Democratization	1979–88	−	+	++	+	−
Trade liberalization	1987–93			+	+	+
Privatization	1981–00			+		+
Regulatory	1991–01	−		+		
Decentralization	1988–95		+		+	− −
Financial sector	1995–05	+	+			+
Education	1995–00		+		+	
Pension	1995–03				−	− −
Social assistance	1988–05		+		+	−
Tax	1988–06	−		− −	−	++
Labor	1988	−		−		
Fiscal and budgetary	1979–01			+		+
Judiciary	1988, 2004–06	−	+	+		
Electoral	1988–2006	−	+	++		−
Anti-corruption	1988–2002			+		
Administrative	1988–98					−

Key: +, positive; ++, strongly positive; −, negative; − −, strongly negative.

macroeconomic stability. The impact on property rights resulted from a mixture of increased judicial activism, misguided legislation, more frequent changes in legal norms, and greater tolerance of crimes against property. The impact on macroeconomic stability resulted from the rise in current expenditure, which relied on support from politicians and voters.

• Trade liberalization, privatization, and regulatory reform have contributed to stronger competition, and the first two to greater macroeconomic stability as well. But regulatory reforms, because they remain incomplete and have even suffered some setbacks in recent years, have not properly secured property rights.

• Decentralization and the reform of social assistance programs have contributed to more equal opportunity and a broader sharing of the benefits of growth, by granting more than proportional power and attention to the country's poorer states, municipalities, and households. This was achieved, however, by raising current public expenditure, thus weakening macroeconomic stability, rather than by diverting resources from the rich. Moreover, no effort was made to establish a clear link between the value and coverage of transfers and output performance, and so the sharing of benefits has failed to strengthen the constituency in favor of market-based growth reforms.

• A similar argument can be made regarding pension reform. The changes enshrined in the constitution have greatly expanded public spending and have disproportionately benefited the better off, by providing more favorable retirement conditions to civil servants and formal sector workers. Although some of the later reforms went in the opposite direction, the net effect on the growth foundations was negative.

• Fiscal and budgetary reforms, changes in the education and financial sectors, and anti-corruption measures have had positive effects on the foundations that were not offset by significant negative effects. In particular, the fiscal and anti-corruption reforms have made political competition fairer, and the education and financial reforms contributed to equality of opportunities, by focusing on access of the poor to basic education and to financial services (such as microcredit).

• Judicial and electoral reforms have made political competition fairer and helped equalize opportunity, notably in the political sphere. But neither reform has contributed to strengthening the security of property rights, and the party fragmentation that has resulted from electoral reform has created collective action problems that favor the expansion and increased inefficiency of public expenditure, as explored later in this chapter.

• Labor regulations introduced by the 1988 constitution benefited mostly formal sector workers, at the expense of informal and unskilled workers.[6] Hence this reform tended to reduce both equality of opportunities and economic competition.

• Tax reform, although a perennial theme in policy discussions in Brazil, has consistently focused on increasing revenue rather than the pursuit of a more rational system that would encourage investment. This has led to uneven competition between formal and informal sector firms, lowering productivity growth. Moreover, much of the more recent rise in taxes has occurred through an expansion in indirect taxes, which harm the poor disproportionately.

The incompleteness of reform to date was a more or less natural outcome of the pragmatic approach taken to reform. One reason why market-oriented reforms went as far as they did is that they were perceived as instrumental in sustaining price stabilization, a popular policy goal. Once this link weakened, so did the drive for greater economic liberalization. Thus, although it has not stopped altogether, Brazil's reform process has greatly decelerated since 2000. The only noteworthy exceptions have been the enactment of a new bankruptcy law, the introduction of more stringent rules for the retirement of civil servants, and a reform of the judicial system. But these were partly offset by a partial reversal of

---

6. The World Bank's Doing Business indicators reveal that labor laws in Brazil restrict contract flexibility and increase the cost of hiring and firing workers more than in most other countries, but this only benefits half of the labor force, while making it more difficult for the other half to get a job or enter the formal sector.

previous regulatory reform in infrastructure and an expansion of state business activities in finance and manufacturing.

Several factors contributed to the reduced pace of the reform process in this decade: a similar slowdown in the rest of the world, the low growth rates recorded in the postreform period, and the opposition's victory in the 2002 presidential elections, which itself in part reflected the unpopularity of reforms. Moreover, the political debate fails to link the recent acceleration in growth to the reforms, because the growth came after the election of political leaders historically opposed to these reforms. At the same time the resurgence in growth has tended to mitigate the urgency of reform. The same is true with respect to the recovery in world economic growth and the ensuing rise in commodity prices, thanks to which Brazil achieved current account surpluses in 2003–07 and a smaller net external debt. Together with an abundance of international financial liquidity, this has reduced the clout of the multilateral development organizations and of foreign investors in pushing reform forward. Even though the pendulum has not swung back toward state intervention as far as it has in some other South American countries, the enthusiasm for market-oriented reform has clearly subsided.

The same has not, however, happened to the anti-market reforms, notably the structural rise in current expenditure made possible by higher taxes and lower public investment. This reform did more than perhaps any other to move the economy away from the kind of market-based economic model that underlay privatization, trade and financial liberalization, and deregulation. To gauge the impact of the recent tax increases and simultaneous decline in infrastructure investment on Brazil's long-term growth, we simulated what would have happened to Brazil's long-term growth path had taxation and infrastructure investment stayed at levels similar to those that prevailed before the new constitution. Our simulation uses a version of the neoclassical growth model that considers infrastructure provided by the public sector as a public good subject to congestion (Barro, 1990). In this model, increases in the tax burden reduce the private return on capital, and a reduction in public investment causes a reduction in the supply of public goods, which are complementary to private capital; both effects, in turn, contribute to reducing income in the long term. The model thus relates the long-term (steady-state) income ratio y_1/y_0 to public investment as follows:

$$\frac{y_1}{y_0} = \left[\left(\frac{\lambda_1}{\lambda_0}\frac{\tau_1}{\tau_0}\right)^{\beta}\left(\frac{1-\tau_1}{1-\tau_0}\right)^{\alpha}\right]^{\frac{1}{1-\alpha}} = \left[\left(\frac{\Lambda_1}{\Lambda_0}\right)^{\beta}\left(\frac{1-\tau_1}{1-\tau_0}\right)^{\alpha}\right]^{\frac{1}{1-\alpha}},$$

where λ is the share of public revenue expenses in offering the public good, τ is the tax on firms' output, and $\Lambda = \lambda\tau$ is public investment as a share of GDP. (See the online version of this chapter for further details of the model and the simulation.)

Our base case calibrates the model using the following values: τ_0, 0.25; τ_1, 0.35; $\Lambda_1/\Lambda_0 = 0.5$; $\alpha = 0.4$; $\beta = 0.09$. Solving for these values gives $y_1/y_0 = 0.82$, which indicates that, by 2006, the adoption of such policies had reduced GDP by 18 percent compared with our counterfactual scenario. Spread across almost twenty years, such a reduction amounts to an annual average decrease of nearly 1 percentage point in the growth rate of GDP. In other words, had it not been for the increase in the tax burden and the decline in public infrastructure investment, average annual growth over 1989–2006 would have been on the order of 3.3 percent instead of the actual 2.3 percent.

How Has Politics Influenced the Selection and Completeness of Reform?

As already noted, the 1988 constitution triggered many of the policies that have undermined growth in recent decades. One way it did this was through its provisions geared at strengthening the role of the state at the expense of greater market orientation. Another was through its concern with establishing legal rights, which led to an expansion in public expenditure while also reducing the flexibility and, to some extent, the security of private contracts. Yet to blame the constitution alone would be to miss the bigger picture. The constitution has already been amended several times over the years, and although some of these changes strengthened the foundations for growth, others went in the opposite direction. The same can be said of some of the legislative and policy changes approved since 1988. Therefore the 1988 constitution should not be seen as a one-time, exogenous decision that went astray, but as the result of a political environment that has systematically produced a mix of market-oriented and anti-market reforms. That is, these policy decisions need to be treated as endogenous to the country's social and political institutions, as choices made by different democratically elected politicians.

We attribute the problem of anti-market reforms to the interplay between democratization—a comprehensive institutional reform in itself—and Brazil's highly unequal income distribution.[7] Under the dictatorship, governments could overlook the political preferences of specific groups, but the return to democracy changed the government's incentives and encouraged a rise in current spending. As the poor acquired voting rights and became more engaged in the electoral process—a development to which rising urbanization and schooling also contributed—the demand for income redistribution increased. Given the ability of the existing beneficiaries to veto cuts in existing expenditure, and even in some cases to raise it (a tendency to which Brazil's fragmented party system also contributed), the end result was a rise in total spending rather than the redistribution

---

7. The sequencing of reforms may also have contributed to this outcome. Countries that liberalize politics before liberalizing the economy are likely to face more difficulties in negotiating a pro-growth set of reforms (Giavazzi and Tabellini, 2005). If true, this would mean that performance should be better in countries that liberalized in a sequence opposite to Brazil's, such as Chile and China.

of a fixed total. This accounts for the inconsistencies observed in the reform process: whereas the desire for economic growth and price stabilization tended to favor market reform, electoral incentives that led politicians to be more concerned with goals other than growth often resulted in an expansion of spending.

A similar argument can be made regarding the protection of property rights. Whereas public sector transfers can only redistribute income, property expropriation by the poor can redistribute wealth. This has been a critical factor in boosting popular acceptance of squatting, whether on rural land by (supposedly) landless peasants or on urban land by (equally supposedly) homeless families. The *favelas,* or shantytowns, also consume much of the electricity destined for non-commercial use in Brazil's cities, usually without paying for it; many households in the *favelas* also access stolen cable TV services. Legislation forbidding these practices—as well as other manifestations of informality, from street vending to the disregard of labor laws—often goes unenforced, because they are seen as practices that attenuate income disparities. A similar argument inspires Brazilian judges to render biased decisions in contract enforcement, tending to favor the poorer party in disputes involving labor, rent, and credit contracts. Although the authorities may turn a blind eye to these illegal practices only to favor the poor, problems of asymmetry of information prevent such fine tuning, and the end result is an environment of weak legal enforcement.

To the extent that more public consumption and transfers, on the one hand, and the weak enforcement of laws and contracts, on the other, are perceived by influential groups as means of redistributing income and wealth, it is plausible that inequality acts as an obstacle to the implementation of pro-growth reforms. Democratization, by giving voice, vote, and power to those who favor redistribution (for example, to judges), even if at the expense of growth, has changed the balance of power from what it was during most of Brazil's high-growth period, and especially the period of centralized decision-making under the military regime. Coming so soon after the debt crisis, this change in the political underpinnings of economic policy has helped to extend the growth slowdown that began a few years earlier. Yet the resulting growth constraints differ from those of the early 1980s, which stemmed from external shocks.

Thus Brazil's experience is consistent with the political economy argument that greater income inequality tends to reduce growth because in unequal economies the income of the median voter is well below the average. If the political system is democratic, election outcomes will favor policies that raise income and property tax revenue and redistribute the proceeds to the poor.[8] To assess Brazil's perfor-

---

8. Bénabou (2006) notes that the empirical evidence points to a U-shaped relationship between inequality and the tax burden: in the descending region of the curve, the relationship is dominated by the insurance aspect of public sector policies, whereas in the ascending region the redistributive goals of the public sector dominate. This explanation is consistent with the prediction that at high levels of inequality the relationship between inequality and the size of the tax burden will be positive.

Table 4. *Regressions Explaining Social Security Expenditure*

Independent variable	*Regression*				
	1	*2*	*3*	*4*	*5*
Constant	−2.03	18.74	44.04	18.52	−3.54
	(−2.09)	(2.20)	(4.47)	(2.20)	(−1.47)
Income per capita	0.07		0.18	0.06	0.07
	(1.57)		(3.52)	(1.50)	(1.44)
Percent of population age 65 or more	0.94	1.00		0.91	1.02
	(8.63)	(7.68)		(6.39)	(7.00)
Gini coefficient		−102.45	−167.32	−101.90	
		(−2.70)	(−3.50)	(−2.72)	
Square of Gini coefficient		120.98	168.13	120.79	5.32
		(2.78)	(2.99)	(2.81)	(0.72)
No. of observations	60	56	56	56	56
Adjusted R^2	0.72	0.73	0.54	0.74	0.71
Log-likelihood	−154.30	−141.66	−156.91	−140.45	−144.24

Source: Authors' regressions.

a. The dependent variable is social security expenditure as a percent of GDP. Numbers in parentheses are t-statistics.

mance in this regard, we estimated a nonlinear relationship in a sample of fifty-six countries (for four of sixty countries in the original sample, Gini coefficients are not available) between social security transfers and the Gini coefficient under different specifications.[9] First we regressed social security expenditure on income per capita and on the population share aged 65 or more (equation 1 in table 4). This simple econometric model predicts that Brazil should be spending only 3.5 percent of its GDP on social security transfers; the actual figure was 12.7 percent, leaving a residual of 9.2 percent of GDP to be explained by omitted variables. We then added both the Gini coefficient and its square as regressors. The results, reported in the fourth column of table 4, show a better fit. Still, the residual for Brazil remains a very high 7.3 percent of GDP.

Thus, Brazil has higher social security expenditures than predicted by its demographic characteristics and its levels of income and inequality. We infer that although the interplay between re-democratization and high inequality explains much of the large rise in public transfers, it does not account for all of it. We believe the difference can be partly explained by the nature of Brazilian political institutions. Brazilian democracy is based on the proportional electoral rule. This rule produces a more fragmented legislature than under a majority-rule system, because it allows for a larger number of minority parties to be represented. Brazil's

9. Our approach follows that of Mello and Tiongson (2006). Data are from the World Bank database and refer to 2002.

system also reduces individual accountability compared with the majority-rule system and expands the number of potential veto holders. The empirical evidence suggests that proportional systems tend to raise social expenditure by up to 3 percent of GDP compared with other systems.[10]

The Way Forward: How to Accelerate Growth?

The Critical Foundations

Macroeconomic stability is the most critically missing growth foundation in Brazil. Even after price stabilization and the floating of the exchange rate, Brazil has had an unbalanced macroeconomic policy mix, which overburdens monetary policy and the tax system to compensate for a lax fiscal policy, a large public debt, and a structure of public spending that is greatly skewed toward current expenditure at the expense of public investment. *The high tax burden is one of the main obstacles to the acceleration of growth.* The high policy interest rate set by the central bank, combined with high taxation of financial intermediation, has limited financial deepening, further weakening the link between this foundation and growth. In addition, the central role played by the state in mobilizing and allocating savings dampens the impact of financial intermediation on capital productivity.

The security of *property rights* ranks second among the foundations most critically in need of streamlining. This foundation has received less attention in the reform process of the last quarter century. Reforms aimed at strengthening property rights moved slowly and were often only partly implemented. Moreover, the greater independence afforded to the judiciary has often translated into weaker rather than stronger property rights, as judges rule according to their political views and to pursue "social justice" through decisions aimed at redistributing wealth to debtors, tenants, employees, and others perceived as economically weak.

The *broad sharing of the benefits from growth* is a third critical foundation in need of strengthening. Since the early 1990s, income-compensating transfers and other types of public social spending have increased substantially, with a large rise in the real value of the minimum salary and an expansion in the coverage of social programs, so that they currently play an important role in reducing poverty. However, the present structure of transfers disproportionately benefits the elderly, whose poverty rate is roughly half the national average and a third of that among children. Thus, as currently structured, these transfer systems weaken the link between growth and its broad distribution, because they foster lobbies in favor of greater public spending and discourage labor force participation, when the latter would make households ineligible for benefits. Had this sharing taken place through the labor market rather than through transfers, the link with growth would

10. Persson and Tabellini (2003, chapters 6 and 9, mainly section 6.3).

Table 5. *Brazil: Expected Impact of Potential Future Reforms on the Growth Foundations*

Reform	Property rights	Equal opportunities	Competition	Broad sharing of growth benefits	Macro-economic stability
Trade liberalization			+	+	+
Privatization			+		
Regulatory	++		++		
Decentralization		+		+	
Financial sector		++	+		+
Education		++			+
Pension		+			++
Tax			+	+	++
Fiscal and budgetary					++
Judiciary	++				
Political and electoral			+		+
Anti-corruption	+	+	+		+
Administrative				++	+
Labor		+	+	+	

Key: +, positive; ++, strongly positive.

have been strengthened. This goal can be best achieved by lowering pension expenditure so as to create fiscal space for more effective conditional cash transfers.

Overall, given what we see as a crucial role for higher investment, we put at the top of the priority list those reforms that would create greater fiscal space for capital spending, a reduction in the tax burden, and a lowering of the public debt. Table 5 helps us connect the critical foundations with the main reforms on the agenda. It lists the reforms currently under discussion and relates each of them to the five foundations for growth, indicating the strength of their expected impact. Based on this list, we have chosen six reform areas as most important:[11]

• fiscal reform, which should combine a reduction in public consumption, especially through pension and social security reform, with an increase in public investment, especially in infrastructure, along with tax reform—all of which should contribute strongly to macroeconomic stability

• judicial reform and measures to deal with juridical insecurity, thereby enhancing the security of property rights

• financial sector reform, which impacts three foundations: macroeconomic stability (most importantly), economic and political competition, and (most strongly) equal opportunity

11. Diagnostics, justification, and motivation for each case are discussed in more detail in the online version of this paper on the CGD website.

- education reform, to achieve greater equality of opportunities and, by moving to tuition-based financing of higher education, to improve the fiscal balance and so increase macroeconomic stability
- regulatory reform, which should have strong impacts on securing property rights and promoting economic and political competition, and
- political reform, to facilitate the enactment of policies that promote macroeconomic stability and to improve the nature of political competition, while also addressing several of the foundations by reducing corruption.

Fiscal Reform: Social Security and Taxation

The improvement in Brazil's fiscal accounts can be seen in the maintenance of a primary surplus in recent years large enough to stabilize the public debt-GDP ratio. But even after almost a decade of consistently meeting primary surplus targets, Brazil's adjustment process is far from complete. The public debt remains very high, as does the real interest rate paid on that debt, so that a large primary surplus is required just to keep the debt-GDP ratio from embarking on an explosive path. This introduces considerable political risk into any medium-term scenario for the economy: the size of the primary surplus, which is determined year by year, depends on the micromanagement of different demands for higher spending, a task that can only be accomplished with backing from the president himself. The fiscal adjustment cannot be considered complete until the debt-GDP ratio falls to around 30 percent of GDP, which in turn would allow for a substantial and sustained decline in interest rates.

Another sign of the poor quality of fiscal adjustment is its dependence on a rising tax burden, which went from a relatively stable 25 percent of GDP in 1968–93 to over 35 percent in 2006. This increase has exceeded the amount necessary to meet the primary surplus target, and thus has also financed a major expansion in public primary spending. This higher spending did not, however, fall on items that would contribute to growth. Rather, it concentrated on pension payments. Public sector investment has fallen almost continuously, with negative consequences for the quality of infrastructure. Another problem is the pro-cyclical nature of fiscal policy due to the earmarking of revenue to specific expenditure items.

Fiscal reform should therefore focus on reducing current expenditure so as to expand public saving and investment and lower the tax burden, while also improving the quality of the tax system. In particular, efforts should be aimed at cutting social security expenditure, which has climbed to a level, relative to GDP, found elsewhere only in developed economies with older populations.[12]

---

12. Although we rank the social security system as the most critical area for expenditure reduction, it is hardly the only one. Other areas include the public sector's payroll and procurement practices. Mention should also be made of the need to improve managerial practices and implement more efficient procedures through another round of administrative reform, continuing the (largely abandoned) reforms that took place just after President Fernando Henrique Cardoso came to power in early 1994.

Social Security Reform

The Brazilian social security system is well known for the generosity of its retirement benefits; this generosity increased with the advent of the 1988 constitution. The main issue concerns the rules governing access to benefits, both for their impact on total expenditure and because they award large subsidies to politically influential groups. There is no minimum retirement age for private sector workers, and so a large proportion retire quite young by international standards. Moreover, under present rules women can retire five years earlier than men, and some professionals, such as teachers, can retire five years earlier than regular workers.[13] The other main issue is the generous way in which benefits are periodically adjusted: for most retirees, benefits increase at the same rate as the minimum wage, which rose by an average of 5.3 percent a year over 1995–2007 in real terms, four times as fast as GDP per capita. The system's rules have combined with a major demographic transition to create a bleak outlook for its finances.

There are two ways to curb the trend toward larger social security deficits: cut expenditure or collect additional revenue. Brazil has traditionally favored the latter, which partly explains its high tax burden and high share of workers in the informal sector. The reform proposals discussed next focus on curbing expenditure growth. This should be done along two main lines. The first concerns the rules for the periodic adjustment of the minimum value of benefits; the second deals with changes in the rules that govern access to benefits, especially retirement benefits. We have intentionally left out increases in individual contributions, because we see the system's main problem as its large size rather than the deficit per se. Specifically, we propose that the backbone of a new round of social security reform consist of five measures:[14]

- *De-link the value of pension benefits from the minimum wage.* Pensions and income transfers should be indexed to past inflation so as to keep the real value of benefits constant. Benefits will then more closely reflect the actual contribution made by retired workers to the system, while freeing the minimum wage to incorporate contemporaneous increases in productivity.
- *Fix a minimum retirement age for access to INSS (Instituto Nacional de Seguridade Social) benefits and increase the minimum age over time,* according to

13. A constitutional amendment approved in 2003 imposed minimum retirement ages for men (60) and women (55) in the civil service but continued to allow teachers to retire five years earlier than other workers: in the public sector, male teachers can retire at 55 and female teachers, who comprise the vast majority, at 50. This rule has no equivalent anywhere in the world, as far as we know, and it greatly burdens the fiscal accounts of state and municipal governments, while at the same time limiting the possibility of better pay for teachers still in the work force, with negative repercussions on the quality of education.

14. See Pinheiro and Giambiagi (2006), Giambiagi (2006), and Tafner and Giambiagi (2007) for additional discussion of these proposals.

a pre-established rule, as average life expectancy increases. This would reduce the ratio of beneficiaries to contributors and would reduce the subsidies given to (mostly formal sector) workers who retire relatively young.

• *Move toward a single set of rules governing access to pensions for men and women.* The present five-year difference should be reduced to two or even eliminated over a reasonable period. Because women's life expectancy exceeds that of men, they would still enjoy a disproportional benefit, since they would receive benefits for a longer period on average.

• *Abolish the special retirement regime for teachers.* We propose that the active life of teachers of both sexes be extended by postponing their retirement, applying to them the same rules adopted for other workers.

• *Change the rules of access to benefits to older workers under the Lei Orgânica de Assistência Social.* Present rules encourage participation in the informal sector among workers with incomes near the minimum wage: these workers have no incentive to join the social security system, since they will earn the same benefit whether they contribute or not. Presently the benefit is unconditionally granted to all persons 65 and older. We propose limiting future concession of old-age benefits to those who have reached the age of 70 and have contributed to the social security system for some time to be determined.

These suggestions, admittedly, have low political viability, in part because of a general opposition to reforms that seek to reduce public expenditure. Without broad public understanding of the link between cutting public spending and accelerating economic growth, strong constituencies will remain against such reform, and support will be very weak. In the case of social security reform, opposition comes mainly from those who benefit from the present rules (teachers, formal workers, pensioners, and women). For those already retired, the likely benefits of reform, in the form of acceleration in output and employment growth, will be relatively small. The main losers from present policy are the younger generations and those not yet born, who do not yet participate in the political process.

What is worse, the federal government, the major agent of change, is itself not convinced that this reform should be pursued. It expects, perhaps self-servingly, that in due course a rise in formal employment will lower the system's deficit, which it perceives to be the central problem. Besides, social security expenditure is regarded as part and parcel of social policy, a politically sensitive area. Yet the prospect for rising expenditure and deficits is such that the accumulated imbalances are bound to require some kind of action eventually.

The way to advance with social security reform in these circumstances is to pursue a piecewise and gradual strategy. Some measures, such as establishing a minimum retirement age for private sector workers, enjoy some support and could be implemented separately. The fact that this rule (but not the sliding lower bound) already applies to civil servants should make approval easier. Although it is unlikely that Congress will allow the minimum salary to rise above the minimum pension benefit, legislation could be passed capping the rise in the real value of the former. The other measures proposed above are even more unpopular, yet even they may be politically feasible if approved only for those who have not yet entered the labor force. This would apply, in particular, to the special regimes benefiting female workers and teachers. As with the remaining changes, political feasibility also hinges on efforts to increase public awareness about the reasons for reform.

Tax Reform

Tax reform should have three goals: lowering the tax burden, simplifying the tax structure, and reducing the earmarking of revenue. Although it is hard to separate the lowering of the tax burden from measures to cut public spending, causation between the two is far from obvious. We believe that capping taxes would help to limit current spending. The tax structure could be simplified by merging various separate taxes and making them more uniform nationally, without the need to devise a whole new regime. In particular, if the mix between indirect and direct taxes is preserved, reform will be more politically palatable, since its impact on revenue will be less uncertain. Along these lines, our set of proposals includes the following:[15]

• *Adopt uniform ICMS (value added tax) legislation and tax brackets for all states,* but with a range, to allow for some discretion by state governments.

• *Establish the principle that the ICMS should be charged where goods are consumed, rather than where they are produced,* with a small tax applied at the origin to encourage compliance.

• *Merge social security contributions (COFINS) with the public employees savings system (PIS-PASEP) into a single "contribution,"* and the *income tax on firms with the Contribuição Social sobre o Lucro Líquido* (a profits tax, with the same base as the corporate income tax) into another single tax.[16]

• *Modify the tax sharing system* to encompass all taxes and contributions instead of just the current three (the income tax, the excise tax on manufactures, and the Contribução sobre Intervenção no Dominio Econômico, or CIDE, a tax on the sale and import of fuels), but without altering total transfers to states and municipalities.

• *Transform the excise tax on manufactures into a tax on a limited range of specific goods* (tobacco, alcoholic beverages, and passenger cars).

---

15. Some of these reforms have been suggested by Afonso and Varsano (2004).

16. The resulting tax brackets would necessarily be high, but by making the high tax burden explicit they might create a constituency in favor of reducing public sector expenditure.

An alternative, more radical, but also less politically palatable reform would further include the following:

• *Reduce the tax burden* by discontinuing taxes earmarked to expenditure that can be more easily eliminated or transferred to the private sector. Natural candidates are reductions in the FGTS (Fundo de Garantia por Tempo de Serviço) and in the contributions to the SESI, SENAI, and SEBRAE,[17] or even their complete elimination (with the activities these taxes finance being paid for directly by the private sector) and, partially, the PIS-PASEP. Direct and indirect taxes on investment expenditure and import duties should be drastically curtailed in the medium term.

• *Replace a group of indirect taxes* (ICMS, PIS-PASEP, COFINS, CIDE, and others that together presently generate revenue of nearly 16 percent of GDP) with a single value added tax, the proceeds of which would be shared among the federal, state, and municipal governments.

• *Enlarge the DRU* (Desvinculação de Receitas da União) so as to gradually discontinue the majority of existing provisions that earmark revenue for specific expenditure items.

Changes in the tax system are rarely neutral from a distributive viewpoint, and there is much uncertainty as to how each group in society will fare. This tends to strengthen the constituency against almost any proposed measure. Since the states and municipalities are most likely to lose under these reforms, the federal government should compensate them appropriately. The existence of state debts to the federal government both provides a vehicle for such compensation and offers an alternative mechanism for promoting regional policies, which is often cited as a reason not to have a uniform national tax system.[18] Thus one way to weaken the opposition to reform would be to compensate the states' losses by lowering the debt service on their loans from the federal government.

Judicial Reform

The weak protection of property rights in Brazil is a consequence of several factors: judicial activism, breaches of contract by the government, slow enforcement of laws and regulations, extreme instability of the existing rules, and a broad bias against creditors, property owners, and employers. Paramount among these are the last three. The traditional reaction to this dysfunctionality has been to expand the public resources allocated to the judiciary. Yet this has

17. These are entities administered by unions of firms that aim at providing training, recreational, and other services to employees (SESI and SENAI) or to the creation and support of small and medium-size firms (SEBRAE).

18. Another alternative is to create an equalization fund for revenue capable of guaranteeing a lower bound for revenue per capita at the state level. The difference between each state's revenue capacity and the respective minimum tax revenue per capita would be paid out of the fund.

not improved matters, because the demand for judicial services has also grown quite rapidly, sometimes as a consequence of an endogenous rise in procedural complexity. The demands on the judiciary have also increased as a result of democratization and the economic reforms of the 1990s, such as the enactment of a new consumer protection law, with the courts being asked to solve more and more complex cases.

This worsening situation encouraged legislators to adopt more significant changes. In December 2004 a constitutional amendment changed several norms, from rules concerning the selection of judges to the obligation of lower courts to abide by some Supreme Court rulings. Congress also approved a number of infra-constitutional reforms that greatly simplified the civil and procedural codes. These reforms aimed mostly at adopting legal measures to speed up the decision process, largely by reducing the endless opportunities for appeal, notably when involving repetitive legal demands. Other important, if less dramatic, measures adopted in this period focused on improving management practices.

The area that has seen the least progress concerns the change in attitudes toward contract enforcement. Judicial decisions often reflect the judge's political views or intention to use the bench to redistribute income in favor of the less well off. This stance, together with the freedom that judges enjoy to reach very different decisions on similar cases, and their power to paralyze government policies, has turned the judiciary into a key actor in most social and political conflicts. The system has few mechanisms by which to mitigate the impact of these politically motivated decisions on property and contract rights, other than allowing universal appeal to the higher courts, a procedure that itself is often abused and contributes to the increasing volume of litigation observed in Brazil. Moreover, erratic judicial decisions become a fertile ground for corruption, as it becomes harder to identify cases in which factors other than the letter of the law or ideology are at play.

The measures adopted so far have been positive, but further changes are needed. Administratively, there is still a need to improve information systems and case flow, to transfer some responsibilities from the judges to professional managers, and to improve case management. Better management practices will speed up the judicial process and allow the judges to dedicate more time to the merits of each case. Regarding legal reform, there is room for further effort to simplify procedures, including speedier notification of parties, maintaining the continuity of the process when a party shows up after its initiation, a reduction in formalism, and a change in the tendency of judges to decide based on procedural details rather than on the merits of the dispute. A greater reliance on verbal procedures and small claims courts would contribute to these goals.

The more challenging reform is to change the culture of the legal profession—lawyers, prosecutors, and judges—so that they place greater value on the speed, predictability, and impartiality of judicial decisions, which should be independent of the identity or social status of the parties. One way to stimulate such change would be to adopt performance indicators as a criterion in judicial promotion, replacing the present seniority-based system. The use of indicators to assess performance would reveal the differences among judges and tribunals and would encourage them to become more efficient. The National Council of Justice could play a central role in this initiative by developing, calculating, disseminating, and stimulating the use of such indicators. One indicator that could be used to foster greater dispatch in judicial proceedings is the time elapsed between the beginning of each case and the final ruling, with cases appropriately grouped by type. The predictability of a given judge's rulings could be assessed by the percentage of his or her decisions that are confirmed on appeal.

In addition to poor judicial performance, the insecurity of property rights reflects gaps in the quality of legislative output and the often opportunistic and ideological stance of the executive. Measures to strengthen property rights in Brazil must therefore go beyond the judiciary. We propose the following additional core set of measures:

• The executive branch should *exercise greater self-discipline* both in changing the legal norms under its jurisdiction and in appealing to the judiciary to postpone the enforcement of judicial decisions, especially in areas where the law is well established. Implementing this recommendation would require a change in culture and a discontinuance of the use of provisional measures.[19] The executive branch, including the state-owned enterprises, is by far the leading litigator in Brazil. Even more frequently than the private sector, it resorts to the intricacies of Brazil's procedural codes to extend the duration of judicial processes, even when it knows it will eventually lose. This practice not only postpones spending and discourages some plaintiffs from suing in the first place, but also reflects the incentives facing public sector lawyers and managers. In recent years this posture has changed somewhat, but more drastic action is necessary to both reduce caseloads and encourage judges to be less lenient on private parties that follow the same strategy.

• *The quality of legislation needs to be improved.* One of the consequences of party fragmentation and weak party discipline is that Congress has a hard time resolving political disagreements, because it is easy for a minority to block the approval of legislation. To deal with this problem, laws are often written ambiguously and in very general terms to make them palatable to all the different contending groups. This, of course, merely passes the responsibility for settling political conflicts to the courts, which have to clarify what the law has left vague. Even then, except where the Supreme Court enacts a *súmula vinculante* (a ruling

---

19. Provisional measures are a type of presidential decree through which the government heavily influences the legislative agenda and which becomes law upon being enacted, even before going through legislative debate.

that is expressly binding on lower courts), insecurity tends to prevail even after the higher courts have established jurisprudence on the matter.

• *Judicial awards should be indexed to the SELIC,*[20] including those of the public sector (*"precatórios"*), so as to reduce the financial incentive to delay final court rulings. One reason a party to a lawsuit will often spend resources to get a final ruling postponed, even when the outcome is not in doubt, is to secure in the meantime a return on the resources that it will eventually have to transfer to the other party. Raising the interest rate on contested debts would weaken this incentive and thus encourage the speedier conclusion of cases.

• *The burden of proof should be reversed* with respect to decisions made by the board of regulatory agencies and the competition tribunal (CADE), which would continue to hold through the appeals process until a final ruling is handed down by the judiciary.

• *The training of new judges should be extended and strengthened.* Recent reforms have already improved matters by requiring lawyers to have at least three years of practice before being appointed to the bench. However, more training for new judges on their specific responsibilities would improve the quality and predictability of judicial rulings.

• *The syllabuses of law schools should be extended* to include the study of economics, and to emphasize the importance of justice and a sound judicial system for the proper functioning of a market economy.

Experience suggests that the political disputes surrounding judicial reform tend to be argued only among legal professionals themselves. This is unfortunate, because it leaves the users of the judicial system out of the discussion, even though it is they who have the most to gain from improved performance. Increasing popular awareness of the problem, while building on public discontent about the quality of judicial services and especially the slow pace at which decisions are currently rendered, seems to be the best avenue for change. This process would have to be led by business, academia, and the media, which indeed have shown increasing interest. A crucial element is to shed light on performance indicators and the consequences of poor judicial performance for economic development and social fairness.

Within the legal profession, lawyers as a group tend to be the fiercest opponents to reforms that would streamline the judiciary. Lower court judges also tend to oppose reform, because they tend to be more ideologically committed and fear losing the freedom to decide as they please, even if most judges tend to voluntarily abide by the jurisprudence established by higher courts. The Supreme Court justices, on the other hand, tend to be keener about pushing for reform, because they feel more accountable for the overall performance of the judiciary. They also

---

20. The SELIC (Sistema Especial de Liquidação e de Custódia) is the policy interest rate set by the Commission on Monetary Policy at the central bank.

recognize that they are spending too much time deciding matters that should be resolved in the lower courts.

Financial Sector Reform

Brazil has a well-developed financial infrastructure but relatively shallow credit and capital markets, which have historically contributed only modestly to spurring long-term growth (Pinheiro and Bonelli, 2007). Finance is not only scarce, notably for small firms and households, but also expensive. And the incentives faced by financial institutions to select and monitor projects are distorted by norms, institutional weaknesses, and high taxes, so that jurisprudence and patterns of judicial behavior play at least as important a role as the law itself in regulating credit disputes. As indicated in table 5, financial sector reform could improve and strengthen three of the growth foundations: equal opportunities, economic and political competition, and macroeconomic stability. Our reform menu includes measures under five main headings:

• *Improve the quality of information available* to lenders and shareholders, so that they can better evaluate the risks they face. This will require a revamping of accounting practices (a process started in early 2008), better registration of assets, and more stringent disclosure rules. Also important is enlarging credit information registries, which have a relatively wide coverage in Brazil, to include positive information about borrowers as well as the negative information they currently carry. Also needed are better auditing, a strengthening of supervision by the central bank and the securities commission, and more stringent and faster sanctions for those who fail to comply. This may require changes in privacy laws and discussions with judges so that they uphold these changes.

• *Strengthen the rights of creditors and minority shareholders.* Currently, few types of guarantees operate well, in the sense of allowing for a quick and low-cost recovery of the loan. For loans extended with these guarantees as collateral, interest rate spreads are well below the average, which shows the potential for measures in this direction to lower the cost of and expand access to credit, in particular for small firms and poor families. Here, too, cooperation of the judiciary is central, particularly so that collateral offered by the poor may actually be accepted as such by financial institutions. Reforms along this line would be especially important for expanding housing credit.

• *Reduce taxes on financial operations and avoid frequent tax changes.* Implementing this reform would require only political will, but attempts at reducing these taxes will likely be resisted by the executive, as it would force a decline in expenditure and may seem to favor the banks. Moreover, taxes on financial transactions are easy to collect and supervise, and this makes them popular with the tax authorities.

• *Promote competition among financial institutions,* and between them and the capital markets, not least because the current consolidation of the banking sector through concentration among the largest banks is likely to further reduce competition among banks, which also hold a dominant position in the capital markets. The competition tribunal and the central bank should receive a clear mandate to improve competition in the banking sector. This should include a more rigorous analysis of mergers and acquisitions as well as pro-active policies of information dissemination and strengthening of guarantees. Another recommended measure is to make it easier for bank clients to switch their accounts between institutions, by lowering taxes on such changes, and by facilitating banks' access to information on the account history of potential clients.

• *Reduce and restructure the role of the public sector banks* and of directed credit in the financial system. These banks are still responsible for a large share of finance, including many transactions that private institutions or the capital markets could easily handle, but for which they cannot compete because of the subsidies received by the public sector banks. Directed credit, on the other hand, operates as a means of cross-subsidizing certain borrowers, but at the cost of higher interest rate spreads. Both instruments have become inefficient and largely unnecessary with the growing sophistication of private financial institutions, the opening of the capital account, and the expansion of capital markets. The main measures called for in this regard are to significantly lower the subsidies transferred though public banks and to increase the transparency with which they are allocated.

Financial sector reform includes certain measures that are part of other reform areas. One of these is strengthening contract enforcement, which is critical to fostering long-term credit in housing and infrastructure, but in which financial sector reform is just part of a larger effort to improve juridical security and regulation. Likewise, high taxes account for a significant part of bank spreads and financial risk, but changes in this area would be dealt with more properly as part of tax reform. Other areas of reform, such as capital market regulation, access to information in credit bureaus, and better mechanisms for foreclosing on collateral in case of default, can be implemented with relatively less political resistance, as experience in recent years has shown.

The area of strongest resistance will be in reforming the financial subsidy mechanisms embedded in directed credit regulations and the workings of the public sector banks. Recipients of subsidies (for example, large farmers and industrial companies), public sector bank employees, and the politicians connected to them will be the main opponents of reform. The most promising strategy seems to be to concentrate on demanding transparency and accountability in the application of such subsidies and seeking the discontinuance of those that play no social or redistributive role. This would reduce the opposition of public bank employees and of some politicians, while attracting the support of the media and society in general.

Education Reform

Two features of the Brazilian labor market stand out in cross-country comparisons, even with countries at similar development levels: high inequality of wages and low average levels of schooling.[21] The two problems are interconnected, and solving both requires expanding the coverage and improving the quality of basic education. This would primarily foster greater equality of opportunities by extending access to a good education to many who now are deprived of it; it would also have positive spillovers on other areas, such as public health and crime prevention. The average educational attainment of the population aged 15 and over has improved since the 1980s, from 3.1 to 4.9 years, after remaining nearly unchanged in the preceding twenty years. Yet as similar countries, such as Argentina and Chile, have made even greater progress, the gap between them and Brazil has widened.

In recent years several reforms have sought to accelerate the rise in average educational attainment. On the supply side, the FUNDEF (Fundo Nacional para o Desenvolvimento do Ensino Fundamental e Valorização do Magistério) was established to increase the resources allocated to primary education, especially in the country's poorest areas, with noticeably positive effects. Demand, meanwhile, was fostered through the Bolsa Escola program, created in 2001, which pays poor families a stipend to send up to three children aged 6 to 15 years to school. Each child must achieve at least an 85 percent attendance record. Also during this period, several mechanisms were implemented to measure educational performance and supply valuable information for future planning and other focused initiatives.

In the first term of the current president, Luiz Inácio "Lula" da Silva, the policy emphasis shifted from basic to higher education. Leading initiatives included the Programa Universidade para Todos (University for All), which aims at facilitating college entry conditions for poor students, and a proposed reform that, among other provisions, would have reserved 50 percent of vacancies in federal universities to students who attended public secondary schools. In December 2006 the government also created the Fundo de Manutenção e Desenvolvimento da Educação Básica (FUNDEB), which extended the FUNDEF program to pre-primary and secondary education.

These reforms have yielded significant gains, but the education system still faces important challenges, in particular the need to raise equity and efficiency and improve learning. The quality of schooling varies considerably across Brazil. Children attending some public schools lack the basic educational opportunities available in other parts of the country, or even in better-endowed schools within their own jurisdictions. Almost everywhere, repetition and dropout rates remain exceedingly high: only 54 percent of students finish all eight years of primary education, taking an average of ten years to do so. The corresponding figures in the North and the Northeast regions are worse: 39 percent and eleven years.

---

21. This section is based on Ferreira and Veloso (2007).

Even those who complete primary school by no means always receive a good education. Standardized test results for 2001 showed that fewer than half of fourth-graders performed at level 3 on a mathematics proficiency scale of 1 to 10, the same percentage as in 1995. In this context, the recent shift in focus from basic to higher education is an unwelcome development.

Our proposals for education reform seek to address the problems just summarized. Their main thrust is to enhance the coverage and quality of basic education, while reducing subsidies to higher education by shifting from universal free tuition at public universities to a combination of paid tuition and student loans. As already noted, an expanded and improved basic education system would contribute to strengthening the equality of opportunities foundation. A shift to tuition-based financing of higher education would improve the nation's fiscal accounts and so strengthen the macroeconomic stability foundation. The following specific actions are proposed:

• *Achieve universal coverage from pre-school through upper secondary school* by fully implementing the FUNDEB and including families with students aged 16 through 19 in the Bolsa Família program. Indeed, benefits should rise as a function of age, to compensate for the opportunity cost of students staying out of the labor market. Particularly important is expanding coverage and improving the quality of early childhood care, including preschool education, in coordination with other initiatives directed at young children. Evidence shows that investments in early childhood lead to healthier cognitive and emotional development in the early years, which translates into higher overall educational attainment (and hence a more competitive labor force), greater internal efficiency of the formal education system (reduced repetition and dropout rates), and better physical and mental health. All of these, in turn, make students more responsible citizens and better parents as adults, and may produce externalities through role modeling for siblings, peers, and others.

• *Improve the quality of primary education.* Specific proposals include careful periodic evaluation of schools and teachers, possibly with the introduction of an accreditation system, and increased competition among schools. Quasi-market mechanisms, from concessions schools to vouchers, should be introduced at the state and municipal levels, along with better governance structures.

• *Increase efficiency and equity in university education.* Competition among universities should be increased. Facilities should be used more intensively, for example by increasing enrollment in night courses. Public universities should charge tuition and fees, and the federal program of scholarships should be expanded, especially for poor students.

The main advantage of the first proposal is also its main weakness: because it involves allocating more resources to the sector, none of the main interest groups opposes it; on the other hand, its implementation would require the transfer of funds from other activities, which means fighting an uphill battle with mayors and governors, who often argue that too much of their resources are already allocated to education. Yet if continued economic growth produces a parallel rise in tax revenue, even the existing provisions, together with a projected decline in primary enrollment, should allow for universalization at least of preschool education in the medium term. This, in turn, should raise the efficiency of the primary schools, fostering the universalization of secondary education. Evidence suggests that Brazil's high dropout rates in secondary education owe less to the opportunity cost of staying out of the labor market than to learning difficulties and lack of motivation.

The big problem with improving primary education is that its current low quality appears to result mainly from administrative problems, so that merely allocating more resources is unlikely by itself to produce significant improvement (Menezes-Filho, 2003). However, the agenda outlined above is strongly opposed by public school teachers' unions. These unions share a culture of victimization that portrays the low quality of education as due primarily to teachers being paid low wages and working in poor conditions. In fact, although salaries in the public schools are not very high, they are higher than the average salary paid by the private sector (Barbosa-Filho et al., 2008) and are not low by international standards as a share of GDP per capita (Barbosa-Filho and Pessoa, 2008). Furthermore, this culture of teacher victimization has caused administration to be geared to teachers' needs rather than focused on the students. High rates of teacher absenteeism are tolerated (in Sao Paulo state, 13 percent of teachers are absent on a given day), and teachers move freely between workplaces, even in the middle of the school year, impeding rational management.

Fortunately, the public school system is highly decentralized—each state and municipality has its own system—which reduces the unions' power, facilitates support from the federal government, and creates scope for piecewise, incremental change: reform in one jurisdiction can create a constituency for reform in others. Alternative management practices are also possible, including public-private partnerships and the hiring of private firms to provide services.

The main potential ally of reform will be civil society; with its support, governors and mayors will come along. Brazilian society in general has yet to understand that the problem is much more complex than simply a lack of resources, but there are strong signs that this process has begun. Here the main strategy is to provide greater transparency about the problems, to make them more understandable to parents and society at large; in particular, the culture of seeing the teachers as the victims, rather than the children who are deprived of a good education, must be changed. For this it will be critical to enlist the media as an ally.

Finally, the reform of higher education will not be easy: there is no popular support for charging fees at public universities. However, we believe that as primary and secondary education expand and improve, demand for higher education will grow exponentially, making competition for admission to the public universities even more intense. This will raise public awareness and force a discussion about whether a fortunate subset of the population should continue to attend university for free. Either there will be a move to charge fees and so reduce demand, or entry barriers will have to be lowered, resulting in a sharp reduction in the teacher-student ratio, as has occurred, for example, in Argentina's public universities. The sacrifice in quality that the latter would entail may persuade the public to accept the concept that public universities should charge reasonable tuitions for the education they provide.

Regulatory Reform

Many important economic sectors, including telecommunications, electric power, railways, ports, roads, and water and sanitation, experienced not only extensive privatization but also substantial regulatory reform in the 1990s, dismantling an institutional framework that in some cases had been in place for over half a century. Although the reform process evolved independently in each of the various sectors, the diagnosis that motivated it and the principles underscoring the new regulatory model were essentially the same. In particular, bringing private investors in was seen as the best way to raise investment without sacrificing fiscal discipline; but for that to occur, the regulatory framework had to be revamped.

Following international practice, regulatory reform in the area of infrastructure involved the separation of commercial, regulatory, and policy activities. The state-owned enterprises continued to engage in commercial activities but were restructured, often through privatization. As the new regulatory model stressed the introduction of competition, privatization was often accompanied by the vertical or horizontal breakup of the enterprise and the dismantling of barriers to new private entry. To reduce the risk of expropriation, new regulatory agencies, with relative financial and administrative independence from the government, were entrusted with the responsibility of fixing rates, subject to rules set out in the concession contracts and the general principle of "financial and economic equilibrium" established in the Concessions Law. Policy responsibilities were ascribed to the appropriate sector ministry.

Although the evidence suggests that regulatory reform has succeeded in fostering productivity growth and improving the fiscal accounts, much less has been accomplished by way of raising investment. In particular, the new private owners invested in rehabilitation and modernization of facilities, but not as much was invested in greenfield projects, with the result that expansion of capacity was rather limited. The telecommunications sector is apparently the only exception to this rule, in the sense that not only did capacity increase significantly, but this was achieved while the state successfully transferred all commercial activities to the private sector.

The regulatory reform agenda detailed below draws on the successful case of the telecommunications sector. Its starting point is the view that since the state continues to lack the resources to invest directly in infrastructure, it needs to establish a regulatory framework that encourages private investors to do so, allowing them to operate at a reasonable level of risk. Thus our proposals aim at completing the transition initiated in the 1990s, focusing largely on the strengthening of regulatory agencies in infrastructure, but recognizing that these share common problems with other, similar institutions. Thus, the antitrust agencies and, to some extent, the central bank also need strengthening. Specifically, we propose the following:

• *Expand the number of board members in regulatory agencies* to seven, with each member serving a seven-year term. (Every year the president would appoint one member to each board, to take office the following year.) This would replace the present rule—five members serving for five years each—which has proved insufficient to insulate the agencies from the political cycle. Board members would continue to be approved by the legislature. The law should also establish provisions for replacing board members in case of vacancy, so that vacancies do not last indefinitely when the executive and Congress cannot agree. This has happened repeatedly in the recent past, leaving the agencies with too few board members to make formal decisions.

• *A performance contract* should be signed between the agency and the appropriate ministry, fixing performance targets and mechanisms for control and follow-up. This will require the objectives of the agencies to be clearly stated. The performance contract should respect agencies' autonomy to decide on regulatory matters, while obliging them to abide by transparency and administrative norms common to other public institutions.

• *Set fixed terms for central bank directors,* which should not coincide with the term of the president of the republic.

• *Change the law to make mergers conditional on ex ante approval by the competition tribunal.*

• *Complete the regulatory framework* in the areas of transportation (for example, the ports), electric power, and especially sanitation. Conflicts of interest and the overlapping of responsibilities should be carefully disentangled so as to expand the network operated by private investors.

• *In the electric power sector, move toward privatization* as a long-term strategy, while in the medium run fostering competition and improving the quality of management and the mechanisms for supervision and control, limiting political interference, and strengthening the enterprises' commercial ethos.

• *Streamline the operations of the environmental protection agencies,* including speeding up the licensing process. Strengthen cooperation among these agencies, the judiciary, and prosecutors, so as to reduce judicial insecurity and risk over environmental licenses. Improve coordination among the federal, state, and municipal environmental protection agencies.

• *Strengthen coordination among the regulatory agencies,* especially those dealing with the energy sector (the electric power, oil, and water agencies). Similarly, foster cooperation between the regulatory agencies and the consumer protection and antitrust institutions.

• *Develop financial instruments and secondary markets* capable of supplying more financial resources and means of managing the risks of infrastructure projects.

The main obstacles to regulatory reform are neither technical nor political, but ideological. Some of the above proposals will require further refinement (for example, those concerning financial instruments and the design of performance contracts), but the complexities are few. Interest groups will oppose the privatization of the electric power companies and complicate the reaching of a compromise between state and municipal governments in water and sanitation, but the obstacles are not insurmountable. The key challenge, then, is to tilt the balance between pragmatism and ideology to favor the former. This may happen as infrastructure bottlenecks become more critical in the near future. In particular, as economic conditions improve and the cost of capital continues to decline, private operators will be willing to charge lower usage fees, weakening one of the areas of resistance.

Political Reform

As argued above, one cannot fully understand the relationship between reform and economic growth in Brazil over the last two decades without taking the country's politics and political institutions into account. In particular, two of the defining features of Brazil's political system—the reliance on proportional representation and on open lists, rather than majority rule (*voto majoritário*) and closed lists, in the election of Congress has favored the rapid rise in current public expenditure since the return to democracy. Controlling this spending is crucial to improving the quality of macroeconomic policy and thus to strengthening the macroeconomic stability foundation. Therefore one of the priorities of reform must be to bring about change in these institutions.

Brazil is not alone in experiencing high public expenditure under a proportional representation system: the political science literature reports a robust relationship between the two in countries around the world. Persson and Tabellini (2003) show that the ratio of public expenditure to GDP tends to be 5 percent higher, and social security expenditure 3 percent higher, in democracies that rely on proportional representation than in those that do not.

What accounts for this relationship? Persson, Roland, and Tabellini (2003) develop a theoretical model that suggests that higher public spending is a consequence of the greater party fragmentation induced by proportional representation. This also makes intuitive sense. If the executive is elected without a strong legislative majority, it will have to build legislative support for its initiatives issue by issue, constantly assembling new coalitions, if it is to accomplish anything. The more fragmented the legislature, the harder the executive will have to work to build these coalitions, and the more it will have to bargain. Some parties will already be inclined to support a given measure, but others will be at best indifferent; to win their support, the executive will have to engage in "logrolling," giving these parties concessions on issues of more importance to them in exchange for their support on the issue at hand. The cost of these concessions will, of course, be additional to the cost of the executive's own initiative, so that a successful bargain will increase public expenditure above what it would be if logrolling were unnecessary, and obviously it will exceed what it would be if the initiative failed for lack of support. Persson et al. (2003) show that legislative fragmentation (which can be measured in much the same way as concentration in an industry, using Herfindahl's index) is important empirically in explaining the level of public expenditure: they find no direct relationship between the system of government (presidential or parliamentary) and the electoral rule (majoritarian or proportional), on the one hand, and the level of public expenditure, on the other, once they control for the degree of party fragmentation in the lower house of the legislature.

Political institutions also matter for the level of corruption in government and for the ability of the government to take steps to control corruption; anti-corruption reforms, in turn, should contribute to strengthening several of the foundations for growth (table 5). Here, however, the theoretical results are less robust. Persson and Tabellini's analysis would suggest that the best electoral system from the standpoint of minimizing corruption is a proportional representation system with open lists (because it is easier to challenge incumbents) and large electoral districts. Yet this is precisely the system that Brazil already has, and Brazil, at least according to opinion polls and the frequent news reports of political scandal, is clearly a long way from minimizing corruption. Moreover, Italy also had the same system until 1994 yet was considered to have the most corrupt politics in the developed world.

What Persson and Tabellini's analysis seems to overlook is the fact that proportional systems with open lists and large districts tend to have strong *intraparty* competition, which leads to expensive political campaigns. The cost of financing campaigns in turn makes politicians more dependent on wealthy donors, with corruption the result as the winning politicians reward their contributors with political favors once in office (Golden and Chang, 2001; Chang, 2005). Chang and Golden (2006) also report evidence showing that corruption is greater (and increasing) in larger districts (more than fifteen representatives) that use open rather than closed lists; in smaller districts, however, corruption tends to be lower with open lists. Shugart, Valdini, and Suominen (2005) corroborate this finding, showing that in larger districts, candidates have a greater interest in differentiating themselves from other candidates under an open-list than under a closed-list system, and that they do this through pork-barrel spending and corrupt practices. Finally, Tavits (2007) argues that party fragmentation reduces the clarity of responsibility for political outcomes, and that where responsibility is less clear, corruption will be greater. Thus political fragmentation may be a culprit both in Brazil's excessive spending growth and in its level of corruption.

What do these results imply in terms of recommendations for political reform in Brazil? Although the results of Persson and his coauthors indicate that a shift to majority voting might lead to reduced expenditure, this would be a fairly radical change for Brazil. It also appears unnecessary, since the above discussion suggests that the potentially adverse outcomes of proportional representation can be improved simply by changing the parameters of the proportional system. In particular, improvement in government spending decisions might be achievable through a reform that aims at lowering party fragmentation, especially in Congress, so that elected administrations can form the base of support necessary to accomplish their objectives with fewer parties.

A particularly important parameter in determining the degree of party fragmentation is the size of the electoral district. Unless regional parties are strong (Brazilian law makes them almost impossible to form), a minor party will have greater difficulty winning a seat in any given district, the less seats are contested. In Brazil seats in the lower house of Congress (the Câmara dos Deputados) are allotted by state, with the number of seats proportional to its population. But this number is truncated from above and below, with a minimum of eight seats guaranteed to each of the smallest states and a maximum of seventy seats allowed for São Paulo, the most populous state. Even this wide range in number of seats per state (8.75 to 1) is far less than the actual differences in state population: at 41 million in 2006, São Paulo has 100 times the population of the smallest state, Roraima. Thus each legislator from São Paulo represents about twelve times as many voters as a legislator from Roraima.

The studies by Chang and Golden (2006) and by Shugart et al. (2005) indicate that the performance of open-list systems with respect to corruption is not unfavorable in sufficiently small districts. Thus we propose the following reform:

• Divide the states that currently have more than nine representatives in the Câmara dos Deputados into smaller districts (for purposes of congressional voting only) with a minimum of five representatives each. Keep the remaining institutions (proportional representation, open lists, and so forth) unchanged.

This reform would reduce the degree of party fragmentation substantially and thus should have beneficial impacts on public spending. Additionally, the reduction in the number of seats per district in the larger states would reduce intraparty competition without too great an increase in entry barriers. The studies cited above suggest that under this reform, corruption would be reduced as well; measures to reform campaign financing could also help in this regard (Samuels, 2006, pp. 133–53). As a side benefit, this reform would also strengthen the representation of metropolitan areas (Monroe and Rose, 2002). Although critical, this reform should be implemented incrementally, because such changes inevitably generate uncertainty, and it is difficult to predict how the population would react to this change and to other changes in the functioning of institutions generally.

Final Remarks

Brazil has implemented many reforms since the 1980s, without, however, achieving the expected increase in economic growth. These reforms caused a significant rise in total factor productivity growth and made growth more inclusive, but they failed to boost investment or accelerate the lackluster pace of human capital accumulation. Performance in these areas was particularly poor compared with most other countries at similar levels of development. We explain this outcome by the fact that many of the reforms were only partly implemented or were sidetracked into pursuing other objectives, while others strengthened one growth foundation but weakened others. More important, even as Brazil pursued market-oriented reforms in many areas, it also engaged in what we have termed "anti-market reforms": changes in norms, resource allocation, and policies that discouraged investment and productivity growth and weakened the links between the market-oriented reforms and growth. These anti-market reforms severely undermined the impact of the pro-market reforms on growth.

We view the *expansion in public expenditure and the change in its composition—* with a decline in public investment and a rise in current outlays—as the most important of these anti-market reforms. Rising public expenditure was initially financed by rising inflation, then by public sector borrowing, and most recently by expanding tax revenue, in all cases with adverse consequences for macroeconomic stability and with negative spillovers on capital accumulation and productivity growth. The 1988 constitution, which produced a mix of market-oriented and anti-market reforms, was a landmark in this process. Yet the policies embedded in the constitution did not constitute an isolated event, but only the most noteworthy of a series of policy initiatives that continued through the following two decades in the same vein.

This indicates that these policy decisions were endogenous to the country's social and political institutions. In particular, we attribute the problem of poor selection of reforms to the interplay between democratization, itself a major reform, and Brazil's highly unequal income distribution. Democratization allowed voters to express their preference for a large, protective state. The repeated expansion of current public expenditure, notably transfers, is also consistent with a key feature of Brazil's political system, namely, political party fragmentation, notably in the government's congressional support base. Problems of information asymmetry further explain the preference for a large state, as characterized by the fact that the regressive nature of the tax system is less transparent than the progressive character of the more advertised social programs. Voters can assess relatively easily how public funds are spent but find it more difficult to recognize the incidence of indirect taxes.

Looking forward, *macroeconomic stability* is the foundation for growth whose weakness is the most critical. The weakness of this pillar results from an unbalanced policy mix, which overburdens monetary policy and requires a rising tax burden and a low rate of public investment to ensure public solvency. It is crucial that public saving be increased. Thus the most critical reforms are those that reduce current expenditure. We have argued that pension reform is the best way to achieve this goal, but it is extremely unpopular in Brazil: barring a major crisis, we do not see what could make a wholesale reform in this area viable in the short term. Thus, as with other reforms, we suggest that piecewise, incremental reform be adopted. This last point underlines our conclusion that significant curbs on current public spending will have to wait for a change in the political environment, not only to make pension reform more viable, but also because Brazilian political institutions favor party fragmentation, which in turn tends to boost current public spending. Thus, to bring about a political environment conducive to lowering public expenditure, Brazil should pursue a reduction in party fragmentation, particularly concerning the number of parties represented in Congress, so that governments can form majorities with fewer participating parties. We see an expansion in the size of electoral districts as the most promising way to achieve that goal.

The insecurity of *property rights* comes second in our list of weakest foundations. The problem in this case stems from a combination of the poor quality of the laws produced by Congress, an executive that exploits judicial delay as a fiscal policy instrument while underestimating the importance of stable legal norms, and a judiciary that suffers under a procedural code that, despite recent progress, remains cumbersome, and from judicial activism and inefficiencies in its own administrative practices. More broadly, we have identified a national culture that favors pursuing "social justice" over judicial consistency, and which needs to be changed if the rule of law is to be significantly strengthened.

To conclude, we stress three lessons with respect to the challenge of advancing growth-enhancing but unpopular market-oriented reforms while at the same time preventing or even undoing popular anti-market reforms. Needless to say, political will is a necessary condition for success.

First, it is crucial to be pragmatic and avoid risking all one's political capital on a politically unfeasible reform, no matter how sensible it may be from an economic standpoint. Likewise, it makes more sense to pursue piecewise, seemingly uncoordinated reforms than to get bogged down promoting an all-encompassing but unfeasible reform package. The recommendation, then, is to stress those reforms that are politically less sensitive, such as tax reform, or that allow the losers from reform to be at least partly compensated or protected through transition or grandfather clauses. As an example, new rules for pension reform could be designed to apply only to workers entering the labor market after the reform. Nonetheless, it is important to have and follow a general master plan to help ensure consistency.

Second, although Brazil's skewed income distribution is one leading explanation of voters' preferences for big government, another is the fact that voters have an imperfect perception of the consequences of their policy choices. Here a good example is the small redistributive impact of fiscal policy reform. By increasing transparency about the diagnosis that informs the reform proposals, one can likely build a constituency for at least some reforms, without having to wait for the distribution of income to improve—something that will not happen quickly in any case. This highlights the importance of further academic work and a close link with the media, so as to change perceptions about how the majority of voters are affected by current policy choices.

Third, in the past when Brazil has faced severe crises, notably foreign exchange crises, unpopular reforms were approved as necessary evils that helped bring about a greater good. To seize these opportunities, should they recur in the future, it is crucial to have well-developed reform proposals ready on the shelf, well known to the political leadership, that can be rapidly approved. Likewise, some of the reforms discussed here, such as regulatory reform, face a kind of ideological opposition that may wane significantly in the event of a political transition, such as the election of a more centrist president. In that event, too, it would help to have well-developed reform projects that could be brought swiftly before the consideration of legislators.

References

Afonso, J. R., and R. Varsano. 2004. "Reforma Tributária: Sonhos e Frustrações." In F. Giambiagi, J. G. Reis, and A. Urani, eds., *Reformas no Brasil: Balanço e Agenda*. Rio de Janeiro: Editora Nova Fronteira.

Barbosa Filho, F. de H., and S. de A. Pessôa. 2008. "A Carreira de Professor Estadual no Brasil: Os Casos de São Paulo e Rio Grande do Sul." Rio de Janeiro: Fundação Getúlio Vargas.

Barbosa Filho, F. de H., L. A. Afonso, and S. de A. Pessôa. 2008. "Um Estudo Sobre os Diferenciais de Remuneração Entre os Professores das Redes Pública e Privada de Ensino." Rio de Janeiro: Fundação Getúlio Vargas.

Barro, Robert J. 1990. "Government Spending in a Simple Model of Endogenous Growth." *Journal of Political Economy* 98, no. 5, pt. 2: S103–25.

Barros, R. P. de, and R. Mendonça. 1995. "A Evolução do Bem-Estar, Pobreza e Desigualdade no Brasil ao longo das Últimas Três Décadas—1960/1990." *Pesquisa e Planejamento Econômico* 25, no. 1: 115–63.

Barros, R. P. de, M. de Carvalho, S. Franco, and R. Mendonça. 2007. "Determinantes Imediatos da Queda da Desigualdade de Renda Brasileira." In Ricardo Paes de Barros, Miguel Nathan Foguel, and Gabriel Ulyssea, eds., *Desigualdade de Renda no Brasil: Uma Análise da Queda Recente*. Rio de Janeiro: Instituto de Pesquisa Econômica Aplicada. www.ipea.gov.br/082/08201004.jsp?ttCD_CHAVE=2783.

Bénabou, R. 2006. "Inequality, Technology and the Social Contract." In P. Aghion and S. Durlauf, eds., *Handbook of Economic Growth*. Amsterdam: Elsevier, North-Holland.

Carvalho Filho, I., and M. Chamon. 2006. "The Myth of Post-Reform Income Stagnation in Brazil." IMF Working Paper 06/275. Washington: International Monetary Fund, Western Hemisphere and Research Departments (December).

Chang, Eric C. C. 2005. "Electoral Incentives for Political Corruption under Open-List Proportional Representation." *Journal of Politics* 67, no. 3: 716–30.

Chang, Eric C. C., and Miriam A. Golden. 2006. "Electoral Systems, District Magnitude and Corruption." *British Journal of Political Science* 37: 115–37.

Ferreira, S., and F. Veloso. 2006. "A Reforma da Educação." In A. C. Pinheiro and F. Giambiagi, eds., *Rompendo o Marasmo: A Retomada do Desenvolvimento no Brasil*. Rio de Janeiro: Campus/Elsevier.

Ferreira, F., P. Leite, and M. Ravallion. 2007. "Poverty Reduction without Economic Growth? Explaining Brazil's Poverty Dynamics, 1985–2004." Policy Research Working Paper 4431. Washington: World Bank (December).

Giambiagi, F. 2006. *Reforma da Previdência: O Encontro Marcado*. Rio de Janeiro: Campus/Elsevier.

Giavazzi, F., and G. Tabellini. 2005. "Economic and Political Liberalization." *Journal of Monetary Economics* 52: 1297–1330.

Golden, Miriam A., and Eric C. C. Chang. 2001. "Competitive Corruption: Factional Conflict and Political Malfeasance in Postwar Italian Christian Democracy." *World Politics* 53: 588–622.

Kakwani, N., M. Neri, and H. H. Son. 2006. "Linkages between Pro-Poor Growth and the Labor Market." In *Anais do XXXV Encontro Nacional de Economia*. Niterói, Brazil: Associação Nacional dos Centros de Pósgraduação em Economia. www.anpec.org.br/encontro2007/artigos/A07A096.pdf.

Mello, L., and E. Tiongson. 2006. "Income Inequality and Redistributive Government Spending." *Public Finance Review* 34, no. 3: 282–305.

Menezes-Filho, N. 2003. "Trade Liberalization and Inequality in Brazil." Paper presented at the seminar Brazil: Risks and Opportunities of Integration into the World Economy, São Paulo, November 4.

Monroe, Burt L., and Amanda G. Rose. 2002. "Electoral System and Unimagined Consequences: Partisan Effect of District Proportional Rule." *American Journal of Political Science* 46, no. 1: 67–89.

Persson, T., and G. Tabellini. 2003. *The Economic Effects of Constitutions*. MIT Press.

Persson, Torsten, Gérard Roland, and Guido Tabellini. 2003. "How Do Electoral Rules Shape Party Structures, Government Coalitions, and Economic Policies?" Working Paper 10176. Cambridge, Mass.: National Bureau of Economic Research.

Pinheiro, A. C., and R. Bonelli. 2007. "Financial Development, Growth and Equity in Brazil." In R. Ffrench-Davis and J. L. Machinea, eds., *Economic Growth with Equity—Challenges for Latin America*. Houndmills, Basingstoke, U.K.: Palgrave-Macmillan.

Pinheiro, A. C., R. Bonelli, and B. R. Schneider. 2007. "Pragmatism and Market Reforms in Brazil." In J. M. Fanelli, ed., *Understanding Market Reforms in Latin America*. Houndmills, Basingstoke, U.K.: Palgrave-Macmillan.

Pinheiro, A. C., and F. Giambiagi. 2006. *Rompendo o Marasmo: A Retomada do Desenvolvimento no Brasil*. Rio de Janeiro: Campus/Elsevier.

Samuels, D. 2006. *Financiamento de Campanhas no Brasil e Propostas de Reformas—Reforma Política, Lições da História Recente*. Rio de Janeiro: Editora FGV.

Shugart, Matthew Soberg, Melody Ellis Valdini, and Kati Suominen. 2005. "Looking for Locals: Voter Information Demands and Personal Vote-Earning Attributes of Legislators under Proportional Representation." *American Journal of Political Science* 49, no. 2: 437–49.

Tafner, P., and F. Giambiagi, eds. 2007, *Previdência no Brasil–Debates, Dilemas e Escolhas*. Rio de Janeiro: Instituto de Pesquisa Econômica Aplicada.

Tavits, Margit. 2007. "Clarity of Responsibility and Corruption." *American Journal of Political Science* 51, no. 1: 218–29.

4

Colombia's Efforts at Achieving Inclusive and Sustainable Growth

ROBERTO STEINER, IRENE CLAVIJO, AND NATALIA SALAZAR

At the end of the 1980s, Colombia confronted a situation of slow economic growth and unsettled domestic security. To address these issues, a comprehensive reform effort was undertaken starting in 1990. The agenda comprised a set of market-driven reforms aimed at enhancing competition and the role of the private sector, as well as a vast array of institutional reforms aimed at strengthening macroeconomic stability, promoting equality of opportunities in the political and judicial arenas, and sharing more broadly the benefits of growth across regions and individuals. In this chapter we show that this ambitious reform drive proved very challenging. Reforms aimed at strengthening some foundations for growth actually weakened others. Restrictions stemming from the local environment and issues of design prevented many of the reforms from fully delivering on their promise. In particular, the benefits of broadened opportunities achieved through fiscal decentralization, increased social expenditure, and expanded access to the judicial system must be contrasted with the fiscal deterioration and macroeconomic vulnerability that accompanied them.

Starting in 1999, a succession of three administrations tackled some of the salient problems. Although this effort, coupled with a supportive external environment and improved security, delivered a favorable economic outcome, chal-

We have received very useful comments from Liliana Rojas-Suárez, Nora Lustig, Ernesto Stein, Felipe Botero, Mauricio Cárdenas, and Mauricio Santamaria and from participants at a September 2007 workshop at the Center for Global Development in Washington.

lenges remain in further strengthening the foundations for growth. This chapter will offer some proposals to that effect, with an emphasis on the need to remove some of the limitations imposed by the local environment, particularly those arising from a highly activist judicial system.

The Road to a Comprehensive Reform Effort

During the late 1960s and 1970s, Colombia's economic performance was strong. Between 1965 and 1979 real GDP growth averaged 5.6 percent a year, and inflation, although seldom in the single digits, never experienced the sharp rises typical of some other Latin American countries. Prudent macroeconomic policies rather than a particularly stable external environment were behind these developments.[1] Growth in output per worker, which averaged 1.8 percent a year during 1965–79, was led by increases in total factor productivity (TFP), which grew at an average rate of 1.1 percent a year (Cárdenas, 2007). The 1960s and 1970s were also a period of political tranquility and of progress in social indicators. A 1958 power sharing agreement between the two historically dominant political parties had brought an end to political violence, and peace and economic prosperity facilitated a decline in poverty and an improvement in the distribution of income.[2]

Although Colombia was, except for Chile, the only large regional economy not to be devastated by the 1980s debt crisis, performance during that decade was at best mediocre. Average GDP growth declined to 3.4 percent a year, led by a dismal performance of TFP, which contracted at an annual rate of 1 percent during the decade.[3] Most social indicators continued to improve, but at a slower pace. The salient feature of the 1980s was the deterioration in security.[4]

1. A study by the Inter-American Development Bank (1995) characterized Colombia's economic policy as the most stable among twenty-two regional economies. Except during a short period in the early 1980s, the fiscal deficit was always small. Until 1993, public debt had never surpassed 20 percent of GDP.

2. Income inequality declined during the 1960s and 1970s (Londoño, 1995). Recent estimations, although not strictly comparable to the earlier ones, suggest that the distribution of income improved only slightly during the 1980s.

3. As part of the policy package designed to confront the decline in net foreign transfers that followed the Mexican crisis, throughout the 1980s the Colombian economy became increasingly distorted and closed to foreign competition. Whereas in 1980 around a third of imports were prohibited or subject to government approval, by 1984 that share had risen to 99.6 percent. Labor market regulation was inflexible and obsolete. Restrictions and distortions were also prevalent in the financial sector. A vast array of exchange controls supported a crawling peg exchange rate regime, and legislation governing foreign direct investment appeared to be aimed at severing ties with the world economy. The tax system, meanwhile, featured double taxation of distributed earnings and a broad range of exemptions.

4. Drug money emboldened the cartels and Marxist guerrilla movements. In 1982, when the government began to extradite drug traffickers to the United States, the drug mafia declared war. The guerrillas, who had been somewhat active in remote regions in the 1970s, became important actors during the 1980s. It was during the early 1980s that the head of Colombia's main business association memorably said, "even though the economy is doing well, the country is doing poorly." By the end of the decade this decoupling seemed untenable.

Figure 1. *Colombia: Selected Economic and Social Indicators*

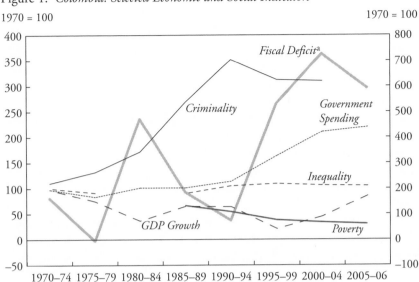

Sources: Ministry of Finance, Departamento Nacional de Planeación, Departamento Administrativo Nacional de Estadística, Banco de la República, Defensoría del Pueblo, Cárdenas (2007), Londoño (1995), MERP (2006).
a. Scaled on the right axis; all other variables are scaled on the left axis.

Figure 1 looks at six dimensions of economic and social issues—GDP growth, public spending, the fiscal deficit, poverty, inequality, and criminality—since 1970, a stretch of time that encompasses the pre-reform period, the decade following the first round of reforms, and the period since the second round of reforms. In a nutshell, growth slowed in the 1980s while security, as measured by the homicide rate, deteriorated markedly in the context of a slow but continuous decline in poverty. Following the first wave of reforms in the early 1990s, the fiscal situation sharply worsened as a result of the hike in public expenditure that was mandated in the new constitution, which went into effect in 1991. Although growth failed to recover, poverty continued to decline; criminality meanwhile remained high. Following the second wave of reforms starting in 1999, the fiscal deficit declined sharply. This, coupled with a remarkable improvement in security and a supportive external environment, has delivered much stronger economic growth.

Over a short period during 1990–92, Colombia—which had been a regional beacon of economic and political stability during the 1960s and 1970s, where policy continuity had been the norm—underwent major economic, political, and institutional change (Edwards and Steiner, 2008). The comprehensive reform process was the consequence of two forces. On the economic front, the slowdown in growth and its association with a contraction in productivity paved the way for the introduction of pro-market reforms—including in trade, finance, and the labor market—during the second half of 1990. On the political-institutional front, in late 1990 a popularly elected Constitutional Assembly was entrusted with rewriting the country's 100-year-old constitution, with the expectation that the new constitution would enhance governance and facilitate both the containment of the drug cartels and the negotiation of a peace agreement with the guerrilla movements. The new constitution significantly expanded expenditure in health and education and broadened access to the judicial system and to the political process. These measures were aimed at sharing the benefits of growth more broadly, so as to make growth more sustainable.

Several analyses of the new constitution support the following general description of its contents:

• It commits the nation to a welfare state, in contrast to the market-oriented reforms being introduced at the same time.

• It mandates that the central government transfer a large and growing portion of tax revenue to subnational governments (departments and municipalities) in order to finance a meaningful expansion of expenditure in health and education.

• It empowers citizens, particularly by establishing the *acción de tutela,* an expeditious mechanism granting immediate access to the judicial system.

• It shifts the policymaking structure from one characterized by a powerful president to one in which subnational governments, the Constitutional Court, and the central bank are key actors as well. In those areas that are "hard-wired" in the constitution—such as the transfers to subnational governments to fund health and education—the executive saw its discretion significantly reduced.

In terms of the CGD framework (see chapter 2), the early 1990s reform drive sought to affect four of the five foundations: fostering *economic and political competition,* promoting *equality of opportunities, broader sharing of the benefits of growth,* and protecting *macroeconomic stability,* the last of these particularly by granting independence to the central bank and introducing fully funded private pension funds. Progress on the fifth foundation, securing *property rights,* might have occurred as a by-product of the pension reform. The prominence given to competition reflected the fact that lagging productivity was viewed as driving the slowdown in growth during the 1980s. Likewise, promoting competition and equality of opportunities on the economic, political, and judicial fronts was a means of dealing with a much deteriorated political and security situation by broadening the pool of beneficiaries from growth.

During the decade that followed the launch of the reforms, the economy underperformed. The fiscal position weakened, the economy became more vulnerable and volatile, poverty reduction slowed,[5] and income distribution wors-

---

5. This statement applies when poverty is defined in terms of unsatisfied basic needs, as in figure 1. When poverty is defined as the percentage of the population living on less than x amount per day, poverty becomes highly pro-cyclical, *increasing* during the second half of the 1990s.

ened. Although several exogenous factors play a role in explaining this turn of events,[6] elements associated with the reform program also contributed. When the Asian crisis of the late 1990s hit Latin America, Colombia found itself in a particularly weak macroeconomic position. An unprecedented output contraction followed, which hit the poor especially hard. More rapid growth and a new, positive trend in poverty reduction have been achieved only recently, after the fiscal imbalance began to be addressed and the security situation started to improve, in the context of a favorable external environment.

Some stylized facts about the performance of the Colombian economy since the launch of the 1990 reforms include the following:

• Performance went from exemplary in the 1970s, to mediocre in the 1980s, to very poor until recently. In 1999 Colombia saw its first economic contraction in seventy years. Since 2002 GDP growth has accelerated, averaging 5.5 percent a year during 2003–07. Estimates by Cárdenas (2007) show that during the second half of the 1990s, and contrary to what was expected following the pro-market reforms undertaken at the beginning of the decade, TFP growth was a dismal −2.7 percent a year. The recovery in growth that followed the second round of reforms, in a context of enhanced security and a benign international environment, has been accompanied by an improvement in TFP, which rose at an annual rate of 0.8 percent between 2001 and 2005, and by significantly more in 2006–07 according to a preliminary update of Cárdenas (2007) undertaken by Fedesarrollo.[7]

• Colombia is the only large Latin American country in which growth during the decade following the launch of reforms was historically low, the fiscal balance weak, and public expenditure particularly high (Sahay and Goyal, 2006).[8]

• Growth also became increasingly volatile during the 1990s and the first few years of the new century (figure 2).

• Inflation declined consistently and now hovers at around 4 to 6 percent a year.

• Colombia strayed from its tradition of a sound fiscal stance. Although the deterioration had a cyclical component, it was to a large extent the result of structural features, in particular the increase in expenditure mandated in the new constitution. In no other large country in the region did social expenditure increase as much, as a percentage of GDP, in the decade following the launch of pro-market reforms, although it remains below that in Argentina, Brazil, and Chile

6. These factors included an unfavorable international environment, a tense security situation, and a profound political crisis in the mid-1990s following allegations that drug money had financed a presidential campaign.

7. Because of a change in 2006 in the employment module of the household survey, the employment index fell considerably, perhaps causing an underestimation of the capital-output ratio.

8. Colombia is one of only three countries—the other two being Paraguay and Venezuela—in the Sahay and Goyal (2006) sample in which the decade with the slowest growth (which can refer to any consecutive ten-year period) happened *after* the early-1990s reform process.

Figure 2. *Colombia: Growth and Volatility of GDP, 1955–2007*

Percent

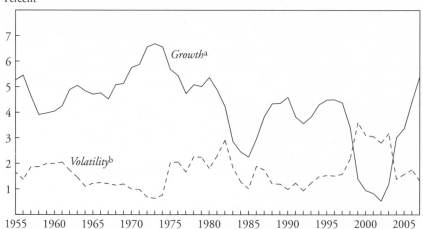

Source: Authors' calculations based on data from the Departamento Administrativo Nacional de Estadística.
a. Average of the past five years.
b. Average standard deviation of growth over the past five years.

(table 1). Since entering into a seven-year agreement with the International Monetary Fund in 1999, three successive administrations have focused on restoring fiscal discipline. Progress notwithstanding, the public debt is still around 40 percent of GDP.

• With regard to income distribution, the progress achieved in the 1970s and the first half of the 1980s was reversed during 1990–2000. Although the distribution has improved lately, in 2005 it was as inequitable as it had been in 1992 (figure 3).

• As measured by the UBN (unsatisfied basic needs) index, poverty declined throughout the 1990s, although at a slower rate than previously. But poverty as measured by the percentage of the population living below the poverty line (a definition that is heavily influenced by the business cycle) increased. Núñez and Espinosa (2005), using data on income per capita from the national household surveys and applying the poverty equivalent growth rate (PEGR) methodology,[9] show that during the worst period in terms of output expansion, growth was anti-poor (table 2): although economic growth was positive, headcount poverty

9. The PEGR is the growth rate that would have resulted in the same poverty reduction as the observed growth rate if everyone had received the same proportional benefits. If the PEGR is greater than the observed rate, growth is pro-poor. If the PEGR is less than the observed rate but positive, growth is defined as "trickle-down": although poverty declines, inequality increases. If the PEGR is less than observed growth and negative, growth is defined as anti-poor: although observed growth is positive, poverty increases because the benefits are distributed only among the non-poor.

Table 1. *Public Social Expenditure in Selected Latin American Countries*
Percent of GDP

Country	1990–93	1999–2001
Argentina	19.7	21.2
Brazil	17.9	19.1
Chile	12.1	15.4
Colombia	7.5	13.8
Mexico	7.3	9.5
Peru	4.7	7.9
Venezuela	8.7	9.9

Source: Authors' calculations from ECLAC database.

Figure 3. *Colombia: Income Inequality, 1978–2007*
Gini coefficient (100 = maximum inequality)

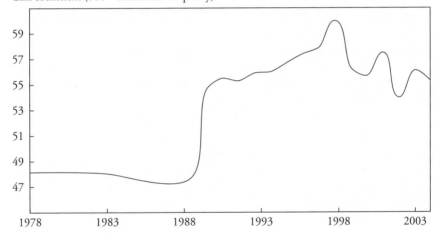

Source: MERP (2006).

Table 2. *Colombia: GDP Growth and Poverty-Equivalent Growth*
Percent a year (simple averages)

Period	GDP growth rate	Poverty-equivalent growth rate[a]
1997–2000	0.625	−2.625
2000–04	2.875	3.1
1997–2004	1.75	0.2375

Source: Núñez and Espinosa (2005).
a. The growth rate that would result in the same poverty reduction as the observed growth rate if every-one had received the same proportional benefits.

increased; thus the benefits of growth were captured by the nonpoor. During the recovery, growth has been pro-poor, as poverty has declined on account of faster growth and an improved income distribution. During the entire 1997–2004 period, the nonpoor benefited more from growth than the poor (growth "trickled down"): although growth contributed to reducing poverty, higher inequality increased poverty on a yearly basis (except in 2000 and 2003).

Colombia's attempt at promoting market-driven reforms while at the same time putting in place measures to enhance economic, political, and judicial inclusiveness proved very difficult, as some reforms turned out to include elements that detracted from the effectiveness of others. Although the renewed impetus since the late 1990s, together with a favorable external environment and a much improved security situation, has delivered an economic dividend, important challenges lie ahead.

The next section describes the main reforms undertaken in the early 1990s and the foundations that they were intended to impact. We then highlight some inconsistencies among elements of the reforms that weakened these foundations. In some cases there were design problems; in others the instruments used were insufficient; in most there were institutional constraints, mainly stemming from the active role of the Constitutional Court and from restrictions imposed by the decentralization effort mandated under the new constitution. Although progress has recently been made in addressing some of the inconsistencies, there is room for improvement. We follow this discussion with some proposals aimed at improving the prospects for achieving a sustainable rate of growth, that is, one consistent with macroeconomic stability and social inclusiveness. We not only try to identify "what" needs to be done; we also offer recommendations for "how" specific initiatives stand a better chance of being implemented. And we do not shy away from acknowledging that some constraints imposed by the local environment appear insurmountable, at least in the short to medium term.

The Reforms and Their Intended Impact on the Foundations

The reform effort launched in 1990 was an attempt to affect, to varying degrees, most of the foundations for growth identified in the CGD framework. Table 3 summarizes both the intended and the actual impacts of the most important reforms; in this section we discuss the intended effects, and in the next we analyze the actual results. Reforms in the economic arena—trade, finance, and labor—were geared mainly at enhancing *competition* so as to foster efficiency and reverse the trend decline in TFP. Financial liberalization also aimed at *broader sharing of the benefits of growth,* and capital account liberalization at promoting *equality of opportunities,* by fostering financial deepening and access to credit. Consolidating *macroeconomic stability* was the goal of two institutional reforms—to the central bank and the pension system—and of several tax reforms, although pension

Table 3. *Colombia: Intended and Actual Impact of Reforms on the Growth Foundations*

Reform	Property rights		Equal opportunities		Competition		Broad sharing of growth benefits		Macroeconomic stability	
	Intended	Actual	Intended	Actual	Intended	Actual	Intended	Actual	Intended	Actual
Trade liberalization					++	++				
Financial reform					++	+				
Capital account liberalization	+	+					+			
Labor reform					++	+				
Tax reform									++	++
Central bank independence									++	++
Pension reform	+	+			+	−	+		++	+
Fiscal decentralization							++	+		− −
Health reform					+	−	++	+		− −
Education reform							++	+		−
Political reform			++	+		−	+			−
Judicial reform			++	+		−	+			− −

Source: Authors' evaluations.
Key: +, positive; ++, strongly positive; −, negative; − −, strongly negative.

reform had other objectives as well. Broader sharing of the benefits of growth was also the main goal of decentralization, which was undertaken together with a hike in social expenditure. Equality of opportunities, and to a lesser extent the broader sharing of the benefits of growth, was the purpose of reforms in the judicial and political arenas.[10]

Enhancing Competition and Lowering Barriers to Entry

The centerpiece of the economic reforms was *trade liberalization*. Launched as a gradual reform in the late 1980s, it was significantly expanded in 1991. The driving force behind this reform was the view that the economy should be exposed to foreign competition as a means of reversing the pattern of declining TFP witnessed throughout the 1980s, which, as noted above, explained most of the growth slowdown. The five-year program that began in early 1990 was geared toward eliminating quantitative restrictions, reducing tariff rates and the number of tariff levels, implementing institutional reforms, and negotiating international trade agreements. In October 1990 a new government issued a three-year liberalization schedule, which included the agricultural sector. But instead of increasing as expected, imports actually declined. Together with an increase in capital inflows, this made monetary management exceedingly difficult. In June 1991 it was decided that the initial liberalization schedule would be carried out by September 1991.

Trade liberalization was accompanied by *financial liberalization*. This reform sought to foster competition and efficiency and to strengthen and deepen the financial sector. It also aimed at a more level playing field in which foreign institutions could compete on an equal footing with local ones, and in which all investors, not only those with connections, could allocate their portfolios across borders.[11] With the enforcement of new capitalization standards and stronger regulation and supervision, it was expected that the financial sector would contribute to economic stability. Specific features of the package included removal of barriers to entry, reduction and rationalization of reserve requirements, liberalization of most interest rates, a reduction in forced investments, and the privatization of some banks. Law 9 of 1991 removed all entry restrictions and established national treatment for foreign direct investment. It also eliminated limits on the profits that foreign firms could transfer abroad.

The authorities held the view that for the country to effectively compete in the global economy, a more *flexible labor market* was needed. The 1990 reform made

---

10. Other than through the introduction of private pension funds, the strengthening of *property rights* does not appear to have been an important goal of the reforms undertaken since the early 1990s.

11. An important component of financial liberalization was the dismantling of capital controls that had been in place for over twenty years. Also, a general amnesty was given to Colombians who had kept foreign exchange abroad.

contracts more flexible and reduced labor costs. Importantly, it attempted to reduce the gap between formal sector workers and those working informally. In order to expand formalization, dismissal costs and nonwage labor costs were reduced and short-term contracts and flexibility in the definition of working hours introduced. At the same time, procedures for establishing a labor union were made simpler, a regulation forbidding them from participating in politics was repealed, and liabilities to workers were granted seniority in the event of their employer's bankruptcy.

Promoting Macroeconomic Stability

To enhance macroeconomic stability, the 1991 constitution granted *independence to the central bank*. Its board of directors is the authority in charge of monetary, exchange rate, and credit policy. The board is composed of seven members: five of these are appointed by the government for concurrent four-year terms, but every four years only two of the five may be replaced;[12] the minister of finance is a member of the board and together with the five appointed members elects the central bank governor for a four-year term that can be renewed twice. The central bank may not extend credit or offer guarantees to the private nonfinancial sector and may extend direct credit to the government only upon unanimous vote by its board. It must strive for a low and stable rate of inflation, in coordination with overall economic policy. In the event that other goals conflict with achieving low and stable inflation, the bank must give priority to the latter.

Another reform undertaken mainly with the purpose of promoting macroeconomic stability was a major transformation of the *pension system* in 1993. The system previously in place exhibited all the limitations of a public pay-as-you-go (PAYGO) scheme: contributions and benefits differed across the various subsystems; the earliest retirees received huge transfers; contributions were weakly linked to benefits; coverage was low; administration was inefficient; and the system lacked adequate reserves and therefore depended on growing fiscal transfers. The reform established a general scheme composed of two subsystems: a public PAYGO regime and a subsidized individual savings scheme using privately managed funds (*administradoras de fondos de pensiones,* or AFPs). Although the subsystems were separate from one another, transfers between them were allowed. The system was made mandatory for employees in the private and public sectors. Until it was reformed again in 2003, participation was optional for the self-employed and for dependents of participants. Although a long transition period was allowed, the reform increased the retirement age,

12. The tenure of the Colombian president is four years, and until 2005 the president could not seek a second term.

raised contribution rates and eligibility requirements, and rationalized benefits. In addition to placing the system in a more sustainable financial position, other objectives of the reform included exposing the public fund to competition, promoting the development of the capital market, and, in the case of the 2003 reform, better targeting of subsidies. A by-product of the reform was greater security of the pension rights of formal sector workers, with rights more clearly defined in individual accounts.

Since the early 1990s Colombia has undergone several *tax reforms*. Unlike the reform of 1986, which brought about a major improvement in the *quality* of the tax code, the reforms undertaken since 1990 have aimed at increasing tax revenue, to finance the increase in public expenditure mandated, for the most part, in the 1991 constitution.

Broader Sharing of the Benefits of Growth and Greater Equality of Opportunities

The second half of the 1980s saw a growing recognition that *decentralization* should play a major role in rebuilding trust in institutions, in the context of a critical security situation. Self-government was seen as a means of consolidating democracy while improving the efficiency of government intervention. The 1991 constitution established the popular election of governors,[13] as well as the ability to remove them and mayors through popular vote. It increased the amount of resources transferred from the central government to subnational governments— and, implicitly, from wealthier to poorer regions—in order to ensure broad access to *health and education*. The constitution went into great detail regarding the distribution of resources among government levels and expenditure categories; widened the base for calculating transfers and increased them significantly; gave local authorities the power to levy taxes; and established that income from monopolies that are the property of regions may not be appropriated by the central government.

The 1993 reform of the *health care system* was mainly geared toward broader sharing of the benefits of growth, by promoting universal coverage and incorporating elements of solidarity and fairness. It also aimed at fostering competition between private and public providers to enhance quality and efficiency. The reform changed the way public hospitals are financed (through the sale of services rather than through the budget), decentralized their administration, and forced them to compete with private hospitals, so that the efficient public hospitals should thrive and others close. The system uses vouchers to subsidize demand, with the costs distributed between employers and employees when the insured has the ability to pay, and the responsibility of the government otherwise. Cross sub-

---

13. Mayors had been elected, rather than appointed by the central government, since 1986.

sidies, both among those who can contribute and between them and those who cannot, promote solidarity.[14]

In addition to introducing the popular election of governors, the 1991 constitution included a major *political reform* focused on enhancing representation, weakening the two-party system, empowering voters, and shifting power away from the executive.[15] The reform aimed at improving equality of opportunities and may contribute to broader sharing of the benefits of growth as well. It established that the senate would be elected on a nationwide basis, on the premise that candidates of minority groups, all but unelectable in small districts, could gather enough votes from across the different regions to win seats.[16] Also, voting in a national district was expected to place at a disadvantage the small regional movements that had become prevalent during the Frente Nacional period (Botero, 2000).[17] The constitution lowered barriers to entry, empowered citizens to organize political parties, and made it easier for voters to directly submit proposed legislation to Congress and to remove elected officials. The constitution also assigned to Congress additional legislative and control functions. An important provision made it much more complicated for the executive to use extraordinary powers to legislate (Ungar, 2003), and Congress can now override a presidential veto with a simple majority.

The 1991 constitution promoted equality of opportunities by expanding *access to the justice system.* All citizens are now in a better position to claim their constitutional rights, which also promotes the broader sharing of the benefits of growth. The constitution enshrined the concept of an *estado social de derecho,* geared

14. The system operates on the basis of an insurance premium (which is calibrated to reflect gender, age, and regional differences) and offers a standard package to workers and their dependents. For self-employed and formal sector workers there is a contributory regime, funded by a contribution from wages. Health promotion firms affiliate individuals and receive contributions. Contributors may choose their own health promotion firm as well as their own service provider. Each firm transfers the contributions it collects in excess of entitled capitation payments to a public fund and is compensated by the fund when contributions fall short of entitled capitation payments. Individuals wishing to enroll in the subsidized regime must come from a household at level 1 or 2 of Sisben (a proxy means test index stratifying households into six levels). One-twelfth of contributions are transferred to the subsidized regime, and those eligible for coverage who remain uninsured (*vinculados*) receive services from public hospitals or from private ones that enter into contracts with subnational governments.

15. Cárdenas, Junguito, and Pachón (2006) provide a good description of how the 1991 constitution redistributed power away from the executive and toward the legislative, the subnational governments, the judiciary, and the central bank.

16. Two of the 102 Senate seats were reserved to those elected in a district reserved for indigenous groups.

17. The Frente Nacional (FN) was a 1958 compromise to end civil unrest between the two historically dominant parties. Although the compromise formally ended in 1974, many of its provisions lasted longer. During the FN, 50 percent of seats in Congress were reserved for each party, excluding all others. Elections thus became a personal contest *within* parties rather than an ideological contest between them. When the FN formally ended, provisions allowing parties to present multiple lists in an election were preserved.

toward ensuring not only those rights labeled as "first generation" (that is, civil liberties, which are ensured through government restraint) but also "second generation" rights (access to certain services that require positive action by the state). Although the constitution defines first-generation rights as "fundamental" and second-generation rights as "social and economic,"[18] it also established a mechanism (the *tutela*) by which any citizen who feels his or her rights have been disregarded may go before any judge and seek restitution, which, if the judge rules in favor, must be provided immediately.[19] The country's highest court, the Constitutional Court, has developed the principle of connectivity (*principio de conexidad*), according to which many rights not deemed "fundamental" in the constitution are to be treated as such. For example, a connection has been established between access to health care (a second-generation right) and the fundamental right to life.

The Reforms in Practice

Table 3 shows that many of the expected effects of the early-1990s reforms on the foundations of growth were indeed achieved. However, in several cases—particularly with respect to decentralization of health and education expenditure, and political and judicial reform—there were also unintended consequences. Several inconsistencies had become evident by the late 1990s, including the following:

• Some policies proved fiscally unsustainable; notable among these was the major expansion of expenditure in the social sectors by subnational governments.

• Some social policies, financed through taxes on labor, fostered the movement of workers to the informal sector.

• Reforms in the political arena geared at broadening representation also fostered party fragmentation and increased political transaction costs.

• Reforms aimed at facilitating access to the justice system also empowered judges and made the Constitutional Court a veto player in economic policy.

This section highlights some of the problems that characterized the reform effort and reports on corrective measures undertaken since. Reference will be made to limitations stemming from the local environment, issues of design, and inconsistencies among elements of different reforms. The picture that emerges is one of tension between policies aimed at enhancing competition and promoting macro-

---

18. Chapter 1 of Title II is "On Fundamental Rights": the right to life (article 11), to religious freedom (article 19), to free speech (article 20), and to due process (article 29). Chapter 2 is "On Social, Economic and Cultural Rights," which include social security (article 48), health (article 49), dignified housing (article 51), and property (articles 58–61).

19. *Tutelas* need not be in writing, and the judge must rule within ten days. Appeals have to be decided within twenty days. All decisions are sent to the Constitutional Court, which chooses those it will review.

economic stability, on the one hand, and institutional arrangements geared toward fostering equality of opportunities and promoting a broad sharing of the benefits of growth, on the other.

The Judicial System: Greater Access to Justice, but at a High Fiscal Cost

Although the growing number of *tutelas* suggests that this new mechanism has broadened access to the legal system, it also raises issues of abuse and inefficiency.[20] The resulting judicial rulings, for example on the indexing of minimum salaries, have redistributed income and thus contributed to the broader sharing of growth. But the added cost to the government of higher salaries and benefits, together with other judicial decisions that forced a lowering of taxes, threatens fiscal balance and thus macroeconomic stability, and much higher minimum salaries tend to make labor markets less flexible, reducing economic competition. An activist judicial system, basing its decisions on a rather simplistic interpretation of the concepts of equality and dignity, has had a profound influence on economic reform and has prevented some reforms from delivering on their promise. The Constitutional Court has gone beyond "legislating in the negative"; it often modifies legislation in an attempt to ensure that the law, as the court sees it, complies with the constitution. It has extended its decisions to apply beyond the regulation in question to others that had not been challenged. In so doing the court has imposed peremptory deadlines on Congress to legislate in accordance with its rulings.[21]

Some of the most important interventions by the Constitutional Court in economic matters include the following:

• *Wages.* The task of establishing the monthly minimum salary is undertaken by a commission on which government, labor, and business are represented. If no agreement is reached, the government sets the minimum salary. Until 1998 it was standard practice to increase the minimum salary periodically in line with *expected* inflation plus some allowance for productivity growth. In 1999, however, the court determined that this procedure violated workers' right to a minimum "vital and mobile" remuneration and determined that "the adjustment must never be lower than the previous year's inflation." In 2000 the court extended this rationale to most public sector wages and determined that "any savings achieved from limiting wage hikes has to go to social investment," even though the constitution establishes that in time of peace only elected bodies may mandate public expenditure.

20. Between 1999 and April 2007, 1.6 million *tutelas* were filed, one-third of them in reference to health care. The judiciary upheld 87 percent of the total (*El Tiempo*, August 31, 2007).

21. The court's activism generates uncertainty and encourages the use of lawsuits to produce changes that politically disadvantaged groups are unable to accomplish through the legislative process, and which may deter many from participating in the political process (Kalmanovitz, 2003; Uprimny, 2001). Politicians might, as a result, find it rational to defer to the Constitutional Court on topical issues, transferring to it the political costs involved.

- *Pensions.* The court struck down a provision in the 2003 pension reform shortening the transition period. It opined that the reform affected not just workers' expectations, but also their acquired rights. In upholding a *tutela* by teachers claiming their right to a fourteenth monthly pension payment each year, the court justified its decision on equity grounds. This payment had been established in 1993 to compensate *some* retirees whose pensions had not been fully adjusted for inflation; the court extended the benefit to *all* pensioners, at a cost of around 12.5 percent of GDP (Cadena, 2006).
- *Taxes.* Stating that it deemed the graduation of VAT rates across different goods to be insufficient, the court overturned a provision in a tax reform that extended the VAT to previously excluded items, but at a very low rate.
- *Health care.* Although the health care law defines the manner in which citizens may exercise their health care rights, judges and the Constitutional Court have allowed citizens to claim much broader rights, at public expense, on grounds of protecting the "right to life."

Interventions by the Constitutional Court in the *financial sector* have been by far the most controversial. In 1998, at a time when the country's mortgage banks were in crisis, the administration declared an economic emergency and issued decrees with the (temporary) force of law. Their review opened the door for the Constitutional Court to play a very active role in a range of financial matters:

- The government introduced a financial transactions tax (FTT) but exempted interbank operations. The court overturned this provision on grounds that it violated the principle of equality. Until a much lower tariff was introduced, the interbank market, including the market for foreign exchange operations, dried up.
- A government proposal, upheld by the court, forced banks to accept, during a twelve-month period, properties returned by mortgage holders in exchange for the complete write-off of their mortgage. The government intended to target this provision to low-income owners, but again citing the principle of equality, the court extended it to all debtors.
- The administrative court ruled that the central bank could not continue linking the *corrección monetaria* to interest rates, but the Constitutional Court ordered that it be fully linked to inflation.[22] It opined that if indexed debts increased faster than inflation, citizens' right to housing would be affected. As a result, a 1999 law established that the real rate of interest (that is, the premium

---

22. Mortgages were defined in terms of a unit of account (UPAC), originally intended to remain constant in terms of the consumer price index. The periodic adjustment of this unit was known as *corrección monetaria*. All assets and liabilities in mortgage banks were indexed to the UPAC. At the insistence of the mortgage banks, the *corrección monetaria* began to incorporate interest rates in addition to inflation. Eventually, the UPAC became fully indexed to interest rates.

Table 4. *Colombia: Proliferation of Political Parties and Electoral Lists*

| Year | Parties seeking seats in the senate | Electoral lists offered | |
		Senate	House
1978	n.a.	210	308
1982	n.a.	225	343
1986	n.a.	202	330
1990	8	213	351
1991	21	143	486
1994	54	251	628
1998	80	319	692
2002	63	322	883

Sources: Roland and Zapata (2005); Botero and Rodríguez (2007).
n.a. = not available.

over the *corrección monetaria*)[23] would be capped and held constant, and that interest payments could no longer be capitalized. The court then determined that all existing mortgages should be re-priced in terms of the new unit of account, and it ordered banks to issue refunds to debtors who had "overpaid."

Political Reform: More Participation, but Little or No Improvement in Policy Outcomes

To facilitate the emergence of new political parties, the 1991 constitution determined that "the law cannot establish conditions for the organization of parties and movements, nor make affiliation in one of them a condition for participating in elections." Lowering barriers to entry and introducing a national senate district ended the monopoly of the two traditional parties: their combined representation in the senate fell from close to 100 percent to around 75 percent. Promoting entry and competition, however, came at a price: an explosion in the number of parties and movements and a sharp increase in registered lists of candidates during elections (table 4). Although the number of lists had already begun to grow before 1991, it shot up during the 1990s. In the 2002 senate, fifty-two parties, movements, and coalitions were represented (Ungar, 2003). Whereas in the 1991 senate the two dominant lists together had held one-third of the 102 seats, in each of the next three elections the top three lists each elected only two senators each. In 2002 the three lists receiving the most votes each received slightly less than 2 percent of the total.

Despite the move to a national district for senatorial elections, politicians did not change their way of doing business, and competition in the political arena was

23. This premium has to be lower than the lowest real rate of interest prevalent in the market, and even lower for low-income housing. The central bank, entrusted in 2000 with periodically setting the rate, is thus forced to negate the principle according to which interest rates reflect expected risks.

not enhanced. Most incumbents managed to obtain enough votes in their traditional regions to retain a seat. Botero (2000) estimates a "regional concentration index" as the percentage of votes raised in their "preferred" department by all elected candidates. The average index value for 1991, 1994, and 1998 was a startling 66.7. Politicians were elected without having to compete beyond their traditional areas of influence, and with no support from a party organization.[24] Problems also emerged with regard to representation. Although the 1991 constitution did away with the practice of voting for alternates, it provided that permanent vacancies would be filled by unelected candidates on the same list as the elected candidate. Of the 263 seats in the 1998 Congress, by the end of 2001 some 247 were held by someone other than the person elected. These were legislators for whom nobody had voted; indeed, their names did not even appear on the ballot, which identifies only the head of the list. Also, assigning seats using the LR-Hare system in the context of list proliferation can lead to huge reallocations of votes. Botero (2000) estimates an index of deviations from proportionality to measure the extent of reassignment. This index, which averaged 23 in 1986 and 1990, reached 60 in 2002.[25] The D'Hondt system, introduced in 2003, brought about a sharp change; the four most voted lists in 2006 received 62.5 percent of the vote and won 68.6 percent of the seats.[26]

The emphasis given to providing equality of opportunities by lowering barriers to entry helped deliver a fragmented political system. This in turn raised transaction costs, probably facilitated capture by interest groups, and undermined the political system's ability to undertake sound long-term policies, which among other things endangers macroeconomic stability. When parties have almost no control over who may run under the party's banner, the result is to promote *intra-party* rather than *interparty* competition, leading to clientelism: those at the top of the list differentiate themselves from other candidates by catering to narrow local interests (Roland and Zapata, 2005). The rules in place until 2003 for allocating seats in Congress appear to have in fact lowered the quality of legislative work. The average number of bills introduced each year rose from 142 during 1982–91 to 215 during 1992–2003, and around 80 percent of bills in the latter period were introduced by legislators with a clear regional orientation. This kind of legislative

24. Besides the flawed electoral rules, other factors that explain this outcome include the increase in fiscal resources at the local level due to decentralization; the influx of drug money into politics; public campaign financing through reimbursements to candidates rather than to parties; and new voting procedures that reduced the value of the logistical capabilities provided by a party organization (Cárdenas et al., 2006).

25. The index is calculated as 0.5 times the sum of the absolute value of the difference, for each list, between the percentage of votes received and the percentage of seats gained. The index value is zero under perfect proportional representation. In 2002 some 60 percent of votes were reassigned among lists in the process of translating electoral results into congressional seats.

26. See Roland and Zapata (2005) for an explanation of alternative electoral allocation systems in a Colombian context.

"inflation" suggests party weakness: when there is no quality control, the bills submitted by legislators lack financial and judicial rigor. Unsurprisingly, the approval rate for legislation submitted by the executive is much higher.

After several failed attempts, a new reform was approved by Congress in 2003. The new electoral rules maintained a system of proportional representation but shifted to a D'Hondt rule with minimum thresholds: a 2 percent threshold in the senate and 50 percent of the quota in the house, in the case of departments electing more than two representatives, and 30 percent in the few departments that elect only two. Parties may present only one list for each chamber, there can be no more candidates on the list than seats to be filled, and voters may not register with more than one party. As a compromise, each party decides for itself whether voters may choose the order of candidates within the list. In 2005 Congress passed a *ley de bancadas* with several new provisions: it established that members of Congress elected from the same list must constitute a group; delegated to the parties the responsibility of issuing rules to ensure that groups act in conformity with the law; and established procedures to enhance the efficiency of legislative proceedings.

The 2003 reform was put to the test at the congressional level in 2006. The introduction of a threshold induced consolidation: only 20 lists contested for the senate, down from 322 in 2002;[27] 10 surpassed the threshold. Although the reform brought order to a situation that some had labeled chaotic, the fate of the 2006 tax reform, perhaps the most important economic issue that Congress has dealt with since, suggests that the greater electoral cohesion has yet to translate into a more structured legislative process, one less prone to capture and better able to deliver sound public policies.

Labor and Tax Reform

Although trade liberalization in Colombia has proceeded almost without interruption, the country's integration into the global economy has been hampered by two factors that should have enhanced it. First, labor reform failed to deliver on its promise of making the labor market more flexible. Second, in order to finance a much higher level of public expenditure, the tax burden has increased quite markedly, to a level deemed at odds with greater private sector competitiveness. Meanwhile, for a host of reasons, financial liberalization has proved to be a more complex and protracted process than originally envisioned.

LABOR REFORM: MEASURES TO ENHANCE COMPETITION NEUTRALIZED BY REFORMS ELSEWHERE

The main goal of the 1990 labor reform was to support trade liberalization by enhancing the flexibility and formalization of the labor force, thus making

---

27. More precisely, in the 2002 elections 63 parties and movements presented 322 lists, whereas four years later 20 parties or movements presented 20 lists.

Figure 4. *Colombia: Nonwage Labor Costs, 1977–2005*[a]

Percent of salary

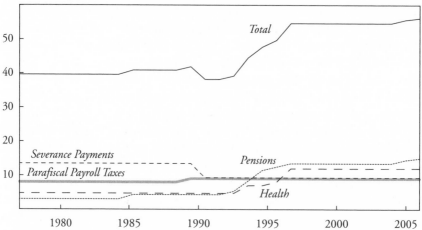

Sources: Cárdenas and Mercer-Blackman (2006); Bernal and Cárdenas (2003).

a. Includes parafiscal payroll taxes (contributions to ICBF, SENA, and CCFs), contributions to social security (health, pensions, severance payments, and professional risks), paid vacations, and mandatory bonuses.

Colombian producers more competitive. The observed reduction in nonwage labor costs would soon be overtaken, however, by the rise in social security contributions stemming from the 1993 social security reform, undertaken for the purpose of promoting macroeconomic stability by placing pensions and health care on a sounder financial footing, and by the rigidity of wages (figure 4). Nonwage costs increased from around 40 percent of payrolls in the 1980s to 56 percent in 2004 (Cárdenas and Meicer-Blackman, 2006; Bernal Cárdenas, 2003).[28] By 1999 Colombia had the second-highest nonwage labor costs in the region. A study by the World Bank (2005) shows that the rise in nonwage costs has constrained the demand for labor while increasing supply. The share of workers in the informal

28. Nonwage costs are composed of the following: parafiscal contributions, which sum to 9 percent of payroll, consisting of 2 percent for SENA (Servicio Nacional de Aprendizaje, the vocational training program), 4 percent for ICBF (Instituto Colombiano de Bienestar Familiar, the family welfare program), and 3 percent for the CCFs (*cajas de compensación familiar,* or family compensation funds), which are private funds involved in a host of activities including cash subsidies, recreation and cultural activities, and unemployment insurance; contributions to severance funds and paid vacations; health contributions, which rose from 7 percent to 12 percent in 1993 and to 12.5 percent in 2007; and contributions to pensions, which rose from 6.5 percent to 13.5 percent in 1993 and to 15.5 percent in 2002, with an additional 1-percentage-point contribution for those with high salaries. Other sources have estimated these percentages to be slightly different. These nonwage labor costs are calculated using author-specific definitions of payroll taxes, mandatory bonuses, and so on. For example, according to the World Bank (2005), total nonwage costs were about 47 percent in the late 1980s and rose to around 60 percent in 2004.

sector, at 58 percent, was higher in 2004, when the economy was in a recovery, than it had been in 1992 (54 percent).

Actions with regard to wages have also stood in the way of enhancing labor flexibility and formalization. Provisions in the law and interpretations by the Constitutional Court have determined that the minimum monthly salary and wage schedules affecting most civil servants must be indexed to inflation. When, after 1999, the central bank's inflation targeting framework started to deliver consistently lower inflation, backward indexation resulted in a continuous rise in real terms in the minimum salary, an increase in the ratio of the minimum to the average salary, and a rise in the proportion of self-employed workers earning less than the minimum. Between 1996 and 2002 the real wages of the self-employed declined, indicating that this sector had adjusted better to the business cycle than the formal sector, where wages increased even as the economy entered a severe recession. World Bank (2005) estimates of Okun equations show that cyclical variations in output have affected unemployment more strongly since 1998 (that is, the labor market increasingly adjusts through quantities rather than wages); this is hardly consistent with the objective of making labor markets more flexible and supportive of an open trade regime.

A new reform was passed in 2002. Its provisions fall into two categories: formalization of employment, and social protection and enhancement of opportunities for hard-to-hire groups. It reduced overtime pay and made the workday and the workweek more flexible; amended apprenticeship contracts, which no longer involve parafiscal contributions or severance payments and are not subject to the minimum salary; further reduced firing costs; and introduced an unemployment insurance scheme. Gaviria (2004) estimates that the reduction in firing costs and overtime pay barely compensates for the increase in pension contributions enacted at the same time. He also reports positive effects on the hiring of apprentices and on underemployment, minor effects on employment generation and formalization, and no impact from the new unemployment insurance scheme. The 2002 reform seems to have marginally enhanced flexibility. However, by failing to address the two critical issues—high nonwage labor costs and inflexible wages—it has done little to promote labor market formalization.

Tax Reform: Strong Revenue Growth, but at the Expense of Competitiveness and Efficiency

At 15 percent of GDP, Colombia's tax burden is not high, given the country's level of income and the well-established tendency of tax burdens to increase with income. However, the present level of taxation reflects the fact that the tax burden has risen faster in Colombia than in any other country in the region, having almost doubled since 1990. Given the upward pressures on spending described elsewhere, the resulting higher revenue has proved vital to keeping the fiscal deficit under control and the macroeconomy stable. On the other hand, taxation remains a source of uncertainty for businesses and workers, with no fewer than ten national tax reforms in the last seventeen years and ample discretion exercised by municipal authorities. The tax regime is also extremely inefficient, combining a shallow base (fewer than 2 percent of the active labor force paid income taxes in 2004, according to Cárdenas and Mercer-Blackman, 2006) with high marginal tax rates on both income (the top marginal rate was 38.5 percent until 2007 and is now 35 percent) and consumption (the VAT). Moreover, the tax system is complicated to administer, and the existence of multiple rates (eight in the case of the VAT, ranging from 2 to 45 percent) and an ever-increasing list of exemptions likely foster avoidance and evasion. Finally, all this is complemented by the second-highest tax rate on the wage bill in the region, the highest FTT, a technically flawed local tax on business turnover, and a distortionary tax on net wealth. Successive tax reforms, aimed at supporting fiscal and macroeconomic stability in the context of an ever-rising level of public expenditure, have had a negative effect on competition and efficiency.

Colombia's business-unfriendly tax regime has its root cause in the fact that the tax burden has had to be raised frequently just to keep pace with growth in public expenditure—throughout the 1990s to comply with mandates in the 1991 constitution, more recently to fund the costs of enhanced security. Although Congress has generally accommodated the executive's need for additional resources, the latter has always found itself at the mercy of the legislature, and therefore of interest groups, regarding the quality of tax changes. A good example has been the fate of the highly distortionary FTT, introduced as a temporary provision at a rate of 0.2 percent in 1999. In each tax reform that the executive has submitted since then, it has requested the phasing out of this tax and its replacement with less distortionary taxes. The results have been dismal: the FTT is now permanent, at a rate of 0.4 percent. Even when Congress has supported attempts to improve the tax code—as in 2002, when it agreed to impose a VAT, at a low rate, on all foodstuffs—the Constitutional Court has ruled that such a move ran counter to any concept of fairness. The administration itself, for example in the failed 2006 reform, has not shied away from making explicit its intention to maintain certain exemptions in order to promote private sector investment. This posture soon led to numerous suggestions for additional exemptions and differential tariff rates, eventually leading the administration to withdraw its reform proposal altogether.

Financial Sector Reform: More Competition and Greater Efficiency, but Access Is Limited and Restrictions Remain

We present several approaches to assessing progress in the financial sector during the reform process to date: a financial repression index, a model gauging the development of competition, and the literature on financial efficiency all suggest room for improvement. An update of Salazar's (2005) repression index suggests that a period of continuous liberalization that began in the late 1980s was inter-

Figure 5. *Colombia: Financial Repression Index, 1960–2006*[a]

5 = most repressed

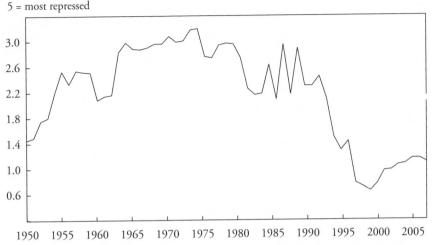

Source: Authors' calculations.

a. Principal components analysis was applied to a set of financial repression indicators. A single indicator was estimated, with the weights of its components set equal to their participation in the variance of the information set. Seven indicators were considered: mandatory investments; reserve requirements; interest rate controls; the difference between the usury interest rate and the average loan rate; revenue from the financial transfers tax; assets of public banks; and assets of foreign banks (the last two measured as a percentage of total assets). The first component was taken as the indicator of repression, as it explains 70 percent of the variance of the information set. The variables most highly correlated with the first component are the importance of public banks, foreign participation, and mandatory investments.

rupted during the crisis affecting both mortgage and public banks in the late 1990s, when an FTT and forced investment were introduced and foreign ownership fell (figure 5).

Although the number of financial institutions increased after the initial reform effort, as a consequence of easier entry, it declined following the crisis that engulfed the mortgage and public banks. The percentage of assets in the largest banks shows a similar pattern. In a contestable market, concentration does not necessarily imply lack of competition. Barajas, Steiner, and Salazar (2000) applied the Panzar-Rosse test for 1985–98 and found that liberalization enhanced competition. In similar estimations for 1990–2007 (results available on request), we found evidence that in spite of a higher concentration of assets, competition has increased but still falls short of being optimal.

There is evidence that efficiency in the banking industry, although still lagging, has increased as well. Labor costs have been on a declining trend, from 4.1 percent of assets in 1991 to 2.3 percent in 2007. Intermediation spreads—which reflect efficiency as well as risk, market structure, and cost of regulation—have likewise fallen, from around 20 percent in the early 1990s to 7 percent recently.

Recent estimates report high levels of cost inefficiency, at anywhere between 30 and 73 percent of total costs.[29]

Progress with regard to credit expansion (a factor potentially affecting the broad sharing of the benefits of growth) has been modest. Bank credit is only 35 percent of GDP, and credit to the private sector barely 24 percent. Results of a vector autoregression (available upon request) show that once capital flows are included, our repression index does not affect financial deepening. These results suggest that in a small, open economy, capital flows play a critical role, and that although quite complex, our index fails to capture aspects that might be critical in fostering financial deepening and access, such as the role of credit bureaus, an efficient guarantee system, and protection of creditor rights.

Although in the regional context Colombia apparently does not fare poorly with regard to access, as of June 2007 only 35 percent of Colombians held at least one financial product. On the other hand, credit to small and medium-size enterprises has grown, but from a low base. Providing banking services to the poor is costly for financial institutions and taxing on the poor themselves. Information requirements can overburden potential customers, particularly if they work in the informal sector. In 2006 the government launched a program, called Banca de las Oportunidades, aimed at enhancing poor Colombians' access to financial services. At the margin, the program has lessened some of the severe constraints that the poor have faced.[30]

Just as macroeconomic stability was compromised by constitutional mandates geared toward broadening the pool of beneficiaries from growth, so the concern for macroeconomic stability in the context of insufficient policy instruments has hampered financial liberalization and might have prevented financial reform from meaningfully affecting the foundations as had been expected (see table 3). First, in response to a sharp rise in capital inflows, the central bank has established reserve requirements on foreign borrowing and increased overall reserve requirements. This curtailed competition and efficiency in the financial sector and increased financing costs. Second, limited budgetary flexibility played a role in the decision to finance public intervention in the crisis engulfing mortgage and public banks through an FTT, a tax that retards financial deepening and access by the poor to financial services. Third, unable to resort to the budget to promote specific sectors, in 1999 the government reintroduced some forced investments, this time in favor of low-income housing.

The expansion of bank credit has also been hampered by a deeply engrained cultural bias favoring debtors over creditors, a bias that is evident in the minds of those who write the laws and of those in charge of upholding them; this arguably

---

29. See Asociación Nacional de Instituciones Financieras (2005) and the references therein.

30. In addition to allowing the creation of nonbanking correspondents, the program established different usury rates for different sectors, increased allowable commissions on microcredit, and expanded FTT exemptions for withdrawals from savings accounts.

amounts to a populist interpretation of property rights by the legislative and judicial branches. We have already mentioned the Constitutional Court's decisions with regard to forcing mortgage banks to bail out debtors. In addition, Law 550 of 1999 attempted to provide lenders and borrowers with incentives and mechanisms to negotiate restructuring programs that would allow businesses under stress to normalize their activities. The bias against creditors became evident, however, and only a few deals were finalized. A major hurdle faced by financial institutions in their attempts at recovering collateral has been the extreme complexity of the judicial process. In addition, the legal system does not allow for the expeditious creation of guarantees, and the existing guarantee registries are technologically obsolete. A 2006 law improves matters but does not fully solve the main problems.

The expansion of credit in general, and to smaller borrowers in particular, is constrained by caps on interest rates. We have already mentioned the decisions by the Constitutional Court that forced banks to decouple interest rates on mortgages from any assessment of risk. In addition, credit operations are subjected to limits imposed by the usury rate of interest, which lately might have become binding for certain operations. Interpretations by the bank supervisory agency have determined that limits shall apply throughout the loan's life span; in other words, if market conditions change and the usury rate falls, the contract has to be renegotiated. Besides producing uncertainty, this inhibits the market for securitized assets.[31] In the case of microcredit, banks may charge fixed commissions on top of the usury rate. In practice, however, this flexibility is not significant. The system in place does not foster the expansion of microenterprises and does not allow banks to cover the operational costs and risks associated with small transactions with agents in the informal sector.

The fact that credit bureaus are underdeveloped also helps explain the low level of access to the financial sector. It was only recently that a "habeas data" law was approved, establishing a four-year permanence for all negative information. This law is now under review by the Constitutional Court. Before the law was passed, the court had ruled favorably on numerous demands from citizens arguing that their rights (to privacy and reputation) had been violated by credit bureaus—another example of a judicial intervention that has impeded the development of the financial sector. The negative view that many have regarding the financial sector, together with widespread lack of knowledge about how information systems work, allowed the notion that "the less information, the greater the access to credit" to flourish.

Fiscal and Budget Reform

During the decade following the launch of the reform program, Colombia strayed from its tradition of prudent fiscal policy and relative macroeconomic stability.

31. The authorities have attempted to introduce some flexibility into this restrictive regime. Recently, the government decided to establish the usury rate by type of credit and at a higher time frequency.

Although having granted independence to the central bank would eventually prove to be a wise move—Colombia now enjoys historically low rates of inflation—the lack of a supportive fiscal policy stance during the 1990s determined that when international financial conditions tightened after 1997, the central bank had to adopt an extremely tight monetary policy stance in order to pursue its mandate of low inflation. To support the currency, during 1998 and 1999 the central bank raised interest rates to unprecedented levels. This proved very costly for economic activity in general and for the mortgage industry in particular. The fiscal deterioration that engulfed Colombia in the second half of the 1990s resulted from a confluence of factors, of which we highlight two: overestimation of the fiscal benefits of the 1993 pension reform, and the rise in expenditure, particularly in the social sectors at the subnational level, mandated in the new constitution. In both cases the Constitutional Court played a critical role in making a difficult situation even worse. In late 1999, for the first time ever, Colombia entered into a financial arrangement with the International Monetary Fund. This IMF program involved some important reforms, mostly geared toward restoring macroeconomic stability.

PENSION REFORM: RECENT ADJUSTMENTS PROMISE A SOUNDER, FAIRER SYSTEM

The 1993 reform adjusted the parameters of the pension system to put it on a sustainable footing more in accordance with demographic trends. The reform, however, provided for a long transition period: workers retiring before 2014 would not be affected.[32] Members of the armed forces, the police, the teacher's union pension fund, and the state-owned oil company were exempted from the general system. It soon became evident that the reform had not achieved the goal of placing public pension liabilities on a sustainable path. After some failed attempts, important changes were introduced in 2003–05 to address this issue, while also improving equity and enhancing fairness:

• Subsidies now benefit only those unable to save enough to fund a minimum pension. Guaranteed minimum pensions in the AFPs are now fully funded.

• Contributions were raised, benefits were capped, and some degree of progressivity was introduced in the determination of the replacement rate.

• The fourteenth monthly payment—an extra benefit for a few public employees that, on grounds of equality, the Constitutional Court had extended to all—was eliminated for those earning more than three times the minimum salary, and for all persons retiring after 2011; all privileged regimes (except for the military)

---

32. The reform involved a twenty-year transition and an increase in the retirement age of just two years, even though life expectancy had increased from 61 years at the beginning of the 1970s to 70 at the end of the 1990s, and the conditional life expectancy of a 60-year-old had surpassed 80 (Cadena, 2006).

were eliminated starting in 2010; and collective agreements may no longer establish more favorable conditions than in the general system.

• The transition was brought forward to 2010 except for those very close to retirement. Congress approved bringing it forward to 2008, but, as noted above, this provision was watered down by the Constitutional Court on grounds that those affected had not only an "expectation" of receiving certain benefits but an "acquired right."

The 2003–05 reforms reduced the unfunded liabilities of the PAYGO regime from over 200 percent of GDP to 140 percent in net present value terms. Yet pension payments will continue to be a drag on the budget. Transfers from the central government are peaking in 2007–08 at slightly less than 5 percent of GDP and are expected to remain close to 4 percent of GDP until 2015 (Ministerio de Hacienda, 2005). The pension regime is not only expensive; it has also proved to be an inequitable use of taxpayer money. The system has involved huge subsidies for many beneficiaries, ranging from those who never contributed but were entitled to a modest pension, to those whose contributions were not enough to cover their pension, to some egregious cases where no contributions were made but where benefits were nevertheless huge.[33] Before the 2003 reform the government subsidized two-thirds of the benefits of those receiving a minimum pension of one monthly minimum salary, and around half of all others (Montenegro and Rivas, 2005). Since coverage is low and biased in favor of the better off, the distribution of the subsidies has been appalling, with the lowest income quintile receiving no subsidy and the highest capturing 80 percent of the total (Lasso, 2006). Notwithstanding the prolonged transition period, the 2003–05 reforms had a major impact on equity by doing away with most of the privileged regimes, the main source of inequality. Solidarity was also enhanced. At the margin, pension subsidies are now well targeted.

FISCAL DECENTRALIZATION: A BROADER SHARING OF WEALTH,
BUT AT THE EXPENSE OF BUDGET BALANCE

Since the entry into force of the 1991 constitution, there has been a significant transfer of resources from rich regions to poor ones, and the bulk of the resources transferred from the central government to subnational governments has been used to fund expenditures in health and education, thereby broadening the pool of beneficiaries of growth. Transfers rose from around 5 percent of GDP in 1990 to over 12 percent recently. In the initial stages, however, some subnational

---

33. For example, before the 2003 reform, public school teachers did not contribute to the pension fund, could retire much earlier, and received significantly higher benefits. Borjas and Acosta (2000) estimated that in 2000 this program, benefiting 303,000 active teachers, had generated a liability to the government equivalent to 30 percent of GDP. This was similar to the pension liability generated by 2.3 million nonteachers.

governments began running deficits and accumulating debt, thus compromising macroeconomic stability. Notwithstanding the rise in transfers, expenditure increased even faster.[34] The scheme put in place did not provide enough incentives for local tax effort and allowed for full discretion with regard to indebtedness.[35] Although views differ as to whether there has been "fiscal apathy," tax collection was clearly more dynamic at the national level.[36] Because they were linked to current central government revenue, transfers became highly procyclical, making macroeconomic policy less flexible while tying expenditure on health and education to tax revenue that was sensitive to the business cycle. Distribution formulas were complicated, and few subnational governments could reasonably predict their income flows. The rigidity of the formulas fostered overprovision of certain services in some areas and underprovision in others.

A second round of reforms was driven by the need to make the scheme sustainable, while introducing flexibility into the distribution of transfers so as to produce a better match between the supply of fiscal resources and the effective demand for them. In 1997 borrowing by subnational governments was made contingent on their meeting certain solvency and liquidity criteria. A 2000 law classified these governments into categories and established differing limits on operational expenses, up to a given percentage of revenue (excluding transfers). Legislative Act 01 of 2000 created the Sistema General de Participaciones (SGP), which combined the three existing transfer mechanisms. The SGP will grow with inflation plus a mark-up, which has recently been raised.[37] Law 715 in 2000 made the allocation of transfers more flexible—without a regional dimension, and taking into account potential users as well as standardized costs—and introduced incentives for local taxation. A 2003 fiscal responsibility law affecting all levels of government establishes that the primary surplus must be at least equal to debt service. Even if deficits at the subnational level have been averted, the central government still faces imbalances on account of decentralization. Overlapping functions, a confusing distribution of responsibilities, and weak links between expenditure and financing decisions abound. How expenditures are to be assigned by level of government has never been made entirely clear. Although the 1991 constitution called for Congress to pass a territorial organization law

34. There is evidence of a "flypaper effect," according to which "money sticks were it hits," the most interesting example being the education compensation fund.

35. Local governments with negative current saving were allowed to borrow by pledging transfer receipts, and provisioning rules gave banks incentives to lend to them.

36. A revealing case has to do with the surcharge on gasoline. This 20 percent tax was first established in Bogotá, and later in Medellín. It was expected that these success stories would be replicated throughout the country. Local authorities, however, balked and instead lobbied their congressional delegations to pass national legislation—whose political costs fell mainly on the central government—making the surcharge mandatory.

37. Because of political pressure from FECODE, the powerful teachers' union, transfers to education will receive an additional mark-up on top of the general mark-up.

Figure 6. *Colombia: Health Care Expenditure, 1993–2003*
Percent of GDP

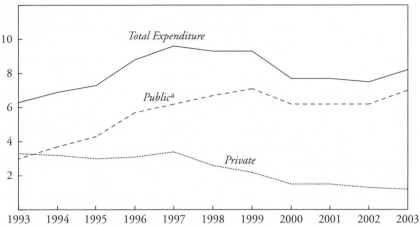

Source: Authors' calculations based on Barón (2007).
a. Includes spending by ISS (Instituto de Seguros Sociales) and all other public sector social security entities.

distributing assignments, this has not happened, and the central government continues to pay for many responsibilities that presumably had already been devolved to subnational governments.[38]

HEALTH CARE: WIDER COVERAGE, BUT COSTS ARE RISING AND QUALITY IS DOUBTFUL

Although the goal of universal health care coverage, originally set for 2001, has yet to be achieved, there has been huge progress: coverage has risen from 47 percent of the population in 1996 to 74 percent in 2005. The 1993 reform (enacted in Law 100) implied a rise in public resources devoted to health care, accompanied by a (smaller) reduction in private expenditure (figure 6). Early evaluations gave Law 100 high marks. Consumer satisfaction was high, and the World Health Organization ranked Colombia first among 191 countries with regard to fairness of contributions and financial risk protection (World Bank, 2003). The system's progressivity is also evident in the estimates of Lasso (2006).

This early success notwithstanding, it soon became evident that the health care system was costly and universal coverage elusive, and that further expansion of coverage would require a curtailment in the quality of service. Law 100 mandated

---

38. Notwithstanding the macro and financial problems associated with the decentralization process, it is important to recognize some important non-economic payoffs to the greater discretion granted mayors and localities in terms of security. For example, recent youth programs and anti-gang policies have contributed to the transformation of Bogotá. Similarly, resource transfers to localities may have helped in restoring greater social peace.

the shifting of subsidies from suppliers to consumers and established a precise schedule by which this should happen.[39] But the schedule was not met. The process of transforming the subsidies into demand subsidies gave rise to a vicious cycle, since payments to suppliers had to be maintained in order to assist the poor and the uninsured. This reduced the resources available to subsidize demand, which in turn hindered the enrollment of new members and consequently prevented a reduction in supply subsidies (World Bank, 2003; Gaviria, Medina, and Mejía, 2006). Although the number of potential users of supply subsidies fell by 54 percent from 1994 to 2000, resources devoted to subsidizing supply increased by 155 percent (Departamento Nacional de Planeación, 2002). These inconsistencies were compounded by the fact that closing an underutilized public facility is always a challenging endeavor.[40] With resources devoted to health care declining after 1997, and coverage increasing, expenditure per capita fell.

To address some of these issues, Congress in 2001 approved Law 715, which more clearly defined responsibilities and rationalized the distribution of transfers. Resources for insurance coverage are now distributed across regions, taking into account the number of beneficiaries and the estimated cost of providing the service. Resources for hospitals are estimated based on each department's number of uninsured. Departments are in charge of executing national policies, running the hospitals, and inspecting and regulating insurers; municipalities are entrusted with running the contributory and subsidized regimes, including selecting the beneficiaries of the latter.[41]

Compounding the problems stemming from poor design, there is ample evidence of system abuse. Being poor is not the only reason for being classified as Sisben 1 or 2 and eligible to participate in the subsidized regime. Individuals classified in levels 4 to 6 have also joined,[42] and political patronage seems to have played a role (Gaviria et al., 2006). Sisben fails to expeditiously capture changes in a household's true condition. A 2000 review found that type I errors (failure to classify a poor household as such) happened 15 percent of the time, but type II

39. However, under the decentralization law (Law 60 of 1993), transfers to subnational governments to fund health care were conceived as supply subsidies, with departments entrusted with administering hospitals.

40. Law 100 had internal consistency problems. Although the idea was that there would be three main actors acting independently from one another (the insured, the insurer, and the service provider), in many instances the same entity acted as both insurer and provider, even though the integration was hardly justified on efficiency grounds. Departments, which own the public hospitals, have been involved in insurance activities. This has given rise to conflicts of interest, reduced competition, and impaired accountability, and has generated demand for providers that otherwise would have been redundant and should have been shut down.

41. In fact, only "certified municipalities" (those with 100,000 or more inhabitants) and smaller ones with a proven track record play this role.

42. Gaviria et al. (2006) estimate that in 2003 more than half of individuals classified as Sisben 1 or 2 were not affiliated with the system, whereas some 20 percent of those classified as Sisben 3 and 4 were.

Table 5. *Public Expenditure on Education in Selected Latin American countries, 1990–2004 Average*

Country	Spending per pupil as percent of GDP per capita	Total spending as percent of GDP
Argentina[a]	13.8	4.3
Brazil[b]	13.8	4.2
Chile	15.3	4.0
Colombia	18.4	4.7
Mexico[a]	17.5	5.1
Peru[b]	8.6	3.1

Source: Authors' calculations based on UNESCO data.
a. Data are for 1990–2003.
b. Data are for 1990–2002.

errors (erroneously classifying a nonpoor household as poor) occurred 25 percent of the time. Unfortunately, the changes that were introduced went in the wrong direction: although type I error was reduced, type II error increased (Peña and Glassman, 2004). The new methodology increased the share of people classified as Sisben 1 or 2 from 21 percent to 56 percent; the number of potential beneficiaries of the system—and other social programs—rose by 15.3 million. Not only is this fiscally costly, but resources will have to be shared among a larger pool of beneficiaries at the expense of the neediest, and perverse incentives to join the formal sector might have been introduced.

In addition, and although the health care law defined in precise terms how citizens may exercise their right to health care, judges have allowed citizens to claim that right under broader terms, and the Constitutional Court has upheld most of these interventions. Sotelo (2000) provides a long and astonishing list of the services that health providers have been forced to make available to patients.[43] In some cases the legal ruling explicitly states that the provider should be reimbursed by the government; in others the provider is left in the dark as to who will bear the costs of these expensive services.

EDUCATION: ENROLLMENT IS UP, BUT COSTS ARE UP EVEN MORE

Colombia now spends more per capita on public education than any other large country in the region (table 5). Public expenditure on education rose from 2.4 percent of GDP to 4.5 percent between 1990 and 2005.[44] There has also been a large increase in coverage, although following the 1999 recession, enrollment stalled at

43. One judge ordered a provider to perform a kidney transplant within forty-eight hours. There are instances of judges expanding the contents of the standard health plan by mandating payment for experimental treatments abroad. Recently, a provider was ordered to pay for dental care, a service not covered in the standard health care program.
44. Private expenditure on education amounts to 4.3 percent of GDP (World Bank, 2003).

Table 6. *Colombia: School Enrollment Rates, Selected Years*
Percent

Year	Pre-primary, gross[a]	Primary, net[b]	Secondary, net	Tertiary, gross
1991	13	69	34	14
1999	36	88	54	22
2002	37	87	55	24
2004	38	83	55	27
Average for Latin America and the Caribbean, 2004	61	95	67	28

Source: UNESCO.
a. Enrollees of all ages as a percent of the population aged 7 to 11.
b. Enrollees aged 7 to 11 as a percent of the population in that age range.

least until 2004 and is still low in comparative terms (table 6). A stock measure of educational attainment (years of schooling completed) also supports the view that Colombia has advanced but remains below the regional average.

Expanded expenditure and coverage have had good results in terms of equity. Data from the World Bank show that:

• Primary school enrollment increased somewhat between 1995 and 2000, but declined afterward. As a result, enrollment in 2005 was roughly similar to that in 1995. Interestingly, it was higher for the lowest quintiles in the income distribution.

• Secondary school enrollment increased throughout the period, and by far the most notable improvement was in the lowest quintiles.

• The bulk of the improvement in enrollment and attainment happened in rural areas and was biased in favor of girls.

• Lasso's (2006) study on targeting supports this favorable assessment: the two lowest quintiles receive two-thirds of public expenditure on primary education; the three lowest quintiles receive three-quarters of expenditure on secondary education. At the tertiary level the situation is reversed: over 70 percent of public expenditure benefits the two highest quintiles.

Enhanced education coverage constitutes progress toward a broader sharing of the benefits of reform. Yet the increase in public school attendance has not kept pace with the resources spent. In constant terms, public expenditure increased by 72 percent between 1996 and 2005, but the number of students enrolled rose by only 43 percent.[45] Furthermore, the quality of education is generally low, particularly in the public schools. Among schools reporting average results on the ICFES (a standardized test for high school seniors), the share with "low" results

45. These rates of increase in expenditure are almost twice as large if one takes the year before adoption of the 1991 constitution as the basis for comparison. Unfortunately, we lack access to reliable data on the number of students attending public institutions before 1996.

rose from 40 percent in 1986 to over 60 percent in 1999 (Fundación Corona, 2003). The 2005 SABER test portrays a similarly worrisome picture in language and math, nationally and across regions, for fifth and ninth graders.[46] Colombian students have not fared well on international tests either.[47] In 2003, 97 percent of students in the lowest income quintile who enrolled in primary school attended public institutions, while only 38 percent of children in the highest quintile did so. There is strong evidence suggesting that the quality of public education is lower than that offered by private schools, even after controlling for socioeconomic differences (Núñez et al., 2002).

Public school teachers are part of the problem. The bulk of the rise in education expenditure following the 1991 boost to decentralization has gone to paying wages.[48] Although there are three types of teachers—municipal, departmental, and national (some 80 percent of public sector teachers were employed by the central government in 2000)—the wages of all are centrally determined. Given that most resources come in the form of transfers from the central government, the level of government that administers the teacher roster is not the same level that negotiates wages and pays for them. Moreover, Law 60 determined that transfers should be based on the number of students and teachers *as of 1993*. This has perpetuated inefficiencies and kept in place whatever inequalities may have existed then. In 2001 Law 715 brought about a major change, making transfers a function of the number of students, with actual costs taken into consideration. Still, with wages set through centralized bargaining and with transfers paying for most of the wage bill, the incentives for a governor to transfer teachers to places where they are most needed do not seem particularly strong.

Until 2002, teaching activities were governed by a 1979 statute that created a ranking of categories in which time in grade and skill upgrading were the main determinants of promotions, together with other incentives that were prone to abuse. Although the 1994 General Education Law established a system to develop procedures to evaluate teachers, it was only in 2002 that a new statute, applicable to those hired *after* 2002, was enacted. It introduced teacher evaluations both for those entering the system and for those remaining and being promoted. Some 274,000 teachers out of a total of around 426,000—295,000 of them in the public schools—were evaluated in 2005.

---

46. Scatterplots (available upon request) with data for all thirty-one departments and special districts suggest no discernible association between the 2005 SABER test results and regional GDP.

47. In the 1995 math and science TIMSS exam, eighth and ninth graders ranked next-to-last among forty-one countries assessed. Colombian students ranked twenty-ninth out of thirty-five countries participating in the 2001 PIRLS reading literacy test. On a positive note, students now routinely participate in international evaluations, including the 2005 PISA exam administered by the Organization for Economic Cooperation and Development and in the 2006–07 versions of TIMSS.

48. Current expenditure (mainly wages) represented 92 percent of total expenditure on education in 1990–94 and 97 percent in 2000–05. Public teachers not only enjoyed a privileged pension regime; they also received some of the most generous wage adjustments.

Regional and national authorities have embarked on efforts with the private sector to enhance enrollment and increase the quality of public education. Because of supply limitations in the public sector, using public resources to take advantage of private sector installed capacity has been a wise move. Recent initiatives include the PACES program at the national level (1991–97), in which poor children were randomly given vouchers to attend private schools; ongoing concession schools in Bogotá and other major cities; and the Escuela Nueva program in rural areas. All have received positive evaluations.[49]

Some Proposals for Further Strengthening the Foundations for Growth

We have attempted to show throughout this chapter that although several of the reforms undertaken since 1990 strengthened some of the foundations for growth, other reforms had unintended consequences (see table 3). One of the most salient examples is fiscal decentralization, particularly of expenditure on health and education, which had adverse effects on macroeconomic stability, even if it contributed to broader sharing of the benefits of growth. A similar judgment can be made with regard to judicial reform, where the welcome expansion of access to the justice system came with a high fiscal price tag. Likewise, several reforms—to health care and pensions, for example—as well as restrictions from the local environment emanating from the political system and the justice system have been conducive to high and distortionary taxes on business and labor, which have weakened competitiveness.

The past eight years have been devoted to making many of the reforms consistent with the goal of restoring fiscal sustainability, which is now widely understood to be a prerequisite for sustainable growth, and to avoid the spikes in poverty associated with sharp economic contractions. The fine tuning of the reforms to make them fiscally sustainable has included elements geared toward correcting design flaws that might have prevented the reforms from fully delivering on their objectives. But much remains to be done. In what follows we offer several recommendations for enhancing the quality of certain reforms, giving particular attention to identifying the political and institutional constraints that have to be dealt with to make the suggested changes feasible.

Removing Constraints from the Local Environment

THE JUSTICE SYSTEM

No other single reform seems as important as a fundamental review of certain aspects of the *acción de tutela* and of the way the Constitutional Court operates. Although citizens' right of access to the justice system must be upheld, it is also of

49. Angrist, Bettinger, and Kremer (2006) evaluate PACES, and Barrera (2006) the Bogotá concession schools.

paramount importance to curtail the system's ability to tamper with economic policy matters in general and with macroeconomic stability in particular. Yet it is difficult to envision a more complicated task, as these are two enormously popular institutions, and the Constitutional Court is itself the final arbiter of any proposed change. The challenge is to creatively provide incentives for the highest court to entertain some of these proposals.

• *Appointments to the Constitutional Court.* Given how the court is organized and how its justices are chosen, the latter face much the same incentives as politicians. There are nine justices on the court, each elected by the senate for a period of eight years, without the possibility of reelection. The senate chooses from groups of three candidates proposed by the executive, the Supreme Court, and the Consejo de Estado.[50] After their term, justices face almost no restrictions on their involvement in politics, and indeed several have launched political careers. Some commentators have proposed that the justices be given life tenure and be nominated by the executive and confirmed by the senate (Kugler and Rosenthal, 2005). We believe a less ambitious proposal would stand a better chance of passage: there should be a "cool-off" period of, say, five years before a justice may run for elected office; in exchange for this concession, tenure on the court could be extended to, say, twelve years.

• *The tutela and "fundamental rights."* In the current debate, economists generally argue that justices should interpret and uphold the constitution rather than rewrite it, whereas the legal profession believes justices may proclaim any right as "fundamental." Common ground on this issue has yet to be found. An avenue worth exploring, therefore, is one put forward by former associate justice Uprimny (2001), who believes that Colombia's level of development should inform Constitutional Court rulings. In his view, some rights should be achieved progressively, over time, rather than immediately. He proposes a consensual definition by all powers of what should constitute an adequate health care plan, so that judges will no longer uphold *tutelas* demanding services beyond what the plan includes. The content of such a program should be enhanced as the country becomes wealthier.

• *Prior constitutional review.* There is evidence that the existing political process routinely produces low-quality legislation. Breaches of procedure often occur, which then become grounds for the Constitutional Court to overturn a law. The court should review laws as soon as they are approved, so that if they are to be overturned on procedural grounds, this is done before they become operational.

THE POLITICAL SYSTEM

Additional work is needed to ensure that the goal of political inclusion is made compatible with a legislature that can deliver high-quality public policies in such a manner that one foundation for growth is not strengthened at the expense of

---

50. Although terms are not concurrent, in 2001 seven out of nine justices were replaced at the same time.

others. Although 20 parties is a much more reasonable number than 322, it is still too many. To be sure, the biggest challenge is to translate the decline in electoral fragmentation into effective cohesion *within* Congress. We offer the following recommendations:

• *Foster additional electoral consolidation.* An obvious step is to gradually increase the threshold for winning representation, from 2 percent up to perhaps 5 percent.

• *Promote stronger political parties.* Campaign finance reform should identify ways to strengthen the links between a member of Congress and his or her party. Public and private funds should go to the party rather than to the candidate. Also, a *ley de bancadas* with more teeth should be enacted, particularly to ensure that the law rather than the party determines the proper sanctions for free-riding members of Congress.

• *Enhance legislative efficiency and transparency.* Kugler and Rosenthal (2005) argue in favor of granting fast-track authority, whereby the president could submit to Congress nonamendable propositions on urgent economic matters for an up-or-down vote. This might be a good mechanism to avoid the watering down of legislation, a recurrent problem in the case of laws related to taxes. The proposal's feasibility would be enhanced by a "sunset clause," so that the authority expires after a set number of years if Congress chooses not to renew it. Transparency would be enhanced if congressional voting were made by roll call and public, except perhaps on issues related to objections of conscience.

Enhancing Labor Flexibility, Promoting Formalization, and Increasing Pension Coverage

Colombia must persist in the elusive goal of enhancing labor market formalization, so as to *enhance competition* and ensure that all workers, not just those currently in the formal sector, *share in the benefits of growth.*[51] Here two constraints seem insurmountable, at least in the short term: high contributions to the funding of health and pensions, and full indexation of the minimum monthly salary. It is therefore essential to reduce nonwage labor costs other than social security contributions (contributions to ICBF, SENA, and CCFs). This is no easy task, given that together these programs administer resources that amount to 1 percent of GDP. In all three, unionization is prevalent, and they are backed by powerful political actors and provide employment to some 25,000 people (Echeverry and Santamaria, 2004). At first glance the solution seems simple: finance ICBF and SENA through user fees or the budget, and end the public funding of CCFs. In fact, this was one of the recommendations of a recent task force on public spend-

---

51. Bustamante (2006) estimates that 21 percent of the Colombian labor force was affiliated with the pension system in 2002, with 89 percent of affiliates coming from urban areas and a similar percentage from the top three deciles of the income distribution.

ing. The government, however, caved in to pressure from interest groups, who argued that if ICBF and SENA were to be funded out of general taxation, their existence would be a matter of debate during each budget cycle. Therefore second-best options have to be considered. We propose the following:

- *Earmark revenue from general taxation to ICBF and SENA.* Funding would preferably come from the VAT, rather than surcharges on formal sector wages. Although revenue earmarking is generally a questionable practice for several reasons, when it is unavoidable it should at least apply to less distortionary taxes.

- *CCFs should be financed through user fees,* particularly given that informal sector workers do not benefit from them. The move away from a tax on labor would be gradually phased in. The reduction in public financing of the CCFs should start by relieving them of the public policy tasks they now administer, such as the unemployment insurance program, which should be run by the government if it is indeed maintained at all.[52]

Promoting Financial Sector Deepening and Access and Further Developing the Capital Market

The following reforms of the financial system and the capital market would contribute to a *broader sharing of the benefits of growth* throughout the economy:

- *Adopt a more liberal policy with regard to the usury interest rate and a less restrictive definition of microcredit.* Although it is politically impractical to try to eliminate the usury rate, the executive has ample room to make it less restrictive.

- *Strike a better balance between creditor and debtor rights.* The legal system should facilitate the structuring of guarantees by removing restrictions on the assets that can serve as collateral, and foster the unification and updating of registries. Expeditious legal and paralegal procedures that speed the execution of guarantees should be put in place.

- *Provide incentives that promote the expansion of data bases,* once the Constitutional Court upholds the "habeas data" law. Utility companies should be allowed to report to credit bureaus the (generally favorable) information they have on their subscribers.

- *Better regulate AFP investments.* Regulations have skewed investments toward public debt. As proposed by Laserna (2007), AFPs could be required to maintain a minimum degree of diversification. Given the long-term nature of their liabilities, they should be matched to long-term assets such as investments in infrastructure (Asociación Nacional de Instituciones Financieras, 2007). A plausible way forward is a scheme in which each AFP defines a reference portfolio against which its performance can be assessed.

---

52. The World Bank (2005) raised concerns with regard to conflicts of interest involved in CCFs administering the unemployment insurance program, and it questioned the merit of focusing this insurance on workers previously employed in the formal sector.

Designing a More Business-Friendly Tax Code

On no other topic does there seem to be greater consensus than with regard to taxes, and this is not the place to repeat the specifics of what a "good" tax system should look like. The problem is not with the "what," but rather the "how." To be sure, a less fragmented Congress should be of much help, as it would allow the executive to negotiate the reform with a few strong parties rather than with each member of Congress individually. Also, the administration has to negotiate from a position of strength. In our view a structural tax reform should be submitted only in the context of a buoyant fiscal situation, so that the executive can propose *improving* the tax code while at the same time *reducing* the overall tax burden. A fairer and more business-friendly tax system would contribute to *strengthening competition* in the economy.

Clarifying the Distribution of Responsibilities among Levels of Government

Putting in place a decentralized political system in a country with a long tradition of political and fiscal centralization has proved to be a challenge, and any further effort in that direction is bound to confront risks and costs. The changes introduced in 1997–2003 have addressed many of the problems that followed the 1991–93 reforms. One key issue, however, remains unresolved, namely, the delegation of responsibilities. Given the lack of a well-developed framework on territorial organization—Congress has never passed a territorial organization law—efforts to devolve responsibilities have become bogged down in details.[53] Behind the label "public expenditure" stand all the intricacies of the business of providing public goods, particularly in the areas of health and education. There are many actors, among whom teachers are the most visible, who benefit from duplicate expenditures and from ill-defined responsibilities.[54] Without such a framework, full devolution will take a long time, and many of the benefits of decentralization for the *broader sharing of growth* and *equality of opportunities* will be delayed, and *macroeconomic stability* will continue to be undermined. Inasmuch

---

53. The lack of a well-defined framework for devolution of resources and responsibilities has also made it all but impossible to entertain the possibility of sharing tax bases among levels of government, thus establishing a constraint on allowing subnational governments to have an important say on tax issues.

54. An influential senator recently argued that ". . . a Congress with regional and national representation is in no position to approve a substantive law that affects regional interest with regard to territory, financial resources and responsibilities" (Pérez, 2006, p. 76, our translation). Soon after Congress approved Law 715, in 2001, the secretary general of FECODE wrote an interesting piece objecting to the new framework for decentralization (Arroyave, 2002). What emerges clearly from this document is the opposition of teachers to the decentralization of education. The document complains that "the [central government] will no longer administer nor provide educational services"; that "headmasters will be made responsible for the quality of education"; and that "the regional reallocation of teachers is now at the discretion of each [subnational government]." The conclusion that we reach is that FECODE opposes decentralization because the union stands to obtain better working conditions under a centralized decision-making process.

as many local public goods are provided by the central government, subnational governments do not face a hard budget constraint; to instill discipline, therefore, the central government must have an important say in how expenditure is undertaken. Local governments are more accountable to the central government than to their constituents, and voters hold the central government accountable for problems with the provision of public goods, and they react by demanding more resources from it.

Attempts at correcting the health care system's structural flaws should address three issues: generating adequate incentives at the subnational level, improving targeting, and setting limits on the health care rights of individuals (as discussed above in reference to the Constitutional Court):

• *Increased accountability at the local level is a must.* With the central government providing most of the resources, local authorities face weak incentives to enhance the efficiency of their health care institutions. Instead of being driven out of the market, inefficient providers are kept in operation and become a fiscal burden. In the end, the question boils down to enforcing responsibilities acquired by the governors. Public hospitals must be placed under close supervision to pinpoint and correct efficiency problems and to avoid capture by elites through corruption.

• *Improving targeting systems is key for the sustainability and effectiveness of the subsidized regime.* Aside from creating a fiscal burden, flawed targeting is detrimental to the quality of the assistance provided. Although it would be costly and technically demanding, an upgrade to the Sisben targeting system that allows households who have overcome poverty to be removed from the system should be a priority. The long-run cost of doing so will be far less than that of subsidizing the nonpoor.

• *Strengthen incentives to improve the quality of public education.* Recent notable efforts to this effect—including with regard to the evaluation, training, and promotion of teachers; a better formula for distributing transfers; and the involvement of private schools in the provision of public education—can be constrained by the fact that most teachers are paid at the national level, thus limiting the extent of devolution and enhancement of responsibilities and accountability at the local level.

Concluding Remarks

In 1990 Colombia embarked on a comprehensive reform program that should have had a positive impact on the foundations for growth, making economic growth both fiscally as well as politically sustainable. We have shown that the initial drive for reform failed to deliver on many of its expected promises, and a number of reforms actually weakened some of the foundations, in particular Colombia's long-held adherence to macroeconomic stability. The 1990s were thus a decade of unfulfilled promises. Starting in 1999, the reform agenda was reinvigorated, and many of the design problems of the initial reform drive have been addressed. This process, coupled with a benign external environment and a much-improved security situation, has of late produced enormous benefits in terms of economic growth and a renewed decline in poverty. The job is far from complete, however, and in many areas additional reforms need to be undertaken in order to make growth sustainable and even more inclusive. In this chapter we have offered policy recommendations along many dimensions, taking care to acknowledge that what is technically advisable is not always politically or institutionally feasible.

References

Angrist, J., E. Bettinger, and M. Kremer. 2006. "Long-Term Educational Consequences of Secondary School Vouchers." *American Economic Review* 96, no. 3: 847–62.

Arroyave, R. 2002. "La Ley 715 de 2001: Hacia la Privatización Total de la Educación." *Deslinde* no. 30 (February).

Asociación Nacional de Instituciones Financieras. 2005. "Mergers and Acquisitions in the Colombian Financial Sector: Impact on Efficiency (1990–2005)." Bogotá.

———. 2007. "Los Fondos de Pensiones y la Financiación de la Infraestructura." *Carta Financiera* 137: 7–12.

Barajas, A., R. Steiner, and N. Salazar. 2000. "The Impact of Liberalization and Foreign Investment in Colombia's Financial Sector." *Journal of Development Economics* 63, no. 1: 157–96.

Barón, G. 2007. "Cuentas de Salud de Colombia 1993–2002: El Gasto Nacional en Salud y su Financiamiento." Bogotá: Ministerio de la Protección Social.

Barrera, F. 2006. "The Impact of Private Provision of Public Education: Empirical Evidence from Bogotá's Concession Schools." World Bank Policy Research Report 4121. Washington: World Bank.

Bernal, R., and M. Cárdenas. 2003. "Determinants of Labor Demand in Colombia: 1976–1996." Working Paper 10077. Cambridge, Mass.: National Bureau of Economic Research.

Borjas, J., and O. L. Acosta. 2000. "Educational Reform in Colombia." In A. Alesina, ed., *Institutional Reforms: The Case of Colombia*. MIT Press.

Botero, F. 2000. "Circunscripción Nacional y Practicas Electorales." In E. Bonilla, ed., *Formación de Investigadores II*. Bogotá: Ediciones UniAndes-Colciencias-Tercer Mundo.

Botero, F., and J. C. Rodríguez. 2007. "Escepticismo Optimista: La Reforma Electoral Colombiana de 2003." In C. U. Santander and N. Penteado, eds., *Os processos eleitorias na América Latina*. Brasilia: Editorial LGE.

Bustamante, J. P. 2006. "Factores que Inciden en la Cobertura del Sistema Pensional en Colombia." Archivos de Economía 312. Bogotá: Departamento Nacional de Planeación.

Cadena, X. 2006. "The Next Step for the Colombian Pension System." Princeton University.

Cárdenas, M. 2007. "Economic Growth in Colombia: A Reversal of 'Fortune'?" *Ensayos Sobre Política Económica* 25, no. 53: 220–59.

Cárdenas, M., and V. Mercer-Blackman. 2006. *Análisis del Sistema Tributario Colombiano y su Impacto sobre la Competitividad*. Cuadernos de Fedesarrollo no. 19. Bogotá: Fedesarrollo.

Cárdenas, M., R. Junguito, and M. Pachón. 2006. "Political Institutions and Political Outcomes in Colombia: The Effects of the 1991 Constitution." Working Paper R-508. Washington: Inter-American Development Bank.

Departamento Nacional de Planeación. 2002. "Autorización a la Nación para Contratar Empréstitos con la Banca Multilateral." Documento Conpes 3175. Bogotá.

Echeverry, J. C., and M. Santamaria. 2004. "The Political Economy of Labor Reform in Colombia." Documento CEDE 2004-22. Universidad de los Andes.

Edwards, S., and R. Steiner. 2008. *La Revolución Incompleta: Las Reformas de Gaviria.* Bogotá: Editorial Norma, Colección Vitral.

Fundación Corona, Corpoeducación. 2003. *Informe del Progreso Educativo en Colombia.* Bogotá: Preal.

Gaviria, A. 2004. "Ley 789 de 2002: Funcionó o No?" Documento CEDE 2004-45. Bogotá: Centro de Estudios sobre Desarrollo Económico.

Gaviria, A., C. Medina, and C. Mejía. 2006. "Assessing Health Reform in Colombia: From Theory to Practice." *Economía* 7, no. 1: 29–72.

Inter-American Development Bank. 1995. *Overcoming Volatility.* Economic and Social Progress in Latin America series. Washington.

———. 2002. "Evaluación de la Política Económica en Colombia: Una Aproximación desde el Análisis de las Políticas Públicas." Washington (June).

Kalmanovitz, S. 2003. *Ensayos sobre Banca Central: Comportamiento, Independencia e Historia.* Cali: Grupo Editorial Norma.

Kugler, M., and H. Rosenthal. 2005. "Checks and Balances: An Assessment of the Institutional Separation of Political Powers in Colombia." In A. Alesina, ed., *Institutional Reforms: The Case of Colombia.* MIT Press.

Laserna, J. M. 2007. "Una Propuesta para Mejorar el Manejo de Riesgo, la Diversificación y la Eficiencia de los Portafolios de los Fondos de Pensiones Obligatorios." Banco de la República.

Lasso, F. J. 2006. "Incidencia del Gasto Público Social sobre la Distribución del Ingreso y la Reducción de la Pobreza." In Misión para la Erradicación de la Pobreza y Desigualdad, *Misión para el Diseño de una Estrategia para la Reducción de la Pobreza y la Desigualdad.* Bogotá: Departamento Nacional de Planeación.

Londoño, J. L. 1995. *Distribución del Ingreso y Desarrollo Económico: Colombia en el Siglo XX.* Bogotá: Tercer Mundo.

MERP (Misión para la Erradicación de la Pobreza y Desigualdad). 2006. *Misión para el Diseño de una Estrategia para la Reducción de la Pobreza y la Desigualdad.* Bogotá: Departamento Nacional de Planeación.

Ministerio de Hacienda. 2005. "Colombia, Surpassing Expectations: Growth, Pensions and the Fiscal Deficit." Bogotá.

Montenegro, A., and R. Rivas. 2005. *Las Piezas del Rompecabezas: Desigualdad, Pobreza y Crecimiento.* Bogotá: Taurus.

Núñez, J., and S. Espinosa. 2005. "Pro-Poor Growth and Pro-Poor Programs in Colombia." Documento CEDE 2005-51. Bogotá: Centro de Estudios sobre Desarrollo Económico.

Núñez, J., R. Steiner, X. Cadena, and R. Pardo. 2002. "Cuáles Colegios Ofrecen Mejor Educación en Colombia?" Documento CEDE 3. Bogotá: Centro de Estudios sobre Desarrollo Económico.

Peña, X., and A. Glassman. 2004. "Comparación entre Medidas de Pobreza en Colombia: La Nueva Metodología de Sisben." Washington: Inter-American Development Bank.

Pérez, O. D. 2006. "El Saneamiento Fiscal de los Departamentos y Municipios." In M. Cárdenas and C. Aguilar, eds., *Reformas Fiscales para el Nuevo Siglo.* Bogotá: Fedesarrollo.

Roland, G., and J. G. Zapata. 2005. "Colombia's Electoral and Party System: Paths for Reform." In A. Alesina, ed., *Institutional Reforms: The Case of Colombia.* MIT Press.

Sahay, R., and S. Goyal. 2006. "Volatility and Growth in Latin America: An Episodic Approach?" IMF Working Paper 06/287. Washington: International Monetary Fund.

Salazar, N. 2005. "Represión Financiera y Márgenes de Intermediación." *Carta Financiera* 131 (September).

Sotelo, L. C. 2000. "Los Derechos Constitucionales de Prestación y sus Implicaciones Económico-Políticas." Archivos de Macroeconomía 133. Bogotá: Departamento Nacional de Planeación.

Ungar, E. 2003. "Repensar el Congreso para Enfrentar la Crisis." In A. Mason and L. J. Orjuela, eds., *La Crisis Política Colombiana.* Bogotá: Ediciones UniAndes.

Uprimny, R. 2001. "Legitimidad y Conveniencia del Control Constitucional de la Economía." *Revista de Derecho Público* 12: 154–83.

World Bank. 2003. *Colombia: The Economic Foundation of Peace.* Washington.

———. 2005. *Colombia: Labor Market Adjustment, Reform and Productivity: What Are the Factors That Matter?* Report 32068-CO. Washington.

5

Political and Institutional Obstacles to Reform in Costa Rica

JORGE CORNICK AND ALBERTO TREJOS

From Near Success to Reform Paralysis

With a population of 4.4 million in 2006 in an area of just 51,000 square kilometers, Costa Rica is one of the smallest countries in Latin America. Yet it is an interesting case to analyze in the context of the CGD project. In recent decades Costa Rica has applied some but not all of the conventional policies pursued by the rest of the region, with varying degrees of intensity, while protecting and enhancing social policies—including but not limited to welfare policies—that were not discussed as part of the Washington consensus, except perhaps as sources of fiscal deficit. The results can be characterized as a near success: steady but not spectacular growth; reduced but still comparatively high inflation; and a rapid reduction in poverty in the aftermath of the early-1980s crisis—all in a context of economic and democratic stability.

Yet the pace of reform has consistently slowed in recent years, while the capacity of many public institutions to deliver essential services has diminished. The fall in the poverty rate has stagnated in recent years, and income inequality has increased. And, to add paradox to an already interesting story, recent growth has been robust, foreign direct investment (FDI) is growing, the central bank is quickly accumulating reserves, and for the first time in decades there is a fiscal surplus—all precisely at the same time that the public sector seems to be verging on

Laura Muñoz provided excellent research assistance throughout the whole project.

paralysis.[1] Clearly, although the new reforms under discussion are extremely difficult to approve and implement, the results of the old reforms, and of day-to-day
economic management, have been positive. Yet problems remain: the political system and public sector administration move very slowly and often ineffectively, as
a result of self-imposed rules that have transformed "checks and balances" into
"chokes and strangleholds." Both for its achievements and for its failures, therefore, Costa Rica seems to be a promising ground on which to apply the CGD
framework.

Growth Performance since the Early 1980s

According to cross-country data from the International Monetary Fund, Costa
Rica recorded the second-highest economic growth rate, corrected for purchasing
power parity (PPP), in Latin America over the 1983–2007 period, lagging behind
only Chile. Real annual GDP growth averaged 5.1 percent and even reached 6.1
percent in the last five years. GDP per capita in 2007 surpassed $5,560; corrected
for PPP, that figure is equivalent to almost $11,300, one of the four highest in
Latin America. According to household survey data from the National Institute
for Statistics and Census, real wages more than doubled between 1983 and 2003;
meanwhile the poverty rate fell from 55 percent during the 1982 crisis to 32 percent in 1986 and 17 percent in 2007. Compared with other countries in the
region, Costa Rica has enjoyed not only comparatively high but also quite stable
growth. There has not been a single fiscal, balance of payments, exchange rate,
banking, or political crisis since 1983, and growth has been positive in every
single year during the same period.

Costa Rica's economy has grown even though total factor productivity (TFP)
has risen very little; the increase in output is due almost exclusively to the accumulation of inputs. Rodríguez, Sáenz, and Trejos (2002) performed a TFP
decomposition for the second half of the twentieth century and found that productivity increases were rarely a driving force over that long period, and in fact
TFP growth was negative for the sluggish 1995–2000 period. Although a similar
exercise for the 2000–07 period would be far beyond the scope of this paper, there
is some evidence of TFP recovery after 2002.

Zettelmeyer (2006) highlights a number of stylized facts that characterize Latin
America's disappointing growth of the last few decades. Costa Rica shares some
of these features, notably the lackluster performance in TFP before 2000 that
Loayza, Fajnzylber, and Calderón (2005) found for the region as a whole. With
respect to some other stylized facts, however, Costa Rica is an outlier: as already
noted, it has not shared with other countries in the region the pattern of frequent

---

1. These paragraphs were written in early 2008. As of July of the same year, the country's economic prospects seem distinctly less positive, as a consequence of high international commodity
prices and the global economic downturn.

output collapses, nor has the current expansion been short lived. Rather, Costa Rica has been on a single sustained "growth spurt" for a quarter of a century, with growth in GDP per capita between 1983 and any given year since then exceeding 2 percent a year. Thus, Costa Rica has managed to escape the pattern of isolated, short-lasting growth spurts, frequent crises, and high output volatility described by Zettelmeyer. This is the case even though the national income accounts are probably biased downward, as that author suggests, by the fact that the country reduced its barriers to trade very quickly and maintained pre-opening relative prices in valuing output (as mentioned above and quantified in Rodríguez, Sáenz, and Trejos, 2002).[2]

Earlier, in 1980–82, Costa Rica went through a deep economic crisis, which resulted in a cumulative loss of income per capita of nearly 20 percent. The crisis was the consequence of structural problems similar to those afflicting the rest of Latin America, of external shocks that exposed these internal weaknesses, and of internal financial mismanagement that exacerbated them. After the crisis, Costa Rica decided to pursue a more prudent fiscal policy, to open the economy to trade and capital flows, and to gradually do away with some of the heavy-handed economic planning instruments in use at the time. Some timid attempts at deregulation were made, but, over all, red tape has probably increased rather than decreased since the 1980s.

Unlike in many other countries in the hemisphere, public utilities (water, electric power, and telecommunications) were not privatized, and the budget for key social services was protected. Costa Rica thus implemented a somewhat heterodox reform package, but one that, broadly speaking, fit within the policy consensus of the time.

Opposition to reform was vocal but politically weak. Critics denounced the reforms as "inequitable" and "neoliberal" and claimed that economic adjustment was increasing poverty, when in reality the poverty rate fell 20 percentage points during the stabilization phase.

Despite the depth of the crisis, the bipartisan political system that had been in place since the 1948 civil war remained intact. Democratic discourse enjoyed widespread legitimacy; governance was, if not outstanding, at least good enough; and major policy initiatives could be successfully negotiated between the government and the opposition. The "sensible center" seemed to have won the day, and the only viable political choice seemed to be between two centrist, ideologically broad parties, the social democratic Partido Liberación Nacional and the slightly more conservative Partido Unidad Social Cristiana. To their extreme left, the

---

2. Costa Rica's story also fits the Zettelmeyer growth covariates: besides having the region's second-highest growth rate, Costa Rica has had comparatively less growth volatility, has one of the region's most equitable income distributions, and is fairly open to trade. Political crises have also been extremely rare. Of course, when compared with the developing world as a whole, Costa Rica's record is not particularly exemplary in terms of growth, volatility, or equity.

Marxist political parties were in retreat, and although they managed to hold some seats in the legislature, all the wide-ranging far-left alliances imploded. At the other extreme, not a single far-right political party ever had any strength. Occasionally, small regional parties, content to offer their support of the government in power in exchange for regional earmarks, would get a few members elected to Congress.

The Recent Near Paralysis of Reform

Despite the mostly positive performance of economic policy since the 1980s crisis, progress with economic reform has lately become increasingly difficult: reform fatigue seems to have set in. This section attempts to identify both the key reforms that still need to be implemented and the key constraints that have slowed or halted implementation. More fundamentally, we try to explain the economic and political processes that have generated reform fatigue despite the positive performance of past reforms.

REFORM FATIGUE

If the results of reform in terms of economic growth have been so good, why has further reform become so difficult? The situation is all the more puzzling because the reform agenda has succeeded in other areas besides growth: inflation, while remaining persistently above 10 percent, seldom strays much higher; the public finances have been significantly strengthened, both in the government itself and at the central bank; the liberalization of key sectors and a profound transformation of the structure of the economy have been achieved in a short time, while exports and FDI have grown rapidly; unemployment has been consistently low.

Three factors seem to account for Costa Rica's turnabout from solid progress at reform to almost complete reform paralysis. First, the distribution of income has worsened, robbing the political and economic system of some of its legitimacy. Second, a necessary transformation of the public sector was simplistically confused with mere downsizing, rendering the Costa Rican state ineffective and breeding new opponents of reform. Third, political events, including some high-level corruption scandals and their consequences, have reshaped the ideological and party structure of the political system, leading to congressional atrophy and paralysis.

PERSISTENT POVERTY AND WORSENING INCOME DISTRIBUTION

Although economic growth was steady and poverty fell rapidly in the late 1980s and early 1990s, since then the decline in the share of the population living below the poverty line—currently 16.7 percent—has been much slower. This is low by Latin American standards, but that is little solace for those Costa Ricans who remain poor and have little hope of escaping poverty. Figure 1 shows both the poverty rate (the fraction of the population living in households that cannot afford the minimal consumption basket) and the extreme poverty rate (the fraction that

Figure 1. *Costa Rica: Alternative Measures of Poverty, 1961–2008*

Percent

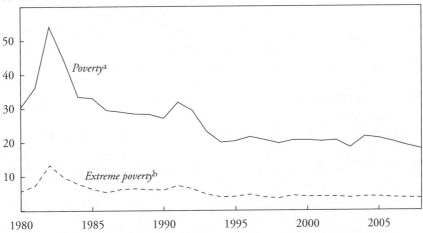

Source: Annual Household Survey, National Institute for Statistics and Census.
a. Fraction of the population living in households that cannot afford the minimal consumption basket.
b. Fraction of the population living in households that cannot afford the minimal food basket.

cannot afford the minimal *food* basket), both baskets as defined by the National Institute for Statistics and Census.

Inequality has always been a significant problem in Costa Rica, even if less so than in neighboring countries. The country's Gini coefficient,[3] already high in the 1970s, increased dramatically during the 1980–82 crisis, but then fell back below historical levels during and immediately after the postcrisis stabilization. The Gini then gradually crept up again during the 1990s, and in the last few years it has oscillated wildly. Other indicators of income dispersion display similar patterns.

Does this mean that the relatively rapid growth enjoyed in the last two decades was not pro-poor? In a loose sense, following Leipziger (2005), growth has been pro-poor by definition, given that the poverty rate fell; in the very strong sense used by Kakwani and Pernia (2000), however, growth was not pro-poor, because the segment of the population below the poverty line saw its income per capita grow at a slower rate than average income per capita. To be precise, in the 1988–2007 period, according to the family income data reported by the national household survey, the poorest 40 percent of the population (the relevant group for this purpose, as the poverty rate varied between the current 16.7 percent and 33.1 percent in that period) saw its income per capita grow by an average of about 1.9 percent annually, while the population as a whole enjoyed average annual

3. The following discussion is based on analyses by Juan Diego Trejos with data from the household survey and the national census.

growth of 3.3 percent, and the richest 40 percent saw annual growth of 3.6 percent. Had all income brackets enjoyed the same rate of growth, the fall in the poverty rate would have been larger, especially since a large number of people had incomes within a few percentage points of the poverty line. But this result does not hold throughout the period. For example, between 2004 and 2007—years of unusually rapid growth—average household income among the poorest quintile grew by 28 percent, while that for the population as a whole grew by 19.1 percent; thus, growth was extremely pro-poor in those years, even by the strong definition.

One should be careful, however, in interpreting this result. On the one hand, comparison with other Latin American countries is not easy, because in some of those countries, unlike in Costa Rica, "the poor" (as conventionally defined) represent a majority of the population. On the other hand, one should take into account the immigration into Costa Rica of between 300,000 and 450,000 Nicaraguans during precisely the same period (Consejo Monetario Centroamericano, 2004). According to Lizano and Monge (2006), 89.3 percent of immigrants in 2005 were in the poorest fifth of the Costa Rican population and accounted for 24.3 percent of Costa Rica's poor. If one corrects for the effects of immigration, which include not only the numbers of poor immigrants but also their competition for jobs with the poorest locals, the fall in the poverty rate in the period under consideration was larger, and it is easier to argue that growth has been pro-poor.

Even if one accepts the interpretation of the data that growth has *not* been pro-poor, it is not necessarily the case that the pro-growth reforms caused poverty. In our opinion, the incomes of the poor would have been no higher in the absence of these reforms; on the contrary, the poverty rate would have been higher. And the main reasons (besides immigration and the worldwide increase in the education premium) why income redistribution was not more successful are some of the same ones we highlight below as limitations on growth: congressional institutions that delay the legislation required to further economic reform; low government revenue that forces the postponement or cancellation of public investment, both social and economic, required to strengthen the growth foundations; and administrative restrictions that render the public sector, or at least large portions of it, increasingly ineffective.

A WEAKER PUBLIC SECTOR AND A MORE CONTENTIOUS POLITICAL SYSTEM

Costa Rica's relatively strong economic growth record is more than matched by its remarkable record on social policy: literacy, at 97 percent, and life expectancy at birth, at 78.7 years, are at developed-world levels; 98 percent of the population has access to drinking water; net primary and secondary school enrollment rates are 98.6 and 66.1 percent, respectively. Also, by our calculations 87.6 percent of the population has health insurance, 98.3 percent has electricity in their homes, and there are 575 telephone lines (main and mobile combined) per 1,000 people. None of this could have been achieved without a public sector capable of both designing and implementing effective public policies, including the construction of large infrastructure projects. Strong institutions and a political system dominated by two political parties alternating in power, with sufficient common ground to reach agreements on the broad outlines of public policy, form the background of these accomplishments.

However, in recent years Costa Rica's public sector seems to be slowly collapsing. Many government agencies are less and less capable of discharging their duties. Years of cost-cutting efforts and administrative atomization, the misdirection of anti-corruption and other regulations, and financial and personnel problems are taking their toll. Whole areas of government activity, especially those that involve investment and a long-term mindset, have been weakened. The most notable examples are education and transportation infrastructure (the latter is discussed in detail below).

Public sector reform in Costa Rica has too often been simplistically confused with downsizing. The resulting loss in public sector effectiveness has turned the same public servants who would ordinarily be in charge of implementing policy and reform into an active and aggressive political force against reform. Meanwhile a drastic reduction in public sector capital expenditure, particularly in infrastructure and education, ensured that after the crisis was over, public expenditure would continue to be managed under a crisis mindset. Thus, a perception that government does not deliver became widespread, weakening the mandates of reform-minded administrations.

To make matters worse, a new political reality emerged. Since the mid-1990s, Costa Rica has witnessed the emergence of a new political opposition, fiercely globaphobic, highly organized and vocal, electorally successful, and including an influential strand of what, in our opinion, can only be described as a hard core of well-organized groups that do not believe in the democratic system.

In the two-party political system that prevailed before this change, both sides shared ample common ground, an ability and willingness to negotiate and execute agreements, and an expectation of alternating in power. The executive also possessed some effective tools—such as control of disbursement of earmarks—to enforce party discipline. After the change, new parties have emerged to capitalize on the anti-system mentality, while the old ones have been considerably weakened; there is now a multiparty Congress and very little basis for consensus. Yet meanwhile the country has kept the same parliamentary procedures and political habits as before. The combination of these old rules with the new composition of Congress has led to near paralysis, which can only be overcome through time-consuming and presumably costly negotiations, as each individual member of Congress has the ability to delay any vote almost indefinitely. It is extremely hard for both the executive and individual legislators to get any bill passed within a

reasonable time frame, even if it enjoys the support of a strong majority: the status quo is king.[4]

How did this change in the country's politics come about? Although the poor
were protected during the postcrisis stabilization phase, and in fact a broad segment of the working classes thrived during the recovery, thus partly addressing the
broad sharing of the benefits of growth (one of the five growth foundations identified by the CGD framework), a large portion of the middle class did not share in
the fruits of the rapid growth achieved in that period. These were mainly people
who worked or expected to work in the public sector, but also some professionals
and clerical workers in the private sector. As it happens, these middle class workers were the backbone of the Costa Rican political system. Neglect of their economic needs and aspirations, compounded by political mistakes, weakened
political support for the traditional, "sensible center" political parties. This, in our
opinion, is the key element that explains both the emergence of the new, anti-
reform political organizations that now enjoy broad electoral support and the current impasse in public policymaking.

Successes, Near Successes, and Failures: Which Policies Matter Most for Future Growth?

As argued above, Costa Rica has arrived at a juncture at which the design,
approval, and implementation of growth-enhancing, middle class–strengthening
reforms are almost impossible, unless Congress somehow recovers its ability to
produce legislation at a reasonable pace and the rest of the public sector recovers
its effectiveness. The congressional rules that worked, almost in spite of themselves, for decades have ceased to work in the wake of the political realignment.
Consequently, the legislature is paralyzed, and any reform requiring legislation is
so likely to be delayed indefinitely that many proposed bills are simply shelved
without ever being put to a vote. To the extent that this problem can be solved, it
is this reform that opens the door to many other areas of reform that address one
or more of the foundations of growth identified in the CGD framework. Hence,
we will begin our analysis of reform by looking at *legislative reform,* because of its
importance for progress across the whole spectrum of growth foundations.

Meanwhile the public sector, as a result of botched reforms in the past, is no
longer able to deliver the services expected from it efficiently and on time. Thus,
administrative reform is the second area addressed in our analysis. This administrative weakness is manifest in several areas, but none more important than the
provision of transportation infrastructure. Our discussion of administrative
reform therefore focuses on that sector, both because the administrative difficul-

---

4. Recently, a "fast track" rule has been approved and now has been tested at the Constitutional
Court. Although not exactly "fast," this rule allows Congress to set a definite number of sessions after
which a bill must be put up for a vote.

ties encountered there are emblematic of those observed across the whole public sector, and because the poor present state of the country's transportation infrastructure specifically affects performance on each of the growth foundations. Just as Costa Rica's entire reform agenda today is being thwarted in Congress by procedural potholes, detours, and gridlock, so, too, in the most literal sense, its progress on growth-enhancing reforms is being held up by an outdated and inadequate transport network.

Once Congress, the executive, and the rest of the public sector are able at some point in the future to discharge their duties effectively, the most salient weaknesses in the Costa Rican growth foundations can be addressed. These have to do with lack of *equality of opportunities*, insufficient *economic competition*, and the fact that the gains in terms of *macroeconomic stability* have been significant but not complete. Thus, our other three priority reforms relate mainly to those weaknesses.

First, government needs more revenue, both to consolidate the *macroeconomic stability* already achieved and make it sustainable (for example, by reducing debt, absorbing the quasi-fiscal deficit of the central bank, and reducing inflation) and to strengthen the public networks and institutions that are critical to improving the country's income distribution and thus to improving *equality of opportunities* and to *sharing more broadly the benefits of the country's growth*. Improved tax collection has already not only reduced the public sector deficit but also, more recently, generated fiscal surpluses. Nevertheless, existing revenue is still far from sufficient to finance the country's long-postponed and direly needed public sector investments. Thoroughgoing tax reform is necessary to attend to these needs while preserving stable public finances. *Tax reform* is therefore our third area of study.[5]

Second, an area of particular importance for greater *economic competition* and a more dynamic business environment is reform of the country's antiquated and clearly inadequate telecommunications regime. Telecommunications is an area in which strong political sensitivities have prevented progress for years. As a consequence, the system's performance is so poor that it is affecting most of the other growth foundations, including *macroeconomic stability*, because so large a share of the state's resources is tied up in this public sector monopoly, and *equality of opportunity*, because the existence of this monopoly excludes would-be entrants. On the bright side, the years of stagnation have left many low-hanging fruit for reform to pick. The current system clearly delivered major achievements in the past, but standards in several parts of the market are very low; *restoring a competitive telecommunications system* is thus vital for a series of critical industries, ranging from software to business services, and from tourism to computing.

---

5. It has been suggested to us that given the paramount importance of education in Costa Rica, this chapter should examine reform in that area as well. We agree that education is a high priority for the growth foundations and that it has deteriorated in Costa Rica, but we believe that most of the problem in this field, just as in infrastructure, is a manifestation of the country's fiscal and administrative problems rather than a separate problem with its own distinct origins.

Third, although the successful reform of the trade and investment regime has been perhaps the most critical element in the country's postcrisis recovery and growth, a significant pending agenda in *trade liberalization* remains, with overwhelming obstacles in its path. As with telecommunications, reform in this area is primarily aimed at strengthening *economic competition*, but by lowering entry barriers to a range of activities, it is also important for enhancing *equality of opportunities.* Success in the foreign markets opened to trade should also contribute positively to Costa Rica's balance of payments, thus assisting *macroeconomic stability.*

Table 1, which identifies the relationship between each of the above sets of policies and the foundations of growth (following the authors' admittedly somewhat subjective judgments), is intended to clarify the connection between these reforms and the CGD framework. The table groups a number of specific reforms into several policy areas. We think this organization is useful for understanding some of the paradoxes of Costa Rica's economic performance. For example, rapid economic growth in the country that possesses Latin America's last remaining telecommunications monopoly seems easier to understand when placed in a context of market-based policies in which, over all, the "progress score" is not bad, even if telecommunications reform lags behind the rest.

The question marks in table 1 identify those cases where the impact of reform is unknown or ambiguous. In many cases this ambiguity is the result of a definition of reform that is, perhaps, a bit too broad. For example, privatization of the telecommunications monopoly would be expected to strengthen macroeconomic stability, all else equal. But liberalization without privatization, leaving the public utility to compete with private providers (and thus facing the possibility of bankruptcy), could create potentially large contingent liabilities that would work against macroeconomic stability.

Economic Reform and the Growth Foundations

In the previous section we used the CGD framework to identify five areas of reform that are key to Costa Rica's future economic performance. Here we pursue a deeper understanding of these reforms, their relevance to the foundations of growth, the steps necessary to move them forward, and the barriers likely to be confronted in the process. As already noted, we find that political and institutional obstacles to implementation are particularly important, and therefore we begin with those.

Legislative Reform

A coherent body of law and respect for the rule of law are obvious prerequisites for economic growth and development in a modern market economy. Only slightly less obvious is the need for an effective, representative, and efficient system for revising and updating the laws and promulgating new laws as needed. A

Table 1. *Costa Rica: Importance and Actual Impact of Potential Future Reforms on the Growth Foundations*
5 = most important

Reform	Property rights		Equal opportunities		Competition		Broad sharing of the benefits of growth		Macroeconomic stability	
	Importance	Actual impact	Importance	Actual impact	Importance	Actual impact	Importance	Actual impact	Importance	Actual impact
Public sector reform[a]	5		5		5		4		2	
Legislative reform	5	2	5	2	5	2	5	2	5	2
Administrative reform	5	2	5	2	5	2	5	2	1	2
Anti-corruption	5	2	5	2	5	2	4	2	1	2
Judiciary reform	5	2	5	2	5	2	2	2	?	2
Tax and budgetary reform	n.a.	—	4	3	4	2	5	3	3	3
Developing competitive markets	3		5		5		?		?	
Trade liberalization	1	4	5	4	5	4	3	4	?	?
Financial liberalization	3	4	5	4	5	4	2	4	?	?
Privatization[b]	1	5	5	5	5	5	1	5	?	?
Telecommunications demonopolization	2	5	5	1	5	1	3	1	5	?
Insurance demonopolization	3	4	5	1	5	1	2	1	?	?
Antitrust policy	3	4	5	2	5	2	2	2	?	?
Public services development	4		5		4		5		2	
Education	4	4	5	4	4	4	5	4	4	4
Health	4	4	5	4	4	4	5	4	1	4
Security	5	3	3	3	1	3	2	3	1	3

Source: Authors' analysis.

n.a. = not available; ? = unknown or ambiguous impact.

a. Scores for broad policy areas (in italic) indicate overall importance of that area.

b. Other than utilities.

well-functioning legislature is thus vital for the proper functioning of the economy, which it affects through every one of the growth foundations. If the laws are flawed and cannot be rewritten without interminable delay, *property rights* are at risk of being usurped, either outright or by exploiting that delay. A legislative body whose makeup is poorly aligned with the actual distribution of the population will be prone to decisions that favor those who are better represented; this inevitably impacts both *equality of opportunities* and *the broad sharing of the benefits of economic growth.* The rules under which the legislature operates determine whether *political competition* leads to open debate and good-faith negotiation, and so to legislation that serves the national interest, or to gridlock and paralysis. And both *macroeconomic stability* and healthy *economic competition* frequently depend on timely and responsible legislative decisions on the government budget, fiscal stimulus, fair taxation, antitrust, and a host of other matters.

The existing congressional system in Costa Rica has two major problems. One is the inefficiency of the existing rules of order and parliamentary procedures and the ease with which they can be used to delay or block action. The other is the unrepresentative manner in which members of Congress are elected.

Cumbersome Rules and Procedures

The formal parliamentary procedures of the Costa Rican Congress give political minorities enormous power to make themselves heard by indefinitely delaying votes that they oppose. This creates a power vacuum that is often then filled by judicial activism, as new interpretations of the existing law substitute for new legislation. Delay also leads the executive to abandon efforts at reform that require new legislation, and instead to push reform through executive action, only to find that its power to do so is extremely limited. Because most reforms require supporting legislation to some degree, the extreme difficulty in passing laws is obviously an obstacle to growth.

The most controversial areas of political debate in the last few years have been the worst victims of congressional deadlock. These include a variety of laws to enhance *economic competition,* for example through telecommunications reform or trade liberalization. Also affected have been laws linked to *macroeconomic stability,* such as fiscal initiatives. Finally, the existing programs that seek to alleviate poverty and reduce the gap between the rich and poor, thus generating *equal opportunities,* were designed many years ago, in response to a different distributional challenge in a very different country and economy. It is necessary not only to inject fresh resources into these programs, but also to create *new* programs designed for the new order. The topic is naturally controversial, and as long as parliamentary procedures require near unanimity, it is very unlikely that changes of the necessary scope and magnitude will be enacted.

Among the most problematic of Congress's rules and procedures are the following. A two-thirds quorum is required not only when votes are cast but even during debate: written discussion and submissions for the record are not allowed. Bills must be voted on once in committee and then twice by the full Congress. Questions concerning a law's constitutionality are referred to the courts between the first and the second vote; a minority of members may even send the bill to the courts before the first vote. Every member may propose an unlimited number of amendments to a bill and is allocated a certain amount of time to argue for each proposal. Each motion to amend is debated and voted on separately, may be raised and re-raised in committee, and then raised and re-raised again before the full house.

Bills before Congress are discussed on a first-come, first-served basis unless a supermajority agrees otherwise, so a new and urgent proposal may have to wait years before being discussed. During some months every year, bills are discussed in the order the executive requests, but, unlike in other countries with a similar rule, the executive cannot force a vote on those bills. The chair has some tools to accelerate the proceedings, provided a two-thirds majority agrees, and even then the mechanics are very fickle and the dissenting minority can easily prevail. Any member may question the procedure and raise it before the Supreme Court. If the court finds any procedural mistake, even in form, the process must go back to the point where the mistake happened, even if this implies the invalidation of a vote.

These rules, cumbersome though they are, did not impede decision making for many years because they operated in a bipartisan setting, in which the two major parties used the rules of order as a bargaining tool, not as a means to paralyze a polarized Congress. The two leading parties held most of the seats in Congress and usually alternated the presidency. Because each party expected that it would someday be taking the place of the other, neither perceived any benefit from obstructionist practices. Both parties had knowledge of how public sector institutions worked, and the skills necessary for effective public management were preserved in a semi-professional political class. Although the parties had real and nontrivial ideological differences, they also shared core ideological values that made negotiation and agreement possible. Even the small regional parties that occasionally won seats in Congress could be brought to the table through the executive's authority to block the disbursement of local budgetary allocations. Anti-system parties, when they reached Congress, were weak enough to be easily neutralized.

These same rules in a Congress that is both multipartisan and ideologically polarized lead not to negotiation but to near paralysis. Even if the major players reach agreement on the agenda and on the content of key bills, any single member can filibuster any bill, because cloture requires a supermajority, which can rarely be achieved. Several parties in the current opposition are ideologically rather than regionally based, and so their agenda is nonnegotiable. Their members have very little high-level government experience and little expectation of winning actual power, so they have no vested interest in keeping things moving. On the contrary, some members respond to a constituency that, finding no basis of agreement with the majority, *wants* to see things blocked and the system collapse.

A Representative Process that Does Not Represent

Congressional elections in Costa Rica take place every four years, concurrently with presidential elections. Incumbents may not run for reelection—Costa Rica is one of the very few countries in the world where this rule applies.

Each province is allotted a number of congressional seats in proportion to its census population. Parties field lists of candidates for each province, and each party is awarded seats roughly according to the fraction of the total vote that its list receives.[6] These seats are assigned starting from the top of the list, regardless of how the votes are distributed across the province. Thus, members are not elected as individual representatives of a specific geographic area but represent the province at large.

Candidates on the lists are selected by party national assemblies, akin to party conventions in the United States. Although it is not compulsory, the candidates whose names end up on the list often have won nonbinding internal elections in their counties or regions. Nevertheless, the final decision of who shall appear on the list is made by the assembly as a whole, including the representatives elected from other regions. The all-important order of names on the list usually follows the size of the counties represented. Hence, the largest city or county in each province usually gets the top several spots on the list in each party, and thus several seats in Congress; candidates from smaller regions are usually put lower on the list, and thus these regions get no representation.

In the case of San José, the largest province by far and the one where most government, professional, and academic activity takes place, the top of the list is dominated not by local representatives, but rather by nationally known figures who are not linked to a particular county or town. Once elected, these members are even referred to as *diputados nacionales,* although on paper they represent San José.

What is wrong with these arrangements? One problem is that they make members of Congress largely unaccountable to the population. Most representatives are thought of as representing a county, and act accordingly, but in fact they are elected from a provincial party list. It is quite possible for a given candidate's party to lose in the candidate's county but (thanks to the votes cast for the other members on the list) win the province as a whole, in which case that candidate is sent to Congress instead of the candidate who actually won in that county, and instead of some of the candidate's fellow party members who won in their counties. If the reader finds this totally confusing, that is the point—so does the electorate. Nor

6. The formula used to calculate how many seats are allocated to each list assigns them relatively close to proportionality among those parties that meet a certain minimum vote. The minimum vote is smaller, the larger the number of seats allocated to the province.

is it surprising that, under this system, the representative's allegiance to his or her county often weakens once in Congress, all the more because the representative may not run for reelection and thus will not be facing the voters again.

In addition to this lack of accountability, there are marked asymmetries in party representation between different places in the country. The basic electoral unit is the province, and the country's provinces vary greatly in population (and thus in the number of representatives). Limón, the province with the smallest population, elects four members of Congress, and San José, with five times the population, elects twenty. As a result, what it takes to get elected to Congress differs from one place to another: small parties are viable in San José, but not in the rest of the country.

There are also large differences in the representation of different localities. Many places in Costa Rica effectively have no congressional representation at all, in the sense that nobody who actually campaigned there got elected. Thus, residents of these places have no local leader to turn to for support or intercession, and the result is limited *political competition,* which in turn limits the *broader sharing of the benefits of growth.* In other countries, small towns may not have a congressional seat of their own but are part of larger geographic units that do. In parts of Costa Rica, for example the sparsely populated counties in the north of Alajuela province, the answer to the question "Who is your congressman?" is, quite frankly, "Nobody."[7]

How to Deal with These Obstacles

The fundamental problem facing legislative reform in a system like Costa Rica's is that any such reform would take power away from those now impeding action, and they will surely use the power they have to prevent that from happening. Legislative reform requires legislative action, which, ironically, is almost impossible without legislative reform. The only way to resolve this catch-22 is through public awareness of the problems and their consequences, so that those who insist on preserving the status quo realize the ultimate political cost. Costa Ricans in general know that their political system is not producing the results they desire, and they are fairly discontented with it, but most are not well informed about the specific problems or the possible solutions, which in our view include the following.

The rules for elections should be changed. Electoral units should be smaller and all of uniform size, rather than coinciding with provinces. Then candidates who happen to come from smaller towns and counties will be running for office in a unit that is larger than their base community, rather than for unelectable spots

---

7. As an illustration of these asymmetries, consider the contrast between Puntarenas, the largest county in the province of that name, and Tibás, a large suburb north of San José. Because Puntarenas is always at the top of the provincial list for each party, Puntarenas County usually has three or four congressional seats. Tibás, with the same population, rarely holds one.

on provincial lists. This would leave no doubt about which members of Congress represent which voters. Accountability would be strengthened, and each citizen, no matter where he or she is from, would have equal representation in Congress. There is no reason in such a scenario to forbid reelection.

If the institution of *diputados nacionales* is to be preserved, as is probably convenient, these members should be explicitly elected from the country at large, rather than from the top of the San José list. This would require a separate ballot listing candidates for a specified number of national at-large seats, with all voters choosing individually from that list. The relationship between the citizen and the local member of Congress should apply no differently to residents of San José than to the rest of the country.

The above proposals relate to how representatives are selected. Obviously, something also needs to be done about the rules under which they operate once seated in Congress. First, bills before Congress should be subject to a fixed time period within which a vote on the bill has to be held. This period could be shortened under a cloture rule or extended, but only by explicit vote and with a supermajority; otherwise, debate should cease when time has expired. Rules limiting the ability of members to filibuster or otherwise block legislation should be strengthened.[8] Filibustering should not be completely outlawed, as it provides a means for a determined minority to be heard on matters of critical importance to it. But neither should it be easy, and in particular it should not be the mechanism that routinely determines the outcome of any debate.

Second, the executive should have the authority not only to set the congressional agenda during part of the year, but also to require that any initiatives that it introduces be voted on (not just debated) by the end of that period. The executive should also have a limited power to declare certain bills urgent, and subject to a shorter deadline, as is done in Chile, for example.

Third, members should be granted alternative ways of putting forward their positions on legislation before the house and of placing them on the record, for example by filing their opinions in writing, or presenting them orally during sessions when a quorum is not present. A quorum should be required only for votes, not for debate. There should also be a mechanism for proposing amendments that does not delay the proceedings of the full Congress.

Also in need of attention is the new law that allows matters to be settled by referendum. This law passed its first test with flying colors on the CAFTA (Central American Free Trade Agreement) vote. Of course, because the law requires that a minimum of 30 percent of voters (40 percent for certain types of laws) participate in order for a referendum to be binding, as a practical matter few issues can be

---

8. Recently, Congress instituted a new practice (rule 41.bis) that allows a limited version of cloture to be applied when two-thirds of the members so decide. This is a step in the right direction but still falls short of what is needed.

taken to a referendum between national elections.[9] But a number of issues could be decided by referendum on the same day as a national election, thus securing the minimum participation. The elections themselves may provide an opportune environment for those matters to be discussed, and for the people to empower a new government by passing beforehand some of its desired legal reforms, or to limit it by rejecting them. The advantage of a referendum is clear: the vote happens on a fixed date with no possibility of filibuster, the results are binding and highly legitimate in the eyes of the population, and, by construction, vocal minorities are less important than silent majorities.

Public Sector Administrative Reform

For all its past (and some current) achievements, the Costa Rican public sector has become a slow, cumbersome, and inefficient machine. Whereas financing was the binding constraint on the public sector in the immediate aftermath of the crisis of the 1980s, it is clear that an acute deterioration of managerial abilities, loss of talent to the private sector, a tangled web of regulations and audits, atomized authority, and overlapping jurisdictions are now crippling the public sector, even as the country's fiscal constraints have eased considerably. As a result, the Costa Rican public sector has lost much of its ability to deliver the services expected of it promptly and efficiently. Insofar as public sector action is needed to strengthen the growth foundations, the managerial and administrative problems just listed clearly have an impact on all of them.

Among the government agencies most affected by these problems are those in charge of education, public infrastructure, and social assistance. This has a direct impact on two of the foundations: *equality of opportunities* and the *broad sharing of the benefits of growth,* both of which are obviously connected to those areas of policy. *Economic competition* is also affected: for example, in a country like Costa Rica, which despite its small size has areas that are remote and physically isolated, the failure of the state to provide an adequate road network allows local providers of goods to enjoy considerable monopoly power. More generally, failure by the public sector to provide the essential services expected of it, and for which taxes have been paid, effectively dilutes *property rights,* as does arbitrary and time-consuming decision making by government agencies on matters that affect business operations. Inefficiencies in public administration also raise the cost of government itself, thus contributing adversely to *macroeconomic stability.*

How did this loss of public sector effectiveness come about? During the 1980s, and to some degree during the 1990s, government expenditure was severely restricted as the government struggled to rescue the economy from the

---

9. Initiating a referendum requires the signatures of at least 15 percent of the adult population, or a two-thirds vote of Congress, or the approval of the president and at least half of Congress. Tax bills and constitutional amendments may not be taken to referendum.

crisis of the 1980s and to restore fiscal and monetary equilibria. However, the indisputable fact that the public sector deficit had to be brought under control, together with the undeniable failure of heavy-handed state interventionism, was confused with the quite different and controversial thesis that government should simply be made smaller. What was really needed was to make government more efficient.

Making matters worse, it proved too difficult politically to conduct this downsizing according to well-defined priorities. Instead, restrictions on expenditure were imposed across the board, and a "voluntary labor mobility" program was put in place to reduce the number of public sector workers. Not surprisingly, those who decided to participate were by and large the best qualified, who had a reasonable chance of finding a good job in the private sector, and the most recently employed, who did not benefit from the *anualidades* (annual bonuses) that increase public sector wages each year, independent of performance or inflation adjustments. As the best, the brightest, and the youngest left, the general perception that public workers were less than competent was validated, thus supporting a trend toward government salaries dramatically lagging incomes in the private sector. In turn, the reduced prestige and pay of a government position made it difficult to recruit new talent into public service. Those workers who have remained in the public sector are entrenched by civil service legislation that conspicuously lacks performance-based incentives.

Only those institutions funded outside the general budget of the executive branch, such as the health care system and the state enterprises, were spared from this drain of human resources, and then only partly: legislation was passed that allowed the central government to put caps on investment and expenditure even on theoretically decentralized or autonomous institutions. Meanwhile hostile sentiment prevailed among those public servants who remained, prompted by feelings of persecution, the frustration of limited resources, and the stigma of being seen as "the ones who could not leave." Consequently, opinion among government workers started shifting toward the anti-reform camp, making it very difficult to implement policy.

At the same time, in an effort to better control corruption and pursue more advanced management techniques, an increasingly complex set of horizontal control regulations was put in place. Rules regarding public sector purchases became stricter, and rules regarding the formulation and execution of public sector budgets became more sophisticated in theory, but increasingly unmanageable in practice for a bureaucracy that was now much less talented than that for which the rules had been designed. Ironically, as the downsizing did not seem to follow a clear pattern, in some cases new institutions had to be created to manage the new controls and fill the most salient voids. These new supervisory agencies became politically important, as a perception of generalized corruption within government became widespread. As a result, controls became more rigid, making the interaction between private parties and the government more difficult.[10] The result, in short, has been paralysis, waste, and inefficiency, even in the provision of such basic functions of the state as public security and the administration of justice.

An Example: Bureaucratic Gridlock in Public Transportation Infrastructure

A case study will illustrate the kind of administrative ordeals that now afflict the public sector. Although several examples could be used, perhaps none is more telling than the case of the institutions that provide transportation infrastructure, and in particular the Ministry of Transportation and Public Works (Ministerio de Obras Públicas y de Transportación, or MOPT). The problems described here are not unique to MOPT; rather, it is used here as an example of a malaise that affects many agencies of government.

Historically, Costa Rica's infrastructure has been quite acceptable for a country at its level of development. The quality and density of roads, ports, power networks, telephone lines, and potable water systems were among the best in Latin America by the 1960s and 1970s. This infrastructure was built in a very bottom-up fashion, with the result that key "arteries" were often barely sufficient, but small-scale and regional "capillaries" were abundant, dense, and of high quality. Even today, what remains of these works is a valuable national asset; for example, Costa Rica still leads Latin America in kilometers of paved road per square kilometer of territory.

The slowdown and eventual halt of infrastructure development during and immediately after the 1980s debt crisis was hardly unique to Costa Rica. The building of public works came to a standstill everywhere in Latin America. What is peculiar is that Costa Rica continued on a path of very low investment even after the crisis was over.

The poor quality of roads and other public works today is a commonly expressed concern.[11] This is not surprising: between 1984 and 2005 the share of households that own a car rose from 14.1 percent to 35.1 percent, the population itself grew from 2.4 million to 4.5 million, and GDP climbed from $4.9 billion to $27 billion, yet not a single major road or highway was built. No one has gained any political capital by creating this problem. Tourists' complaints about potholes and road quality finally became so commonplace that the tourism industry, unable to do anything about the roads themselves, started advertising "adventure driving" as an attraction.

---

10. We are not arguing here that controls are unnecessary, but rather that the ones in place are very poorly designed. To give an example: a public works project may not start as soon as a bid has been awarded; instead, all grievances and appeals must first be resolved by the comptroller's office. In other countries such damages are settled and any guilt assessed and punished *after* the project has been completed.

11. According to the competitiveness index published annually by the World Economic Forum, Costa Rica ranked 52nd (among 125 countries) in overall competitiveness in 2006, but 73rd in infrastructure and 102nd in perceived road quality.

Not only are few road projects even attempted; those that are started frequently get frozen in their tracks. Public bids for the San José–San Ramón highway (the busiest part of the Inter-American Highway as it crosses Costa Rica) have been solicited several times, never to be completed. Perhaps even more dramatic is the construction of the highway from San José to Caldera, the country's main port on the Pacific. Half of the road (from San José to the exurb of Ciudad Colón) has existed for thirty years; the other half remains to be built, despite several attempts. Year after year has passed, and the section of the highway that connects Ciudad Colón with Caldera, plus all the main exchanges, remains unbuilt. Under a separate contract, several bridges were built (and paid for) and today stand idle, awaiting the road that someday will connect them. The project was funded by the Inter-American Development Bank almost thirty years ago; the loan was disbursed and was, in principle, payable. The problem was not the money: the contract has been awarded—twice, to no avail. At the time of this writing, after the highway has been contracted out for the third time in thirty years, there are reasons for mild optimism, yet the work has not begun.

Even small-scale projects are often delayed. After the need for a series of pedestrian bridges on the main highways near San José was given priority and notoriety in 2003, only in 2007 were the bridges finally built. Again the delay was caused not by lack of money, but rather by a series of institutional, legal, and administrative impediments that thwarted progress every time. The problem is the result of a strategic shift in the operation of MOPT that was only partially implemented, and of a growing web of verifications and approvals, which a downsized public sector lacks the capacity to handle.

During the downsizing of the public sector, the decision was made to transform the MOPT from a large construction company into a planning and supervising agency, contracting out some projects and overseeing build-operate-transfer (BOT) contracts where feasible. It was expected that this would result in significant efficiencies and savings. The ministry would no longer need such a large payroll, as private contractors, not the ministry, would hire construction workers and civil engineers. Nor would there be any need for the ministry to maintain a large stock of construction equipment.

This change in direction might have made perfect sense in a favorable fiscal situation. However, many crucial elements needed to make the strategy successful were not put in place. In particular, it was easy to strip the ministry of the resources it had needed in its former role, but what proved much harder was setting out the laws, rules, practices, and administrative capacities that would enable the institution to perform its new functions.

Building a road is not just a matter of engineering. It is, first of all, an administrative and legal problem. In Costa Rica the appeal of administrative decisions is a particularly lengthy process, the cost of filing frivolous appeals is negligible, and often public works construction is halted until the issues are solved. In other countries the works are continued and any damages paid ex post if the appeal is successful.

The operation of the legal system is costly and cumbersome. Until very recently, oral statements were invalid in civil matters; everything had to be in writing. Private written documents are also generally invalid unless notarized, yet only lawyers may notarize a document. Thus, a formality that costs about a dollar elsewhere can cost 1 percent of the value of the contract in Costa Rica. Requirements about form are unclear, and form very often prevails over content. The authorities may not, even for good reason, waive unneeded prerequisites or allow the correction of clerical mistakes. Mistakes in form either invalidate a bidder or take the project back to square one; efforts to expedite the process, even in good faith, put the public officials responsible in danger of criminal prosecution.

Audit procedures have also become increasingly cumbersome, in the mistaken belief that this makes them more effective. The Costa Rican public sector works under an ever-increasing and ever more complex set of horizontal verifications. The state comptrollers verify every aspect of policy and every step taken. The budget authority oversees everything and must preauthorize even the smallest expenditures. The planning ministry publishes each year an intractable National Development Plan, and by law every proposed investment must be justified in relation to the priorities and designs of that plan. Every government agency has its own internal auditor with extensive powers, with whom it is dangerous to honestly disagree. The National Secretariat for the Environment must approve many economic initiatives, even if the environmental effect is negligible.

The cost and difficulty of compliance are constantly increasing, and considerable administrative resources have to be devoted to these tasks alone. Whether or not these controls are actually necessary, it is clear that they could be made simpler with no loss of effectiveness. The requirements imposed on public sector management have been increasing at the same time that its capabilities have diminished. The result, quite predictably, is decreasing effectiveness of the public sector.

Finally, the personal and civil responsibilities and the potential for criminal liability faced by poorly paid public sector workers (including those at the cabinet level) who make the final decisions are daunting. In an attempt to prevent corruption, the law now punishes the bureaucrat who makes an honest mistake almost as harshly as one who profits illegally. The consequence is that even small decisions become daunting, and decision-makers are tempted to take any opportunity to annul or delay a public act, or to make decisions on formalistic grounds rather than on content.

DEALING WITH THE OBSTACLES

There is universal agreement that the nation's public services have serious problems, but the solutions are controversial and cut across several political debates. Private sector participation in some services is a big part of the answer, but unfortunately, enough political power still lies with those who miss the old, state-centered system that any proposal along these lines becomes a matter for interminable dispute. At the same time, however, strengthening public institutions will require additional resources and perhaps a larger public sector payroll, both of which are opposed by those who still regard the downsizing undertaken to date as an important and difficult achievement. Finally, freeing the process from unnecessary audits and redundant rules might be perceived or portrayed by some as an attempt to facilitate corruption, especially in the context of recent, widely publicized scandals. Indeed, in the wake of these scandals, the conventional wisdom seems to be that even more regulation is needed, when in fact the reverse is true.

Nevertheless, it is clear that in order to recover the ability of the state to implement policy and provide the services expected of it, actions need to be taken on several fronts. First, the *administrative, managerial, and technical capacities* of the public sector need to be strengthened. This will require a different system of selection, recruitment, and retention of civil servants, one that facilitates the firing of corrupt and incompetent employees and the hiring of honest and capable ones. Among other things, this implies both paying higher wages and raising the public perception of government service.

Second, the *legal framework* needs to be modified. This includes, but is not limited to, minimizing the number of opportunities for appeal; revising the procedures governing BOT and other public-private contracts along the lines that have worked in other countries; and simplifying red tape by making all defects of form more readily solvable, while encouraging officials to base their decisions more on substance and less on form. It also means making comptroller, audit, and court decisions punitive in nature rather than preventive: legal controversies should be dealt with through ex post settlement rather than ex ante delay, except in areas, such as the environment, where this would be dangerous.

Third, although the government no longer faces the same stringent fiscal constraints as in the past (in part precisely because worthwhile public investments were delayed), increasing spending will not solve the problem by itself. More resources are needed, but it is also important to restore some notion of *budgetary priorities,* so that direct provision of services by the state in key areas does not come at the expense of hard-won fiscal stability. No solution is going to work if it has to be applied across the board.

Tax and Budgetary Reform

Although Costa Rica has made significant progress toward macroeconomic stability and has avoided financial crisis for over twenty-five years, the job is not complete. As we have already seen, fiscal balance has been achieved at the cost of reducing and postponing capital expenditure, and the consequences have built up over the years. "No matter what we do, it is always a war economy," complained a former president. Even after enormous sacrifice, government finances have often been frail. There is also a persistent quasi-fiscal problem in the form of a central bank deficit; this has fueled inflation, which, although lower than in the past, stubbornly remains between 10 and 15 percent year after year. Costa Rica went from having the second-lowest inflation rate in Latin America in the mid-1980s, to the second-highest in 2005.

According to official data, Costa Rica emerged from the 1980–82 crisis with a public debt in excess of 135 percent of GDP, most of which was owed abroad. This debt burden fell consistently in the 1980s and early 1990s and has fallen very quickly since 2005, so the debt burden is expected to be under 40 percent by the end of this year, and only a third of that is foreign debt. Central government deficits have averaged around 3 percent of GDP since stabilization—at the cost of very tight budgeting—and have turned into surpluses in the last couple of years. As a consequence of administrative improvements in the tax authority, central government revenue as a fraction of GDP has risen consistently in the last ten years, although it still barely reaches 15 percent.[12] Despite this progress, revenue still falls short of what is needed to raise infrastructure, education, and social expenditures to adequate levels and further secure financial stability.

Impact on the Growth Foundations

Stated quite simply, the revenues of the Costa Rican state are insufficient to its needs, and this fact has a negative impact on all of the growth foundations. In particular, true *macroeconomic stability,* under a government that fulfills the expectations of its population, will require that more resources be directed to the government. A substantial tax reform is needed.

Some of the other growth foundations would benefit from tax and budgetary reform. The *broader sharing of the benefits of growth* requires a government that can afford to make certain public investments, including in education and transportation infrastructure. An increasingly equitable income distribution will require expenditure on a variety of support and redistributive activities and the provision of basic services. A government that can attend to those needs without sacrificing fiscal stability is perhaps the key to bringing about sufficiently *equal opportunities.* But it is precisely these types of investments and expenditures that are being sacrificed in Costa Rica, at an enormous cost, in the pursuit of preserving an erratic macroeconomic stability in the absence of higher tax collections.

Yet even that frugality is not enough. Congress has frequently passed small tax adjustments, barely enough to maintain the status quo, only to be followed by a

12. This number does not include all parts of the Costa Rican public sector, which contains a series of institutions that are funded separately from the central treasury and function somewhat better. Notable among these is the national health care and social security system, managed by the Caja Costarricense del Seguro Social, which gets its resources from a tax on wages and handles them independently of the central government. Another separately funded agency is the job training institution (the Instituto Nacional de Aprendizaje, or INA).

new tax bill a few years later, usually at the beginning of a new administration: every new administration but one in the last twenty-four years has submitted a tax bill to Congress early in its tenure. The finances of the other nonfinancial public institutions have also been kept under tight control, at the very significant cost of postponing for decades necessary investments in infrastructure as well as upgrades and improvements in social services, so as to keep public sector deficits within narrow margins.

The pursuit of stable public finances without adequate tax collection also causes political difficulty. The government that most Costa Ricans expect, and that many anti-reform forces—including public sector workers—remember fondly, is much bigger than the government that the country can currently afford. The government of that earlier era also had the flexibility to budget strategically and according to priorities, which today's government does not have.

This lack of flexibility is due to the fact that an overwhelming majority of fiscal revenue is needed just to cover payroll, debt service, pensions, and other preallocated expenses that are fixed by law or, in some cases, by the constitution itself, and therefore difficult to change. Budgetary stability has thus been achieved at the expense of any discretionary spending that can be postponed in the short run, including strategic projects and, of course, investments in sustained long-term growth. Preallocated expenditures include, among other things, not only spending on social programs but also government salaries and collective action agreements with public sector unions; special, treasury-funded pension regimes; interest payments; legal mandates (earmarks) to transfer certain percentages of specific taxes to predetermined uses (such as road construction or certain special social programs); and constitutional mandates to transfer fixed percentages of revenue to the public university system, the judiciary, and local governments. Figure 2 shows the fraction of tax revenue spent annually on these entitlements over the last two decades. In many years over 90 percent of revenues were precommitted under these provisions, and even then some of the constitutionally mandated items were in fact not met.

Meanwhile the central bank has incurred losses every year since the mid-1980s, usually well above 1 percent of GDP. The government has been able to absorb only part of the resulting quasi-fiscal debt, and these payments, together with greater exchange rate flexibility, have allowed the central bank to bring down inflation somewhat in recent years. But it is becoming difficult for the central bank to sterilize the impact of its financial losses even to the tune of 1 percent of GDP, because it has had to adopt a more contractionary stance to offset other sources of money creation in the economy. Either the government will have to absorb a larger share of the central bank's losses, which means raising taxes since it cannot do much to lower expenditure, or inflation will remain high. As with several other reforms, the technical solution is plain, but the political solution has been so far impossible to discern.

Figure 2. *Precommitted Government Revenue, 1987–2007*

Percent of total revenue

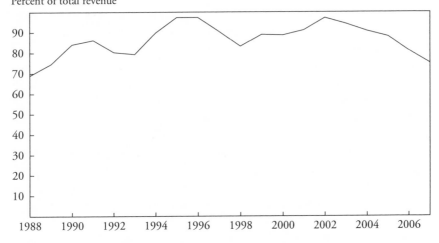

Source: CEFSA, using statistics from the Central Bank of Costa Rica.

The recurring theme here is that fiscal balance, although a good thing in and of itself, has been achieved at the expense of investment in the country's long-term growth, and at the cost of moderately high inflation, which grows out of the country's quasi-fiscal problems and the choice of monetary policy. To recover the capability of the national government to spend—without sacrificing stability—on infrastructure, education, and income redistribution; to deliver on the broad set of public goods and services that Costa Ricans expect from the state; and to lower inflation to international levels, taxes need to be raised by perhaps 2 or 3 percent of GDP or more. This increase in revenue, moreover, should not come solely from higher tax rates, but mainly from an expansion of the tax base and the closing of loopholes, which might even allow for rate reductions in some cases. The adjustment should be fair, thus eliminating the odd asymmetries in the tax burdens often confronted by Costa Ricans with similar incomes. It should certainly be progressive, because income distribution has worsened significantly over the years. It should allow for further improvements in the effectiveness of tax collection, of the kind that has been enjoyed in the last three years. Finally, it should be politically viable, not only because any reform will have to pass Congress, but also because a broad discussion of the costs and benefits of government is important if the country is to return to cohesion in national politics and chart a clear path forward.

OBSTACLES AND SOLUTIONS

Taxes can be modified only through changes in the law, and this means going through Congress. As we have seen, in Costa Rica the perception that government

should do more is so widespread that a majority of parties already agree in principle to a progressive and comprehensive increase in the tax burden. Yet as we have
also seen, current parliamentary rules and procedures make it very easy to postpone or even prevent a vote on any law that faces forceful opposition, even one
that has majority support.

And tax increases do face forceful opposition. At the very least, the Libertar-
ian Party, for which lower taxes are the dominant issue on the agenda, is large
(five members in Congress) and vocal enough to act as a severe bottleneck. Past
experience also indicates that even when the two largest parties agree on the general principle (in this case, a progressive increase in the tax burden), they find it
impossible to agree on any of the important details. Other parties that have
acted as allies of the administration on other issues, but that have no expectation of returning to the presidency any time soon, probably would not support
tax reform. These problems loom all the larger because tax laws cannot be passed
by referendum.

Other obstacles lie ahead on the path to tax reform. First, such reforms tend to
be complex, because part of what is needed relates to administration, collection
procedures, and the structure of the tax authority. Second, any tax reform also
tends to have large numbers of small winners (the many citizens who would like
government to do more) and small numbers of large losers (those who today enjoy
exclusions and loopholes), and the latter usually win. Third, tax reforms easily run
afoul of ideological divisions, and even parties that agree on the general principle
of progressive taxation have never failed to disagree on which taxes are progressive
and which are not. Fourth, many Costa Ricans may feel that the problem will fix
itself, given that tax revenue has grown faster than the economy since 2000, without any new taxes being enacted, because of administrative improvements in the
tax authority, technological changes (collection becomes easier as more transactions involve credit cards, bank instruments, or international payments instead of
cash), and the virtuous cycle that sets in as government borrows less, interest rates
fall, the deficit falls further, and so on.

But even all these factors together will not be enough to provide the needed
revenue; new taxes are necessary. Their approval in Congress will depend, of
course, on the political attractiveness of their design and on finding a solution to
the legislative procedural problems discussed above. The following strategic considerations may help to make tax reform politically viable:

• It is important in any tax reform to create winners. There have to be identi-
fiable groups that benefit from the expansion of the tax base, the lowering of the
tax rate, or the funding and credibility of any earmarked expenses.

• It may be easier to pass tax changes individually rather than as a comprehensive reform. The argument that no government has enough political capital for
more than one tax reform, and that therefore it is better to load everything into
one package, has yet to be validated in practice.

• The weaknesses of the current tax system allow some profound changes to the system to be defended as "closing loopholes" (always a popular argument) rather than levying new taxes. For example, under current law a company paying sales tax on the purchase of an input may not claim a credit for that tax payment when it sells the resulting output, and this creates incentives for both parties to hide the transaction. Allowing the credit would likely generate more net revenue by bringing more of these transactions into the open. It is also hard to defend the present exemption of several hundred products from sales tax. Another example is Costa Rica's territorial tax treatment of foreign income: residents pay Costa Rican income tax only on income generated in Costa Rica. This made sense when the country's tight balance of payments situation provided a reason for the government to encourage Costa Ricans to earn money abroad. But a move to worldwide taxation, in which all income is taxed whether generated in Costa Rica or abroad, would raise more needed revenue without raising tax rates or introducing "new" taxes. Although returns to offshore capital would be hard to identify, returns to labor would not be.

• Under the present income tax structure, each source of personal income is taxed separately, impeding true progressivity. For example, in Costa Rica, a worker with a full-time job faces a higher marginal tax rate, and thus pays more tax, than another worker who earns the same amount at two part-time jobs, because the tax system treats the latter the same as if he or she were two separate individuals. This system needs to be replaced with a global personal income tax in which each individual reports all income from all sources on a single tax form and pays accordingly.

• The current corporate income tax regime has too many deductions and exemptions. Eliminating these would both make filing simple and allow a lower tax rate, which would be politically popular as well as easier to administer. Depending on the rate chosen, it could also generate more revenue, especially if the base were broadened at the same time.

• Taxing obvious displays of wealth and ostentatious consumption at higher rates would be popular, progressive, and a quick, effective way of raising revenue. A proposal is already before Congress to increase the tax rate paid on houses that exceed a certain value and on second homes.

• Current penalties for tax evasion, even when it involves flagrant misrepresentation and perjury, are weaker than they should be, and limited to fines rather than prison sentences. Strengthening these penalties and their enforcement would be not only politically tolerable but even popular, except of course among those who get caught.

Telecommunications Reform

Telecommunications is the most important economic activity still operating as a monopoly in Costa Rica, and therefore reform in this area is key to promoting *economic competition*. Reform should aim not only at increasing the number of participants in the provision of telecommunications services. It should also seek to improve market access, reduce risk, and lower transaction costs, so as to extend access to better telecommunications services to the general population, with positive effects on competition throughout the economy. These reforms also would reinforce *macroeconomic stability,* as the contingent liability resulting from the state monopoly's operations currently poses a threat to fiscal balance.

Telecommunications is also one of the few areas in which a broad problem of undefined *property rights* exists in Costa Rica. The effort to sustain a legal monopoly in the sector after the economic and technical foundations of a natural monopoly disappeared has led to the emergence of a gray (and in some cases a black) market. Operators in this market lack secure rights to conduct their business, whether through an explicit concession, for services that exploit goods in the public domain, or a clear-cut legal permit, for other services. Some of these services include Internet cafés, Internet telephone (VoIP) services, and direct satellite access to the Internet.[13]

It now looks as if, finally, competition in some telecommunications services will happen in 2009 or 2010, as part of the implementation of CAFTA. However, attempts to liberalize the sector go all the way back to the administration of José Figueres in 1994–98, which raises the question of what has taken Costa Rica so long to get rid of a technologically obsolete monopoly. By many measures, the performance of the government monopoly, Telecomunicaciones ICE, in the more modern telecommunications services, especially cellular phones and Internet access, has been quite disappointing. Freeing the company from some of its current financial and administrative constraints will quite probably not be enough, and it involves some risk. It is worth noting that the repeated attempts at telecommunications reform under the last three administrations not only all failed but also turned the issue into the most heated topic in the political debate.

Costa Ricans are Fond of Their Public Utilities

Reform efforts in the telecommunications sector have aimed at moving from a state monopoly to regulated competition. The arguments against a publicly owned monopoly have been twofold: a privatization argument and an anti-monopoly argument:

• Privatization arguments are of different kinds: ideological (the government is incapable of running a large business efficiently), fiscal (the sale of public assets will reduce the public debt), and opportunity cost–based (if the private sector is willing to invest in telecommunications, public resources should not be devoted to the sector but instead focused on areas where private investment is not forthcoming).

---

13. DirectTV is offered in the country, but the company may not offer Internet access. Some companies set up their own antennas, and the telecommunications monopoly spends considerable resources trying to prevent such illegal connections.

• On the other hand, standard economic theory provides very sound efficiency arguments against monopolies, which need not be repeated here, but these have nothing to do with privatization.

Unfortunately, these two lines of argument have frequently been confused in discussions of privatization in Latin America, and this helps explain why reform has proved so difficult in Costa Rica.

Privatization arguments have not had much traction in Costa Rica, and for good reason: the publicly owned telecommunications company delivered services of good quality cheaply, with extensive coverage and access to at least some services (public telephones) for a large percentage of the population. Meanwhile the opportunity cost argument had no merit: the telecommunications utility has consistently funded itself from its own operations, not from general government revenue. Nor has the fiscal argument had much relevance, or at least it has not today: the public sector debt is shrinking and the government finances are in surplus.

However, three factors eventually resulted in a growing sense of frustration with telecommunications services and in support for market liberalization (but not for privatization):

• investment restrictions placed on the telecommunications utility as a means of restraining central government deficits;

• changes in technology that turned a natural monopoly into a potentially competitive market; and

• "capture" of the company both by its unions and by corrupt politicians, resulting in (to put it euphemistically) inefficient resource allocation.

Technological change seems to have posed a particularly difficult challenge: in the absence of competition, the public telecommunications company had no incentives to adapt, innovate, and learn. It even tried to prevent the adoption of new technologies (such as VoIP) and clung to old-fashioned technology (switches instead of routers). Mobile services were cheap but of low quality, cumbersome to acquire, and with long waiting lists.

Why hasn't telecommunications reform advanced in Costa Rica at the pace it has in other countries? First, since for most of its history the state monopoly had provided adequate service, especially in fixed lines and electricity (the same company also operates the electric power monopoly), many assumed that the problem was not the lack of competition, but rather the details of implementation. Meanwhile, in the heated political debate, confusion was created between opening to regulated competition, on the one hand, and privatization, on the other. Aware of ill-designed and poorly executed privatizations in other countries, many Costa Ricans opposed any reform, fearing it was a Trojan horse for privatization. Furthermore, corruption scandals involving two former presidents, among other public officials, raised suspicions about any and all reform proposals. All these reasons were craftily exploited by a well-organized and well-funded union in the state monopoly with a vested interest in preventing competition, and by disgruntled anti-reform leaders on the left and in the public sector, who saw the state monopoly in such an important business as the most visible survivor of the former, more statist economy they still venerated.

How to Deal with the Obstacles to Reform

With the approval of CAFTA by popular referendum on October 7, 2007, liberalization of some segments of telecommunications (mobile telephone services, private networks, Internet services) has become a legal mandate. The implementing legislation was passed on June 4, 2008. Because this came after a popular vote on this specific subject, and after a thorough debate, the political momentum indicates that regulated competition is finally going to happen. It is equally important that the implementation of this new legislation be technically flawless, that regulators perform the tasks prescribed in the laws, and that the leaders of the public company, which will remain in business but no longer as a monopolist, prepare it to thrive under the new reality.

Transparency in this process is key. Any hint of wrongdoing in the liberalization process—in particular, in the assignment of the first concession for mobile services—will be cited by opponents as proof that they were right and that liberalization should be reversed. The necessary institutions are in place to make the process transparent, with no political tampering. If the authorities want this process to succeed, they should exercise exceptionally close oversight to make sure the process works as expected, without so much as a hint of corruption.

Also, the introduction of one private operator does not by itself create a competitive market; true competition will emerge only with broad market entry. International experience demonstrates consistently that mobile telephone services retain a highly concentrated structure, especially, and for a longer period, when the starting point is a dominant operator with sole control of all the infrastructure and very strong incentives to deny, delay, or otherwise hinder interconnection with the backbone. Therefore, a *strong regulatory authority* that is not shy about using its power is crucial to prevent abuses or anticompetitive practices on the part of either the incumbent or new entrants.

Finally, the key element that may tip the balance in favor of a liberalized market is *customer education*. Unlike foreign investors and locals with foreign exposure, most Costa Ricans have no experience of anything beyond the service that the government monopoly now provides. They have nothing to compare it with and therefore do not know what they have a right to expect and demand. A better-informed public will exert stronger market discipline on all participants in the sector.

Trade Policy Reform

Trade liberalization (in particular, export promotion) and the attraction of FDI have been key policy initiatives over the last twenty years, and the results have been mostly successful. Despite this progress, however, trade policy remains a critical area for further reform, because it affects all of the growth foundations, although some more than others.

Any business environment in which new products are constantly emerging, producers are forced to compete, and activities with high employment potential are unleashed is conducive to greater *equality of opportunities.* Such an environment is more likely to develop in a dynamic, diversified economy that is open to foreign trade. Unskilled workers in such an economy—for example, in the textile sector—find manufacturing employment where before they only had access to lower productivity jobs in the services or in agriculture; professionals in certain fields find private sector jobs where in the past only government jobs existed.

THE FIRST FRUITS OF TRADE AND INVESTMENT REFORM

In Costa Rica, export-led growth has been accompanied over the last decade by widespread job creation, and the emergence of dynamic, internationally competitive technology and services sectors has allowed a trained and educated workforce to command a higher premium for their human capital, thus allowing the *benefits of growth to be shared more broadly.* A recent study by PROCOMER (Costa Rica's export promotion agency) indicates that out of a workforce of 1.5 million, 294,000 workers have jobs in firms that export directly 20 percent or more of their output. According to the national income accounts, export value added accounted for 50.6 percent of GDP in 2006. It is well established that labor, the relatively abundant factor in a poor country, is better rewarded under trade than under autarky.

High import barriers turn small markets into oligopolies, limiting *economic competition.* They also make the protection of those barriers the main driver of profitability, allowing concentration of political power and reducing *political competition.* Also, in several key services –telecommunications, electric power generation, and insurance–where the government has monopoly rights and the lack of competition is very damaging, the path to more competition goes through trade. Meanwhile export-led growth has helped improve the fiscal balance, stabilize the foreign exchange market, and allow the central bank to accumulate reserves, thus also contributing to *macroeconomic stability.*

Costa Rica was a largely closed economy from the 1950s until the mid-1980s. Since then the country has pursued integration into international markets, promoted export-led growth, and sought to attract FDI. This shift in policy was originally prompted by the urgency of the balance of payments situation during the 1980s debt crisis, and by the aspiration toward export-led growth at times when the local market was under tight financial constraints. Over time these objectives evolved, and Costa Rica came to focus more on the diversification and sophistication of its exports and on using FDI to pursue the transition to a knowledge-based economy.

The results have been fairly impressive; indeed, trade has been the main driver of economic growth. Since the early 1980s, exports have multiplied twelvefold and have diversified and become much more sophisticated; FDI per capita is among the highest in the hemisphere—and eight times China's. Real growth in goods exports accounted for 64.7 percent of total GDP growth between 1995 and 2004, with exports of services accounting for an extra 19 percent.

Even as traditional exports (coffee, bananas, and sugar) doubled between 1982 and 2007, a series of new agricultural products (mostly tropical fruits, tubers, ornamentals, fish, and processed foods) emerged, making Costa Rica the world's sixth-largest agricultural exporter on a per capita basis. Manufacturing exports were less than $300 million in 1982 and went entirely to the protected Central American Common Market; by 2007 they had grown to over $7 billion, including a number of high-technology products, both from local firms and from affiliates of foreign multinationals. Costa Rica has also become an important worldwide provider of services ranging from ecological and adventure tourism to business services, "nearsourcing," and information technology. As they have grown, exports have become more diversified: traditional commodities fell from 61 percent of total exports in 1982 to only 13 percent today. They have also become more sophisticated: many of Costa Rica's goods and services exports are intensive in human capital, technology, and advanced inputs.[14]

The stock of FDI has been estimated at nearly $6.7 billion in 2006; FDI inflows rose from around $200 million annually in the 1980s, to $600 million in the 1990s, to $1.4 billion in 2007. These flows have been of fairly high quality, involving relatively sophisticated companies, dominant in their markets, in sectors that are considered strategic for the country. Most of this FDI is greenfield—new capital entering the country to create new private productive capacities—rather than the acquisitions, purchases of mining rights, and privatizations prevalent in the rest of Latin America.

Trade policy reform since the mid-1980s has been implemented gradually but consistently through a variety of instruments. Much liberalization has taken place through unilateral reduction of import barriers: tariffs fell from an (unweighted) average of 54.9 percent in 1986 to 3.3 percent in 2005. Like many other countries, Costa Rica offers tax incentives for investment in the form of a free trade zone (FTZ) regime, for mobile FDI that meets a minimum export performance requirement. Companies in FTZs pay no indirect taxes on domestic purchases, international trade, profits, or dividends and have access to special, simplified administrative procedures for all imports and exports. Exporters also have enjoyed a competitive exchange rate: to avoid overappreciation of the local currency and volatility in export returns, from 1984 to 2007 the central bank maintained a nearly constant real exchange rate by applying a system of daily small corrections

14. Lall, Weiss, and Zhang (2006) develop an index of export sophistication, which relates products to the income per capita of the country that exports them. They find that Costa Rica's exports are more than one standard deviation more sophisticated than predicted by its income per capita—despite the fact that the index treats tropical agricultural products as unsophisticated.

in the nominal exchange rate, targeted to offset the differences in inflation between Costa Rica and its trading partners. Before 1998 there were also incentives for exports, in particular a subsidy (known as CAT) for exports of new products equivalent to 15 percent of the gross exported value. This controversial instrument eventually became too expensive and distortionary and a temptation for corruption; early on, however, it was an effective incentive for local firms to enter international markets.

More strategically, the Costa Rican government has procured preferential market access to most of its major export markets, through participation in preference regimes established by developed nations, membership in the Central American Common Market, bilateral free trade agreements with a majority of its trading partners,[15] two dozen bilateral investment treaties, and active engagement in multilateral negotiations. It has also developed a series of support institutions for trade, including a dedicated ministry (the Ministerio de Comercio Exterior, or COMEX) for trade policy and international negotiations. Within COMEX a specialized office oversees the implementation of the country's international trade agreements, and PROCOMER, a hybrid public-private institution, is in charge of export promotion, logistics and tax collection in the export-import process, and the administration of the FTZ regime. A private nonprofit institution, CINDE, is charged with the tasks of attracting FDI, promoting the country "brand," identifying and luring potential investors, and acting as a think tank on issues of business climate and competitiveness.

THE REMAINING REFORM AGENDA

Past achievements notwithstanding, the pending trade and investment agenda is very important. National productivity and competitiveness require further attention and a fully articulated national policy where now only certain uncoordinated elements, for example in tourism and nontraditional exports, are in place. Also needed is an enhancement of PROCOMER's activities in helping small and medium-size producers reach the international market, as well as more technical assistance from other agencies.

A variety of measures of bureaucratic costs and barriers indicate that these are on the rise (see World Bank, 2007). Most important, the weakness of the government agencies in charge of infrastructure and education, plus the lack of competition in telecommunications and problems with the national energy strategy, significantly increases the cost of doing business in Costa Rica and limits

---

15. Free trade agreements are in place with Mexico, Canada, Chile, the Dominican Republic, and CARICOM; pending ratification with the United States; and pending implementation with Panama. Negotiations have been started with the European Union. These agreements have also been instrumental in obtaining commitment to some necessary reforms and establishing competitive rights for investors. Once all these agreements are implemented, Costa Rica will have secure, enhanced market access in the countries that currently absorb 93 percent of its exports.

competitiveness. A number of recent projects by the private sector offer some hope of filling the gap left by the public sector's lack of capacity. These projects include, among others, the analysis of competitive clusters by INCAE, a prestigious business school; efforts by CINDE to reduce the backlog in second-language education; and a strategy for national technological development proposed by a leading group of scientists. But sufficient momentum is so far lacking.

A more pedestrian, but urgent, need is to fix the FTZ regime. Rulings by the World Trade Organization indicate that middle-income countries like Costa Rica will no longer be in compliance with GATT regulations if they maintain a regime of tax incentives based on an export performance requirement after 2013. Although this presents a difficult legal problem, it also provides an opportunity to give the regime a needed overhaul. This could include differentiated incentives for firms established in less developed regions of the country: FDI (except for tourism and agriculture) has tended to concentrate in the San José metropolitan area, where infrastructure is better and human capital more abundant. Another important task is to eliminate the extra administrative burden when inputs are of local origin, which acts as a disincentive for FTZ firms to source locally. Finally, there are currently no instruments linked to training, R&D, or other strategic activities. The problem, here as elsewhere, is that any solution has to go through Congress.

Some FTA negotiations are still pending. The Association Agreement with the European Union has huge potential and promises to reduce dependence on the U.S. market. Central America is one of the world's leading providers of bananas, sugar, fruits, and textiles, and the EU market is large. The challenge is not just to achieve an agreement, but to ensure that it provides adequate market access. Central America would be the first FTA partner of the European Union that directly competes with former European colonies, so there is pressure to avoid the erosion of their preferences. Another negotiation that will require much thought is that on the transformation of the Central American Common Market into a customs union. Although this is bound to be a lengthy process, recent progress has been remarkable. Finally, the enactment of CAFTA is, as of this writing, almost complete but not guaranteed. Even after the popular vote ratified the agreement into law, the implementing legislation was successfully delayed by an opposition filibuster in Congress.

Another challenge is to reduce market concentration in the logistics and commercialization of imported goods. The oligopolistic organization of these markets implies that some of the gains from the phase-out of trade barriers will be appropriated by importers and fail to reach the final consumer. The government institutions that oversee and regulate competition need to be strengthened, and anti-competitive practices in international trade need to be more clearly contained.

Finally, further success in international trade requires progress in the other areas of reform discussed in this chapter. The legal and administrative constraints choking much of the Costa Rican state affect specifically the provision of education and infrastructure. Certain plant-level manufacturing skills are becoming increasingly scarce, because the education and training systems cannot churn out graduates fast enough in areas such as metal mechanics. The scarcity of some white-collar skills, including in information technology, at both the professional and the pre-college level, is also becoming acute. Also prominent is the need to enhance investment in the foreign language skills of the country's technicians and professionals. Similar weaknesses afflict logistics and transportation infrastructure.

An important step toward maturity has been reached in some industries for a broad spectrum of firms, where it is no longer a case of looking for a pioneer investor or the first exporter, but rather trying to integrate backward or to develop strategic linkages. These broader industry objectives will require strategic policy action.

In Costa Rica, as in all countries, there are opponents to market-oriented reform. They have a large variety of motivations and objectives but are increasingly focused on halting or reversing trade liberalization. Anti-globalization feelings seem to outrank other political objectives. Policy opposition to further market-driven reform—and electoral opposition, in the form of new parties hoping to get elected by capturing the anti-reform vote—see trade reform as the front line; to stop it is to stop other reforms.

Broad consultation within the country and internal negotiation with key local commercial interests are key to overcoming these political obstacles. The consultation process must be conducted in a way that benefits participants, first of all, by listening to them, and then keeps them politically committed to what they have said and accepted. Documenting the process is perhaps just as important.

Meanwhile the opportunities generated by trade should be made more widely accessible. There has been significant progress: many small agricultural producers are now exporters, for example, and many jobs have been created, through trade and investment, for professional, skilled, and unskilled workers alike. But geographic barriers remain to be overcome: the dynamic new sectors have concentrated in the country's central valley, because incentives, infrastructure, and training facilities are lacking in the rest of the country. And those with access to better education certainly gain more than the rest.

Lessons from the Costa Rican Experience

The previous section analyzed five areas of reform that we consider particularly relevant and interesting, both in the context of explaining Costa Rica's growth performance and in the context of applying the CGD framework. We now focus our attention on the latter.

Latin America's economic performance seems, at first glance, to fit the framework. In the case of Costa Rica, *property rights* are comparatively well established, even in the most complex areas such as intellectual property. Costa Rica has also improved its *macroeconomic performance* quite dramatically since the crisis of the 1980s, achieving stability in terms of debt reduction, fiscal performance, financial market regulation, and balance of payments sustainability. The result has been twenty-five years without a macro-financial crisis. More important, Costa Rica built a broad network of infrastructure and government services throughout the twentieth century, including significant investments in human capital, which allowed a much *broader sharing of the benefits of growth* than its neighbors enjoyed, as well as political stability and huge potential for raising productivity. *Political competition* has long existed in this old democracy, which is full of mechanisms for allowing minority opinions to be heard. Once a degree of economic liberalization had taken place, along with aggressive and successful trade and investment policies, Costa Rica also saw greatly enhanced *economic competition,* whose benefits, through massive job creation and the higher valuation of human capital, were widely (but unevenly) shared. As a result, growth was relatively rapid. In these matters Costa Rica ranks, in our opinion, second only to Chile in the hemisphere in the post–debt crisis period. And the fact that Costa Rica also ranks second only to Chile in accumulated growth is a strong endorsement, again in our opinion, of the CGD framework.

Yet the paradox that we pointed out at the beginning of this chapter—how success at reform has been accompanied by strong (but still minority) hostility to further reform—also fits this theoretical framework. What explains the paradox, in our view, is the fact that, in the last few years, the two most salient characteristics that separate Costa Rica from the pack of Latin American countries—the broad sharing of growth benefits and the country's relatively equitable income distribution—have eroded.

As we have seen, Costa Rica did a fairly good job of protecting the poor and reducing the poverty rate in the aftermath of the 1980s crisis. Although progress in reducing poverty later stagnated, social programs were protected, so that even the poor had access to health care, education, potable water, and other support services. But pressures on the equality of income distribution have grown worldwide in the last few years, and policies aimed at confronting them have not emerged at the same pace.

We should underline that it is neither economic growth itself nor the policies that Costa Rica has enacted in the pursuit of that growth that have allowed the income distribution to deteriorate. Other countries with more lackluster growth performance have also suffered a rise in inequality. And in Costa Rica, as shown above, the subperiod of the last twenty-five years that recorded the fastest growth (2003–07) was also one in which growth was pro-poor, even under a strong definition. Those with little human capital and serious social problems, who as a consequence find themselves in the bottom 20 percent of the income distribution, require more than employment opportunities and overall economic growth to improve their lot. We believe that reversing the policies that have increased growth would do nothing to enhance equity; instead, what is needed is to complement these policies with stronger and more innovative social policies aimed directly at the distribution problem. This has not happened, perhaps in part because of the real financial constraints faced by the Costa Rican state (and the perception on the part of some that the state needs to remain small and neutral), but also in part because of the institutional and political barriers to action that we have described and that affected not only economic policy reform but reform of social policy as well.

Although Costa Rica's income distribution deteriorated during most if not all of the last twenty-five years, the *broad sharing* foundation also weakened, as another group in the population besides the very poorest has failed to share fully in the benefits of growth, namely, the segment of the middle class that works (or expects to work) in the public sector. This group has been affected by the slow-down of job creation in the public payroll, by the relatively low wages that the government pays its skilled workers, and by the weakening of their benefits and of their standing in society. Their active opposition to reform, their participation in the "globaphobic" sentiments now being widely voiced, and their attraction to anti-democratic political forces are easy to understand in these circumstances, and these factors have given rise to new parties that could flourish in the country's unique institutional and political milieu.

In conclusion, both the rapid and accelerating economic growth that Costa Rica enjoyed during 1983–2007 and the political and institutional limitations that have hindered policy reform and challenged the prospects for future growth are successfully explained by the CGD framework. The framework is also a rich one in that it allows an explicit role for profound changes in society, including political change, such as greater democratization; administrative change, such as the fight against corruption; distributional change, such as improvements in health care and education; as well as technological and environmental and other types of change. Like mainstream economic theory, which assigns key roles to both productivity and human capital, but unlike the political fashions of the 1980s, the framework stresses these issues as key to *achieving* growth, rather than as luxuries that a society can afford *only after it achieves* growth. On the contrary, Costa Rica—like Chile and Uruguay, the two other countries in the region with the fastest growth over the last two decades—created institutions that put those "luxuries" first; Costa Rica's experience is a reminder that *fundamentals are fundamental.* They are not "second generation" matters that can come later.

We believe that the Costa Rican story offers some other lessons:

• Although the framework does not address these explicitly, the timing, sequencing, and pace of reform, and the interactions between reforms, are critical. The Costa Rican story suggests that it is a good idea to do things sequentially and gradually, building on initial successes. The slow progression of the economic transformation after stabilization may have seemed frustrating, but it may have prevented those reforms from being reversed.

• The framework gives due importance to macroeconomic stability, prominently including fiscal sustainability. This is, of course, correct, and without a doubt Costa Rica has benefited from the rapid improvement in and continued attention to its macroeconomic indicators since the mid-1980s. But Costa Rica's story is also a reminder that not all macroeconomic equilibria are created equal. In the effort to cut expenditure and restore balance in the public finances, extra sacrifices were made in some areas to ensure that other public institutions and social services continued to function well even in times of austerity. Although this strategy might seem to be a sign of lukewarm commitment to achieving macroeconomic stability, it proved in fact to be critical for the political sustainability of reform and for keeping certain other essential growth foundations intact. Countries that pursue fiscal probity and macroeconomic stability in the short run, perhaps under the encouragement and supervision of international financial institutions, without caring about the long-run political sustainability of their reforms, will probably show good economic numbers only for a little while.

• Although Costa Rica preserved essential social services from the cutbacks of the early 1980s, its failure to boost tax revenue implied that fiscal stability could only be achieved by postponing key investments and weakening important institutions. A well-functioning state requires the right people in positions of authority, working under the right incentives, laws, rules, and procedures. The lack of these capable people and sound institutions gave rise to institutional and administrative problems, which became a serious obstacle to growth in Costa Rica. In this, as in all human endeavors, the devil is in the details.

Finally, although the framework does not address politics directly, because the political context varies from country to country, reform will not happen if the political groundwork is not laid correctly, as both Costa Rica's successes and its failures illustrate:

• It is necessary to construct *a base of short-term beneficiaries* from the initiatives of government. When a group of people can clearly and concretely see how they themselves profit from a particular policy, they will lend it legitimacy, fight for it, and increase the political cost of reversing it. They will also act as a buffer and first line of defense for the policy, ahead of the technocrats who originally proposed it for complex analytical reasons, and ahead of the politicians, whose motives may be suspect.

• It is important for *reform-minded political parties to maintain a link with academia and with other groups in society,* so that once in government, politicians can rely on a battery of intellectual support and take advantage of open channels to communicate, explain, and negotiate.

• *Reform should have an ideological underpinning, and leaders should educate for change.* It is not only important for policy to be designed as an instrument to achieve a well-defined goal. It is also critical, if that policy is to be implemented successfully and sustained in the long run, that those well-defined goals be agreed upon as stemming from a common set of values and worldviews.

Costa Rica's economic performance has followed a unique course, full of contrasts and paradoxes, successes and failures, and it is a tall order to understand it well. It is a telling achievement of the CGD framework that it can be applied to understanding this story in a flexible and simple way. Nevertheless, this complex story also requires focusing on issues of implementation, politics, and institutional development that also deserve attention.

References

Consejo Monetario Centroamericano. 2004. "Naturaleza y Situación de las Remesas Familiares en los Países Miembros." Working paper (November).

Kakwani, N., and E. Pernia. 2000. "What is Pro-poor Growth?" Manila: Asian Development Bank.

Lall, Sanjaya, John Weiss, and Jinkang Zhang. 2006. "The 'Sophistication' of Exports: A New Trade Measure." *World Development* 34, no. 2: 222–37.

Leipziger, Danny. 2005. "Pro-poor Growth in the 1990s: Lessons and Insights from 14 Countries." Washington: World Bank.

Lizano, Eduardo, and Ricardo Monge. 2006. "Bancarización de las Remesas de los Inmigrantes Nicaragüenses en Costa Rica." Washington: Multilateral Investment Fund (October).

Loayza, Norman, Pablo Fajnzylber, and César Calderón. 2005. *Economic Growth in Latin America and the Caribbean: Stylized Facts, Explanations, and Forecasts.* Washington: World Bank.

Rodríguez Clare A., M. Sáenz, and A. Trejos. 2002. "Analysis of Economic Growth in Costa Rica 1950–2000." Washington: Inter-American Development Bank.

World Bank. 2007. "Doing Business in Costa Rica." Washington.

Zettelmeyer, Jeromin. 2006. "Growth and Reforms in Latin America: A Survey of Facts and Arguments." IMF Working Paper WP/06/210. Washington: International Monetary Fund (September).

6

How Can Reforms Help Deliver Growth in Mexico?

GERARDO ESQUIVEL AND FAUSTO HERNÁNDEZ-TRILLO

I n the early 1980s, Mexico's inward-looking development strategy collapsed. By then macroeconomic instability—high inflation rates, large fiscal deficits, balance of payments crises, and a huge external debt—had become pervasive, not just in Mexico but also in many other Latin American countries. In mid-1982 Mexico announced that it would default on its external debt, precipitating what came to be known as the Latin American debt crisis and the "lost decade."

The crisis made clear that the country had to modify its development strategy, from one based largely on trade protection and a heavily interventionist state toward a more market-oriented, modern, deregulated economy. Since then Mexico, like many other Latin American countries, has been trying to return to sustainable economic growth by implementing a series of structural economic reforms and by moving toward a full-fledged market economy. During the second half of the 1980s and the early 1990s, the Mexican government managed to approve and implement a series of important economic reforms, including an

We thank Liliana Rojas-Suarez for providing detailed comments on previous versions of this chapter. We also thank Guillermo Perry, Kurt Weyland, and participants in a seminar in Washington for their very helpful comments on a preliminary version. We also thank Marcos Avalos, Sergio López Ayllón, Jorge Chavez, Daniel Chiquiar, Pablo Cotler, Rafael del Villar, Carlos Elizondo, L. M. Galindo, Cesár Hernández, Juan Carlos Moreno, José Antonio Murillo, F. Suárez Dávila, Alejandro Villagomez, and Leo Zuckerman for their comments and contributions on different sections of this chapter. As usual, we are the only ones responsible for any remaining errors.

ambitious privatization program, a partial pension reform, and wide-ranging trade liberalization and deregulation.

It is evident today, however, that Mexico's economic reforms have had relatively disappointing results: income per capita since 1981 has grown at a dismal average rate of close to 0.5 percent a year. Such a low growth rate, together with the generalized perception that economic growth has not been broadly shared, has generated ample popular discontent with economic reforms in Mexico. For that reason, any future reform proposals are likely to face much greater debate and opposition than in the past. In fact, disappointment with previous reforms, in an already difficult political context, has deterred recent administrations from pursuing further economic reform. As a consequence, Mexico has entered onto the path of reform inaction that currently characterizes most of Latin America.

At least two competing explanations have been advanced to explain the relative failure of economic reform in Mexico.[1] The first is that the reforms thus far have been insufficient and incomplete (Gil-Díaz, 2003), and that deeper and broader reforms are needed to achieve positive results. The second argues that, to the contrary, the economic reform process has gone too far and that it has been unable to break the stranglehold of existing economic interest groups, and may even have made them more powerful. This line of analysis concludes that the reform process should not continue and that some reforms may even need to be reversed. Although this point of view is not predominant in academic discussions, it is deeply entrenched in a large segment of the Mexican population.

We follow yet a third line of analysis. We claim that structural reform in Mexico has failed to contribute to more rapid growth because in some cases, such as the initial pension reform of 1992, the reforms were driven by a sense of urgency, and therefore were not actually designed to promote economic growth, whereas in other cases the reforms could have had positive effects but either were badly implemented (for example, privatization) or remain incomplete (for example, financial reform). Some other important economic reforms have not even been attempted, and, most important, in many other cases the sequencing of reform was inappropriate. All of these factors could explain why structural reform in Mexico has had such a limited—sometimes even a negative—impact on the foundations for growth.

In some cases, moreover, powerful interest groups have played an important role in preventing implementation of what might otherwise have been a successful reform. The opponents of further reform were in some cases the winners from the initial wave of reforms and may perceive that further reform could deprive them of those benefits (as described by Hellman, 1998). More recently, however, political and ideological confrontation among the three major political parties in

---

1. See Zettelmeyer (2006) for a recent summary of the evidence and debate on the relationship between reform and economic growth in Latin America.

Mexico has also become an obstacle to further structural reform (Lehoucq and others, 2005). The result has been a political situation in which each major party has veto power over the others, leading to reform inaction as an equilibrium outcome. These considerations, together with reform fatigue, are the main local constraints on further reform in Mexico.

Nevertheless, we believe that reforms can still be implemented in Mexico on a wide array of issues, and that these reforms can and should be designed so as to maximize their impact on the foundations for growth. The reforms that we see as needed in Mexico can be divided into two groups. The first consists of reforms that involve substantial ideological differences and political trade-offs, and therefore will require a much deeper level of discussion. In this group we include issues such as fiscal, energy, and labor reform. Achievement of any of these reforms will ultimately depend upon some agreement being reached among the major political forces, or at least between two of the three leading political parties, so as to guarantee a simple majority in Congress.

We argue here that this set of reforms—especially the fiscal and energy reforms—needs first an underlying institutional framework in order to work; this means, in particular, judicial and competition reform. For example, if Pemex, the state-owned oil company, were fully privatized under a weak competition framework, privatization might not yield the desired results. By the same token, as we argue later, without a judicial reform that includes the modification of the fiscal *amparo*, fiscal reform will not deliver the intended outcomes. For these reasons we focus on these two reforms and emphasize that the sequencing of reforms is important.

This second group of reforms includes those on which there are no major political or ideological differences among the political parties; here we anticipate that a congressional majority could be achieved in the short run. Some of these reforms have not been attempted either because they were considered already completed or because politicians are unsure about their implications for economic growth. This chapter will concentrate on this second set of reforms, since they are the ones that seem to be attainable in the short run and whose implementation depends mostly on political will rather than on ideological compromise.

The main objective of this chapter is to identify why previous reforms failed to generate a higher rate of sustainable economic growth in Mexico, and what can be done to reactivate the process of economic reform in a way that leads to faster growth. We devote particular attention to the specific characteristics and idiosyncratic aspects of the Mexican situation, as well as to the sequencing of the reforms proposed.

We begin in the next section by reviewing recent trends in the Mexican economy. Here we also develop a first approach to the recent evolution of some of the foundations for growth as defined by the CGD framework (see chapter 2). The next section explores the reasons for reform fatigue in Mexico and how this fatigue, in the current domestic political context, has become an obstacle to further economic reform. In this section we also briefly describe some of the economic reforms that have already been implemented, either fully or in part, including trade liberalization, privatization, and pension reform. The next section discusses some areas where the reform agenda might successfully be advanced. In particular, we propose and discuss three areas of reform for which there is some probability of consensus: legal and judicial reform, competition policy, and financial sector reform. Again, the first two sets of reforms are necessary for the other reforms to work. The financial sector is included for illustrative purposes, that is, to show that for this reform to work, a competitive environment and an efficient and adequate rule of law are both needed. The final section concludes.

Economic Growth and Its Foundations

Economic Growth in the Recent Past

The performance of the domestic economy during the past twenty-five years has been quite disappointing, not just for the Mexican population but for all who saw great potential in the economic reforms of the 1980s and 1990s.[2] The slow rate of growth in Mexico's real income per capita from 1981 to 2006 stands in sharp contrast with the country's own economic performance between 1950 and 1981, when real income per capita grew at a pace of 3.4 percent a year. This record of growth is depicted in figure 1, which also shows the structural break in 1981 that was detected statistically by Berg, Ostry, and Zettelmeyer (2006). However, starting in 1995 Mexico seems to have resumed a positive growth trend, with a slump between 2000 and 2003, which can be partly attributed to the U.S. recession of 2001. In any event, average annual growth in real income per capita between 1995 and 2006, at 2.2 percent, was not only slower than in the previous period, but slower than what many had expected given the amplitude and variety of reforms undertaken.

What accounts for Mexico's economic growth slowdown since 1981? Answering this question requires a deeper analysis of the underlying factors. One way to do this is by performing a standard growth accounting decomposition, to investigate whether the problem has been one of factor accumulation or of slow growth in total factor productivity (TFP). Several recent studies have attempted to disentangle the contributions of these different factors to growth in Mexico's GDP.[3] In general, all reach the same basic conclusion: Mexico's economy has grown slowly since the 1980s as a result of a sharp decline in TFP.

2. A large number of papers have explored Mexico's recent economic growth performance, including Tornell, Westermann, and Martínez-Trigueros (2004) and Garcia-Verdú (2007). The Mexican case has also been analyzed in the broader Latin American context in Loayza, Fajnzylber, and Calderón (2005) and Zettelmeyer (2006).

3. See, for example, Loayza et al. (2005) and García-Verdú (2007).

Figure 1. *Mexico: Real Income per Capita, 1950–2006*

Log units[a]

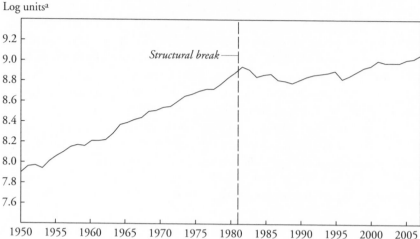

Source: Penn World Tables version 6.2 (Heston, Summers, and Aten, 2006) and author's estimates.
a. In constant dollars.

Table 1 reports the results of a growth decomposition exercise for Mexico during the period 1950–2006, based on a recent study by Garcia-Verdú (2007). The table shows the results for three subperiods: 1950–70, a period of very rapid economic growth with relative macroeconomic stability; 1971–82, a period of continued rapid growth, but accompanied by macroeconomic instability; and 1982–2006, a period of relatively slow growth.

The results are unambiguous: most of the slowdown in economic growth since 1982 has been due to a reduction in the rate of TFP growth, which even turned negative in the last subperiod.[4] A second contributing factor has been a reduction in the rate of capital accumulation, which clearly depends on the foundations for growth being sound. The fact that these two components, capital accumulation and TFP, are contributing far less to Mexico's economic growth than they used to suggests that the foundations for growth are not developing in a positive way. We look next at the recent trends in some of these foundations in more detail.

The Foundations for Growth

In what follows we make use of the analytical framework described in chapter 2 of this volume. This framework identifies five foundations for growth for the

---

4. These results are in line with those of Loayza et al. (2005), who found negative contributions from three alternative measures of TFP during the 1980s and an almost zero contribution during the 1990s.

Table 1. *Mexico: Accounting for Growth, 1950–2006*
Percent a year (annual averages)

Period	Change in GDP	Change in capital stock	Change in composition of human capital	Change in total factor productivity
1950–70	6.10	1.67	0.63	3.80
1971–82	5.97	2.54	1.94	1.49
1982–2006	2.42	1.22	2.07	−0.87

Source: Authors' calculations based on Garcia-Verdú (2007).

Latin American economies: property rights, equal opportunities, competition, macroeconomic stability, and a broader sharing of the benefits of growth. Unfortunately, there are no obvious ways of measuring some of these concepts or of capturing them through proxy variables. However, we do have suitable proxies for three of these concepts, and in this section we briefly review and discuss their track record in Mexico. In each case we use only those variables for which we have data before and after 1982, the year when Mexico's structural reforms got under way.

Property Rights

As a proxy measure for property rights, we use the Legal Structure and Security of Property Rights Index developed by the Cato Institute, which is one of the components of the World Economic Freedom Index computed annually by that organization. Since 1995 the Cato property rights index has been based on five indicators: judicial independence, impartiality of the courts, protection of intellectual property, military interference in the political regime, and integrity of the legal system. Values of all the indicators range from zero to 10, with zero indicating maximum weakness.

Table 2 traces the Cato property rights index for Mexico since 1970. The pattern is erratic, with a slight improvement between 1975 and 1990 followed by a sharp reversal between 1990 and 2000 and then a slight recovery after 2000. The index in 2004 was well below its value in 1980, which means that there was no net progress at all over those twenty-five years; the index actually shows a slight decline since the beginning of the structural reform process. This pattern, as discussed later, could be associated with the negative performance of some of the previous economic reforms.

Macroeconomic Stability

Mexico, like many other Latin American countries, has gone through several macroeconomic crises and has suffered from macroeconomic instability and high vulnerability to external shocks. Mexico has also experienced several devaluations of the peso and has signed several letters of intent with the International Mone-

Table 2. *Mexico: Strength of Property Rights, 1970–2004*
Index, 10 = maximum

	1970	1975	1980	1985	1990	1995	2000	2004
Cato Legal Structure and Security of Property Rights Index	4.7	4.1	6.3	5.4	6.8	5.3	4.2	4.5

Source: Gwartney and Lawson (2007).

tary Fund in an effort to restore macroeconomic stability.[5] Any of a number of variables could be used as a proxy for this foundation for growth. We focus on only two that were at the heart of the regionwide macroeconomic instability of the 1970s and 1980s: inflation and public sector debt.

Inflation in Mexico began to increase in the early 1970s and then accelerated in the 1980s, reaching almost 150 percent at its peak in 1987. Since then inflation has mostly followed a declining trend, with a brief spurt upward in the mid-1990s, when it approached 50 percent as a result of the tequila crisis of 1994–95. After that episode, however, inflation steadily declined, and since 2000 it has been in the single digits; it is close to 4 percent currently.

The ratio of Mexico's total (external and internal) public sector debt to GDP increased substantially in the early 1980s, reaching a peak of 104 percent in 1987; the ratio of external debt to GDP reached a peak of 73 percent that same year. Since then, however, both ratios have steadily declined (again with a small increase during the 1994–95 crisis) and today are at moderate levels.

Together these two indicators allow us to conclude that Mexico's economy has become much more stable in recent years compared with the 1980s and 1990s. This suggests that Mexico's macroeconomic stability foundation has shown significant improvement and could have contributed to increasing the economy's growth potential.

BROAD SHARING OF THE BENEFITS OF GROWTH

We view Mexico's failure to share the benefits of economic growth more broadly as critical to understanding some of the disappointment with structural reform. We focus on two variables as proxies for this concept: poverty rates and income inequality.

Poverty. There are three officially defined measures of poverty in Mexico: food poverty (also called extreme poverty), capabilities poverty, and assets-based poverty (also called moderate poverty); all of these are defined in terms of income

---

5. See Lustig (1998) for more details on the episodes of macroeconomic instability in Mexico.

Figure 2. *Mexico: Moderate and Extreme Poverty, 1950–2004*

Percent of total population

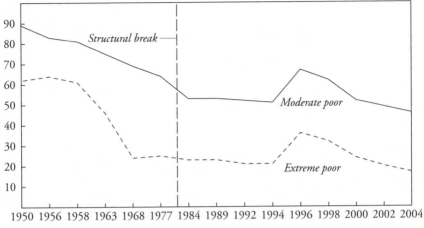

Source: Székely (2005).

thresholds. The longest poverty rate series for Mexico using consistent data and estimation methods was recently published by Székely (2005); this series is available from 1950 to 2004.

Figure 2 shows these series for two of the three measures of poverty: moderate and extreme. Both have declined substantially since 1950, but most of this reduction took place well before the launch of structural reforms in 1981. Indeed, except for the period around the tequila crisis, Mexico's moderate and extreme poverty rates have shown remarkable stability and a certain degree of downward rigidity since the early 1980s and the late 1960s, respectively: the extreme poverty rate in 2000 was the same as it had been in 1968. On the other hand, the number of people in extreme poverty has remained almost constant at around 20 million since 1950, while the number of moderately poor has doubled, from 24 million people in 1950 to around 50 million in 2004.

Inequality. Latin America is well known for having the highest levels of economic inequality among world regions, and Mexico is no exception. Székely (2005) also provides a long time series for income inequality in Mexico, with data available for selected years between 1950 and 2004. The story told by these data, shown in figure 3, is similar to that for poverty: income inequality has been relatively stable in Mexico, with little net change from 1984 to 2004, despite a slight increase from 1984 to 1994 and a reversal thereafter. As with poverty, all the reduction in this indicator occurred before the period of structural reform; no significant long-run improvement is evident since then.[6]

6. There has been, however, an important reduction in income inequality since 1994. Esquivel (2008) analyzes the observed reduction in Mexico's income inequality since 1994.

Figure 3. *Mexico: Income Inequality, 1950–2004*

Gini index (100 = most unequal)

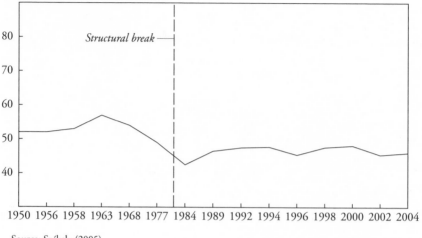

Source: Székely (2005).

To summarize, Mexico's economic reforms have had little substantive effect on the foundations for growth. The only foundation for which there is some evidence of improvement in recent years is macroeconomic stability. Neither the property rights environment nor the broad sharing of economic growth has shown substantial improvement in the recent period. On the contrary, in terms of the Cato property rights index, Mexico is now below its own 1980 level, and poverty and inequality have shown no substantial improvement since the early 1980s. It is therefore not surprising that Mexico's economic growth performance has been disappointing.

Has Growth Been Inclusive?

To analyze whether economic growth in Mexico has been inclusive, we report the results of Munguía (2008), who performed an analysis similar to that of Dollar and Kraay (2002). The latter used a cross-country panel data regression model to estimate the effect of overall growth in income per capita on growth in income per capita among the poorest quintile. They found that the incomes of the poor grew at the same rate as average income per capita: that is, the elasticity of the bottom-quintile growth rate with respect to the overall growth rate was not statistically different from one. Dollar and Kraay concluded from this evidence that "growth is good for the poor."

Munguía (2008) used information from Mexico's income-expenditure household surveys from 1992 to 2006. These surveys are conducted every other year, so that data were available for eight cross sections. The author then computed

Table 3. *Mexico: Elasticity of Income Growth of the Poor with Respect to Average Income Growth*[a]

Sample period	States included in sample	Estimated elasticity	
		With time dummies	Without time dummies
1992–2006	All	1.053	1.054
		(0.050)	(0.041)
1992–1998	All	0.907	0.999
		(0.216)	(0.102)
2000–2006	All	1.052	1.048
		(0.074)	(0.063)
1992–2006	Poor states only	0.864	0.900
		(0.090)	(0.087)
1992–2006	Rich states only	1.001	0.973
		(0.069)	(0.054)

Source: Munguía (2008).

a. Results of a regression of the log of growth in income per capita of the poor on the log of growth in average income per capita, using the system-GMM (generalized method of moments) method. All regressions include two lags of the dependent variable as instruments. Numbers in parentheses are standard errors.

both average income per capita and that of the poorest quintile using state-level data from all thirty-two of Mexico's states, 256 observations in all. The author regressed the log of income per capita of the poor on the log of overall average income per capita, controlling for such variables as education, foreign direct investment, and the share of the maquiladora sector in the state. To reduce the bias associated with the model's specification, following Dollar and Kraay's (2002) methodology, Munguía estimated the model in both levels and first-differences using the system-GMM (generalized method of moments) approach.

Table 3, which summarizes his results, shows that the income growth elasticity of the poor is again very close to one in all specifications. In fact, none of the estimated coefficients is statistically different from one, suggesting that average income per capita at the state level grew at the same rate as income per capita among the poorest quintile. Thus, although economic growth in Mexico was not pro-poor, in the sense that the poorest did not benefit more than proportionally from economic growth than the middle of the distribution, at least growth was not biased against them.

Using a different approach, Esquivel (2008) has shown that, at least since 1994, the income of the bottom part of the distribution has grown faster than that of the rest of the population. This fact explains the reduction in inequality that has been observed since that year. This result, together with our previous discussion, suggests that the problem with the recent trend in income growth in Mexico is mainly its low level rather than its distribution.

Reform Fatigue, the Political Constraint, and Previous Reforms

How did Mexico go from being one of the region's leading reformers in the early 1990s to the "reform paralysis" of recent years? Part of the answer lies in the dismal performance of the Mexican economy, discussed above, after the initial set of reforms. However, this is not a convincing explanation for everyone, since some have argued that the Mexican economy would have done better if further reforms had been implemented. Why, then, are further economic reforms not being as vigorously pursued in Mexico as they were in the 1980s and 1990s? Why have recent administrations been unable to pass a single important economic reform? We see three reasons behind this outcome: first, a generalized perception that the reform agenda had failed to generate faster economic growth; second, a change in political conditions that have made it much harder to implement any further economic reform; and third, the actual failure of some of the first group of reforms. We address each of these issues in turn.

Economic Growth and Reform

The relationship between reform and economic growth is not an obvious one. Often reforms affect growth only indirectly. In any event, Mexico's reforms were expected to have a positive effect on growth, and indeed it was precisely on those grounds that the government justified them. Yet, as we have seen, Mexico's economic performance does not seem to have improved in the wake of the reforms. Indeed, an important segment of the population perceives their overall effect to have been negative, and not without reason. Figure 4 compares an index of structural reform with the ratio of Mexico's GDP per capita to that of the United States for the period since 1970.[7] The figure shows a surprising mirror image between these two variables: when the reform index started to increase in 1982, GDP per capita relative to the United States started to decline, and when the rise in the reform index began to slow around 1989, the GDP per capita ratio started to stabilize as well. Since 1997 both indices have been basically constant.

Although this pattern obviously does not imply causation, that may not matter to the general public, who perceives only the negative association between reform and economic performance. Given these results, it is not surprising that important groups of the Mexican population are less than eager to support a continued pro-reform agenda.

---

7. This index was originally calculated by Morley, Machado, and Pettinato (1999) and was recently updated and revised by Escaith and Paunovic (2004). We are assuming no changes in the index between 2004 and 2006.

Figure 4. *Mexico: Structural Reform and GDP per Capita Relative to United States, 1970–2006*

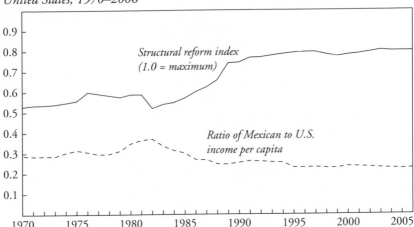

Source: Penn World Tables version 6.2 (Heston, Summers, and Aten, 2006); Escaith and Paunovic (2004); authors' estimates.

The Political Context and the Policymaking Process

Also helping to explain the lack of further reform is the change in the political context and in the policymaking process in Mexico. In the late 1980s and early 1990s, Congress approved some important and technically complex economic reforms without major difficulties, in part because until 1994 Mexican politics was dominated by a single party, the Revolutionary Institutional Party (Partido Revolucionario Institucional, or PRI).

The PRI, which ruled Mexico for several decades beginning in the late 1920s, lacks a clear ideological stance and therefore has been capable of some flexibility in the policies it embraced. It was under the PRI that Mexico adopted, in the 1940s and 1950s, an inward-looking economic development strategy. Later, as this strategy began to show some fragility, successive PRI administrations, beginning with that of President Miguel de la Madrid (1982–88), started to adjust the economic model and proposed several economic reforms to confront some of the emerging problems. These reforms, which included a massive program of privatization, tariff reduction, deregulation, and the initial stage of a financial reform, were deemed urgent and necessary in light of the fiscal, monetary, and balance of payments problems that Mexico faced during the 1980s.

De la Madrid's successor, Carlos Salinas de Gortari (1988–94), continued with these policies and indeed went much further in some areas (Aspe, 1993). It was under his administration that Mexico proposed a free trade agreement with the

United States and Canada, which was implemented as the North American Free Trade Agreement (NAFTA) in 1994. One can appreciate the magnitude of this change of perspective for Mexico by noting that as recently as 1980, the Mexican government had rejected, on purely nationalistic grounds, membership in the General Agreement on Tariffs and Trade (GATT).

The lackluster economic results of the 1980s and the failure (perceived or real) of some of the economic reforms of that period, together with a more open political environment, took their toll on the PRI's popular support. Thus, although PRI candidates won the presidential elections of 1988 and 1994, they faced much stronger competition and barely obtained an absolute majority of the popular vote (figure 5). In those two elections and in the mid-term elections of 1991, the PRI continued to win absolute majorities in both houses of Congress. This facilitated policymaking, and some important economic reforms were implemented without strong opposition in Congress during this period.[8]

However, during President Salinas's administration the PRI had already lost enough seats in Congress that it could no longer make constitutional changes without the support of other parties. (These changes require a qualified majority of two-thirds of the votes in both houses.) Therefore, in order to advance the reform agenda when constitutional reforms were needed, Salinas and the PRI formed a voting coalition with the right-of-center National Action Party (Partido Acción Nacional, or PAN). The PRI could still pass other reforms without having to resort to compromise with other political forces. During this period the leftist-oriented political parties (which in figure 5 are generically labeled as PRD) opposed most of the reforms but were unable to prevent their passage.

In 1997, during President Ernesto Zedillo's administration (1994–2000), the political context underwent a dramatic and important change. For the first time in Mexico's recent history, the governing party failed to achieve a simple majority in Congress, and the country entered an era of divided government. Not surprisingly, this change coincided with the beginning of the period of reform inaction shown in figure 4.

In 2000, for the first time after more than seven decades in power, the PRI lost the presidential election to Vicente Fox, the PAN's charismatic candidate. However, the PAN failed to win either house of Congress, and thus President Fox faced an even more complex situation than had his predecessor. Not only was the PAN unable to approve any reform proposal without support from other parties, but it lacked the PRI's political expertise as well. Not surprisingly, then, the new administration proved incapable of building a majority coalition with other political forces. The result of the mid-term elections in 2003 left the governing

8. This is not to say that economic reform was not debated. In fact, some reform proposals generated a heated debate in the media, and others provoked public demonstrations of opposition.

Figure 5. *Mexico: Results of Presidential and Congressional Elections, 1934–2006*

Presidential elections

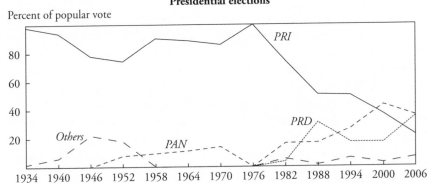

Congressional elections: Chamber of Deputies

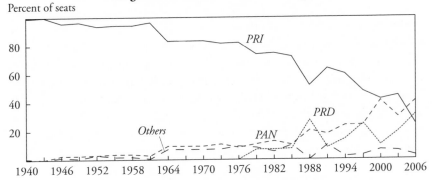

Congressional elections: Senate

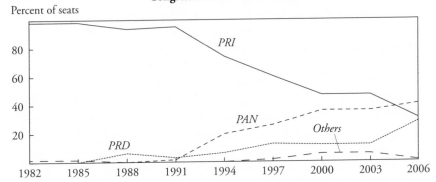

Source: Nohlen (2005) and 2006 official results from Instituto Federal Electoral (http://www.ife. org.mx)

party in an even worse situation, with only 30 percent of the seats in the Chamber of Deputies.

Following a very close presidential election in 2006, Mexico again has a divided government, with the new president, Felipe Calderón of the PAN, facing the same problems that his predecessor, President Fox, did. Nevertheless, as of 2008 two reforms had passed, a public pension reform and a fiscal reform, with the support of both the PRI and the PAN. The fiscal reform, however, is a very weak one, and short of what had been anticipated. An energy reform has been proposed and as of this writing is being heatedly debated in Congress. This reform will probably be either rejected or so diluted as to make it almost irrelevant.

As mentioned above, the new political situation seems to have prevented approval of some important economic reforms that could have contributed to enhancing Mexico's opportunities for economic growth. The next section reviews the performance of some of the reforms that were approved in the 1980s.

Results of Some Previous Reforms

Mexico's recent reform inaction can partly be explained by the apparent lack of effectiveness of the previous reforms in delivering growth. What went wrong? Why did Mexico's economic reforms fail to translate into stronger economic growth? Were they ineffective in terms of influencing the foundations for growth, or were they simply not aimed at influencing them? To answer these questions, we briefly review three of the most important previous reforms in Mexico: trade liberalization, pension reform, and privatization.

TRADE LIBERALIZATION

In 1985, in the midst of a macroeconomic crisis, the Mexican government announced a unilateral reduction in tariffs on foreign goods as well as the elimination of many trade barriers and import quotas. This surprising move represented a substantial change from Mexico's traditional protectionist policy and marked the beginning of a new trade policy. During the early 1990s, to consolidate this new approach to international trade, the Mexican government signed a free trade agreement, NAFTA, with the United States and Canada. Since then Mexico has established free trade agreements with many other Latin American nations and with the European Union, Israel, and Japan.

The objectives of this reform were the following:
- to improve efficiency and resource allocation in the economy
- to attract more foreign direct investment (FDI) and contribute to generating employment
- to contribute to macroeconomic stability by imposing price discipline through lower import prices, and
- to improve the broad sharing of the benefits of growth by reducing prices of imported goods for everyone.

The reform succeeded in achieving many of its original objectives and, together with the achievement of macroeconomic stability, can be considered as one of the most important reform successes in Mexico. Both trade flows and FDI increased considerably after the launch of NAFTA; prices of imported goods helped keep Mexico's inflation in line; efficiency, resource allocation, and productivity in Mexico's industry improved (see López-Córdova, 2003, and Lederman, Maloney, and Servén, 2005).

However, it is also clear that the high expectations about the impact of trade liberalization in general, and NAFTA in particular, have not fully materialized. The following are some problems with the design and implementation of this reform:

• According to Easterly, Fiess, and Lederman (2003), the main factor contributing to the lack of convergence in income per capita between Mexico and the United States is the weaker quality of Mexico's institutions: the rule of law, government integrity and effectiveness, and regulatory quality. Improvement in these areas could help increase the beneficial effects of trade liberalization.

• Despite passage of several other free trade agreements, Mexico's trade is still highly concentrated in the U.S. market. More than 80 percent of Mexico's exports go to the United States, and close to 70 percent of Mexico's imports come from that country. Inadequate infrastructure, together with high fees and lack of investment in Mexico's ports, undoubtedly played a role in this outcome.

• An unintended consequence of trade liberalization has been increased regional inequality. The northern states, already relatively rich, have tended to benefit the most from greater FDI flows, job creation, and lower income inequality, whereas the relatively poor southern states have benefited little (Esquivel et al., 2002; Borraz and López-Córdova, 2007). Lack of adequate infrastructure and human capital in the southern states largely explain these results (see Esquivel et al., 2002).

To deal with these obstacles, we propose the following steps:

• Implement a general reform of many of the institutional aspects of the Mexican economy, including enforcement of the rule of law and regulatory quality.

• Invest in education and infrastructure in Mexico's southern region to help that region catch up and to generate a better business environment there.

• Improve and reform the operations of Mexico's ports and invest in infrastructure throughout the country. Stronger regulation and application of the antitrust laws in the ports' operation may be needed.

• More generally, an adequate and consistent regional development policy needs to be designed and implemented.

PENSION REFORM

In 1996 Congress approved a new social security law and a new law governing the retirement savings system. This legislation brought about a radical change in the retirement conditions of formal private sector workers (around 10 million workers at the time the law was passed). Mexico had previously had a pay-as-you-go pension system, where current workers' contributions were used to finance current pensions. However, demographic changes (especially a substantial increase in life expectancy) and problems with the administration of pension funds in the past made it clear that this system would eventually collapse.

The new laws implemented a change toward a scheme based on individual savings accounts. They mandated the creation of specialized pension fund management firms (*administradoras de fondos para el retiro*, or *afores*), which would administer the workers' savings accounts and invest the accumulated resources.

The main objectives of the pension reform were the following:[9]
- to solve the fiscal crisis associated with the previous system
- to provide an opportunity for workers to increase their retirement income through participation in financial markets
- to increase the national saving rate by giving workers a sense of ownership of their retirement savings, and
- to contribute to the deepening of the domestic financial system.

By helping to prevent a fiscal crisis, pension reform played a fundamental role in ensuring macroeconomic stability and was thus indispensable. However, the reform cannot be considered completely successful, since it has not achieved many of its other objectives, and indeed it is not obvious that most workers will benefit from the reform. Many workers will not save enough to pay for the minimum guaranteed pension. Many others perceive that their retirement savings are being eroded by the high fees and commissions charged by the *afores*. The domestic financial system has not improved as a result of the reform, nor has financial intermediation increased. All this seems to be due to a number of problems of design and implementation, including the following:

- The high administrative costs of individual accounts reduce workers' future retirement income. These high costs will eventually lead to a large number of workers being unable to accumulate enough resources to pay for the minimum guaranteed pension, and this will increase the fiscal burden in the future (Sinha and Rentería, 2005).

- The *afores* industry is highly concentrated, and the government antitrust agency claims that these firms seem to be acting in a noncompetitive manner (Comisión Federal de Competencia, 2006). For example, real net returns on accounts managed by the largest firms over the 1997–2005 period averaged a minuscule 0.8 percent a year. Yet the *afores* themselves have been extremely profitable, with returns on equity much higher than those of most Mexican banks (which are quite high by international standards).

- From the perspective of two of the foundations for growth—the broad sharing of the benefits of reform and equality of opportunities—the reform was only

9. See Grandolini and Cerda (1998).

partial: it included only nongovernment workers in the formal sector, leaving out the bureaucracy as well as the 60 percent of the population not covered by any pension scheme.

- The financial system faces inadequate incentives to increase its role in financial intermediation and needs a reform of its own (see below).

We propose the following steps to allow pension reform to better address the growth foundations:

- Promote competition in the *afores* sector. Remove obstacles to entry into this market. Enforce anticompetition laws in the sector.

- Increase transparency concerning the real costs incurred by workers, by requiring *afores* to reveal complete and comparable information about the accounts they manage and about their own risk position.

- Modify the pricing structure in order to better align incentives. Fees should only be charged for account administration and returns to investment. There is no reason to charge fees on either the stocks or the flows of retirement accounts.

- Pursue a reform of the financial sector to increase its role in financial intermediation.

PRIVATIZATION

In 1982 Mexico began a wide-ranging and ambitious privatization program: by 1988 the government had sold 155 public sector firms, and another 261 by 1995.[10] The first stage of the program focused on relatively small firms, and the second on bigger and more complex operations. Around 98 percent of the total proceeds from privatization were obtained during the second stage. Privatization was part of a more general divestiture program that also included the dissolution, liquidation, merger, and transfer to state governments of many other public entities. The number of public sector entities fell from 1,155 in 1982 to 219 in 1994. The largest privatized firms were Teléfonos de México (Telmex), three banks (Banamex, Bancomer, and Banca Serfín), and two airlines (Aeroméxico and Mexicana). An important infrastructure concession program proceeded in parallel.

The main objectives of the privatization program were the following:
- redefinition of the government's role in the economy
- improvements in efficiency and resource allocation
- a temporary increase in government revenue, and
- a new relationship with the private sector.

Some authors (e.g., Chong and López-de-Silanes, 2005) view the Mexican privatization program as highly successful and beneficial. Although perhaps true in many cases, there were also several cases of mismanagement leading to very poor economic outcomes. The main problem, however, was that the least successful

---

10. For more details on the privatization reform see Rogozinski (1998).

cases were those related to the largest firms or to key sectors of the economy: examples include telecommunications, banks, ports, and highways. Problems of design or implementation included the following:

• The selection of bidders was often plagued by irregularities and was highly discretionary and opaque. In the case of bank privatization this was documented in a report commissioned by Congress (the Mackey Report).

• Inadequate sequencing was also a problem. In some key cases, privatization took place with insufficient or even no regulation for the post-privatization stage. Again the privatized banks are a prominent example. The absence of appropriate prudential regulation and supervision led to extreme cases of "related lending" (Laporta, López-de-Silanes, and Zamarripa, 2003) and to an uncontrollable credit boom during the early 1990s (Sachs, Tornell, and Velasco, 1996). Both factors played a key role in the 1994–95 tequila crisis.

• In other cases, such as telecommunications and the ports, a public monopoly was transferred to the private sector without an appropriate regulatory and institutional framework. (As discussed later, the federal agency regulating competition was established only at the end of 1993.) In the Telmex case, the results have been relatively high tariffs, predatory behavior, and the abuse of monopoly power (Del Villar, 2007). In the case of the ports, lack of regulation has led to high tariffs, underinvestment, and inefficient operation (Paredes, 2007).

• The National Highways Concession Program was a complete disaster. According to Rogozinski (1998), director in chief of the Office for Privatization, the program "was not a success. Owing to design flaws, costs were higher both during construction of the original design and during the post-construction phase. Fares and traffic volume were merely rough estimates and or were determined at discretion."

• These problems eventually led to the renegotiation of the concessions' original conditions, and the terms of half of the concessions (twenty-six out of fifty-two) were extended to the maximum length allowed. Later, with the onset of the crisis, the government launched an extremely costly road recovery program.[11]

• After the tequila crisis, a large segment of the newly privatized banking sector had to be bailed out. The cost of the bailouts is very difficult to estimate, but some authors put it at nearly 15 percent of GDP. The bailouts were the natural outcome of a grossly mismanaged privatization process and contained important irregularities of their own, according to the Mackey Report. Not surprisingly, the whole process has been questioned for its opacity and abuse of discretion (Haber, 2005).

This brief review indicates that in some key sectors of the economy, privatization was far from successful, and in some cases it was a complete failure, with

11. Guasch (2004) has analyzed the determinants of renegotiation in concession contracts in Latin America. He finds that macroeconomic shocks, the quality of the regulatory framework, corruption, and the timing of elections, among other variables, help explain the probability that a contract would be renegotiated.

negative implications for the whole economy. However, some steps can be taken to reduce these negative effects:

- Improve supervision and regulation in the privatized sectors. In particular, strengthen the supervisory and regulatory capabilities of the National Banking and Securities Commission and the Federal Telecommunications Commission.

- Avoid the renegotiation of infrastructure concessions in the future. Any renegotiation represents a violation of the original terms and conditions, affecting perceptions of the strength of the rule of law.

- Promote greater competition in the privatized sectors and improve antitrust law and its enforcement.

Previous Reforms and the Foundations for Growth

Our review of some of the reforms implemented in Mexico during the 1980s and 1990s has shed some light on why they failed to generate sustained economic growth. Many of the reforms suffered from serious problems of sequencing or implementation, or both. Some failed to have any positive effect on the foundations, and some even had a negative effect.

A prime example is privatization, whose impact on every one of the foundations was negative. Privatization effectively harmed competition in many sectors, because without adequate regulation, private firms with monopoly power could exercise this power without restrictions. The property rights foundation was weakened by the constant renegotiation of contracts in infrastructure concessions and by the opacity and abuse of discretion in many official decisions. The equal opportunities foundation was affected in that privatization did not seek to level the playing field for participants in some of the privatized markets; instead winners were hand picked, resulting in the consolidation of new privatized and export-oriented elites in place of the old statist and import-competing groups (Tornell and Esquivel, 1997). Also, inadequate regulation and supervision of the privatized banks contributed to the 1994–95 crisis and to its worsening, thus affecting the macroeconomic stability foundation. Finally, since the large losses associated with the bank and highway bailouts were socialized, privatization also had a negative effect on the broad sharing of the benefits of growth.

Pension reform also had a negative effect on economic competition and on the broad sharing of growth benefits. The reform gave rise to a highly concentrated market of pension fund management firms (the *afores*), which seem to be extracting enormous economic rents from the fees and commissions paid by millions of workers. Pension reform also seems to have adversely affected the equal opportunities foundation, since workers with similar wages but different degrees of financial sophistication may end up receiving very different benefits in retirement. This outcome is due in part to the complexity of administering this type of resource, but also to the heterogeneity and magnitude of fees and commissions charged by the *afores*.

Table 4. *Mexico: Intended and Actual Impact of Reforms on the Growth Foundations*

Reform	Property rights	Equal opportunities	Competition	Broad sharing of growth benefits	Macroeconomic stability
Trade liberalization					
Intended		+	+ +	?	?
Actual		~	+	+	+
Pension reform					
Intended	+	+ +		?	+ +
Actual	~	–	–	–	+
Privatization					
Intended	+	+		+	+
Actual	–	–	–	–	–

Key: +, positive; + +, strongly positive; –, negative; ~, mixed; ?, unclear.

Finally, trade liberalization is the only reform that has had positive effects both on the macroeconomic stability foundation and on competition and the broad sharing of growth benefits. However, this reform, too, had some negative effects—both unintended and unexpected—on the equal opportunities foundation, since it increased the already large regional disparities in Mexico.

Table 4 summarizes the effects of each reform on the foundations for growth in Mexico. For each reform, the first row shows the potential effect according to the CGD framework, and the second row the actual effect as described above.

How to Advance the Reform Agenda?

Some additional reforms, if correctly implemented, could have important positive effects, not just by themselves but also by helping the previous reforms have a real and positive impact on the foundations for growth. A careful reading of the implementation and design problems of previous reforms suggests three areas that need to be addressed: the rule of law, competition, and the financial sector. Each of these issues has already been mentioned in the discussion of at least two of the reforms above. For that reason, but also because they may strengthen some of the foundations for growth that have been the most weakened, in the next section we discuss three reforms that could, in our opinion, contribute to generating sustained economic growth.

What Reforms Should Be Pursued?

Three reforms that we consider both important and viable in the short run in Mexico are legal reform, reform of competition policy, and financial reform. Again we stress that the appropriate sequencing of these reforms is important.

Legal and Judicial Reform

The Mexican legal system is well known for its complexity and inefficiency.[12] Its complexity derives from the interaction of the three branches of government (legislative, executive, and judiciary) and the three levels of government (federal, state, and municipal). Its inefficiency is evident in the fact that a large number of cases go unresolved or are subject to extremely long delays before a final decision is reached. In general, complexity in itself should not necessarily be regarded as dysfunctional, since the existence of a diversity of actors, conflicting interests, and institutions is typical of any democracy. In Mexico, however, this complexity reinforces the inefficiency of the legal system. As mentioned above, Mexico's property rights index, which encompasses several aspects of the legal system, has not shown any significant improvement since 1980.

Legal enforcement in Mexico is also weak. This may be due to several factors, including an inefficient judicial structure, lack of resources, lack of independence from the executive branch (at both the federal and the state level), ineptitude, and corruption. Even the Mexican Supreme Court, where eleven judges are responsible for solving the most important disputes in the nation, usually lacks the necessary support of professionals specialized in certain areas. Furthermore, unlike many other countries, Mexico lacks an adequate system of specialized tribunals in economic and regulatory matters, such as competition and regulation. This often leads tribunals to base their decisions on procedural aspects rather than on the substance of the case.

As a federal republic, Mexico has courts at two levels of government: state and federal. Here a recurring problem is the lack of independence of some state courts with respect to the state's executive power. In many cases the court's appointments overlap with gubernatorial terms of office, thus facilitating political intervention. In fact, such overlapping of appointments (the so-called *sexenio judicial*) is prevalent in about half of Mexican states. This situation leads to excessive use of one of the key features of the Mexican legal system: the *amparo*.

The *amparo* is a multifaceted concept in Mexican law that summarizes several procedures designed to protect citizens from the authorities' inappropriate application of the law. Some of these are the following:
- habeas corpus
- the administrative *amparo*, which applies to the first- and second-level judicial review of federal administrative cases, and
- the judicial *amparo*, which serves as the third-level federal appeal for local cases.

Hence the lack of independence of the state courts accounts for the existence of a third-level federal appeals procedure, which leads some cases to drag on for years.

---

12. See López Ayllón and Fix-Fierro (2003) and Magaloni and Negrete (2000).

Members of the federal judiciary have no incentive to eliminate this appeal procedure, since it allows them to oversee the state courts.

There is also a strong tendency toward excessive use of the administrative *amparos.* These are used mainly in fiscal cases, where individuals dispute tax charges, usually on the grounds that some tax law or regulation violates the definition of equity and proportionality established in the constitution. The overuse of these *amparos* results in severe losses of tax revenue and high administrative costs for the government.

There are two main explanations for the excessive use of this type of *amparo.* First, the Mexican Supreme Court, unlike its counterparts in other countries, has accepted the principle that it should rule on issues of equity and proportionality and has adopted very shallow interpretations of these concepts; in other countries, such as the United States and Spain, the high court may decide on such a basis but only in extreme situations (Elizondo and Pérez, 2006). Second, as a result of an established legal principle called the "formula Otero," *amparos* in Mexico do not establish a general precedent but apply only to the individual filing the case. This leads to the awkward situation where a fiscal regulation may be declared unconstitutional for one or more individuals, but others in the same circumstances still have to pay the tax.

As a result of the growing demand for *amparos* in Mexico, they have become increasingly complex and technical, and thus relatively expensive. As a consequence, they have tended to disproportionately benefit high-income people and large firms (Enrigue, 2006).

OBJECTIVES

A comprehensive legal reform in Mexico should aim at the following objectives, among others:
- improved efficiency of the judicial system
- increased predictability of the legal process
- enhanced access of the population to the judicial system
- increased independence of the judicial branch with respect to both the local and the federal executive powers, and
- increased transparency and accountability of the judicial system.

EXPECTED EFFECTS ON THE FOUNDATIONS FOR GROWTH

Legal reform could have important effects on several of the foundations for growth.

Property Rights. Legal reform could improve the definition and protection of property rights, including greater protection against expropriation without fair compensation, a stronger guarantee of the efficient enforcement of contracts, and better protection for individuals against biased decisions by politically controlled judiciaries. Improving the efficiency and predictability of the legal process could have a significant impact on property rights in Mexico. Mexico has a long tradition of expropriation (the whole banking system was expropriated in 1982, for example), and individuals and firms have usually had limited rights to challenge government decisions.

Equal Opportunities. In principle, all legal systems are designed to protect everyone in society. However, participation in and access to the legal system in Mexico are relatively costly, and therefore access to the system is highly unequal, which in turn reinforces economic inequality. One survey found that 40 percent of Mexicans believe that the law is mainly used to "protect the interest of powerful people." A legal reform that includes a reduction in the cost of access could increase participation, reduce inequality, and increase trust in the legal system.

Competition. The legal system should promote competition by preventing capture of regulatory authorities. It can also increase competition directly by improving efficiency in the enforcement of regulatory rulings, such as those by the federal competition and telecommunications commissions. It may also help to improve the regulatory process and to avoid regulatory capture by dominant firms in specific markets. In fact, empirical evidence shows that the quality of the legal system affects firm size at the state level in Mexico (Laeven and Woodruff, 2007).

Macroeconomic Stability. Since the government loses tax revenue through the *amparos* and spends a fair amount of resources (both monetary and human) in legal proceedings responding to them, a legal reform that would regulate and diminish the incentives for excessive use of *amparos* could improve the fiscal balance, by discouraging tax evasion and reducing the legal and administrative costs of enforcing the tax laws.

Obstacles to Successful Reform

Several obstacles may impede the successful implementation of legal reform and should be taken into account when designing any new reform:[13]

- the poor quality of public property registries: in 2003 the total value of unregistered properties in Mexico was about $245 billion
- extremely long resolution periods in local judicial procedures, and an absence of alternative dispute resolution mechanisms
- strong incentives for excessive use of the administrative *amparo,* as discussed above
- a lack of specialized tribunals with jurisdiction over economic and regulatory issues
- lack of independence of the state courts from the state executive
- absence of an incentive for the federal judiciary to eliminate the federal appeals procedure, and

---

13. Parts of this section draw on Hernández Ochoa (2006).

• lack of appropriate incentives for local judges to reform the existing dispute resolution mechanisms.

Overcoming the Obstacles

Successful implementation of legal reform will likely require the following steps:

• Reform of the *amparo* law is needed to reduce incentives for the excessive use of both administrative and judicial *amparos*. Stricter criteria for granting *amparos* and stronger sanctions for frivolous lawsuits are also needed.

• *Amparos* could be allowed to set general precedents, eliminating the "formula Otero." This could have important consequences for the Ministry of Finance. All three leading candidates in the most recent presidential election supported this proposal, suggesting that a consensus on this issue can be built.

• The Supreme Court should avoid intervening in matters of equity and proportionality with respect to tax laws and regulations. This authority properly belongs to the legislative power.

• Specialized tribunals in areas such as competition and economic regulation should be created.

• State judicial branches should be granted independence from both the federal judiciary and state executive authorities. The simultaneous appointments of court members and state executive authorities should be eliminated.

• Public property registries should be modernized and updated with the latest technology. This is critical for adequate property rights protection and may provide greater certainty in some economic transactions.

• The civil and commercial procedure codes should be reformed to allow different tracks for simple and complex cases.

• Alternative dispute resolution mechanisms should be introduced, to reduce the cost of access to the legal system and shorten judicial delays. For example, commercial arbitration mechanisms and conciliation procedures could be used in the initial stages of disputes.

Competition Policy Reform

In December 1992 Congress promulgated the Federal Law of Economic Competition (Ley Federal de Competencia Económica, or LFCE).[14] This law mandated the creation of the Federal Competition Commission (Comisión Federal de Competencia, or CFC), which began operating in 1993. The CFC is the Mexican federal agency in charge of competition policy, including the investigation of anticompetitive practices, the supervision of vertical and horizontal mergers, and the defense and promotion of competition in the economy.

From the outset, the appropriate level of autonomy of the CFC has been subject to debate. One option was to create an administrative entity within what is

---

14. Parts of this section draw on a background paper prepared by Marcos Avalos.

now the Ministry of Economy. This ministry, however, had a reputation for being protectionist, and some feared that it might tend to protect strong local monopolies as part of an industrial policy program. Another option was to create a completely autonomous competition authority, but no consensus could be reached. As a compromise, the CFC has been since its creation an administrative entity associated with the Ministry of Economy, but enjoys technical and operating autonomy.

OBJECTIVES

The main objective of the LFCE is to increase the overall efficiency of the economy. To that end, the law seeks to generate the appropriate conditions for effective competition. It tries to protect and promote competition through the prevention and elimination of monopolies, monopolistic practices, and other restrictions that may hinder the efficient operation of markets. In some aspects the LFCE acts as a regulatory law, for example when evaluating whether vertical or horizontal mergers should be allowed. In other instances the LFCE is not strictly speaking a regulatory law, in that it can only be applied ex post, after a company or industry has violated some aspect of the competition law.

In applying the LFCE, the CFC interacts with other government agencies and regulatory bodies and must take into account many other Mexican laws and regulations with important implications for economic competition. These laws and regulations must be applied along with the LFCE.

In 2004 the Organization for Economic Cooperation and Development reviewed the performance of Mexico's competition policy during its first decade of operation. The study (OECD, 2004) found that the CFC had been relatively successful: "The accomplishments of the Commission have been noteworthy . . . taking into consideration the harsh conditions under which the Commission operates." In recent years, however, the juridical and organizational framework governing competition policy in Mexico started to show some weaknesses. Implementation of the LFCE also began to encounter problems when a series of judicial rulings revealed deficiencies in the law, in terms not only of its procedures but also of its constitutionality. This situation led to a proposal to modify the legislation, and a new LFCE was approved by Congress in mid-2006. This reform had three main objectives:

• to make the CFC's recommendations (in terms of regulations, norms, and policies) binding on public sector institutions

• to strengthen the CFC's authority to sanction anticompetitive market behavior

• to solve certain procedural deficiencies.

The reform solved many of the problems identified under the old LFCE, but the law remained far from perfect. In the next section we discuss how this reform may affect the foundations for economic growth, and we identify some problems of design and some local factors that may undermine its success. Finally, we discuss some proposals that could improve the economic impact of this reform.

Expected Effects on the Foundations for Growth

As previous studies have shown, competition policy can enhance the intensity of competition in an economy and thus have a positive effect on economic growth. For example, Krakowski (2005) showed that competition policy strengthened economic competition in a sample of more than 100 countries; Dutz and Hayri (2000) showed that the intensity of competition is positively associated with an economy's rate of growth. Other studies have shown similar effects of competition policy on economic growth, employment rates, the level of FDI, and income distribution (OECD, 2006).

In terms of the CGD framework, competition policy reform could have a direct effect on three of the five foundations: economic competition, equal opportunities, and property rights. It could also have an indirect effect on the broad sharing of growth benefits.

This reform, if successful, will have a positive effect on economic competition in Mexico, by guaranteeing the existence of competitive markets and adequate rules for a competitive economic environment. Today, the absence of effective antimonopoly legislation allows firms with monopoly power to exercise it in ways that reduce both social welfare and economic efficiency. By strengthening the CFC and adjusting the LFCE to make it more effective, competition policy reform could increase competition, thereby having a positive impact on one of the main foundations for growth.

Competition reform would also benefit the equal opportunities foundation. The LFCE is designed to protect producers in cases where the behavior of one or more competitors puts competition at risk. In other words, it does not protect producers if they lose market share because of lack of efficiency or innovation, but only when they are being affected by anticompetitive behavior. A successful reform would level the playing field for all competitors in markets where the absence of an effective competition policy allows dominant firms to engage in anticompetitive behavior.

If successfully implemented, this reform could also have a positive effect on the competition, equal opportunities, and property rights foundations in several key regulated sectors. This is a major issue since many of the CFC's opinions on the regulations, procedures, legislation, and norms established by some regulatory authorities have been highly controversial. More important, the regulatory authorities were not obliged to abide by the opinions or recommendations of the CFC.

Under the new law that was approved in 2006, the CFC's opinions regarding the effects on competition of government programs, proposed legislation, or policies became binding for these public sector institutions. Also, the regulatory framework of various sectors of the economy now requires a favorable opinion from the CFC as a prerequisite for the authorization of concessions, permits, or transfer of rights. Since the implementation of the LFCE, laws in key sectors such as telecommunications, commercial aviation, airports, toll roads and bridges, transportation vehicles, and natural gas have been modified, so that any deregulation or privatization initiative in these sectors now requires the approval of the CFC.

In addition, the relevant federal regulatory agency will control rates if the CFC rules that the effective level of competition is insufficient. Finally, some laws now require that potential bidders for public services franchises obtain the approval of the CFC. For all these regulated sectors, an efficient CFC and an effective implementation of the LFCE are key to promoting competition, leveling the playing field for participants, and protecting the rights of those already involved in (or wishing to enter) these markets.

Finally, the effectiveness of competition policy could also have had a positive effect on the broad sharing of growth benefits, since it is expected that enhancing competition in key sectors of the economy will have a disciplinary effect on prices and on product quality, thus making it likely that larger segments of the population will participate in some of these markets.

Obstacles to Successful Reform

Some possible obstacles to and constraints on successful reform are the following:

• *An institutionally weak competition agency.* The CFC's ability to promote and protect competition is deeply constrained by several factors: a lack of full institutional autonomy, which could result in its capture by other government agencies; inadequate financial autonomy, which increases the risks of inefficient implementation of competition policy; and lack of clarity in the allocation of responsibilities between the CFC and some other regulatory agencies, such as the Federal Telecommunications Commission.

• *Lack of an appropriate design for collecting relevant market information.* As mentioned above, one of the main tasks of the CFC is to investigate possible monopolistic practices. There are two ways in which the CFC can begin a formal investigation of such practices. The first is by formal accusation (*denuncia*) by a firm operating in the relevant market that considers itself harmed by the practices of another market participant. The second is by the CFC initiating its own ex officio investigation if it considers that a firm is engaging in monopolistic practices.

Table 5 shows the number of monopolistic practices investigations, both those following accusations and those undertaken ex officio, since 1993. Between 1993 and 1997, the numbers of accusations and of ex officio investigations were almost equal (72 and 70, respectively). Since 1997, however, investigations stemming from accusations have far outnumbered ex officio investigations (380 versus 87).

Table 5. *Mexico: Results of Investigations into Anti-Competitive Behavior, by Type of Procedure, 1993–2006*

Period	Total investigations	By accusation			Ex officio		
		No. of investigations	Investigations resulting in sanction or recommendation		No. of investigations	Investigations resulting in sanction or recommendation	
			Number	Percent		Number	Percent
1993–94	30	19	4	21.1	11	6	54.5
1994–95	16	6	1	16.7	10	6	60.0
1995–96	27	14	5	35.7	13	10	76.9
1996, 2nd half	17	8	0	0.0	9	2	22.2
1997	52	25	2	8.0	27	13	48.1
1998	50	33	9	27.3	17	5	29.4
1999	41	26	3	11.5	15	6	40.0
2000	63	55	7	12.7	8	4	50.0
2001	64	46	6	13.0	18	7	38.9
2002	68	59	20	33.9	9	3	33.3
2003	38	33	6	18.2	5	0	0.0
2004	42	34	6	17.6	8	2	25.0
2005	62	58	9	15.5	4	2	50.0
2006	39	36	1	2.8	3	2	66.7
Total	609	452	79	17.5	157	68	43.3

Source: Comisión Federal de Competencia (2007a), statistical appendix.

The fact that a much smaller fraction of accusations (17.5 percent) than of ex officio investigations (43.3 percent) result in sanctions suggests that such an imbalance may be undesirable and inefficient. It also suggests that the CFC lacks adequate criteria to establish its own priorities.[15]

The main problem with ex officio investigations is that the ability to gather the necessary information then depends on the competition agency's own capacity, rather than on that of consumers or competitors. The CFC uses three sources of information to detect anticompetitive practices: indirect sources, such as newspapers, magazines, and Chamber of Commerce bulletins; suggestions by the Ministry of Economy; and information given in an accusation. The CFC gathers information for specific cases but does not have a permanent monitoring system for gathering information on monopolistic practices.

• *Lack of consideration of efficiency gains.* One crucial aspect of the application of competition policy to mergers is the potential for efficiency gains. This is not a minor point: many competition authorities around the world focus on efficiency gains when discussing merger activity. Therefore it is important to explicitly include efficiency criteria in the Mexican LFCE, because even if legislation does consider the possibility of efficiency gains, the law is not clear on this point and lacks specific evaluation criteria to prove the existence of these gains. In fact, empirical evidence suggests that Mexican merger policy involves the delicate balancing of anticompetitive effects against possible efficiency gains (Avalos and De Hoyos, 2008). In assessing this trade-off, the antitrust authority often relies on very limited and imperfect information, since not only is the evaluation of market power inherently imprecise, but the merging parties usually have better information on the potential efficiency gains than the regulator. Although the merger review process is designed to extract as much information as possible from the parties involved, it is reasonable to assume that some asymmetries remain.[16]

• *Lack of a specialized legal system.* Mexican courts lack experience in implementing competition policy. In general, judges lack economic training and, specifically, training in specialized areas such as competition and economic regulation.

• *Procedural deficiencies.* A crucial aspect of competition policy is how the competition law is implemented. In the United States, for example, the competition authorities evaluate the possible anticompetitive aspects of mergers and other practices and then take their case to the courts, which are the ultimate decisionmakers. In contrast, in Mexico the CFC may issue a sanction or a fine in the first

---

15. Davies and Driffield (1998) report that in the case of the U.K. Monopoly and Merger Commission, ex officio investigations have priority over accusations.

16. In practice, most mergers claim to achieve some efficiency gains, or "synergies." Fisher (1987) argues in favor of establishing very high standards for proving such gains and cites examples where these gains were claimed but did not materialize.

instance, after which the CFC allows the sanctioned firms to appeal the decision. This device used in the appeal is an administrative, not a legal, procedure, under which the CFC must review its own decision and then decide whether to ratify, modify, or revoke it. If the CFC decides to ratify or modify the original resolution and the sanctioned firm remains unsatisfied, it can resort to a legal process called *juicio de amparo* (judicial review) through the local district court. However, this court may only challenge the legality or constitutionality of the commission's decision, not the merits. In any event, the court can give the firm an *amparo,* which suspends the application of the resolution. This process can take a long time (five to seven years),[17] during which the CFC may not apply its resolution until the court decides either to ratify it or to challenge its constitutionality. The whole procedure is very costly and slow and absorbs a substantial amount of the CFC's resources. Not surprisingly, this device has basically become a mechanism for delaying enforcement.

• *Further delays in the judicial process.* Besides seeking a *juicio de amparo,* firms can challenge a ratified resolution by presenting a formal appeal to the Federal Tribunal of Fiscal and Administrative Justice (Tribunal Federal de Justicia Fiscal y Administrativa, TFJFA). These two alternatives have been used more intensively in recent years as a way of avoiding the effective application of fines by the CFC. Not only can the sanctioned firm contest the fine in the administrative court, but the court can also evaluate the internal proceedings and the competition analysis that justified the fine. Thus, the TFJFA has become an additional step in the review of competition proceedings. This generates a vicious circle, where the revision by the TFJFA generates additional paperwork, unnecessarily drawing out the procedure and reducing the efficacy of the CFC's system of fines. The fact that judges lack specific training on competition issues gives firms even stronger incentives to appeal, using either of these two legal channels. This has slowed the implementation of competition policy in Mexico.

Overcoming the Obstacles

The following proposals may improve the effectiveness of competition policy reform:

• *Grant full autonomy to the CFC.* This should include financial autonomy, under which the CFC would request its own budget. Greater autonomy would make the CFC less vulnerable to capture by other government agencies.[18]

• *Create a specialized court.* A court specializing in economic issues, and competition and regulation in particular, is necessary for the proper implementation

---

17. Sometimes it can even take longer. For example, judicial review in the case of the CFC versus Telmex (the dominant firm in the telecommunications sector) took almost ten years.

18. There are several examples of autonomous competition authorities in less developed countries, including El Salvador and Honduras (Rivera and Schatan, 2008).

of competition policy. Such a court would offer many benefits in the implementation of competition policy, since it would eliminate long and costly administrative procedures and free up human, physical, and financial resources at the CFC. This court could be designed in a manner similar to Chile's Tribunal for the Defense of Free Competition.

• If the preceding recommendation is not possible or would take too long to implement, two others could be considered. The first would *internalize judicial risks in the design and implementation of competition policy.* In practical terms, the judicial system is the main obstacle to an effective competition policy. In the infamous Telmex case, the judicial process obstructed the proper implementation of competition policy through procedural delays and through judicial protection mechanisms (*amparos*). This case shows that there is always the risk that a case will become stalled in the judicial system, rendering the CFC ineffective. Legal problems have also limited the collection of fines: only 10 percent of fines due have been paid since the CFC's creation. This is disturbing, since fines are an important disincentive to monopolistic practices. The lesson is that judicial risks should be internalized in the design and implementation of competition policy. For example, if monopolistic predatory pricing is difficult to prove in a given case, the competition authority must opt for a different approach.

• *TFJFA proceedings should not constitute a review of LFCE procedures.* The TFJFA is not a specialized entity in anticompetitive policies and does not have any formal authority in those matters, according to Article 28 of the constitution. Therefore its use as a mechanism for reviewing LFCE procedures should not be allowed.

• *Improve the mechanism for conducting investigations of monopolistic practices.* A monitoring system for the generation and gathering of information on monopolistic practices should be created. Investigation of these practices should switch from the present reactive policy to a proactive one. At present the following are the main criteria used to determine whether to conduct an investigation: probability of success; the pursuit of certain anticompetitive practices that economic agents themselves have not reported; and the number of cases that the CFC can handle. This organizational scheme must be changed; the competition agency should be able to define priorities in order to carry out relevant ex officio investigations.

• *Define appropriate and specific methodologies.* Little is known about the evaluation criteria or the weight given to each variable in the decisions of the competition authority. Competition policy can hinder rather than foster economic activity if it increases transaction costs for both the government and economic agents. For instance, in trying to evaluate the potential efficiency gains of a merger, the CFC faces two limitations. The first is asymmetric information, in that the companies proposing the merger have an incentive to overestimate how much the merger will reduce marginal costs. The second is that the CFC lacks the instruments and the methodology to estimate marginal costs on its own and to accurately evaluate the likely efficiency gains of a merger. The commission should take a more assertive stance on this matter and not leave the corroboration of these possible gains to the companies. Since its creation, the CFC has taken steps to improve its methodology, but it has not yet developed the advanced quantitative techniques that would help it make better decisions.

Financial Sector Reform

Financial sector reform in Mexico is essential, because it has the potential to improve several of the weakest foundations for growth simultaneously, in particular the broad sharing of growth benefits, equal opportunities, and competition. The impact of this reform would be enhanced if it were preceded by legal and competition policy reform along the lines discussed above. These reforms are thus complementary; however, we believe that some measures can be taken independently.

Mexico has already been through several stages of financial reform. The previous reforms, however, were motivated by either macroeconomic stability or financial deregulation concerns. The first set of reforms sought the deregulation of the sector and included the privatization of banks, as discussed above. The second was launched in reaction to the tequila crisis and included the recapitalization of banks, improvements in prudential regulation, and new legislation oriented toward securing property rights and improving contract enforcement (in particular, the ability to foreclose on collateral).[19]

As already mentioned, the first set of reforms actually had negative effects on several important foundations for growth, such as macroeconomic stability, economic competition, and property rights. Neither set of reforms impinged in any significant way on the broad sharing of growth or on equal opportunities. Thus, financial reform to date cannot be considered successful, since it has not had a positive influence on the foundations for growth.

The financial sector in Mexico today is characterized by inadequate access and low financial deepening. In what follows we focus on the banking sector, which is still the most important source of financing and intermediation for the private sector (Stephanou and Salinas, 2007).

In terms of access, Mexico's financial sector ranks near the bottom worldwide. In a recent study (Beck, Demirgüç-Kunt, and Honohan, 2008) that measured financial access as the share of the adult population with access to an account with a financial intermediary, Mexico ranked 101st out of 157 countries, with just 25 percent of adults having access to an account. Among upper-middle-income countries (by the World Bank classification), Mexico has the lowest level of finan-

---

19. See Aspe (1993) and Murillo (2005) for a description of the first and second reform stages, respectively.

Figure 6. *Prevalence of Deposit Accounts and GDP per Capita, 2003–2004*

Accounts per person

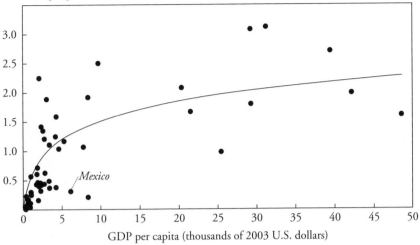

GDP per capita (thousands of 2003 U.S. dollars)

Source: Beck, Demirgüç-Kunt, and Honohan (2008), table A.2.

cial access of any country except Romania, and Mexico is well behind many other countries with lower income per capita.

A second measure of access to financial services is the number of deposit accounts per 1,000 people. According to Beck et al. (2008), Mexico's figure of 300 accounts per 1,000 is below that for many poorer countries, such as Guatemala, Ecuador, and El Salvador (around 400 per 1,000), about half that of Brazil and Colombia (600 per 1,000), and far below that of Chile, which has as many accounts as people. Figure 6 shows that Mexico has only about one-fourth the number of accounts that one would expect given its income per capita. Only Saudi Arabia performs worse on this measure.

Access to the banking sector in Mexico is not just a problem on the deposit side; there are also important problems both on the credit side and in the system of payments. Unfortunately, there are no comparable data available on the number of loans per capita. However, cross-country data on banking credit to the private sector show that although credit has started to increase in recent years, and is now around 22 percent of GDP, it is still only about half what one would expect given Mexico's income. In addition, 70 percent of localities in the country do not have a formal bank branch, which means that nearly 30 percent of the population lacks convenient access to any kind of financial service.

What explains this poor performance? The short and most popular answer in Mexico is that the banking sector is highly concentrated, not very competitive, and highly profitable, extracting economic rents from bank users. We present below some empirical evidence regarding these claims.

Table 6. *Mexico: Concentration in the Banking Sector, 2007*
Percent

	Share accounted for by		
Indicator	Two largest banks	Four largest banks	Six largest banks
Assets	43.7	68.9	82.2
Deposits	43.4	70.6	85.9
No. of branches	36.6	62.7	84.2
Income from fees[a]	54.7	81.8	93.8
Credit cards issued[a]	67.7	87.3	92.5
Consumer credit	52.0	77.2	87.7
Profits	55.4	80.0	92.1

Sources: National Banking Commission and Banco de México.
a. Data are for 2006.

Concentration. The Mexican banking sector is indeed highly concentrated. Although thirty-nine banks now operate in the country, the two largest control around half of the sector (table 6). The four largest banks account for around three-quarters of the sector, and the six largest for almost 90 percent. Although some other countries have concentration measures as high as or even higher than Mexico's, few of these countries are of comparable size or level of development.[20]

Competition. Of course, high concentration does not necessarily imply lack of competition. The generalized perception in Mexico, however, is that the banking sector is insufficiently competitive. This is supported by a recent report (Banco de México, 2007) suggesting that at least some important segments of the banking sector do not behave in a manner consistent with competition.[21] The study analyzed the degree of competition in the bank credit market by type of loan (consumer, mortgages, and commercial) from 2000 to 2005 and found that the intensity of competition across these types of loans is not homogeneous. In particular, for at least one type (consumer credit), the researchers could not reject the hypothesis of perfectly collusive behavior, and for another (commercial credit) they could not reject the hypothesis of monopolistic competition. The only segment of the market that seemed to behave competitively was the mortgage credit market. Avalos and Hernández-Trillo (2008) have argued that this segment of the market has faced increasing competition from nonbank entities (the so-called SOFOLES). As these authors show, mortgage rates have declined substantially in recent years as competition between banks and other financial intermediaries has intensified.

20. See Caprio, Levine, and Barth (2007) and CFC (2007b).
21. See also Negrín et al. (2008) and Solís (2008).

Figure 7. *Mexico: Profitability of the Banking Sector, 1999–2007*

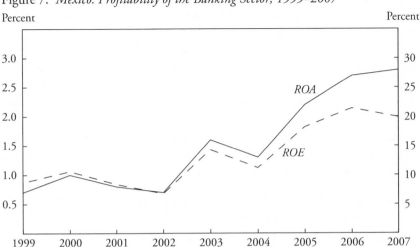

Source: Comisión Federal de Competencia (2007b); authors' estimates.

Profitability. The perception that Mexican banks are highly profitable is not without basis. Figure 7 shows two standard indicators of profitability for the banking system, return on assets (ROA) and return on equity (ROE), for 1999–2007. The figure shows good levels of profitability and, more important, a rising trend in the past few years. By way of comparison, Negrín et al. (2008) show that average ROA in 2000–03 and 2004–06 for a sample of emerging market economies was close to 1.0 and 1.8 percent, respectively, below the ROA for the Mexican banking system in those same periods (CFC, 2007b).

The high degree of concentration in Mexico's banking sector and the lack of competition in certain segments of the credit market certainly help explain the recent increase in the sector's profitability. To see how these aspects are related, however, we need to consider two additional pieces of information: interest rates by type of loan and the composition of banks' loan portfolios.

The implicit average interest rate on consumer credit is almost three times that on mortgage and commercial loans (28.4 percent versus 10.4 and 9.9 percent, respectively). The difference in total costs, which include bank fees, between consumer credit (on credit cards) and mortgage credit is even greater: 47 percent versus 13 percent.[22] Of course, part of this difference is due to the higher risks and operating costs associated with consumer credit; however, lack of competition in the consumer credit subsector could also be playing a role, as suggested by the CFC (2007b).

---

22. Data are for April 2007. For more details see CFC (2007b).

In terms of portfolio composition, it is interesting to see how the Mexican banking sector has switched substantial resources away from commercial and mortgage loans and toward consumption lending (the segment in which the sector seems to behave collusively). This segment, which used to represent about 5 percent of the banks' total loan portfolio, now accounts for about one-third.

To sum up, more resources are now devoted to consumer loans, where banks usually charge much higher fees and interest rates, resulting not only in a highly profitable banking sector, but also in one where commercial lending has lost relevance and where social exclusion is still quite important. In that sense the banking system does not seem to be contributing to the development of the economy; this alone could justify a new financial reform.

Objectives of the Reform and Their Impact on the Foundations for Growth

Financial reform should seek to achieve the following objectives:
- Enhance competition (which in turn could have positive effects on competition in many other sectors).
- Increase access to both sides of the industry (deposits and loans), without compromising financial stability.
- Improve conditions of access to financial services and, more important, level the playing field with respect to access to financial resources.

As already mentioned, financial reform along these lines could have a positive effect on the following foundations: broad sharing of the benefits of growth, equal opportunities, and greater competition. Appropriate prudential regulation and supervision are also important, so that achieving these objectives does not harm the macroeconomic stability foundation.

Achieving the above objectives will undoubtedly have positive effects that go well beyond the financial sector. Indeed, financial sector reform can be considered a prerequisite to faster economic growth.[23] For example, providing greater and better access to financial resources for small and medium-size firms may contribute to reducing the gap between these and larger firms, which can usually borrow on better terms or in foreign financial markets. In fact, many large non-exporting companies are also in need of domestic currency credit. Leveling the playing field for small and medium-size firms is therefore crucial so that these firms can not only survive, but also invest and grow and become more competitive in their own sectors (Beck and Demirgüç-Kunt, 2006).

For microenterprises, the fact of access to financial resources may be even more important than improving the terms of that access. Most microentrepreneurs (60.8 percent) seeking start-up capital resort to their own savings; other sources of credit include savings and loan institutions (15.7 percent), friends and relatives

---

23. See, for example, Aghion, Howitt, and Mayer-Foulkes (2005).

(13.7 percent), carryover business capital (5.1 percent), moneylenders (2.1 percent), and suppliers and clients (2.0 percent). Only 0.6 percent seek financing from commercial banks.[24]

OBSTACLES TO SUCCESSFUL REFORM

At least three main local constraints or obstacles stand in the way of successful reform: the judicial system, competition policy, and the potential for misguided diagnosis. We review each of these in turn.

The Judicial System. The inefficiency and corruption of the judicial system threaten to undermine the efficacy of financial reform. Reform is likely to have better results if it is accompanied by a properly functioning judicial system.

An appropriately designed financial system will have a strong influence on the protection of property rights. Making this happen will require not only sound law but also the ability to enforce it. For example, when extending a loan, a bank needs a strong legal and judicial system in order to be able to seize collateral in case of default. Most banking and financial transactions take the form of contracts, which the judicial system has to be efficient at enforcing. This is particularly important in situations of financial distress, when interest rates may become more volatile and financial risks increase. The protection of property rights and the efficiency of the judicial system are therefore essential conditions for financial reform to be effective.

The recent literature on financial reform emphasizes the relationship between financial and legal institutions. For example, Laeven and Majnoni (2005) found that an efficient judicial system helps reduce the costs of credit. Beck, Demirgüç-Kunt, and Maksimovic (2005, 2006) found that the interaction between legal and financial variables explains firm size in a sample of countries, and that weakness in these variables may act as a constraint on the growth of small and medium-size firms. The interaction between financial reform and judicial reform is important for leveling the playing field for smaller firms.

Competition Policy. A strong CFC would be very helpful in implementing financial reform in Mexico, since it may have to confront one of the most important, concentrated, and powerful sectors of the Mexican economy: the banks. A weak CFC could become an obstacle to successful implementation. It would therefore be highly desirable to proceed with financial reform only after competition policy has been reformed along the lines discussed above. This, however, should not become an impediment to proceeding with this reform.

Errors in Diagnosis. A wrong, incomplete, or misguided diagnosis of the situation could lead to a poorly designed reform. Enhancing competition in the consumer credit market is a necessary but not sufficient condition for this reform to be successful. Although improving the conditions of consumer credit is important

---

24. For more details see Hernandez-Trillo, Pagán, and Paxton (2005).

in and of itself, another fundamental issue should not be overlooked, namely, the need to promote, through appropriate market incentives and regulations, the channeling of additional resources toward productive and profitable projects of small and medium-size firms. This is probably one of the most important channels through which the financial sector can have an effect on economic growth, and it should not be underestimated.

Promoting competition in the financial sector actually has several dimensions that should be addressed simultaneously: promoting interbank competition, creating a more pro-competitive environment within the banking sector, and promoting competition between banks and nonbank institutions in certain areas. The last of these is critical, since there is evidence, both international and domestic, that when nonbank institutions are able to contest the monopoly power of banks, margins are reduced and banks behave more competitively. This was the case in the United States (Allen and Santomero, 2001), where pension and investment funds have been the main competitors with banks in recent decades. A similar situation occurred recently in Mexico, where the appearance in 1996 of the institutions known as SOFOLES led to a substantial reduction in mortgage interest rates (Avalos and Hernández-Trillo, 2008).

A multidimensional approach to the promotion of competition in the financial sector is justified not only by the evidence described above, but also because competition is necessary to reduce banks' incentives to use their resources in a manner that is relatively unproductive in terms of social welfare. Almost two-thirds of the profits of the Mexican banking system between 1999 and 2005 came from fees, commissions, and investments in securities (mainly government bonds), and only about one-third from interest on loans. Of the latter, almost 70 percent came from consumer credit, where credit cards are the most important instrument. This means that banks have restricted their activities to those that are either risk-free (securities) or risky but highly profitable (consumer credit). This behavior has undoubtedly taken a toll on commercial credit, which has largely disappeared from bank portfolios.

Of course, such behavior is absolutely rational and consistent with the incentives and regulation that banks face. For that reason, competition must be promoted on many fronts so that banks return to their original role as financial intermediaries between savers and firms willing to carry out productive and profitable projects.

Overcoming the Obstacles

What needs to be done to achieve the objectives of reform and to avoid the obstacles just identified? We offer the following specific suggestions:

• *Promote competition throughout the financial sector,* and specifically in commercial and consumer bank credit. In general, this competition should come from various sources: from a larger number of banks, from a more pro-competitive environment within the banking sector, and from nonbanking institutions. The following are specific proposals in this direction.

• *Reduce barriers to entry.* Even after a recent 11 percent reduction, Mexico's initial capital requirements for new banks remain among the highest in the world, at around $330 million. As the CFC (2007b) has noted, this is about nine times the amount required in Canada, five times that in Europe, four times that in Chile and Brazil, and more than twice that in Japan. Although the so-called niche banks now have separate requirements starting as low as $130 million, this is still a high figure and may act as an important barrier to entry.

• *Develop an appropriate framework of regulatory and prudential supervision for niche banks.* This new type of bank was approved with a modification to the Law of Credit Institutions in mid-2006. However, as of May 2008 the financial authorities had not yet developed an appropriate regulatory framework for these institutions. As a consequence, although many applications have been submitted, none has yet been approved. It is urgent that the appropriate regulatory framework for these banks be put in place.

• *Improve the competitive environment in the banking sector.* This could require a much more decisive intervention by the competition authorities on issues such as collusion in the consumer credit market, as well as in the determination of banking fees, which today appear quite high. If the competition authorities are unable to intervene directly and establish sanctions for noncompetitive behavior in this sector, because of the absence of further competition policy reform, then compelling testimony on this issue like that offered in CFC (2007b) could be very helpful in convincing the financial authorities to intervene.

• *Promote the development of nonbank financial institutions.* It has been shown that when banks face competition, either from other banks or from other financial intermediaries, they react as one would expect: they reduce their margins and compete on the basis of both price and quality of service. It is therefore essential to promote the development of new financial institutions.

• *Eliminate or reduce monopoly power in certain activities.* For example, there seem to be important barriers to entry into specific activities such as credit card issuance and government bond sales. Recently, some retail stores such as Wal-Mart have opened their own banks in order to participate in the consumer credit market, and in particular the credit card market. Although this outcome is desirable from the point of view of greater competition, it raises an important question: should it be necessary to become a formal bank in order to get access to the credit card market? We believe that lowering barriers to entry into the credit card industry is necessary. A similar story applies to government bond sales. Most financial institutions require a minimum purchase of between $30,000 and $50,000. Of course, this excludes small savers from the market, who must then purchase mutual funds, where high fees and commissions are charged, in order to participate. Here a scheme similar to that in the United States could be implemented, where government bonds are sold even over the Internet and participants can invest as little as $1,000.

Conclusions

In this chapter we have analyzed the relationship between economic reform and economic growth in Mexico. We have discussed why some of the reforms of the 1980s and 1990s might have failed to generate rapid and sustained economic growth. We argue that the main reason was that some of the reforms did not positively affect the foundations for growth in Mexico, either because they were not intended to do so or because they failed in their design or implementation. That was the case with both privatization and pension reform and, to a much lesser extent, with trade liberalization. These outcomes, together with a negative popular perception of the reforms and the emergence of a more complex political environment, have given rise to reform inaction and reform fatigue in Mexico since the late 1990s.

The second part of the chapter analyzed how this inaction might be overcome, and how some specific reforms might help to restore economic growth in Mexico. We proposed and discussed reforms in three areas—legal reform, competition policy reform, and financial reform—that we believe are politically viable and that should positively affect the weakest foundations for growth in Mexico. These reforms, besides being relevant in their own right, may also help some of the earlier reforms work better. The proposed reforms may also interact with and reinforce each other, and together they could have a positive effect on the foundations for growth of the Mexican economy.

References

Aghion, Phillip, Peter Howitt, and David Mayer-Foulkes. 2005. "The Effect of Financial Development on Convergence: Theory and Evidence." *Quarterly Journal of Economics* 120 (February): 173–222.

Allen, Franklin, and Anthony M. Santomero. 2001. "What Do Financial Intermediaries Do?" *Journal of Banking and Finance* 25, no. 2 (February): 271–94.

Aspe, Pedro. 1993. *Economic Transformation the Mexican Way.* Lionel Robbins Lectures. MIT Press.

Avalos, Marcos, and Rafael De Hoyos. 2008. "An Empirical Analysis of Mexican Merger Policy." Policy Research Working Paper 4527. Washington: World Bank.

Avalos, Marcos, and Fausto Hernández-Trillo. 2008. "Competencia Bancaria en México." In E. Rivera and C. Schatan, eds., *Centroamérica y México: Políticas de Competencia a Principios del Siglo XXI.* Mexico City: CEPAL.

Banco de México. 2007. *Reporte sobre el Sistema Financiero 2006.* Mexico City.

Beck, Thorsten, and Asli Demirgüç-Kunt. 2006. "Small and Medium-Size Enterprises: Access to Finance as a Growth Constraint." *Journal of Banking and Finance* 30, no. 11: 2931–43.

Beck, Thorsten, Asli Demirgüç-Kunt, and Patrick Honohan. 2008. *Finance for All: Policies and Pitfalls in Expanding Access.* World Bank Policy Research Report. Washington: World Bank.

Beck, T., A. Demirgüç-Kunt, and V. Maksimovic. 2005. "Financial and Legal Constraints to Growth: Does Firm Size Matter?" *Journal of Finance* 40, no. 1: 137–77.

———. 2006. "The Influence of Financial and Legal Insitutions on Firm Size." *Journal of Banking and Finance* 30: 2995–3015.

Berg, Andy, Jonathan Ostry, and Jeromin Zettelmeyer. 2006. "What Makes Growth Sustained?" Washington: International Monetary Fund.

Borraz, Fernando, and J. E. López-Córdova. 2007. "Has Globalization Deepened Income Inequality in Mexico?" *Global Economy Journal* (International Trade and Finance Association) 7, no. 1: 1–55.

Caprio, G., R. E. Levine, and J. R. Barth. 2007. "Bank Regulation and Supervision Database." Washington: World Bank.

Chong, Alberto, and Florencio López-de-Silanes. 2005. "Privatization in Mexico." In *Privatization in Latin America: Myths and Reality.* Stanford University Press and Inter-American Development Bank.

Comisión Federal de Competencia (CFC). 2006. "Opinión con el Fin de Promover la Aplicación de los Principios de Competencia y de Libre Concurrencia en el Sistema de Ahorro para el Retiro (SAR)." Mexico City (November).

———. 2007a. *Annual Report 2006.* Mexico City.

———. 2007b. "Opinión con el Fin de Promover la Aplicación de los Principios de Competencia y de Libre Concurrencia en los Servicios Bancarios al Menudeo." Mexico City (April).

Davies, Stephen W., and Nigel L. Driffield. 1998. *Monopoly Policy in the UK: Assessing the Evidence.* Cheltenham, U.K.: Edward Elgar.

Del Villar, Rafael. 2007. "Competencia y Equidad en Telecomunicaciones." Banco de México, Mexico City (November).

Dollar, David, and Aart Kraay. 2002. "Growth Is Good for the Poor." *Journal of Economic Growth* 7, no. 3: 195–225.

Dutz, Mark, and Aydin Hayri. 2000. "Does More Intense Competition Lead to Higher Growth?" Policy Research Working Paper 2320. Washington: World Bank.

Easterly, William, Norbert Fiess, and Daniel Lederman. 2003. "NAFTA and Convergence in North America: High Expectations, Big Events, Little Time." *Economia* 4, no. 1: 1–54.

Elizondo, Carlos, and Luis M. Pérez. 2006. "Separación de Poderes y Garantías Individuales: La Suprema Corte y los Derechos de los Contribuyentes." *Cuestiones Constitucionales: Revista Mexicana de Derecho Constitucional* 14: 91–130.

Enrigue, Hilda G. 2006. "La Suprema Corte y la Desigualdad en el Acceso a la Justicia: ¿A Quién Sirve el Amparo en Materia Fiscal?" Thesis, Instituto Tecnológico Autónomo de México.

Escaith, Hubert, and Igor Paunovic. 2004. "Reformas Estructurales en América Latina y el Caribe en el Periodo 1970–2000: Indices y Notas Metodológicas." Documento Electrónico LC/W.10. Santiago, Chile: CEPAL (October).

Esquivel, Gerardo. 2008. "The Dynamics of Income Inequality in Mexico since NAFTA." El Colegio de México.

Esquivel, Gerardo, Daniel Lederman, Miguel Messmacher, and Renata Villoro. 2002. "Why NAFTA Did Not Reach the South." Office of the Chief Economist for Latin America and the Caribbean, World Bank, Washington.

Fisher, Franklin M. 1987. "Horizontal Mergers: Triage and Treatment." *Journal of Economic Perspectives* 1, no. 2: 23–40.

García-Verdú, Rodrigo. 2007. "Demographics, Human Capital and Economic Growth in Mexico: 1950–2005." World Bank, Washington (June).

Gil-Díaz, Francisco. 2003. "Don't Blame Our Failures on Reforms That Have Not Taken Place." In *Fraser Forum.* Calgary, Alberta, Canada: Fraser Institute.

Grandolini, Gloria, and Luis Cerda. 1998. "The 1997 Pension Reform in México." Policy Research Working Paper 1933. Washington: World Bank.

Guasch, J. Luis. 2004. "Confirming Anecdote and Theory: Empirical Analysis of the Determinants of Renegotiation." In J. L. Guasch, *Granting and Renegotiating Infrastructure Concessions,* chapter 6. WBI Development Studies. Washington: World Bank.

Gwartney, James, and Robert Lawson. 2007. *Economic Freedom of the World 2007 Annual Report.* Economic Freedom Network.

Haber, Stephen. 2005. "Mexico's Experiments with Bank Privatization and Liberalization, 1991–2003." *Journal of Banking and Finance* 29: 2325–53.

Hellman, Joel S. 1998. "Winners Take All: The Politics of Partial Reform in Postcommunist Transitions." *World Politics* 50, no. 2: 203–34.

Hernández Ochoa, César E. 2006. "La Seguridad Jurídica en México: Seis Problemas y Seis Propuestas de Solución." Mexico City: Centro de Investigación para el Desarrollo.

Hernández-Trillo, Fausto, José A. Pagán, and Julia Paxton. 2005. "Start-up Capital, Microenterprises and Technical Efficiency in Mexico." *Review of Development Economics* 9, no. 3: 434–47.

Heston, Alan, Robert Summers, and Bettina Aten. 2006. *Penn World Table Version 6.2.* Center for International Comparisons of Production, Income, and Prices at the University of Pennsylvania (September).

Krakowski, Michael. 2005. "Competition Policy Works: The Effect of Competition Policy on the Intensity of Competition: An International Cross-Country Comparison." HWWA Discussion Paper 332. Hamburg Institute of International Economics.

Laeven, Luc, and Giovanni Majnoni. 2005. "Does Judicial Efficiency Lower the Cost of Credit?" *Journal of Banking and Finance* 29, no. 7: 1791–1812.

Laeven, Luc, and Christopher Woodruff. 2007. "The Quality of the Legal System, Firm Ownership and Firm Size." *Review of Economics and Statistics* 89, no. 4: 601–14.

Laporta, Rafael, Florencio López-de-Silanes, and Guillermo Zamarripa. 2003. "Related Lending." *Quarterly Journal of Economics* 118, no. 1: 231–68.

Lederman, Daniel, William F. Maloney, and Luis Servén. 2005. *Lessons from NAFTA.* Stanford University Press and World Bank.

Lehoucq, F., G. Negretto, F. Aparicio, B. Nacif, and A. Benton. 2005. "Political Institutions, Policymaking Processes, and Policy Outcomes in Mexico." Working Paper R-512. Washington: Inter-American Development Bank (September).

Loayza, Norman, Pablo Fajnzylber, and César Calderón. 2005. "Economic Growth in Latin America and the Caribbean: Stylized Facts, Explanations and Forecasts." World Bank Latin American and the Caribbean Studies. Washington (April).

López Ayllón, Sergio, and Héctor Fix-Fierro. 2003. "'Faraway, So Close!' The Rule of Law and Legal Change in Mexico, 1970–2000." In Lawrence M. Friedman and Rogelio Pérez-Perdomo, eds., *Legal Culture in the Age of Globalization: Latin America and Latin Europe.* Stanford University Press.

López-Córdova, José E. 2003. "NAFTA and Manufacturing Productivity in Mexico." *Economía* 4, no. 1: 55–88.

Lustig, Nora. 1998. *Mexico: The Remaking of an Economy,* 2nd ed. Brookings.

Magaloni, Ana Laura, and Layda Negrete. 2000. "Desafueros del Poder: La Política Judicial de Decidir sin Resolver." *Trayectorias: Revista de Ciencias Sociales de la Universidad Autónoma de Nuevo León, México* no. 2.

Morley S., R. Machado, and S. Pettinato. 1999. "Indexes of Structural Reform in Latin America." Serie Reformas Económicas 12. Santiago, Chile: ECLAC.

Munguía, Luis. 2008. "Crecimiento Económico y Desigualdad de Ingresos en México." Thesis, El Colegio de México.

Murillo, José Antonio. 2005. "La Banca Después de la Privatización. Auge, Crisis y Reordenamiento." In G. del Angel-Mobarak, C. Bazdresch, and F. Suárez, eds., *Cuando el Estado se Hizo Banquero.* Mexico City: Fondo de Cultura Económica.

Negrín, J. L., E. Bátiz, D. Ocampo, and P. Struck. 2008. "Competition in the Mexican Banking Credit Market." Banco de México, Mexico City.

Nohlen, Dieter. (2005). "Mexico." In D. Nohlen, ed., *Election in the Americas: A Data Handbook.* Vol. 1. Oxford: Oxford University Press.

Organization for Economic Cooperation and Development. 2004. *Report on Regulatory Reform: Regulatory Reform in Mexico.* Paris.

———. 2006. *OECD Economic Outlook.* Paris.

Paredes, Víctor. 2007. *Privatización de Puertos en México.* Estudios de Competencia y Regulación. Mexico City: Centro de Investigación para el Desarrollo.

Rivera, Eugenio, and Claudia Schatan. 2008. "Los Mercados en el Istmo Centroamericano y México: ¿Qué Ha Pasado con la Competencia?" In E. Rivera and C. Schatan, eds., *Centroamérica y México: Políticas de Competencia a Principios del Siglo XXI.* Santiago, Chile: CEPAL.

Rogozinski, Jacques. 1998. *High Price for Change: Privatization in Mexico.* Washington: Inter-American Development Bank.

Sachs, Jeffrey D., Aarón Tornell, and Andrés Velasco. 1996. "Financial Crises in Emerging Markets: The Lessons from 1995." *Brookings Papers on Economic Activity* no. 1 (Spring).

Sinha, Tapen, and Alejandro Rentería. 2005. "The Cost of Minimum Pension Guarantee." Instituto Tecnológico Autónomo de México.

Solís, Liliana. 2008. "Analysis of Banking Competition in Mexico." Ph.D. dissertation. Universidad Complutense de Madrid.

Stephanou, Constantinos, and Emanuel Salinas. 2007. "Financing of the Private Sector in Mexico, 2000–2005: Evolution, Composition and Determinants." Policy Research Working Paper 4264. Washington: World Bank (June).

Székely, Miguel. 2005. "Pobreza y Desigualdad en México entre 1950 y 2004." *El Trimestre Económico* 72, no. 288 (October-December).

Tornell, Aarón, and Gerardo Esquivel. 1997. "The Political Economy of Mexico's Entry into NAFTA." In T. Ito and A. O. Krueger, eds., *Regionalism versus Multilateral Trade Arrangements.* University of Chicago Press.

Tornell, Aaron, Frank Westermann, and Lorenza Martinez-Trigueros. 2004. "NAFTA and Mexico's Less-Than-Stellar Performance." Working Paper 10289. Cambridge, Mass.: National Bureau of Economic Research.

Zettelmeyer, Jeromin. 2006. "Growth and Reforms in Latin America: A Survey of Facts and Arguments." Working Paper WP/06/210. Washington: International Monetary Fund (September).

7

Helping Reforms Deliver Inclusive Growth in Peru

EDUARDO MORÓN, JUAN FRANCISCO CASTRO, AND CYNTHIA SANBORN

The performance of the Peruvian economy in the last half century has been less than stellar in terms of achieving inclusive growth, even during the recent boom. Although Peru has had spells of faster growth than the rest of the region, none lasted long enough to significantly reduce poverty and inequality. For decades the majority of Peruvians have lived at or below the poverty line, and in the past twenty years social and economic inequalities have worsened, fueling social discontent and leading to calls for radical change.

This is not to say that major economic reforms have not been attempted. On the contrary, dramatic swings between market-oriented and state-oriented policies have been part of the problem. In the late 1960s and the 1970s, a military-led "revolution" attempted radical transformation of the country's inequitable economic and social structures, but internal and external crises put an end to that experiment. In the 1980s the introduction of more heterodox policies ended up deepening the economic crisis and fomenting political violence. This episode was followed by dramatic, market-oriented reforms under more authoritarian rule in the 1990s; these, too, ultimately failed to put the country on a more sustained and

We wish to acknowledge a very thoughtful discussion of an earlier version of this document with Martín Benavides, Mauricio Cárdenas, Elmer Cuba, Eduardo Fernández-Arias, Ana María Rodriguez, Mayen Ugarte, and Gustavo Yamada. As usual, these are our personal opinions and should not necessarily be taken as the institutional view of the Centro de Investigación de la Universidad del Pacífico.

inclusive growth path. Growth in both decades was even more volatile than in the region as a whole. Peru's most recent growth spurt, which began in 2002, has occurred in the context of a world economic upturn of uncertain duration, accompanied by a revival of political movements denouncing the lack of "trickle down" and advocating a return to more statist and nationalist policies.

This chapter uses the CGD framework to evaluate Peru's recent reform efforts and determine their impact on the foundations for inclusive growth, and to analyze how to proceed with further reform. To many observers, Peru today seems ready to join the ranks of Chile and Mexico, countries that have achieved considerable macroeconomic stability and embarked on a positive growth path. However, we will argue that Peru still faces significant obstacles to truly inclusive growth.

The chapter is organized as follows. In the next section we present some stylized facts on growth, poverty, and inequality in Peru. We then discuss which of the growth foundations were addressed and which were ignored in the reforms of recent decades, and we select three areas for further analysis—public administration reform, education reform, and political reform—that we believe are largely "missing ingredients" in Peru's reform recipe to date. After summarizing the reforms of the 1990s, we discuss each of the above three areas in detail, analyzing their impact on the growth foundations. The final section offers some concluding remarks.

Growth, Poverty, and Inequality: Some Stylized Facts

A key difference between Peru and other countries in the region is that Peru reformed late, and when it did reform, often went to extremes (Frieden, 2007). But Peru's reforms were not those of the Washington consensus, but rather more fundamental political and social reforms, involving the creation of a legitimate national state and national identity, the extension of the voting franchise to all adults, basic land and labor reforms, and the provision of public education and health services, among others. Economic growth in the early twentieth century had not resulted in the development and modernization of the country's rural areas, even when the sources of growth were located there. Economic and political power has always been concentrated in Lima; indeed, one notable characteristic of the country is the absence of other large cities.

Through most of the twentieth century, political exclusion and economic and social exclusion ran in parallel. During much of its history since independence, Peru has been under military dictatorship; full political democracy with universal suffrage was achieved only in 1980. Throughout its modern history, Peru has had only one strong political party, the Alianza Popular Revolucionaria Americana (APRA), which for long periods operated secretively. The party system has remained weak and fragmented, based on individual *caudillos* (strongmen) rather than lasting

Figure 1. *Real GDP per Capita in Peru and Six Other South American Countries,*
1950–2004

Index, 1950 = 100

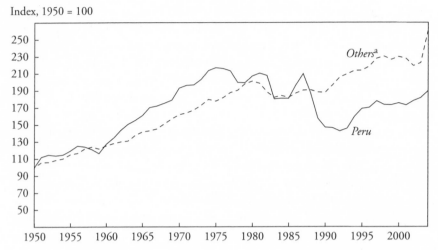

Source: World Bank data.

a. Average of the six major Latin American economies (LAC6), Argentina, Brazil, Chile, Colombia, Venezuela, and Uruguay.

institutions. Unlike some of its neighbors, Peru has no strong regionally based political movements, and significant political decentralization began only in 2001.

During the quarter century up to 1975, Peru's economic growth surpassed that of its largest neighbors (figure 1), with GDP per capita more than doubling in real terms, to almost 80 percent of the average of the six most developed economies on the continent. The Peruvian economy then got off track, compared not only with its neighbors but also with the rest of the world, and GDP per capita fell to only about half that in the above six countries. As Llosa and Panizza (2007) put it, Peru lost three decades of growth while the region as a whole lost only one. Growth resumed in the 1990s, however, and real GDP per capita returned to its previous peak in 2006.

These stylized facts raise two obvious questions: How did Peru manage to lose one-third of its GDP per capita? And what changed to allow Peru to make up that lost ground in a decade and a half? The potential explanations are, of course, the usual suspects: domestic policy decisions, external shocks, and initial conditions.

Peru, like most of the region, has faced significant problems in raising growth through increased productivity. A standard growth decomposition finds that over the last fifty years, only 10 percent of Peru's growth was due to higher total factor productivity (table 1). Perhaps the most obvious of many reasons for this poor performance is mistaken domestic policy decisions. GDP growth was close to zero in the "lost decade" of the 1980s. In that same period, the Peruvian economy

Table 1. *Peru: Accounting for Growth, 1950–2006*

Period	Growth of GDP (percent a year)	Contribution of (percentage points)		
		Labor	*Capital*	*Total factor productivity*
1950–60	5.73	1.34	1.20	3.19
1960–70	5.57	1.79	1.28	2.49
1970–80	3.12	2.19	1.81	−0.89
1980–90	0.36	2.63	0.89	−3.18
1990–2000	2.78	2.04	1.02	−0.28
2000–06	3.85	1.85	0.83	1.16
1950–2006	3.53	1.98	1.20	0.34

Source: Morón and Bernedo (2007).

reduced its openness (imports plus exports as a share of GDP) by half, from 60 percent to 30 percent, while fiscal imprudence and the absence of an independent central bank led to hyperinflation.

In the last twenty years, the poverty rate has varied between 45 and 55 percent, closely following the economic cycle. Yet even when growth has been accompanied by reduced poverty, it has not necessarily been inclusive. We will illustrate this by measuring the extent to which changes in poverty during the expansions and recessions of the last twelve years were accompanied by reduced inequality.[1]

Following Datt and Ravallion (1992), we decompose changes in poverty into growth and inequality components. The first of these components measures the change in poverty that would have occurred had inequality remained constant while mean household income grew at the observed rate. The second measures the change in poverty that would have occurred had mean household income remained constant while inequality changed as actually observed. We then construct pro-poor indices and classify our results, presented in table 2 and summarized in figure 2, according to the method of Kakwani and Pernia (2000).

The pro-poor index (last column of table 2) measures the extent to which changes in inequality have contributed positively to reducing poverty. For a given growth component, the pro-poor index will rise as the inequality component becomes smaller. Clearly, a negative inequality component (meaning that the distribution of income improved during the period) will imply a pro-poor index larger than one. According to the threshold values and classifications proposed by

---

1. For this exercise we use a strong definition of "pro-poor": we expect poverty to fall by more than it would have if all incomes had grown at the same rate. Other, weaker definitions regard growth as "pro-poor" if all households enjoy the same proportionate increase in income (thus maintaining inequality unaltered), or even if it is accompanied by a reduction in the poverty rate (which could well entail an increase in inequality).

Table 2. *Peru: Growth and Inequality Components of the Change in Poverty*

Period	Domain	Poverty rate (percent) In initial year	In final year	Change in poverty rate (percentage points)	Growth component	Inequality component	Pro-poor index[a]
1994–97	National	53.42	50.69	−2.7	−21.73	19.00	0.13
	Urban	46.88	42.95	−3.93	−24.19	20.26	0.16
	Rural	65.56	64.85	−0.71	−15.23	14.53	0.05
1997–2001[b]	National	42.72	54.80	12.08	9.68	2.40	0.80
	Urban	29.72	42.04	12.33	10.81	1.51	0.88
	Rural	66.33	78.44	12.11	7.73	4.38	0.64
2001–2006[b]	National	54.80	44.53	−10.2	−8.65	−1.62	1.19
	Urban	42.04	31.20	−10.84	−8.55	−2.30	1.27
	Rural	78.44	69.33	−9.11	−10.02	0.91	0.91

Sources: Encuesta Nacional de Hogares sobre Medición de Niveles de Vida (ENNIV) for 1994 and 1997; Encuesta Nacional de Hogares sobre Condiciones de Vida y Pobreza (ENAHO) for 1997, 2001, and 2006; authors' calculations.

a. Calculated as the change in the poverty rate divided by the growth component except for the period 1997–2001, which used the inverse because of the increase in poverty incidence.

b. Despite observed discrepancies, the 1997–2001 period was analyzed using the 1997 poverty rate reported by ENAHO to maintain consistency between databases.

Figure 2. *Peru: Pro-Poor Index, 1994–97, 1997–2001, and 2001–06[a]*

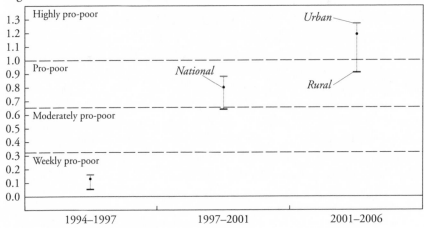

Source: Authors' calculations; see table 2.

Kakwani and Pernia (2000) and used in figure 2, this will, in turn, imply that growth is "highly pro-poor." What table 2 and figure 2 show is that although the incidence of poverty has followed a cyclical path, the "pro-poorness" of Peru's growth exhibits a clear positive trend, indicating that the benefits of growth are being enjoyed more broadly today than in the recent past.

Several caveats are necessary, however. First, the term "highly" can be misleading: strictly speaking, the 2001–06 period is the only one in which the term "pro-poor" can be related to a reduction in inequality. Second, figure 2 also reveals that urban-rural differences in "pro-poorness" are growing. Although expansions in income are now more evenly distributed on a national basis, urban-rural disparities are worsening.[2] Finally, and most important for this project, it is difficult to relate this recent reduction in poverty and inequality to any particular reform effort. This raises doubt as to whether this single "pro-poor" growth episode marks the beginning of a permanent reduction in poverty or is vulnerable to a future reversal. An important question, then, is what further reforms are still required to prevent another sharp increase in poverty and inequality, like that experienced during the mild recession of 1997–2001, when the next negative shock occurs.

As we have seen, until very recently Peru has been unable to achieve sustainable growth that also reduced poverty or inequality on a long-term basis. The current growth spurt has unique characteristics that call the previous path into question. The economy has now grown for more than six consecutive years, and poverty in 2007 was lower than in 2004 in all regions (table 3). Even extreme poverty (defined as the share of the population living on less than one dollar a day) has declined in all regions, although by more on the coast and in urban areas.

A striking feature of the Peruvian economy, as of many others in Latin America, is the government's apparent inability to alter the income distribution through fiscal policy. In developed economies the distribution of income does not necessarily follow the distribution of assets, because fiscal policy serves as a potent equalizer of opportunities (Goñi, López, and Servén, 2008). In Latin America, however, the income distribution after taxes and transfers is usually worse than before. The region's opportunity equalizer mechanism is broken.

The main problem for Peru is how to achieve relatively rapid economic growth that can be sustained not only across long periods but also across the country. As the next section will show, some reforms have been achieved, and the fact that Peru has enjoyed solid growth in the last six years speaks for itself. However, most of these reforms failed to focus on the bottom of the income distribution. The unspoken macroeconomic strategy in the last two decades has been to let economic growth trickle down. Apparently, gravity is not enough.

---

2. In fact, the inequality component in rural areas remained positive in 2001–06, and rural poverty has remained stagnant at around 70 percent in the last three years, while urban poverty has fallen by almost 6 percent. Rural poverty would have fallen more had rural growth been more pro-poor.

Table 3. *Peru: Poverty Rate by Geographic Area*
Percent of population

Area	2004	2005	2006	2007
All Peru	48.6	48.7	44.5	39.3
Urban versus rural				
Urban	37.1	36.8	31.2	25.7
Rural	69.8	70.9	69.3	64.6
Natural region				
Coast	35.1	34.2	28.7	22.6
Highlands	64.7	65.6	63.4	60.1
Forest	57.7	60.3	56.6	48.4
Geographic domain				
Urban coast	37.1	32.2	29.9	25.1
Rural coast	51.2	50.0	49.0	38.1
Urban highlands	44.8	44.4	40.2	36.3
Rural highlands	75.8	77.3	76.5	73.3
Urban forest	50.4	53.9	49.9	40.3
Rural forest	63.8	65.6	62.3	55.3
Metropolitan Lima	30.9	32.6	24.2	18.5

Source: Instituto Nacional de Estadística e Informática (INEI).

Foundations for Growth in Peru: Promise and Reality

This section focuses on the reforms attempted during and since the 1990s and their potential for delivering inclusive growth. We use the proposed CGD framework to guide our discussion of a set of reforms that, working through the foundations identified in the framework, should have yielded inclusive growth but failed to do so. Given that all five foundations have (in principle) similar weight as growth engines, we focus our analysis on the most critical foundation for each reform, comparing what could have been achieved with what actually happened.

Table 4 summarizes the differences between promise and achievement using a simple notation. The first column under each foundation shows whether the indicated reform has a strong (✓✓) or a modest (✓) positive potential impact on that foundation. The second column indicates what impact the reform actually had, whether strongly positive (✓✓), modestly positive (✓), mixed (✓✗), negative (✗), or strongly negative (✗✗). To illustrate the rationale behind these assessments, we focus briefly on five reform areas where the stakes were particularly high: fiscal, labor, education, judicial, and political reform.

Fiscal reform is fundamental to restoring *macroeconomic stability,* which is essential for sustainable and inclusive growth. A government that has problems financing its expenses can reduce the economy's growth potential. A large debt

Table 4. *Peru: Potential and Actual Impact of Reforms*

Reform	*Property rights*		*Equal opportunity*		*Competition*		*Broad sharing of growth benefits*		*Macroeconomic stability*	
	Potential	*Actual*	*Potential*	*Actual*	*Potential*	*Actual*	*Potential*	*Actual*	*Potential*	*Actual*
Trade	✓	✓	✓	✓	✓✓	✓✗	✓	✗		✓✗
Financial	✓	✓	✓	✓	✓	✓	✓	✗	✓✓	✓✗
Labor	✓	✗	✓✓	✓✗			✓	✗		
Pension	✓	✓	✓	✓			✓	✗	✓✓	✓✓
Fiscal							✓	✗	✓✓	✓✓
Public administration							✓✓	✗✗	✓	✓
Education			✓				✓✓	✗✗		
Judiciary	✓✓	✗✗	✓	✗	✓	✗	✓	✗		
Political			✓	✗	✓	✗	✓✓	✗✗		

Source: Authors' evaluations.

a. ✓✓, strong positive impact; ✓, modest positive impact; ✓✗, mixed impact; ✗, negative impact; ✗✗, strong negative impact.

burden can likewise conspire against growth, by diverting the country's resources to debt service. A growing debt also increases the risk of default, which in turn raises interest rates and the cost of financing the debt. This increases macroeconomic volatility and crowds out private investment.

Labor reform should work to increase *equality of opportunity* in society, by reducing the information asymmetries that hinder equal access to job opportunities. If it does not, political or family connections, rather than skills, might dominate the matching of workers with job vacancies, leading to reduced productivity and ultimately slower growth.

The main promise of education reform in this framework is in promoting a *broader sharing of the benefits of economic growth.* A significant market failure occurs when individuals cannot finance their education by borrowing against their expected higher future income stream. Without that education they cannot accumulate enough human capital to command high earnings in the labor market. This market failure and the strong positive externalities from the provision of education justify government intervention in the market for education.

The judicial system is both a guarantor of basic rights, including *property rights,* and a mechanism for resolving conflicts. To serve those functions, the judiciary must be reliable, predictable, and accessible to all, or else individuals and firms will seek alternative means of securing their rights. Failure of the judicial system thus impairs a key element of growth, because property rights must be secure in order for agents to find it profitable to accumulate capital.

The establishment of a democratic political regime should positively affect at least three of the five growth foundations: *equal opportunity, competition,* and especially the *broad sharing of the benefits of growth.* The essence of a democracy is equal rights and opportunities for all citizens in the public sphere. Through universal suffrage, freedom of expression and association, and direct participation in politics and the election of representatives, the less privileged members of society can influence the state and the market and achieve a fairer distribution of resources and opportunities. Democracy is also characterized by competition for public office and for the definition of policy priorities, making it less likely that the state will be captured by a privileged elite. For the same reason, democracies are more likely than dictatorships to share the benefits from growth broadly, through greater responsiveness of government to voters and a stronger capacity of broad-based parties and interest groups to influence budgetary and other policies.

As table 4 suggests, the reforms since 1990 had the potential to transform Peru's economy. These reforms and the links between them and sustainable growth are quite standard and could apply to any emerging economy.[3] What is distinctive about reform in Peru is not its potential but the real impact that reform has had.

---

3. As acknowledged in chapter 2 of this volume, the first three foundations apply to any market economy, whereas the last two refer specifically to Latin America.

Before summarizing the impact of the reforms undertaken (and avoided) since 1990,[4] it is worth highlighting that Peru's reform process was not undertaken as a comprehensively thought out and fully detailed plan. The urgency of the country's situation profoundly influenced the choice of economic reforms. In fact, it was only the widely shared sense of emergency that allowed President Alberto Fujimori to secure special legislative powers to implement the first set of reforms (Kenney, 2004), which were soon followed by the interruption of constitutional rule and restrictions on democratic institutions and processes. Unsurprisingly, the bulk of the economic reforms were attempted in the first part of the decade. After that, Fujimori became less enthusiastic about policy change and more concerned with holding on to power. Only very recently, in June 2008, were new reforms adopted as part of the legislative package implementing the new free trade agreement with the United States. We do not include these reforms in our analysis because, as of this writing, the details have not been approved.

Table 4 presents a mixed overall picture of the impact of reform: although in some areas the reforms delivered as expected, in others they underperformed. Because some reforms are clearly more important than others, rather than assess each individual reform, we will measure the gap between promise and results on a foundation-by-foundation basis. This will allow us to focus on what remains to be done to secure growth and to assess a subset of reforms on this basis.

To begin, we can identify some progress in securing *property rights,* through reform of the financial markets and the pension system. However, a broader concern for citizens' rights and an adequate reform of the judicial system did not accompany this process, leaving the majority of Peruvians without sufficient access. In fact, during the 1990s the executive branch manipulated the workings of the judiciary for political ends. By the end of the decade, the judicial system remained highly unpredictable, inefficient, exclusionary, and corrupt. (See the appendix at the end of this book for more details).

Some progress was also made toward *equality of opportunity,* as a result of reforms in the trade regime and in financial, labor, and pension markets. However, the net gain is unclear, as there was no progress in other areas, such as education and justice.

The picture is also mixed with regard to increasing *competition.* The partial gains from trade and financial reforms were again blurred by the lack of progress in the judiciary and the semiauthoritarian concentration of political power.

Perhaps the clearest picture emerges in terms of the last two growth foundations. The reforms of the 1990s did partly restore *macroeconomic stability,* a key priority at that time, and were particularly successful in restoring fiscal and price stability. On the other hand, it is striking how completely the reforms ignored the

---

4. The assessments in table 4 benefited from the discussions with the group of experts mentioned in the acknowledgments.

broad sharing of the benefits of growth. Despite widespread demand for more equitable growth, none of the reforms took into consideration that progress on this foundation could avoid a backlash against the whole reform process and the new economic model. The apparent explanation is that the concerns at the time were more basic, and the focus was on reshaping that part of the economy that was easier to fix, namely, the more modern and urban part. The rest of the country was left mostly out of the picture.

Our attention to this foundation might seem at odds with the empirical evidence presented in the previous section, and in particular with the fact that Peru's current growth is clearly more pro-poor than that of the previous decade. However, reform thus far has done little to secure a *permanent* reduction in poverty and inequality; thus, the possibility of another sharp increase in these indicators remains. In fact, the absence of specific reform efforts aimed at greater inclusion in the long run suggests that the current "pro-poorness" of growth is more a consequence than a driver of growth. The latent risk of a negative shock reversing these recent positive trends undermines the sustainability of growth, because it translates into a danger of backlash.

Thus, in what follows we analyze more deeply what was done and what were the reasons behind the gap between promise and reality regarding this foundation. In particular, and given that the largest gaps in terms of this foundation are found in administrative, education, and political reform, we focus our attention on these three areas. The framework suggests that such gaps might be explained either by faulty design (technical inadequacies, inappropriate sequencing, lack of complementary reforms, or inadequate fit to the local context) or by local obstacles (institutional constraints, lack of legitimacy, or lack of implementing capacity). We will try to explain on this basis why the above three reforms failed to achieve their potential.

First, however, a brief assessment of Peru's reform successes is in order, because our analysis would be incomplete if we overlooked the importance of preserving what reform has already accomplished in terms of improving respect for property rights, increasing competition, and, especially, stabilizing the macroeconomy. As explained in chapter 2, macroeconomic stability has proved to be a necessary (although not sufficient) condition for growth throughout the region. Moreover, in Peru it is the accomplishments of reform with respect to these other foundations that has allowed private investment to benefit from the current boom.

Recent Economic Reforms: A Brief Assessment

In 1990 the Peruvian economy was in shambles. The monthly inflation rate was running at a four-digit pace without any sign of coming under control. Government revenue plummeted by a full three-quarters, leaving roads without maintenance, public hospitals without basic supplies, and many civil servants having to work two jobs. Growth was completely out of the picture. GDP plunged 25 percent in real terms between 1988 and 1990. The outlook was bleak.

In a surprising turn of events, a political outsider, Alberto Fujimori, won the presidential election without the support of any well-established political party. Even more surprising, he ended up implementing most of the economic plan outlined by his right-wing opponent, Mario Vargas-Llosa. The plan was an aggressive bet on liberalizing the economy in order to spur growth, once an austere stabilization package had halted the hyperinflation.

Although the plan achieved dramatic turnarounds in terms of both stabilization and restoration of access to international capital markets, the most significant changes came in the area of structural reform, which completely reshaped the Peruvian economy. Both labor and capital markets were liberalized, almost every asset in public hands (except the water utilities and the oil companies) was privatized, and new laws were passed protecting and fostering private investment. Foreign investment was attracted through special contracts with specific clauses forbidding surprise changes in the tax code or in regulation. A new regulatory system was also put in place, including a new antitrust agency, a regulatory authority for each newly privatized sector, and a much stronger tax authority.

The political process that accompanied these economic reforms, however, was increasingly authoritarian. Although Fujimori enjoyed initial support for his hardline postures, his concentration of power and the widespread corruption that was eventually revealed among top civil and military leaders ultimately tainted the whole reform process. The process was further discredited when, in late 2001, Fujimori abandoned the presidency and left the country after being accused of running a corruption ring through his spymaster, Vladimiro Montesinos.

These scandals and Fujimori's departure notwithstanding, the governments that succeeded him kept the main thrust of the macroeconomic reforms intact. After decades of government intervention and lackluster results, the common perception was that state intervention had been responsible not only for deterring growth, but also for provoking Peru's worst economic crisis ever. The economic reforms of the 1990s focused on using market forces to restore growth. In some cases markets were created; in others market rules were entirely rewritten. The problem was that the reach of market institutions is not homogeneous throughout the country. The modern economy predominant in Peru's coastal areas and major cities is quite different from the more traditional economy of its rural areas and highlands. Markets in these areas are full of rigidities, which explain why liberalization was not enough to spur growth in these areas, or indeed even for the change to be noticed.

For example, the public pension system was overhauled, creating private fund administrators (*administradoras de fondos de pensiones,* or AFPs) following the Chilean blueprint. However, the labor markets of these two countries are dissimilar. Whereas in Peru two-thirds of the working population is in the informal sector, in Chile the figure is not more than a third. The reform failed to address the needs of these workers, a problem inherited from the previous pension system design. Now, almost twenty years after the reform, opinion about it is mixed. The new system works well for those with stable jobs in the formal sector. For other formal sector workers, however, it is not delivering the promise of a pension closely related to their salary history. And for the majority of Peruvians, the new system was irrelevant, as they were never part of the reform.

Reform of the financial system had similar results at first. Before 1990, the system was severely affected by inflation and by financial repression, which, together with legislation that did not guarantee the rights of lenders, produced a small financial sector from which many individuals and firms were rationed out. There were few long-term transactions, even in the mortgage market.

The 1990s saw a radical change, with a new banking law and the lifting of all price controls and restrictions. These changes attracted major international players into the banking system. The improvement in macroeconomic conditions allowed a credit boom, which, however, went bust with the Russian crisis of 1998. Yet even at the peak, many potential borrowers remained rationed out of the credit market, including many informal sector firms and many poor individuals with no collateralizable assets. Fortunately, over time new microfinance institutions of various kinds found ways to serve this market. It is unlikely that this could have happened in the absence of stabilization and financial market reform.

The first efforts at reform were thus a steppingstone toward the improved growth of later years. The most important reforms were the conquest of inflation, tariff reductions, financial sector reform, and a new framework for attracting private investment. However, rural poverty was not reduced at the same pace as in urban areas. The following section focuses on three areas that might be called the "missing ingredients" of future reform efforts: reform of public administration, education reform, and last but not least, political reform.

Missing Ingredient #1: Public Administration Reform

One of Peru's main obstacles to achieving inclusive growth has been the lack of a well-functioning state apparatus. As is widely known, the Peruvian state before the reform process was bloated, bureaucratized, inefficient, and lacking in professionalism. Its profusion of red tape represented a significant deterrent to private investment. Above all, it was clearly biased against the rural population, as most of the public sector was located in Lima, and no significant effort was made to decentralize its power to the provinces.

As argued by Ugarte (2000), the administrative reforms of the 1990s were maintained only to the extent that they were viewed as necessary for keeping the concurrent economic reforms in place. The central bank regained its independence, the tax authority was given budgetary and operational autonomy, the customs office was completely overhauled, and new regulators began to oversee the many newly privatized enterprises. Three characteristics were common to all of these cases. First, salaries in these agencies were de-linked from those of the rest of the public sector: employees were hired under rules similar to those in the private sector, with productivity bonuses and defined career tracks. Second, the institutions were well funded through sources of revenue not connected with the general government budget. Third, the new public officials were in most cases highly qualified.

The intense macroeconomic volatility of previous decades was tamed not only through much stricter macroeconomic policies but also through several mechanisms expressly designed for that purpose. These included the adoption of a multi-year budgeting framework and fiscal prudence legislation with explicit rules. The government also managed the public debt more actively, leading to Peru's achieving investment grade status. Although this turnaround was significant, so were the reforms still pending, including in particular the professionalization of the civil service and effective mechanisms for national integration.

The Lack of a Professional Civil Service

Before 1990 there was no such thing as a public career within the Peruvian state, and the situation is hardly any better today. Most public sector entities (the central bank is an exception) have nothing resembling a merit-based hiring system. Throughout the 1990s, public servants were part of a minority within the labor force whose paychecks may have been shrinking but who nevertheless enjoyed all basic labor rights as well as virtually complete job stability.[5] Therefore, politicians were eager to use public employment as a source of patronage.

Another factor that has conspired against building a well-defined public career is the short duration in office of the highest-ranking officials. The average tenure of a cabinet minister since 1980 has been less than a year. Usually each new minister comes with his or her own team and imposes a career ladder, with the steps reserved for political appointees, rather than a merit-based system. This discourages the best of the permanent employees, who are likely to see their careers stagnate.

Finally, it is symptomatic of Peru's problems that degree programs in public administration have historically been absent from the university system. None of Peru's eighty universities offers public administration as an undergraduate major, and only a few graduate programs in the field have opened since 2001.

---

5. Permanent job stability was introduced by the military government in 1970, after a three-month trial period. By 1978 the government had increased the trial period to three years, but in 1986 this was reversed. See Saavedra (2000).

The last two decades have seen attempts to reform public administration and introduce a professional civil service. The first attempt was aborted after the 1992 "self-coup," when President Fujimori dissolved Congress and suspended the constitution. The group designing the reform quit, and the project was forgotten. None of the ministries was closed, and only a few small public institutions (including the National Institute of Public Administration) were dismantled. Hyperinflation was the main incentive encouraging people to leave public employment: the real value of public sector salaries fell by more than 75 percent in the 1980s. The most significant change in terms of reducing the public payroll occurred in the state-owned enterprises, which were rapidly privatized.

At the end of Fujimori's first term, a major reform of public administration was attempted, and Congress granted the executive branch broad powers in this area. A group of specialists prepared a serious proposal under the auspices of the prime minister's office. However, the population was easily turned against the reform, as the political opposition claimed it would lead to a series of massive layoffs. There was also opposition within the government, and by the end of 1996 the idea had been abandoned. Eventually the impetus for reform faded, and all plans to reform public administration came to be perceived as too politically controversial.

Obstacles to Building an Integrated Nation

All governments in developing countries face a trade-off between reforms that focus on economic growth and those that focus on reducing inequality. When the starting point is one of persistently slow growth, the focus is unlikely to be on the latter. Once the economy is back on its feet, however, pressure to address inequality increases. Peru has been in this situation for some time now, yet the government's actions to reduce inequality have been neither well articulated nor systematic, nor have they been very effective.

Because inequality in Peru has so much to do with the gap between the capital and the rest of the country, perhaps the obvious first step is to decentralize power and decision-making. The Peruvian state has embarked on a rather disorganized decentralization process since 2001. Although municipal authorities have been elected rather than appointed since 1981, and new regional-level authorities were elected in 2002, this was done without approval of the basic legislation intended to guide the process, and meanwhile another election was held in 2006. Decentralization today remains a work in progress. There have been none of the major fiscal problems that many had feared, primarily because very strict fiscal rules were centrally imposed. However, there have been significant problems in budget execution. Regional and municipal authorities lack the administrative capacity to spend their allocated budgets, and this inhibits the sharing of responsibility across levels of government. Delays continue, and the perception is still widespread that money is not being well spent. The National System of Public

Investment (SNIP) has its hands tied, as responsibility for most investment decisions lies with the regional governments.

But perhaps the most notorious problem is that Peru's twenty-five regional
governments have not pursued any real integration. Decentralization merely
changed the names of the existing national departments to regional departments;
the idea of combining the regions into macroregions, although built into the law,
has not been carried out. The reality is that some regions are simply too small to
build an effective government. Nor do all regions have mineral, gas, or other natural resources to serve as a source of tax revenue, and so tension between poor and
rich regions has increased substantially.

The main tool used by the government to reshape the income expectations of
poorer families is social policy. Better nutrition, health, and education are key to
improving the living standards of these families, who rely on the state to help meet
their needs in these areas. But the role of the state goes beyond fulfilling these basic
needs. The state can become an obstacle to inclusive growth if it does not also provide basic infrastructure, justice, and a minimum of peace and security. Although
the state must exercise its vital regulatory functions, excessive red tape and bureaucracy can put a wrench in the wheels of growth. In sum, a growing economy needs
an efficient and effective state apparatus, ready to work with the private sector in
achieving economic growth.

Basic infrastructure is a powerful equalizer of opportunities, and given the disparities in public infrastructure across the country, there is much that public
expenditure could do in this regard. It is hard to start a manufacturing business if
there are no roads to connect with a larger market, no electricity, and no telephone
network. Yet the technological progress that Lima takes for granted is simply
absent in large parts of the country, and as long as the government grappled with
large fiscal deficits, it could not cope with the mounting problem.

The prolonged economic crisis actually caused public investment to decline as
a share of the economy, as cuts in investment spending were used to fend off fiscal deficits. From 55 percent of total investment outlays in 1975, public investment plummeted to less than 20 percent in 1990. The consequences were a
significant deterioration of all public infrastructure (schools, roads, hospitals) and
of the salaries of public employees. The collapse was even more pronounced in the
1980s, when terrorist groups repeatedly attacked the public electricity network.

How to Move Forward?

This review of the challenges to public administration reform suggests several areas
where the need is critical to work toward a better state apparatus.

MERITOCRACY SHOULD BE THE RULE

Peru has long lacked a professional civil service with merit-based career paths.
Many reform efforts have been blocked as policymakers focused on the existing

stock of personnel instead of building up a new group of professional public ser-vants. A well-defined public career system would make it possible for the public sector to retain the talent it needs.

In June 2006, under the legislative powers granted by Congress to implement the free trade agreement with the United States, the executive issued a legislative decree implementing a civil service system with many desirable features. This cir-cumvented the main obstacle, which was that the executive lacked a majority in Congress and therefore the reform had a slim chance of passage. The new system is based on merit, and its governance structure establishes a politically indepen-dent board that will manage the whole civil service.

A complementary legislative decree in June 2008 breaks the link between the salary structure of elected officials and that of a small group of key public man-agers, whose salaries as a result may now be set higher than the president's. Until now, in the existing "islands of efficiency" in the state apparatus, employees were offered market-based salaries so as to attract the best talent, but the salary struc-ture for these public servants was tied to that of elected politicians. These two structures should not be determined together, as only the market for the former has a relevant shadow price. Of course, it remains to be seen whether this reform will get beyond the design stage.

Focus on Results, Not Just Procedures

Another problem is that the whole state system has been geared toward fulfill-ing a long list of procedures instead of a short list of goals. Bureaucrats feel pres-sured to follow every single requirement imposed by the rules, even if the desired outcome is accomplished less efficiently or not at all. If they deviate from the rules, public employees can face judicial scrutiny, even prosecution, whereas they will never face prosecution for not meeting goals. This way of doing business gener-ates enormous inefficiencies at every step, from unnecessary procedures and doc-uments, to high administrative costs, to sluggishness and interminable delay. The system makes bureaucrats accountable not to the citizens they serve, but to inter-nal audit bodies focused on procedures instead of goals.

The whole budgeting system should serve as a mechanism for making pub-lic expenditure more effective. For that to happen, budget programs should only be approved once a proper system of monitoring and evaluation is in place. Until then, bureaucrats will have little incentive to improve the quality of pub-lic expenditure.

One mechanism that has been implemented as a pilot process in recent years is results-based budgeting (Alvarado and Morón, 2007). A small group of pro-grams have been selected in priority areas (including nutrition and education) and given explicit goals. The idea is to get the bureaucracy to think about what is needed to achieve those goals, instead of focusing on how much money is avail-able for each task. So far only 5 percent of the total budget is subject to this initiative. The rest is basically driven by inertia and without any evaluation of efficiency or goal fulfillment.

Proper use of results-based budgeting could partly resolve many of the issues related to lack of accountability. When clear outcome indicators are required, it will be much easier to educate citizens about what they have a right to expect from government. Today, for example, the state's "clients" have no clear idea how poor public education really is, or how inefficient the delivery of health services has become. True accountability requires linking inputs with outputs, and outputs with outcomes. For that, a proper monitoring system must be put in place as part of the results-based budgeting system.

Decentralize Talent, Not Just Problems

The government needs to empower local and regional governments as a fundamental step toward improving both the efficacy and the coverage of basic social programs. For that to happen, the capacities of these levels of government must be strengthened. A more pressing reform is to establish macroregions out of the current smaller regions, as mentioned above. The central government can more easily focus on helping seven or ten macroregional governments than twenty-five at once. The distribution of public resources should be linked to the creation of these macroregions. Here incrementalism is the best strategy. For example, a single pilot macroregion could help deliver the message that consolidation is possible, desirable, and replicable. Unfortunately, the current commodity boom has created a division between rich and poor regions. Ninety percent of the canon proceeds (revenue levied based on the premise that those regions in which natural resources are being extracted should receive part of the proceeds) go to just twelve regions, and more than half goes to just four. Thus, there are few incentives to reduce the number of regions.

Missing Ingredient #2: Education Reform

Several endogenous growth models rely on human capital to provide an analytical link between economic growth and educational variables (Lucas, 1988). However, empirical evidence at the aggregate level remains inconclusive. A stronger consensus emerges when we connect educational attainment and quality with households' ability to maintain a high, steady income (Hanushek and Wöbmann, 2007; Castro, 2006). In fact, strong linkages can be found at the household level between the stock of human capital and both the level and the variability of income and consumption.

As already mentioned, households seeking to accumulate human capital face a significant market failure in their inability to pledge their increased future income stream; this is what justifies public intervention in education. We therefore expect education reform to exert its growth potential through the *broader sharing of the benefits of growth,*[6] by expanding access to an asset that the market values but fails to offer on an egalitarian basis. Obviously, reform is not just a matter of guaranteeing the existence of this valuable asset (public education of good quality) but also of providing it to households with poor initial endowments.

Why Has Education Failed to Contribute to the Broader Sharing of Growth?

Public interventions in the education system may fail in their goal of spreading more broadly the benefits of growth in either of two ways. First, they may result in services of little value delivered to those with poor initial endowments; second, they may deliver valuable services, but only to those with an already large endowment.

Regarding basic education in Peru, we argue that the problem has been mainly of the first type. As documented in Yamada and Castro (2007), attendance at publicly provided primary and secondary schools is concentrated among the poor.[7] Coverage and attainment have increased, but because spending has been unchanged relative to GDP (around 3 percent over the past ten years), the result has been lower educational quality.[8] To accommodate all enrollees within the existing physical and human infrastructure, public schools have resorted to teaching in three daily shifts of less than five hours each. Clearly, in these circumstances the same nominal educational attainment implies less real human capital accumulation than before, and thus smaller future income gains.

In fact, national school performance measures for 2004 show that only 12 percent of students complete primary school with age-appropriate reading comprehension, and only 8 percent can solve basic logical and mathematical problems (Ministerio de Educación, 2005). These students will need to extend their education if they are to command the same earnings as earlier graduates, thus compensating lower quality with larger quantity.

As documented in Yamada and Castro (2007), the flip side of this result emerges when we examine the probability of being poor for a given educational attainment: data from the national household surveys show that this probability was greater in 2004 than in 1985 for all levels of basic education (figure 3). This reveals to what extent the education sector has weakened as a mechanism of social mobility in the past twenty-five years. The average probabilities shown in figure 3, however, disguise strong differences between publicly and privately

---

6. The channel from education to growth can be traced analytically if we consider human capital as a production factor. Within the proposed framework, the link we propose is between education reform (understood as reshaping public intervention in the education sector) and growth via the "broad sharing" foundation.

7. Among Peruvians with access to publicly provided primary education, 72 percent can be regarded as poor or extremely poor, as are 60 percent of those with access to publicly provided secondary education.

8. As documented in Cotlear (2006), gross enrollment rates in primary and secondary education are now nearly 100 percent and 90 percent, respectively.

Figure 3. *Peru: Probability of Being Poor by Educational Attainment, 1985 and 2004*[a]

Percent

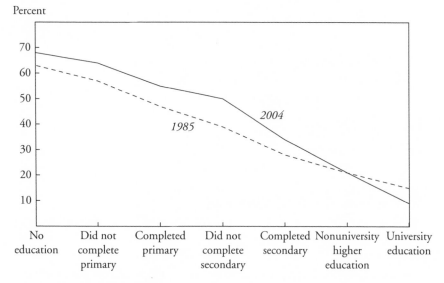

Source: Yamada and Castro (2007).
a. Estimates apply to the adult population only.

provided basic education. Whereas private basic education reduces the probability of being poor by 48 percentage points, the comparable figure for public basic education is only 36 percentage points (figure 4).[9]

The situation is different for tertiary education, which, as figures 3 and 4 show, appears to be a safe escape route from poverty, whether the institution attended is public or private. In addition, the steady increase in real wages for skilled workers in recent years proves that the market does value the assets acquired through tertiary education. Meanwhile several empirical studies (Castro and Yamada, 2006; Yamada and others, 2007) show that universal basic education may not suffice for Peru to achieve the Millennium Development Goal of halving the incidence of poverty by 2015—another strong argument for expanding access to higher education. Unfortunately, higher education today is being provided in a clearly regressive way (figure 5), delivering the promise of increased earnings

9. The results in figure 4 were obtained from a logit regression using the sample of the adult population captured in the 2006 household survey. This comparison is particularly prone to misspecification. The marginal contribution (in terms of poverty reduction) of a private school education can be biased upward by failure to control for the household's initial endowment. To reduce this bias, we extended the analysis proposed in Yamada and Castro (2007) and introduced an additional control variable available in the 2006 household survey: the educational attainment of the household head's parents. Absent such controls, the predicted probability of being poor after completing primary education in a private school would fall to 7 percent.

Figure 4. *Peru: Probability of Being Poor by Educational Attainment,*
Public versus Private, 2006[a]

Percent

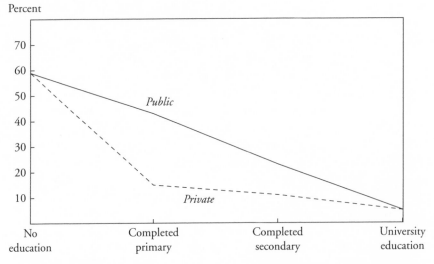

Source: Authors' calculations based on Encuesta Nacional de Hogares sobre Condiciones de Vida y
Pobreza (ENAHO) data for 2006.
a. Estimates apply to the adult population only.

mainly to households already well off. Two out of every three students enrolled
in publicly provided nonuniversity higher education, and almost eight out of every
ten students enrolled in public universities, come from nonpoor households.

To summarize, reforms addressing public intervention in the education sector
should seek to improve its ability to guarantee a more egalitarian distribution of
human capital. This should, in turn, help secure faster economic growth through
two channels: by reducing the risk of backlash against reform, as the benefits will
be shared by a larger population; and by increasing the benefits to be shared, as
the economy's human capital stock increases.

Specifically, education reform in Peru must address two critical issues: the poor
quality of public basic educational services, and unequal access to higher education. Obviously, the two are interconnected, since better public basic education
will give more students from poor households the chance to progress to higher
education. In fact, given that public higher education is practically free, the low
quality of public basic education conspires against more egalitarian access: many
who finish their basic education in a public school have neither the resources to
enroll in a private university or institute nor the skills to gain admission to the
nation's highly selective public universities.[10] It is with these issues in mind that

10. As documented in Rodríguez (2008), the average acceptance ratio at Peru's private universities is as high as 80 percent, but only 17 percent at their public counterparts.

Figure 5. *Peru: Enrollment of 17- to 20-Year-Old High School Graduates in Higher Education by Household Income Quintile, 2006*

Percent

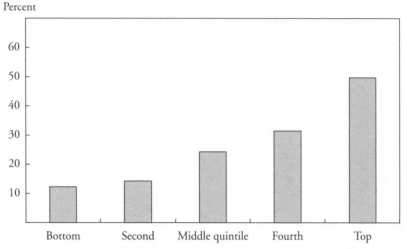

Source: Authors' calculations based on Encuesta Nacional de Hogares sobre Condiciones de Vida y Pobreza (ENAHO) data for 2006.

the following section explores Peru's recent education reforms, analyzing their constraints and obstacles through the lens of the CGD framework.

Education Reform: A Play in Three Acts

ACT ONE: FAILURE TO IMPLEMENT

Following the 1992 self-coup, as part of its attempts to reshape the economic role of the state, the Fujimori government proposed a dramatic new education reform. Although the proposal was highly controversial and ultimately failed to be implemented, it is worth assessing, in terms of the CGD framework, its main components and the process by which it was put forward and then defeated.

As established in three legislative decrees issued in December 1992, the reform comprised three different aspects. First, it proposed reforming the administration of public education by transferring management of the public schools to local representatives convened in Municipal Education Councils (Comuneds), which would hire teachers under a private scheme, and by allowing private organizations (such as teachers' or parents' associations) to manage schools. Second, it proposed changing the funding scheme to one in which the Ministry of Finance would make monthly payments to each Comuned according to the number of regular students attending school; schools would be allowed to generate additional resources by charging tuition. Finally, a performance evaluation system would have allowed the Ministry of Education to monitor the quality of services.

As documented in Webb and Valencia (2006), by 1991 public school teachers' salaries had reached a historic low. After a short-lived expansion during the first three years of President Alan Garcia's first administration (1985–88), salaries had fallen by more than 75 percent as a result of the decline in public expenditure and the hyperinflation of 1988–92. Webb and Valencia argue that low salaries, combined with weak demand, the government's inability to enforce contracts, and an increasingly powerful teachers' union (SUTEP), led to a "low level equilibrium." Teachers compensated for their low salaries by taking second jobs, which reduced the time and effort they devoted to public school teaching. SUTEP's leaders meanwhile negotiated contract terms that reduced teachers' obligations and the government's ability to impose discipline, while building an organization to serve their own radical political agenda. Students and their parents failed to complain, since they remained unaware of how poor the services provided actually were.

Clearly, public education was failing to contribute to the broad sharing of the benefits of growth. Again, coverage was not the problem: gross enrollment rates at all levels were unaffected by the 1988–92 crisis and, as revealed in Cotlear (2006), have remained above the Latin American average for decades. Enrollment in elementary and secondary schools actually experienced a steady increase from 1970 onward. The problem, rather, was low quality, a direct consequence of the "low level equilibrium" described by Webb and Valencia.

The need for reform was thus compelling, and, in principle, the main features of the proposed reform arguably would have created the incentives to allow the educational system to deliver on its potential, both through the "broad sharing" foundation and, indirectly, by facilitating competition and enhancing macroeconomic stability. The proposed transfer of management of public schools to local representatives and the creation of a performance evaluation system were aimed at building a more efficient and accountable administration, where quality would emerge in response to local demand. In addition, decentralization would have allowed for better management of resources, which could, in principle, have alleviated the fiscal burden. In fact, the proposed reform of the funding scheme in favor of a voucher-type system was aimed at this objective. The scheme was also expected to foster competition between privately managed schools. The resulting improvement in quality would have helped the public schools deliver on their primary goal as a driver of growth by equalizing access to human capital.

A critical view of the ability of decentralization to deliver on these objectives must address potential problems of design (related to technical inadequacies) and particular obstacles arising from local conditions, such as lack of implementation capacity. In particular, success will be compromised if the reform lacks a proper balance between greater local autonomy and stronger central administrative capacity. This equilibrium is required to guarantee several things: first, that the funding scheme and contractual arrangements create effective incentives for schools and teachers on the basis of performance (and not just increased coverage and seniority, respectively); second, that information generated by the performance evaluation system is used and disseminated so as to foster competition and demand for quality; and third, that disparities in the managerial abilities of local actors (which are typically correlated with the local poverty rate in a regressive way) are recognized so that capacities and funds can be transferred appropriately.

The proposed reform was flawed on some of these fronts, and this alone would have compromised its success. Although the proposal was based largely on the Chilean model, some effort was made to account for the poorer administrative capacity of Peruvian municipalities and to favor the decentralization of responsibilities from state actors to school actors, and not across bureaucracies. (Comuneds were supposed to convene local representatives, not just local authorities.[11]) Moreover, the idea was to transfer public school management to communities gradually. However, the proposed funding scheme was based only on the number of students in regular attendance, no incentives were provided to foster quality-oriented reform at the school level, and no detail was given about how the evaluation system would be implemented or whether further incentives would be given to schools and teachers on the basis of merit. Furthermore, no specific acknowledgment was made regarding potential disparities among beneficiary communities. Thus, it seems the balance would have tilted in favor of local autonomy, with little emphasis on the need to strengthen administrative capacities or expand central funding. This bias probably stemmed from an excess of confidence in the market, combined with the compelling need to downsize the state and reshape its role in the economy.

Although these design problems failed to manifest themselves because the reform was never implemented, they permeated into the main obstacle to this reform, namely, its lack of political legitimacy. As documented in Ortiz de Zevallos et al. (1999), educational experts and veto groups with different motivations joined ranks to oppose the reform, persuading the public that its main purpose was privatization rather than decentralization and that it threatened the constitutional right to free and universal schooling.

The authoritarian nature of the regime, the top-down way in which the reform was proposed, and the absence of any prior public debate or dissemination strategy involving potential beneficiaries (including parents) all contributed to the reform's failure. In the public's mind, the transfer of educational responsibilities to local governments, which were (and remain) hardly synonymous with efficient administration, raised fears rather than enthusiasm. Further fueling these worries was the lack of any pilot experience that, if successful, could have reassured the

---

11. Some would argue that this decision was driven not only by the objective of overcoming obstacles from local conditions, but also by President Fujimori's discontent with the 1993 municipal elections, where independent candidates won in the majority of provinces and districts (Ortiz de Zevallos et al., 1999).

public of the reform's potential. At the end of 1993, amid strong public opposition that nearly cost the government the approval of the new constitution, President Fujimori abandoned the effort, and in May 1994 Congress repealed the three decrees that had launched the process.

It is worth noting that the rapid erosion of political capital observed in this episode is not a necessary attribute of education reform. In fact, Peru's experience contrasts sharply with that of Argentina, where education reform helped bring together political actors from different factions within the ruling party, thus fostering cooperation on later economic reforms (Corrales, 2006). Argentina's "provincialization" of education was packaged with promises of increased infrastructure spending, which helped soften the appearance of a reform that sought to reduce the central government's fiscal burden by delegating responsibilities. The political context in Peru was very different, and the general public came to believe that this reform was just another attempt to cut spending, this time by eroding a hard-won fundamental social right.

ACT TWO: COPING WITH THE STATUS QUO

By mid-1993 the Fujimori government's emphasis regarding public education had already changed in favor of the provision of basic infrastructure through the recently created Instituto Nacional de Infraestructura en Educación y Salud (INFES). The idea was to lower school dropout rates, especially in rural areas, by providing new schools. Several empirical studies relying on cross-sectional data (Castro and Yamada, 2006; Yamada et al., 2007) have indeed found that the number of students per school is a significant determinant of school achievement (in terms of enrollment and graduation rates), and that the provision of infrastructure and the quality of education can be highly correlated. But Peru's low-quality educational equilibrium was not just a matter of inadequate infrastructure. In fact, alleviating disparities in access to basic education infrastructure is only a necessary, not a sufficient, condition for improving quality in an equitable manner, because strong complementarities exist between physical and human resources in providing educational services. Moreover, mere provision of infrastructure can help perpetuate this perverse equilibrium, if users become contented with visible outputs and fail to develop a proper demand for overall quality.

In the years that followed, and especially during the administration of President Alejandro Toledo (2001–06), emphasis was given to developing training programs for teachers, accompanied by a revision of the national curriculum, provision of standardized textbooks, and improvements in teachers' salaries (by 57 to 69 percent, depending on category and level served). However, the higher salaries were largely due to pressure exerted by SUTEP, rather than a coordinated effort to reward performance and merit. Although low salaries were one of the main culprits behind Peru's "low level equilibrium," indiscriminate wage increases were not the solution. Moreover, failure to link wage negotiations to performance will inevitably contribute to maintaining this undesirable equilibrium, by fueling the union's ability to negotiate contract terms in which obligations and discipline are of secondary importance.

The teacher training programs, the revised national curriculum, and the dissemination of standardized textbooks, meanwhile, had problems of their own, related to technical inadequacies that led to inadequate implementation. As documented in Benavides and Rodríguez (2006), little is known about the effectiveness of training programs, and several studies reveal that the new methodologies were not articulated around the objectives and contents of the new curriculum. The training programs thus failed to transfer the capacities required to take full advantage of the distributed material, and many teachers ended up discarding the official textbooks or "adapting" their content to their own pedagogical abilities and their students' intellectual capacity. A comparison of 1998 and 2004 performance evaluation results (Ministerio de Educación, 2005)[12] reveals little progress, despite spending of nearly $500 million in more than 3,000 schools from 1992 to 2000.

ACT THREE: REFORM REDUX

Setting the urgency of education reform aside, one could argue that delaying reform for nearly fifteen years may yet have positive consequences, but only if Peruvians take stock and learn from their experience and that of other Latin American countries. Soon after returning to office in 2006, President Garcia revived the idea of a thorough reform of the education sector, and of decentralization (which he called "municipalization") in particular. Three milestones characterize the beginning of this third act, which is still under way: the introduction of a pilot decentralization program in October 2006; the regulation in July 2007 of the Sistema Nacional de Evaluación, Acreditación y Certificación de la Calidad Educativa (SINEACE), created in May 2006 under President Toledo; and the approval of a new Teachers' Labor Code (Ley de Carrera Pública Magisterial) that same month.

The pilot decentralization program involves fifty-six of the country's more than 1,800 municipalities during 2007–08. The proposed strategy involves creating in each municipality a Municipal Education Council (Consejo Educativo Municipal), led by the local authority with representatives (school principals, teachers, students, and parents) from all public schools in the district. The usual disclaimers related to design and implementation capacity apply, and just how funds will be transferred to local governments remains unclear. But what is new about this ini-

---

12. As reported in Ministerio de Educación (2005), no significant differences were found between 1998 and 2004 in the verbal communication performance of primary and secondary school students. In mathematics, primary school students performed no differently in the two years, and secondary school students did slightly worse in 2004.

tiative is precisely the fact that it is a pilot experience. This signals not only that the transfer will be gradual, but also, if correctly monitored and successful, that it will provide evidence of the potential gains from delegating school management to local actors.

The regulation of SINEACE is another important reform, since this office is now charged with evaluating and certifying quality and determining standards at all educational levels. As discussed later, this office could play a crucial role by providing the information required to tie incentives to quality and foster demand for better services.

Reviving the idea of decentralization led, not surprisingly, to the teachers' union again raising the privatization specter. Their concerns, however, were rapidly diverted toward two other policy initiatives that impinged directly on their interests: the system of teacher evaluation and the new labor code. The most important features of the new code are the recognition of merit and performance as the main determinants of promotions and raises, and a new system of individual evaluations to assess whether teachers should be retained and promoted.[13] In an atmosphere of increasing mistrust toward this type of policy initiative, fueled by low salaries, poor working conditions, a limited budget, and government's failure to meet the objectives established in the previous labor code, opposition groups and union leaders easily convinced many teachers that this new code was nothing but an attempt to deprive them of their job stability. Massive public demonstrations nationwide followed passage of the law.

How to Move Forward?

We have already identified the two critical issues that any successful reform must address if the education sector is to fulfill its role as a vehicle of social mobility: the quality of public basic education and equality of access to higher education. On the quality front, the recent initiatives just described seem to point in the right direction. However, their success will depend crucially on policymakers' awareness of and skill in avoiding several of the constraints and obstacles noted in chapter 2.

The first of these is the potential lack of legitimacy, made worse by the fact that the costs of reform will be concentrated on a group with considerable veto power (the teachers' union), while the benefits will be dispersed throughout the population and difficult to observe and measure in the near term. A second issue is lack of adequate implementation capacity and problems of design related to technical inadequacies, which make it difficult to attain a proper equilibrium between local autonomy and central administrative capacities. As already mentioned, the for-

---

13. The first type of evaluation is compulsory and takes place every three years. Teachers who fail this evaluation will be provided further training and up to two chances to be approved; those who fail three times at the same career level will be dismissed. The second type of evaluation is not compulsory, occurs every three years, and must be passed for promotion to the next career level.

mer should promote efficiency and accountability, while the latter ties incentives to quality, gathers and disseminates information regarding performance, and promotes equity by recognizing and correcting local disparities.

Several policy recommendations follow. First, further confrontations with the teachers' union should be avoided, now that a new labor code that rewards merit and explicitly uses performance evaluation results has been approved. In fact, the code is a major breakthrough,[14] and any new elements that cause distress to teachers could put the whole reform at risk. The central authorities must acknowledge that, given past experience, teachers will be wary of the new rules being abused, despite great efforts to ensure that the new code emphasizes training and rewards good performance. Second, efforts should now focus on defining the specific criteria and indicators to be used in monitoring quality and performance. Now that laws and basic regulations have been passed, this second, more technical stage is particularly prone to design problems that can end up disconnecting incentives from proposed objectives.

The primary objective of a basic education system is to provide children with the essential cognitive skills to interact effectively in society and possibly to pursue a college degree. Thus, quality must be measured in terms of whether such skills are being taught. The Ministry of Education, via its Quality Measurement Unit, has already conducted several performance evaluations, measuring students' reading comprehension skills and their ability to solve logical and mathematical problems. Several well-defined benchmarks also already exist: for example, after finishing second grade, students should be able to read with understanding at a rate of 60 words per minute. These benchmarks could be readily applied and the results disseminated.

As mentioned, SINEACE is charged with designing indicators and standards to measure educational quality nationwide. Here two important issues must be considered. First, visible outputs (training for teachers, textbooks, infrastructure, and even enrollment and completion rates) should not be confused with outcomes (learning of basic skills), although the two can be correlated. Second, SINEACE must rapidly take stock of measurement techniques and simple standards already available to proxy such learning. It is important to determine and publicize, as soon as possible, how many and which public schools are meeting the standards.

Once this has been established, special recognition in the form of bonuses should be given promptly to well-performing schools, using the quality standards established by SINEACE. Waiting to award these bonuses until decentralization proceeds and funds are transferred to local governments could cause unnecessary delay in tying incentives to quality. Such rewards will create incentives for schools to implement quality-oriented reforms, thus promoting local capacity building.

---

14. Corrales (2006) identifies the failure to reform teachers' labor codes as one of the major design shortcomings of education reform in Latin America.

The rewards will also complement the reforms already introduced in the new labor code. A system of rewards is also important because although SINEACE's governing regulation establishes incentives for school certification, the accreditation process will be time consuming and remains voluntary.

The new labor code also establishes that SINEACE will play a role, together with the Ministry of Education, in designing indicators and measurement instruments for monitoring teachers' performance. This provides an opportunity to tie teachers' retention and promotion to the criteria and standards used to measure quality: well-performing teachers are those whose students demonstrate basic reading, mathematical, and logical skills. Giving more weight to these objective criteria will minimize the risk of corruption and help shelter the education system from politics.

Finally, performance results should be disseminated as a means of encouraging households to demand higher quality. Transparency and simplicity are essential to building public support: the expected benefits will become clearer, the better the population is informed about the outcomes they can expect from reform and the progress made. A string of successful teacher and student performance evaluations evidencing the impact of new selection criteria, training, and decentralization efforts will then build legitimacy for further reforms.

In this regard, the Ministry of Education recently announced that parents and teachers will be given the results of students' evaluations, and that parents will have access to a guide explaining the skills that their children should attain in each semester. Policymakers should be aware that, initially, this can have some costs in terms of parents' perception of the quality of service. However, it remains crucial to foster consensus around the need to persist with the reform.

The recent reform milestones and the recommendations so far point toward improvement in the quality of public basic education. Unfortunately, there has been little discussion of the second reform front: equalizing access to higher education. In fact, SINEACE's efforts currently emphasize the design of criteria for the accreditation of higher education centers that train basic education teachers. Although this is also a priority given the mixed quality of the existing centers, this effort is focused on the first reform front.

The primary objective of higher education is to increase future consumption by building a more highly skilled labor force. Unfortunately, performance evaluations and indicators like those available for basic education do not exist for higher education. As proposed in Yamada and Castro (2007), efforts to assess the quality of higher education must include not only periodic faculty evaluations, but also transparent, market-based indicators that reveal to all potential students the possible economic gains from studying at a given institution for a particular career.

If the benefits of growth are to be broadly shared, however, the most compelling issue for higher education is unequal access. Nearly nine out of ten high school graduates from the poorest 20 percent of Peru's population are effectively excluded from higher education. Yet the empirical evidence demonstrates that access to such education, whether public or private, offers the best chance of escaping poverty.

Although quality improvements in public basic education should help equalize access to higher education, this is a long-term endeavor. Some complementary measures are therefore needed in the near term. Given that public higher education in Peru is currently free for anyone who can access it, charging tuition to nonpoor students would arguably be a sensible first step, because it would reduce demand from nonpoor households while also providing funds that could be used to expand coverage.[15]

However, the lessons learned from past reforms and the obstacles identified by the framework argue against this recommendation for the near term: legitimacy problems would inevitably arise and generate confrontation. Instead we propose an expansion of higher education credits. Publicly provided credit for higher education is currently managed by the Ministry of Education's Oficina de Becas y Credito Educativo, which currently offers close to $10 million in credits annually. However, a look at the schemes currently offered suggests that they fail to promote long-term investment in higher education. Students must begin repayment only a month after funds are transferred, making the current scheme more of a transitory shock absorber than an effective instrument for long-term financing.

An improved higher education credit scheme could help alleviate the problem of unequal access. In such a scheme, funds would be provided by the financial market and oriented to poorer households. Thus households would have to demonstrate their ability to repay not from current income, but rather from the increase in their future income stream resulting from the student's higher education. Second, the state should play a subsidiary role by, for example, providing the collateral that poor households are unable to pledge, thus assuming a contingent liability.

Realizing the promise of a larger incremental income stream depends, of course, on the quality of the education provided. To ensure that borrowed funds are spent on high-quality education, countries such as Chile lend only to students admitted to accredited universities. Since Peru's accreditation system is still in its inception, some other risk-sharing mechanism would have to be devised: for example, the participating universities could be asked to share the burden of providing collateral; the better universities would then self-select. Incentives for doing so (from a private point of view) could be provided by guaranteeing that the credit scheme will cover all educational expenses. Private universities would find this attractive, since they would otherwise charge poor students a modest tuition. In fact, most private universities in Peru already vary their tuition depending on the student's

15. As documented in Bejar and Montero (2006), charging tuition fees to nonpoor students can significantly increase the resources available to public universities. Working with the University of San Marcos (the most important public university in Peru), the authors show that collecting tuition from the richest 60 percent of the student population could secure up to $9.3 million a year, or around 11 percent of the university's annual budget.

socioeconomic background. Although this implies that the credit scheme would be smaller in scope than one might wish, it could prove successful as a transitory mechanism until SINEACE can fulfill its larger role.

Finally, it is worth emphasizing that the legitimacy and design problems stressed throughout this chapter are interconnected. Although the former arise mainly when the government first puts forward a reform, and the latter when it is implemented, the latter also feed back into the former. Ambiguous messages about how the reform will be implemented and what outcomes are to be expected tend to foster impatience and discontent with the reform process.

In the 1990s both public administration reform and educational reform faced significant legitimacy problems related to the nature of the political regime, after President Fujimori concentrated power and exercised it in an authoritarian and arbitrary manner. In both cases the weakness of representative democratic institutions could itself be considered an obstacle to reform, and this helps make the case for the third "missing reform," which we take up next.

Missing Ingredient #3: Political Reform

Comparative research suggests that in addition to their intrinsic value, democratic political systems tend to outperform dictatorships at adjusting to external shocks, investing in human development, protecting the property rights of the majority, and achieving economic stability and social equity over the long run. The elements of democracy considered most important for these ends include universal suffrage, a bill of rights, separation of powers, respect for the rule of law, and the existence of strong, autonomous institutions, including political parties, unions, and other interest groups (Karl, 1996; Rodrik, 1997; Sen, 1999).

Historically, of course, democracy in Peru has not worked this way. Authoritarianism has prevailed during most of Peruvian history, and until recently democracy was considered by both conservatives and radicals an obstacle to various national development goals. Political power has been highly concentrated and at the same time highly unstable, exercised arbitrarily with only limited checks and balances. Although separation of powers is constitutionally mandated, in practice both Congress and the judiciary have been weakly institutionalized and ineffective; political parties and most interest groups have also been weak and fragmented.

In our view, the volatility of Peru's politics and the weakness of its representative institutions have been obstacles to laying the foundations for inclusive growth. They have made it difficult to enforce basic rules and rights, ensure government accountability, and promote sustained collaboration among key actors toward major policy goals, whether they be reducing poverty, reforming the educational system, or reforming the state apparatus. This situation, in turn, favors the emergence of popular "outsiders," who propose to suspend democratic politics in order to establish order and attempt bold social change (Sanborn and Panfichi, 1996; Morón and Sanborn, 2007).

Can the reform of Peru's political institutions improve the prospects for inclusive growth? If so, which institutions, and what kind of reforms? Over the last quarter century, numerous changes have been made in the formal rules and institutions of Peruvian politics, through new constitutions (1979 and 1993), electoral and party legislation, executive decrees, and extra-parliamentary agreements. Although diverse and piecemeal in nature, these changes have largely sought to strengthen the executive, expand electoral participation and competition, and regulate the political party system. Some of these reforms directly or indirectly addressed the foundations for inclusive growth, but only a few have made progress toward that end, while others have been ineffective and some clearly counterproductive.

Here we briefly examine the main challenges that political reformers have faced in Peru in recent years, highlighting some problems of design as well as difficulties in implementing institutional change in the volatile Peruvian context. The main question is: How has it been possible politically for Peru to continue so long without significant economic and social inclusion, and why has inclusion not been a top priority on the political agenda, at least between elections? We examine how various institutions and rules may have helped prolong this situation.

The Political Challenges to Building Inclusive Growth

WHO GETS ELECTED? WEAK PARTY STRUCTURES AND WHAT SUSTAINS THEM

Free and fair elections with universal suffrage were first held in Peru only in 1980 and were interrupted during the 1990s. Hence, although voting is obligatory and turnout high, informed electoral participation and constructive competition remain weak. Political parties in Peru have not served as effective vehicles for citizen education or representation of interests.

Although politics in the 1980s was marked by competition among three main parties or blocs—the centrist APRA, Acción Popular, and the Partido Popular Cristiano (PPC) on the right, and the Marxist United Left alliance—all were characterized by arbitrary and personalistic leadership and fraught with internal disputes, and each was widely rejected by voters after failing to govern effectively during its brief spells in power.[16] During the 1990s these groups were overtaken by a plethora of smaller movements and splinter parties. The triumph of

16. In 1980–95 Acción Popular governed in alliance with the minority PPC, and APRA under Alan Garcia governed from 1985 to 1990; meanwhile the United Left held numerous municipal governments, including Lima's. For more on Peru's parties in the 1980s see Sanborn (1991) and Tanaka (1998).

Alberto Fujimori, a political outsider who refused to build a solid party of his own, accelerated the downfall of the then-existing parties. Although low barriers to entry and other electoral rules facilitated this outcome, it was voter disgust with party performance that created the opportunity (Morón and Sanborn, 2007; Tanaka, 2006).

To varying degrees, Peruvian parties since 2001 have continued to revolve around personalities rather than programs or ideology; they have few roots in society and little institutional life between elections. They lack the ability to aggregate citizens' interests effectively and represent them in the public sphere, and they lack the professional cadres and cohesion necessary to manage the state or undertake effective oversight of government. Thus, although civic association and collective action are relatively strong in Peru, partisan identification is low (around 5 percent of the population), and parties are highly unpopular even by Latin American standards. Indeed, comparative analyses rank Peru as having the weakest party system in the region (Mainwaring and Scully, 1995, pp. 16–17; Payne et al., 2002, p. 143).

Why have Peru's political parties remained so weak? Part of the answer lies in their lack of historical continuity and their ideological and political sectarianism (Sanborn, 1991; Morón and Sanborn, 2007). The rejection of market economics by much of the Left, and the lack of consideration of human rights and equity concerns by most of the Right, made it especially difficult to forge working agreements through the 1980s or to respond to the violence of the Shining Path guerrilla movement. These factors have been compounded by electoral rules that, in the interest of pluralism, continue to encourage personalistic politics and party fragmentation.

Low legal barriers for the registration of parties and candidates, for example, encourage the proliferation of loosely knit movements with few lasting ties to voters. The majority runoff election format also encourages small parties to run separate candidates in the first round rather than form broad coalitions, and second-round alliances tend to be opportunistic and short-lived. The open-list, proportional representation electoral system without a threshold also encourages a proliferation of contenders (only since 2006 have parties had to win at least 4 percent of the total vote to gain a seat in Congress), as does the *voto preferencial doble,* which allows voters to choose their two favorite candidates from a party slate. These features, designed to enhance voter choice, also undermine party discipline and reward personality politics. In 2001, thirteen parties competed for power and eleven were represented in Congress.

REPRESENTATIVES THAT DO NOT REPRESENT

Once elected, Congress should serve as an intermediary between the citizens and the executive, while also producing legislation and preventing abuses of power by the other branches. Although presidents in Peru are also popularly elected, members of Congress should be empowered to challenge or modify the executive agenda if it strays from campaign promises, or if they believe their constituents' voices are not being heard. For this to happen, several reforms are needed.

To begin with, links between citizens and their elected representatives are weak or nonexistent. The downsizing of Congress after 1993 to just one chamber with 120 members is cited by some analysts as contributing to its lack of popular responsiveness. In 1990 there was one member of Congress for every 30,000 voters, but by 2006 this had increased to 137,500, the highest ratio among the Andean countries. Because the number of members is constitutionally fixed, the ratio will continue to widen. However, the creation of twenty-five separate electoral districts in 2001 was designed to offset this problem, reducing the ratio of voters to members in most of the country and ensuring that all regions have some representation. Today twenty-two of the twenty-five districts are small, with two to five representatives each, and 40,000 to 80,000 voters per representative; these twenty-two districts elect 60 percent of all members of Congress. There are also two medium-size districts (La Libertad with seven members, and Piura with six), and one very large one, Lima, with thirty-five members, or 29 percent of the total, and over 152,000 voters per member. Proposals for dividing Lima into smaller districts are still on the drawing board.

Even in those districts with reasonable citizen-to-member ratios, members have few incentives to be attentive and accountable to their constituents. With few exceptions, members elected from the provinces move to Lima and soon become engaged in the capital's political life and in issues that may secure them more media attention than the bread-and-butter needs of voters back home. In practice, they have little time to return home while Congress is in session, unlike in Chile, for example, where the plenary sessions of Congress leave one week of every month free so that representatives can stay in touch with their districts.

Realistically, members of Congress can do very little to directly deliver what many voters back home want most, such as infrastructure projects or improved social services. Peru's last two constitutions stripped Congress of the "power of the purse," or the ability to amend the executive's annual budget proposal. Members may propose changes in the budget's composition, but not specific outlays. This limits their ability to transfer resources to their constituencies and encourages them to gain power and voter attention by other means.

In theory, an open-list, proportional electoral system should increase members' responsiveness and accountability. Accountability should be further enhanced by such elements as electronic voting boards and a congressional website, established in the late 1990s, where citizens can follow legislative decisions and members' voting records (Carey, 2003). In practice, however, Congress's public approval ratings have remained among the lowest for all public institutions, and turnover among individual legislators remains high.[17] Since 1980 the average legislative experience of a member of Congress has been 4.4 years, and most current members have no prior experience in this arena.[18] For the most part, the media pay little attention to their voting records, and relatively few voters have access to the legislature's website or the motivation to review it. The media *have* paid attention to "scandalous" increases in congressional salaries and benefits and questionable hiring practices, which reinforce the public perception that members are basically rent-seekers rather than honest public servants.

Furthermore, Peruvians often do not view legislation as the best means to advance their interests and proposals. Real power is seen as residing with the president and members of the cabinet. However, the power of the media to deliver popular messages to the executive has increased substantially in recent years, and the semi-autonomous ombudsman's office (Defensoría del Pueblo) is widely seen as a more legitimate mechanism for investigating and documenting abuses of power, even though it lacks the authority to apply sanctions.

Legislators Who Prefer Not to Legislate

Under the 1993 constitution, Congress retains considerable formal authority. It can debate and pass legislation, including changes to taxes as well as approval of the budget, and it can still amend the president's budget proposal during the appropriations process. With a simple majority, Congress can also override a presidential veto of legislation and repeal decrees made under delegated authority, and the constitution itself can be amended by a supermajority. Although the president selects the cabinet, ministers can be formally questioned and censured by Congress. The president, cabinet members, and other high officials can also be impeached by a simple majority of the Permanent Commission (see below) and convicted by a simple majority of the remaining legislators (Schmidt, 2004).

What do Peruvian legislators actually do? And why is their performance so poorly evaluated? A lack of empirical research makes these questions difficult to answer. What is known is that legislators do not even do most of the legislating; as table 5 shows, more than half of all legislation from 1980 to 2001 was issued by executive decree, including most major initiatives affecting the economy, the labor market, and the provision of social services.

When Congress does legislate, as in the more proactive 2001–06 period, it has passed some important measures, including the legal framework for decentralization, public sector pension reform, a new law governing mining royalties, and the

---

17. In 2003 Congress had a public approval rating of 10 to 12 percent, which by 2006 had fallen to 8 percent. Approval of the new Congress in mid-2008 was around 10 to 20 percent. Individual parties received approval ratings of just 6 to 9 percent in 2003. See Apoyo, *Opinion y Mercado,* Opinión data: *Resumen de Encuestas de la Opinion Pública,* año 6, número 83, December 11, 2006; año 8, número 101, June 23, 2008; and año 8, número 102, July 21, 2008.

18. Sixty-two percent of members in the 2001–06 Congress were newcomers, and 85 percent had less than five years of experience. The majority of the 2006–11 Congress are also first-timers (Santiso, 2004).

Table 5. *Peru: Decrees and Legislation by Presidential Term, 1980–2006*

| Legal instrument | Fernando Belaúnde, 1980–85 | | Alan García, 1985–90 | | Alberto Fujimori | | | | | | Valentín Paniagua, 2000–01 | | Alejandro Toledo, 2001–06 | | Total |
| | | | | | First term, 1990–92 | | Second term, 1992–95 | | Third term, 1995–2000 | | | | | | |
	Number	Percent of total	Number	Percent of total	Number	Percent of total	Number	Percent of total	Number	Percent of total	Number	Percent of total	Number	Percent of total	Total
Legislative decrees	348	20	263	13	156	20	174	15	119	9	10	4	41	3	1,111
Emergency decrees[a]	667*	38	1,033	53	562	72	744	62	507	38	122	49	210	15	3,845
Laws	724	42	665	34	67	9	275	23	725	54	117	47	1,122	82	3,695
Total	1,739	100	1,961	100	785	100	1,193	100	1,351	100	249	100	1,373	100	8,651
Laws vetoed (percent)[b]	38	5.2	60	9	35	52	46	17	88	12	16	14	320	29	

Source: Morón and Sanborn (2007).

a. Before 1993 this type of legislation (decrees issued under the legal protection of Article 211-20) was not formally called by this name but had the same legislative value.

b. Percent of all laws passed by Congress in the indicated period.

law on political parties discussed below. However, Congress also devotes large amounts of time to passing laws of minor importance, as well as introducing numerous bills that have little chance of passage.[19] Rules allowing legislators to sponsor projects individually, rather than by party blocs, or *bancadas,* have favored this trend. In mid-2006 the new Congress changed the rules to require party sponsorship of legislative proposals, with a minimum number of members signing on. In its first eighteen months this rule appears to have reduced the number of bills, although over 2,000 were still in the works. Of the 427 laws and resolutions approved in this period, 48 percent had been proposed by the executive (Campos, 2008).[20]

The broader problem of party discipline also makes it hard for party blocs to maintain a firm stance on key policy issues or negotiate with other groups to advance needed reforms. Once elected, members have few incentives to follow the party line. Since competitive primary elections are still uncommon, each elected legislator may feel that his or her personal agenda has priority over any broader agenda. The *voto preferencial doble* encourages this, as does the fact that some "parties" are actually loose-knit collections of individual candidates, some without clear agendas. The lack of sanctions on legislators who renounce or change their parties after election further exacerbates these tendencies. Although the new voting rules may have reduced the total number of bills proposed, they have not resolved the general lack of party discipline.

Policymaking by Decree and Lack of Effective Balance of Powers

An essential part of a well-functioning democracy is horizontal control over presidential authority and policymaking, ideally by a solid party system, an experienced Congress, and an impartial and autonomous judiciary. Weak and unstable democracies, however, tend to concentrate power in the executive and encourage government by decree.

One legacy of Peru's long period of military rule in the 1970s was a new constitution in 1979 that gave the civilian executive strong budget prerogatives and the ability to legislate by decree, bypassing the deliberative role and accountability of Congress. The 1993 constitution expanded the president's powers to dissolve Congress and to pass emergency decrees; it also reduced the number of members by half. In the current design, a Permanent Commission of twenty-five members convenes between the two annual sessions and has the same powers as the whole Congress, although its agenda is supposed to be defined and limited in advance.

19. More than 10,000 *proyectos de ley* were presented (and 1,200 approved) in the 2001–06 Congress, compared with fewer than 1,000 in Colombia and fewer than 300 in Chile.

20. Under President Toledo, 82 percent of laws were actually passed by the legislature. The president retained a key role, however, as 78 percent of bills presented by the executive were approved, and 29 percent of bills passed by Congress were vetoed (Morón and Sanborn, 2007; Campos, 2008).

The constitution empowers the executive to issue two types of decrees, legislative and emergency. Besides restricting legislators' ability to increase the proposed budget or insert line items, it stipulates that if the new budget is not approved by a set deadline, the executive's proposal automatically becomes law. Designed to neutralize opposition and avoid deadlock, this measure "significantly diminishes the legislature's bargaining power" and oversight capacity (Santiso with Garcia Belgrano, 2004, p. 14).

However, the current asymmetry in executive-legislative relations derives not only from the constitution's design, but also from electoral outcomes—the existence of a pro-government majority in Congress—and the relative institutional weakness of the legislative branch. In the 1990s Fujimori resorted to both licit and illicit means to control Congress and the judiciary, including generous salary increases, bribes, and blackmail (McMillan and Zoido, 2004). Although a lack of significant opposition or oversight facilitated the initial economic reform efforts of the 1990s, it also permitted unprecedented corruption and unchecked abuse of power by both civilian and military leaders. Once exposed, the scandals greatly undermined the credibility of government and brought widespread demands to restore the rule of law and place more effective checks on executive power. Since 2001 the challenge has been to do this without returning to the polarization and policy stalemates of the past.

Congress also tends to function poorly as a forum for informed public debate: the delegation of legislative authority in practice means ducking public deliberation. Furthermore, as mentioned above, Congress largely fails to hold other agencies of government accountable for their actions. This is notable in public budgeting, where the constitution limits what Congress can do, but it is also true in taxation, where Congress regularly delegates authority to the executive and rarely monitors the latter's tax initiatives (Santiso with Garcia Belgrano, 2004).

Many members of Congress lack the technical capacity or the political incentives to hold government accountable, because of the weakness of their parties, their own limited experience and high turnover, and the limited institutionalization of the committee system (Santiso with Garcia Belgrano, 2004). Each of the 120 legislators serves on three to five committees, on average, whose membership changes annually, and even the budgetary review process is not governed by stable rules or personnel (Santiso with Garcia Belgrano, 2004, p. 20; Campos, 2007b). Most parties do not provide expert advisers to their congressional blocs, and although individual members may hire their own advisers, they often do so based on nontechnical criteria. Once the budget is approved, Congress also has little say in how public resources are actually spent. The authority to issue emergency decrees gives the executive discretion over subsequent budget changes, and legislators lack the skills or the motivation to monitor spending closely. Although limited resources may partially explain the lack of a professional congressional research service or reliable partisan think tanks, the parties have shown little interest in changing this situation or challenging executive dominance.

Although Congress became more active after 2001, when presidents lacked majority control, legislators with short time horizons and little party support or discipline remained reluctant to engage in complex and potentially controversial policy matters. Furthermore, given that legislators lack authority to initiate spending, they depend primarily on contacts with and favors from the executive to provide benefits to their constituents; hence they often agree to delegate authority to the president in exchange for these favors (Morón and Sanborn, 2007; Santiso, 2004, p. 11).

Poll results and qualitative evidence suggest that Peruvians today perceive most legislators as ineffective, corrupt, or both. In the popular stereotype, a legislator is someone who aspires to Congress in order to enrich himself or herself (as quickly as possible, given the general volatility of politics), obtain jobs for friends and family members, and secure other sources of income and power through political contacts or outright corruption. Although members' motivations are more complex than that, and some are genuinely motivated by ideology, party militancy, or commitment to public service, the clientelism and corruption of the parties in power during the past twenty-five years tends to confirm the stereotype. Because many of the weaknesses of Congress stem from those of the party system, reformers since 2001 have focused on trying to address this situation directly.

Political Party Reform: "Hecha la Ley, Hecha la Trampa"?[21]

After the Fujimori debacle, the country's more experienced party leaders came to agree that the country's weak and fragmented party system seriously undermined the quality of governance and their own legitimacy. Although an array of measures was proposed to correct this situation, ultimately the leaders agreed on a more concerted effort to regulate parties directly. The Political Party Law of 2003 (PPL) aimed to raise barriers to party formation and competition, encourage alliances among smaller movements, and promote internal democracy and transparency.

Until 2001, Peru was one of the few countries in Latin America without specific legislation regulating parties and party competition. From 1980 to 2002, proposals to reform the party system were repeatedly thwarted in Congress. According to Fernando Tuesta (1996), political scientist and former head of the National Office of Electoral Processes (Oficina Nacional de Procesos Electorales, or ONPE), competitors formed an implicit pact to avoid setting clearer and stricter rules in this arena. Although party reform had been discussed before the 2001 election, it took twenty months to negotiate a law acceptable to a majority of contenders. The draft proposal was produced by a small group of congressional

---

21. Roughly "make the law, make the loophole." Unidad Nacional candidate Lourdes Flores used this common phrase to describe the implementation of the Political Party Law (cited in Crabtree, 2006, p. 50), and Tuesta and Mendieta use it to title their recent article on party finance (2007).

leaders, including Jorge del Castillo of APRA and Henry Pease of Perú Posible, working with experts from ONPE and several nongovernmental organizations (Crabtree, 2006, p. 43). The final proposal was approved by a close vote in Congress and promulgated on October 1, 2003.

The new law covers three main issues: the constitution and recognition of parties, internal party democracy, and party finance and access to media. Under the law, to register for electoral competition, a party must have a set of internal rules, a government program, and a list of supporters totaling no fewer than 1 percent of voters in the last election (128,000 as of 2001). Parties are also required to demonstrate the existence of local committees in at least 65 of Peru's 194 provinces and 17 of its 25 departments. Each party committee must have at least fifty members, who are legally inscribed in a *padron partidario* and have rights and obligations in the organization; this list must be published on the party's website (Tuesta, 2005). This rule was designed to discourage what Martín Tanaka has called "electoral franchises," in which local personalities are temporarily recruited to run on party slates—often paying for the opportunity—without being party regulars or having established ties to the main organization. The PPL also introduced an electoral threshold (*valla electoral*): a party must receive at least 5 percent of the total vote cast in a general election to be awarded congressional seats and retain its electoral registration.[22]

To promote internal party democracy, the PPL requires that parties hold democratic elections in which all registered affiliates have the right to participate, and that they hold leadership elections at least once every four years. This was one of the more controversial provisions, and the original proposals had to be modified to win approval in Congress (Crabtree, 2006, p. 44). The law also expands a preexisting gender quota—at least 30 percent of candidates on a party's slate must be women—and extends it to internal party leadership positions as well. The law requires that parties present detailed reports of their income and expenditure, sets restrictions on the amount and sources of private campaign finance, and for the first time establishes direct public financing for parties that attain congressional representation. Negative public opinion, however, forced Congress to postpone this measure indefinitely.

In the short term, the PPL did not have the desired effect of raising barriers to entry and reducing fragmentation. Before its passage, twenty-two parties and movements were legally registered; in 2006, thirty-five were registered, and twenty-four fielded candidates in that year's elections. Although the media reported deliberate falsification of signatures and nonexistent committees in at least eleven organizations, the National Election Board (Jurado Nacional de Elec-

---

22. In September 2005 Congress lowered the barrier to 4 percent for the 2006 race (700,000 votes), with an exception for parties winning at least two seats in separate jurisdictions. The difference is important, since members can be elected from some departments with fewer than 10,000 votes.

ciones, JNE) ultimately approved the registration of all that applied (Keller, 2006).[23] The main problem was not the law itself, but the inability of the electoral authorities to implement it effectively and the lack of sanctions for noncompliance. Critics also charge that the JNE had little desire to confront the parties and therefore basically practiced conflict avoidance (Tuesta, 2005). Experts have estimated that had the law been applied correctly, no more than eight parties would have been legally registered.

The effect of the electoral threshold is more ambiguous. Seven groups made it into Congress in 2006, compared with eleven in 2001, and 111 of the 120 seats were won by the four main blocs. However, the threshold itself apparently had little effect, as only one potential congressman was eliminated as a result of his party not passing the bar. The small parties of the Left, which might have passed the threshold had they formed a single alliance, nevertheless failed to do so.[24] Four of the seven winning slates were formed hastily for the 2006 election, including the UPP-PNP coalition, created to back the "outsider" candidate and first-round winner, Ollanta Humala. Fujimori's Alianza por el Futuro was also hastily forged by three different *fujimorista* movements. Although seventeen parties failed to make the cut and were de-registered, it remains to be seen whether this will have a lasting effect on the next elections in 2011.[25]

Changing the rules also had little immediate effect on party cohesion or construction. Apparently, a considerable number of reported party committees were fraudulent or were deactivated soon after registration. The practice of selling party slates to the highest bidder and making deals with local power brokers seeking a trampoline to Congress remained widespread. This was clearest in the case of Humala's electoral operation. Humala used the existing UPP to back his presidential bid and list of newcomers, after failing to register his own Partido Nacionalista. Although they held the largest single voting bloc, the forty-five individuals who reached Congress on his coattails began to distance themselves even before inauguration, and the head of his list soon broke ranks to form a party of his own.

Various parties did hold internal elections to select or ratify their leaders, a positive step that was encouraged by heightened media attention. However, the media also reported numerous cases of party leaders ignoring or overturning the results of internal elections. It was harder for civil society to monitor transparency in campaign finances, because numerous parties delayed submitting their accounts

23. Only the Si Cumple movement was denied the right to compete, because its presidential candidate, former president Alberto Fujimori, had been banned from holding public office until 2010.

24. According to Rici (2006), only César Acuña of Alianza para el Progreso in La Libertad was eliminated by the *valla*. Running separately, the leftist parties received 3.2 percent of the total vote.

25. By late 2007 eleven parties were represented in Congress in six parliamentary groups (Campos, 2007b). As of February 2008, 137 groups had requested party registration forms, including groups seeking re-registration after being excluded by the 2006 results, according to *El Comercio*, February 12, 2008.

until well after the elections, and in many cases the information presented was of dubious credibility. The electoral authorities were equally ill prepared to review and verify parties' financial reports: ONPE had just three auditors to supervise all party finances (Keller, 2006). Because the main sanction for noncompliance is the loss of public funding—under a rule that had yet to be approved as of late 2007, and that applies only to those parties with elected representatives—there are few incentives for the rest to comply.

No Silver Bullet: How to Move Forward with Political Reform

Peruvian democracy today is certainly competitive. Civil liberties have been largely restored since 2000, free and fair elections are held, and dozens of parties and movements have competed for and held public office in recent years. In this sense the opportunity to participate in the electoral process is "broadly shared." However, the majority of citizens do not participate in or identify with any party, and voter preferences remain highly volatile. Citizen discontent is reflected in the rise and fall of presidential approval ratings, in congressional turnover rates of 75 to 80 percent each term, and in negative public opinion regarding virtually all representative institutions.[26] For many Peruvians, the institutions and rules of democracy are not working, and many would be willing once again to trade them away for a promise of greater social and economic benefits (see table 6; Programa de las Naciones Unidas para el Desarrollo, 2005; Camacho and Sanborn, 2007).

Although it is not the only factor, the weakness of the party system contributes to political volatility, the recurrence of unpredictable "outsiders," and a Congress characterized by inexperience and improvisation, in which the desire to be reelected apparently plays a limited role in shaping behavior. These traits, in turn, make government less accountable and less responsive to citizens' needs and demands.

Although few of the institutional reforms undertaken in the past quarter century can be called irrelevant, some did have design problems, and there were contradictions between different rules and reforms. For the most part, changes were made piecemeal rather than as part of an integrated package. The granting of greater authority to the executive, for example, was not accompanied by measures to guarantee the autonomy and effectiveness of the other branches. The virtues of inclusion and pluralism were overshadowed by the weakness of the multiparty system and the frequent changes in leadership, traits that the electoral system and other factors tend to perpetuate. The effort to reform parties from the supply side provided inadequate incentives for voluntary compliance.

---

26. *Latinobarómetro 2006* reported that only 20 percent of respondents said they thought the government works for the well-being of the whole nation and not just the elite. By mid-2008, Garcia's approval ratings placed him among the least popular presidents in the region. See the Consulta Mitovsky website, www.consulta.com.mx.

Table 6. *Peru: Popular Views on Democracy, 1995–2007*
Percent of all respondents

Year	Support for democracy[a]	Satisfaction with democracy[b]
1995	52	44
1996	63	28
1997	60	21
1998	63	17
2000	64	24
2001	62	16
2002	55	18
2003	52	11
2004	45	7
2005	40	13
2006	55	23
2007	47	17

Source: Latinobarómetro.
a. Share of respondents agreeing with the statement "Democracy is preferable to any other government system."
b. Share responding "very satisfied" or "more or less satisfied" with the functioning of democracy.

In addition to these design problems, both external and local constraints have inhibited effective reform. One of these constraints, especially during the 1980s, was ideology, although the country has become significantly less polarized since the 1990s. Another major constraint is the state itself and its limited capacity to uphold the law and apply sanctions, as in the case of the PPL. A third constraint is the structural weakness of the civil society organizations that monitor the government and defend the interests of those who most need its attention.

Although the country's leaders have agreed in principle on a range of broad policy objectives, moving from declaration to action remains difficult. Political and social sector reforms still have few effective and sustained advocates, and public opinion remains uninformed in key areas. The weakness of parties and interest groups and the inexperience and short time horizons of most politicians continue to hinder congressional action; meanwhile the executive continues to take the credit when things go right and the blame when they do not. Between elections, the lack of connection between local communities and national politics is tremendous. The political system still offers few incentives to focus on longer-term development needs or to engage in public dialogue about them.

If political reform is a priority in Peru, how to move forward? To achieve inclusive growth, ultimately it is the state that has to change, not just by encouraging private economic activity but by effectively taxing and redistributing wealth, changing public investment priorities, and expanding opportunities. But reform of the state is itself a political process. When done from the top down, its effectiveness and duration have been limited. When done through a more democratic process and rooted in society, it tends to endure. Measures to reduce poverty and increase equity cannot simply be decreed from above; they require political negotiation and the engagement of diverse interests.

What more could be done to strengthen the role of the political system in this process? The first step is to give democracy more time to work, however imperfectly. Comparative research suggests that the ability to deliberate, resolve conflicts, and play by the rules tends to improve with practice (Rodrik, 1997; Schmitter and Karl, 1995). Hence it is encouraging that an unpopular president without majority support was able to complete his term in 2001 and transfer power to an elected successor. It is also encouraging that the main "anti-system" candidate in 2006, Ollanta Humala, opted for the electoral route and was ultimately spurned by a majority of voters.

Beyond merely "waiting and seeing," more could be done to strengthen the party system and encourage more-solid party organizations, with a broader reach in society and enhanced capacity to select and retain competent members. At a minimum, the capacity of electoral authorities to monitor compliance with the existing party law should be increased, as well as the sanctions for noncompliance. Various changes in the electoral rules are also being debated in Congress. These include eliminating the *voto preferencial doble,* making voting voluntary, dividing Lima into smaller and more representative voting districts, holding staggered or separate elections for president and Congress, and imposing sanctions on members of Congress who change parties between elections. Some of these proposals have implications for other objectives, such as affirmative action and broad representation of interests.[27] Therefore, there is a need for clearer public discussion of what the core problems are and what changes can most effectively resolve them (Tanaka, 2006). The current legislature has avoided this task and, as of mid-2008, has shelved or postponed debate on all significant political reform proposals.

Although a Congress with fewer, more disciplined parties should be a more effective Congress, further reforms within the legislature itself could also enhance its oversight capacity. In addition to enforcing the requirement that parties screen and approve their members' legislative proposals, important steps would be to institutionalize the committee system and procedures, reduce turnover in their composition and leadership, and encourage greater thematic specialization by members (Campos, 2007b). Establishing more professional criteria for congressional advisers, assigning them to party blocs rather than individuals, and creating

---

27. For example, studies by Schmidt (2004) suggest that the *voto preferencial* tends to favor female candidates. And it is widely assumed that in the short run, voluntary voting would lead to reduced turnout among poor and rural citizens.

a well-endowed congressional research service available to all members would also be steps forward (Tanaka, 2006).

Important as it is to enforce and, where necessary, modify existing rules and institutions, that alone is not sufficient. Given the weakness of the current parties and the reluctance of elected authorities to reform political institutions once they are on the inside, nongovernmental organizations (NGOs) and the independent media must work to monitor politicians' behavior and keep political reform on the agenda. It is important to defend and enhance their capacity to do so. NGOs of different orientations involved in research and advocacy are monitoring public agencies, trying to hold leaders accountable, and providing public education to improve the quality of citizen demand. They have also provided dozens of trained professionals to the public sector. In recent years NGOs have been created specifically to promote various aspects of good government, including fair elections, voter education, stronger parties, budget transparency, and the monitoring of local governments and Congress. Although these organizations share some of the same traits as political parties, they may be better organized and more disposed to form alliances. Combining citizen vigilance with promotion of policy alternatives, and coordinating with the ombudsman and sympathetic members of Congress, such organizations teach citizens to defend their rights and monitor their authorities. Ultimately, such empowerment of citizens is the best antidote to *caudillismo* and a necessary complement to reform from within.

Conclusions

The CGD framework has allowed us to identify the broad sharing of the benefits of growth as the "missing foundation" in Peru and to focus our discussion of administrative, educational, and political reform accordingly. This in itself is a major and novel contribution of the framework, in our view, as it prevents policymakers from being swamped by a laundry list of reforms, all of them necessary but in the aggregate surpassing the implementation capacity of the country's institutions. With these limitations in mind, we have proposed a short list of policy initiatives that we believe can help advance reform. In closing we will rely on the framework once again to explain the potential role of each of these ingredients in the reform "recipe."

We argue that Peru finds itself today at the vulnerable equilibrium depicted in figure 6. As explained earlier, our analysis of Peru's reform efforts starts from a point when the economy was in a state of emergency. Much of the reform effort of the 1990s was driven (and justified) by this fact. The main concern of government was to return the economy to viability, restoring basic macroeconomic balance and the ability of private business to ignite economic growth. This was the route taken by the stabilization plan, which was accomplished by means of "unbridled presidentialism" (Morón and Sanborn, 2007).

Figure 6. *Peru's Vulnerable Equilibrium*

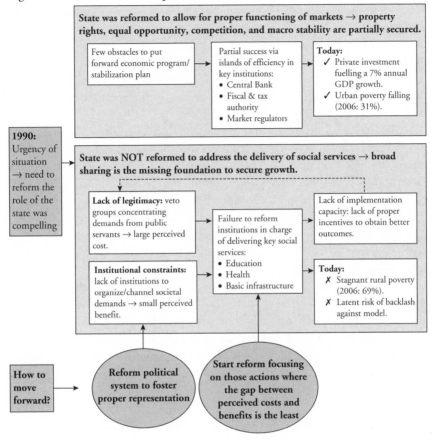

Obviously, the reforms of that period could have also focused on distributive issues or on policies aimed at improving the long-run potential of the less favored share of the population, but this path was not taken. The magnitude of the crisis left by President Garcia and the longer-term failure of state-led development since the 1970s partly explain why the thrust of the reforms of the 1990s had to be thus circumscribed. However, the main reason that the state was not reformed to improve the delivery of social services and encourage expanded opportunities for the majority was a combination of a lack of legitimacy and strong institutional constraints.

Our analysis of the attempted reforms in the education sector showed that reforms that explicitly address the issue of exclusion have concentrated costs but dispersed benefits. From the supply side, reform implies designing the right incentives for a large number of public servants, and it is difficult to build legitimacy for such changes in a public sector where salaries have always been disconnected from results, and where the social sectors have historically been poorly funded. Thus, reform will easily face opposition by veto-wielding groups representing the demands of public servants. From the demand side, although no one living below the poverty line would disagree about the need for better social services, the desired final outcome of any proposed intervention, namely, the more rapid accumulation of human capital, is difficult to measure and invisible in the near term. Thus, the lack of strong institutions to help organize and channel societal demands translates into a small perceived benefit from reform.

As a result, although the reforms undertaken since the early 1990s have partly succeeded in securing property rights, strengthening competition, and improving macroeconomic stability, these have not been secured for all, and meanwhile the broad sharing of the benefits of growth remains the missing foundation. The outcome to date is an economy in a vulnerable equilibrium, capable of sustaining growth but still leaving a large share of the population out of the growth process. As we have seen, the benefits of Peru's current growth may be somewhat better distributed than in the past, but they are still concentrated in the country's urban areas and exclude the rural poor.

We believe the present situation can be characterized as an equilibrium in that it is backed by an economic model in which four of the five foundations for growth are at least partly secured: Peru offers private sector firms the opportunity to thrive in a market-based environment with no significant administrative impediments. In addition, the same problems of representation that thwart organized demand for public intervention in the social arena also contribute to this equilibrium. In fact, the combination of a pervasive centralism and a skewed electoral calculus still tend to leave the poor out of the solution.

However, we also believe this equilibrium is vulnerable, because of the risk of backlash from those who are excluded and those who resent the highly unequal distribution of benefits. This risk is greatest around elections and when adverse economic shocks occur. As we have seen, Peru is characterized by high electoral volatility, where underrepresented groups see each presidential election as an opportunity to revisit all economic arrangements. Between elections, political support for revising the model tends to wane if the economy is performing well; hence the ability to maintain equilibrium depends on the likelihood that the economy will get into trouble. Since a small open economy is certain to get into trouble eventually, the real question is how to minimize the impact on growth and inclusion.

Obviously, part of the answer has to do with further securing the first four growth foundations by, for example, increasing the availability of resources for countercyclical fiscal policies, and further advancing in terms of property rights and competition, to allow new businesses to flourish and promote the diversification of exports. However, because our analysis has focused on broad sharing as the missing foundation, the link we propose between adverse economic shocks and growth has more to do with the danger of exacerbating the risk of backlash against the model. The question then becomes how to distribute the benefits of growth in a more egalitarian way, and a significant part of the answer has to do with reforming the quality and delivery of critical social services.

Before summarizing our answers, we should mention that another consequence of not having reformed the delivery of social services is the current lack of adequate implementation capacity in several key areas. In fact, problems on this front are as much a consequence as a cause of the lack of reform in the social arena: although islands of efficiency were established within key institutions that served the main objectives of stabilization, other sectors, such as justice, education, health, and the provision of basic infrastructure, were virtually ignored, and this, in turn, has contributed to the lack of legitimacy of reform within those sectors.

In concluding, then, we return to the framework and try to take stock of what we have learned about the recent reform processes so as to organize our short list of priority reforms. As discussed above, failure to address the delivery of social services has led to a vulnerable equilibrium characterized by a potential risk of backlash from those excluded. Understanding the role of our proposed policy initiatives requires organizing them in terms of the causes and consequences of this decision.

As explained above, reform in the social arena faced two major obstacles: weak legitimacy and strong institutional constraints. We believe our earlier recommendations for political reform can play an important role by mitigating these obstacles. In particular, working toward a party system that offers better representation should help organize and channel societal demands in a way that reduces fragmentation and raises the perceived benefit of embarking on a reform that addresses the broad sharing foundation. All the individuals involved—politicians, government administrators, and citizens—tend to be short-sighted, and therefore it is hard to set goals that require a longer horizon. In the absence of organizations that can channel societal demands in a responsible manner (and away from electoral calculus), the impatience of the potential beneficiaries can easily influence the planner's own behavior, who then succumbs to the temptation of avoiding policies that will deliver only in the long run.

Fine tuning the mechanisms through which the state communicates with its citizens and attends to their demands must therefore be an essential part of any serious attempt to reform the delivery of social services. Again, political reform cannot be simply decreed from above; it must be accomplished through a process rooted in society for it to endure.

The path toward a new, less vulnerable equilibrium where growth is more broadly shared, however, also requires results in the near term. In fact, the longer-term trickle-down process will surely need more time than remains until the next presidential election, during which the probability of experiencing an adverse shock is rather high. Thus, policy actions aimed at building up legitimacy and reducing institutional constraints must be accompanied by interventions that directly address the delivery of public services. In this respect, we believe our policy recommendations addressing administrative reform and the education sector should play a vital supplementary role. For this to happen, however, reform must be decisive, focusing on those actions where the gap between perceived costs and benefits is the smallest. As already discussed, good examples of such actions include introducing a merit-based career path for new public servants, programming budgetary expansions in a results-based format, focusing decentralization efforts on a pilot macroregion, and avoiding further confrontations with teachers in order to focus on realizing the results to be expected from education reform.

Reforms still pending that address the broad sharing foundation will require changing the process by which public services are delivered, and this, in turn, means dealing with established bureaucracies at the different levels of government. Removing public intervention in markets and creating a new bureaucracy to deal with regulatory issues is one thing; transforming the way the state provides services that have historically come under its purview—and that employ a large number of public servants—is quite another. Thus, if results are to be seen in the short term, it must be acknowledged that reform from within is not easy and that changes must be introduced incrementally. Focusing and persisting on a narrower set of reforms in the social arena, in turn, will make it much easier to avoid potential design problems and foster implementation capacity at lower levels of government.

APPENDIX

Judicial Reform in Peru

One of the main obstacles to inclusive growth in Peru is the lack of a well-functioning state, essential to which is an independent and efficient judicial system. A strong judiciary is indispensable for upholding the rule of law and the rights of all citizens and for ensuring a stable investment climate in which property rights and contracts are respected. The separation of powers and government accountability are incomplete if the judiciary is subordinated to other powers and interests.

Peru's judicial system has been historically weak, and the majority of citizens do not use it to solve their problems. As documented in numerous studies, access to justice is limited by longstanding economic, social, and institutional barriers, including ethnic and gender discrimination, the high cost (direct and indirect) of using the system, extreme delays, and corruption (Bhansali, 2007; Morón and Sanborn, 2007). The judiciary has also been historically subject to external control and manipulation, making it difficult to undertake necessary institutional reforms and give the judiciary greater autonomy. This situation reached a climax in the 1990s, when the executive formally intervened and subordinated the judiciary to its own political agenda.

Since 2001 the judiciary has regained formal autonomy, and some important reforms have been initiated. These include the creation of special commercial courts, increases in the judicial budget and the number of judges, and the introduction of a new penal code in two pilot districts—all measures designed to reduce the excess caseload. Through other, extrajudicial measures, including the awarding of tax stability contracts and the promotion of alternative forms of conflict resolution, those with resources and power are now better able to defend their rights, within the courts or outside them. However, barriers to access remain in place for the majority of citizens—as does political resistance to a broader reform of the system.

Justice in Peru: The Basic Structure

Peru's judicial branch comprises the Supreme Court, superior courts in each of the country's twenty-nine judicial districts, courts of first instance, and justices of the peace. The latter, who account for approximately 76 percent of all judges in the country, are not lawyers or career magistrates but respected community leaders who serve voluntarily and resolve conflicts on the basis of local custom and culture. Their decisions tend to be widely accepted, but they lack the resources to operate effectively in all parts of the country (Bhansali, 2007, p. 791).

The 1993 constitution created several new judicial institutions. The National Judicial Council is charged with monitoring the designation, promotion, and dismissal of judges. To ensure judicial independence, neither the executive nor the legislative branch is represented on the council. A National Judicial Academy is responsible for selecting applicants to judgeships and training judges at all levels. The Tribunal of Constitutional Guarantees is an autonomous organ charged with ruling on the constitutionality of all laws passed. The Public Ministry is responsible for representing society in general and for investigating and prosecuting crimes.

The 1993 constitution also created the Public Defender or Ombudsman as an autonomous position entrusted with the defense and protection of civil rights and oversight of public administration and the provision of public services. Although enjoying broad public legitimacy, the Ombudsman is also politically vulnerable. He or she is elected by Congress, serves a five-year term, and can be dismissed or impeached by a congressional majority. The Ombudsman's office also faces considerable resource limitations that prevent its full presence in all regions.

The Ministry of Justice, which is part of the executive branch, not the judiciary, is charged with defending the interests and rights of the state, advising the executive on legal matters, and overseeing the development and revision of the state's legal framework. The ministry also establishes ad hoc prosecutors when necessary to investigate charges of corruption and abuse of power.

During the 1990s the Fujimori government intervened extensively in the judiciary. After the 1992 "self-coup," the executive disbanded the existing judiciary, dismissed thirteen members of the Supreme Court, named a large number of provisional judges, and formally placed the judiciary under executive control. By 1997, 73 percent of judges had been shifted to provisional status, making them subject to dismissal at any time and hence highly susceptible to political and economic pressures (McMillan and Zoido, 2004, p. 13). Members of the judiciary were coerced, intimidated, and bribed in order to advance the political objectives of the president and his core advisers.

Although Peru's Tribunal of Constitutional Guarantees enjoys broad public legitimacy, it, too, has been politically vulnerable, and it lacks the power to reverse government policies that its counterparts in Brazil and elsewhere enjoy. Congress elects the tribunal's seven members, who serve five-year terms that coincide with those of the president and Congress, may not be immediately reelected, and may be impeached.

Under the interim government of President Valentín Paniagua (2000–01), the Executive Commission in control of the judiciary was deactivated, and another, temporary council was charged with reforming this branch. Anticorruption proceedings were also initiated against leading political and military figures of the 1990s, led by respected special prosecutors named by the executive.

In 2003 judicial reform received a new impetus, led by a Comisión de Reestructuración del Poder Judicial (Ceriajus), and congressional commissions were created to undertake constitutional reform of the system and draft new laws governing judicial careers and public defenders. Yet so far relatively little progress has been made within the judiciary itself toward reducing the main barriers and problems in the system. And according to judicial expert Fernando Eguiguren (2007), reform efforts by Congress have been stalled by disagreement among those who want integral reform of the 1993 constitution, a return to the 1979 constitution, the convocation of a new constituent assembly, or no further reform at all. Hence, although overt executive intervention has been reduced, resource limitations and case backlogs remain severe, many judges and attorneys are poorly qualified, and procedures and technology remain outdated. Incentives for corruption remain great, and experts suggest that it will take considerable time before independent and efficient behavior by the courts can become the norm (Morón and Sanborn, 2007).

Barriers to Access

As emphasized in a recent World Bank report (Bhansali, 2007) and other sources, there are at least three major types of barriers to access to justice in Peru: economic, social, and institutional.

Economic barriers include the official and unofficial costs of judicial services and the resulting systemwide corruption. Costs include the payment of judicial fees and lawyers' fees, the opportunity cost of time involved in litigation, and the cost of bribes for speeding up a case. These costs are especially onerous on the poor and on rural Peruvians generally, who may have to travel and miss work to pursue a case. The scarcity of free legal services exacerbates this situation: according to one recent study, of the 547 lawyers assigned to the justice ministry, only 55 work in the free legal clinics available to needy citizens (Hernandez Breña 2004, cited by Bhansali, 2007, p. 794). The typically long duration of legal proceedings is also a barrier for all users, especially the poor.

Costs are especially high for small and microenterprise owners. Studies show that the costs of litigation are proportionally higher for those with smaller debts, which discourages them from using the system. According to the World Bank report *Doing Business 2005,* it takes 381 days and 35 separate procedures to conclude a commercial contract in Peru. One study cited by Bhansali (2007, p. 794) suggests that if access to justice for small businesses were improved, their economic activity would increase by 25 to 50 percent.

Peru's judiciary is rife with corruption, which is both a cause and an effect of the system's inefficiency, and which undermines the system's legitimacy. According to Transparency International, Peru has one of the highest judicial corruption indexes in the region, and the *perception* of corruption in the judiciary is the highest of all public institutions (Bhansali, 2007, p. 794). Users with the necessary resources can make informal payments to get a case assigned to a specific judge, speed up proceedings, and influence the judge's sentence. Although several specific cases of judicial corruption have been identified by the media and dealt with, those who benefit from the current situation resist proposals for broader anti-corruption reforms.

Social barriers to justice in Peru include language barriers and culture and gender disparities. As with other public services, indigenous people, the rural poor, and especially low-income women lack equal access to the courts. The predominant language in the judicial system is Spanish, and the system is formalistic, complex, and based heavily on written proceedings. Many rural and indigenous Peruvians have an inadequate grasp of Spanish to understand the legal technicalities involved, and have difficulty presenting their cases to lawyers and judges and exercising fully their right to a defense. Efforts to train translators in native languages and to encourage use of such languages in the courts have been limited, as have efforts to incorporate cultural and gender sensitivities into legal and judicial training.

Traditional forms of community justice, although widely respected by the population, remain subordinated to a legal system that is not always appropriate for resolving conflicts. Although the 1993 constitution recognizes special jurisdiction for peasant and indigenous communities, little attention has been paid to its effective and fair implementation (Bhansali, 2007, p. 797). The media frequently cover stories of exasperated community members "taking justice into their own hands" in cases involving robbery, rape, or property disputes.

Gender discrimination and the sexist application of laws are also a serious problem and are aggravated in the case of rural women. The inefficiencies of the system also affect women more, to the extent that they have lower incomes and less education and are less informed about their rights. Men and women in Peru tend to have recourse to the judicial system for different needs, following the roles assigned them by society. Women tend to be plaintiffs in cases related to child support, domestic violence, and the dissolution of marriage. The sheer volume of unresolved cases of this type, the slowness of the proceedings, the lack of prepared judges, and the vulnerability of the system to corruption all take a toll on the women involved. One study shows that 75 percent of demands for child support presented by women in 1998 were still unresolved in 2002 (Bhansali, 2007, p. 798). A recent media report (*El Comercio,* February 16, 2008, p. A2) suggests that a case of domestic violence takes a year or more on average just to get a hearing.

Institutional barriers to access to justice include lack of transparency in the selection of judges and lack of adequate training, resulting in inadequate knowledge of norms and jurisprudence in the material they must resolve. The excessively formalistic and bureaucratic behavior of judges and their often literal and closed interpretation of laws create especially difficult obstacles to the execution of contracts. Many judges are unfamiliar with the fields of law that most affect private economic activity, such as those pertaining to antitrust regulation, banking, insurance, and securities.

The excessive backlog of court cases is another major problem, causing long delays and errors and encouraging corruption. As of June 2007 over 2.2 million cases were pending, including civil and penal cases (and not including the Supreme Court). The largest caseload is in the Superior Court of Lima, and the heaviest backlog of cases is in the administrative area, which includes cases relating to pension benefits. Family courts also have an especially excessive caseload, as do penal courts in the low-income periphery of Lima ("Poder Judicial Emprende Plan de Descarga Procesal, Anuncia Távara," ANDINA, February 14, 2008, citing Távara, 2007). To catch up, each of the country's 1,617 judicial entities would have to resolve 1,376 cases a year—a clearly impossible task.

The precarious, provisional status of most judges is another major problem. Although efforts have been made to formalize judicial hiring through the National Judicial Council and to extend to legal professionals the kind of job stability that an independent judiciary requires, a report in December 2007 claimed that 51 percent of judges and 34 percent of prosecutors still held provisional positions (Villavicencio, 2007). Among them are judges temporarily assigned to cover a vacancy for which they may not be prepared, and judgeships temporarily assigned to lawyers who are not career judges or prosecutors. Although this precariousness is partly the result of efforts to expand coverage and address the backlog of cases, it poses continued problems for judicial independence and leaves judges vulnerable to internal and external pressures

Reform Efforts and Their Limitations

One of the most celebrated recent reforms has been the creation of a set of commercial courts to resolve conflicts facing private business. According to various reports, the initiation of negotiations toward a free trade agreement with the United States underscored the need for improvement in the administration of commercial justice, given the lack of specialization of civil judges in this area as well as the excessive case backlog.

In 2005 a pilot program of seven commercial courts and one superior court began in Lima, as part of a larger program supported by the U.S. Agency for International Development. Civil society organizations initially questioned the credentials of these judges and the lack of transparency in their selection, and it remains unclear whether the judges hired have the skills and experience needed to resolve commercial, banking, and tax controversies involving large sums. Nonetheless, in their first year of operation these courts resolved 80 percent of the 6,437 cases submitted to them, and after two years their superior efficiency and greater transparency were cited by judicial experts and business leaders alike as a model for the rest of the system (Bhansali, 2007, p. 803, reports that they have reduced the duration of commercial proceedings by 70 percent). According to *Doing Business 2007*, this is one of five reforms that have placed Peru among the ten countries that have undertaken the most reforms to facilitate commercial activity ("Firma del TLC Obliga a Estructura una Agenda Interna para su Implementación, opinan," ANDINA, December 25, 2007; "Premio 20007 Buenas Prácticas Gubermentales: Ganadores 2007" [www.ciudadanosaldia.org/premio bpg2007/ ganadores_2007.pdf]). The main limitation so far has been their limited scope, and the challenge now is to expand their number and reach beyond the capital.

Another recent reform, also in the pilot stage, is the introduction of a new penal code that will replace the traditional, inquisitional system with a more agile system with impartial judges and both sides entitled to an equal and separate defense (*Ideele* no. 184, December 2007, pp. 42–43). This system was introduced in the districts of Huaura and La Libertad in 2007, with promising results, and is set to go into effect in Tacna, Moquegua, and Arequipa in 2008. It will not be introduced in Lima until 2013.

In May 2007 the judiciary launched a new National Plan for Caseload Reduction, involving the review and updating of files on existing cases and the creation of 116 new judicial organs in the 29 superior courts, as well as 120 transitory jurisdictional organs. Yet it is widely recognized that creating more temporary courts is not enough. The system also needs to be modernized and endowed with more effective controls.

In 2007 Congress also approved (but the president did not sign) new legislation regulating the judicial career. That same year a respected female judge was named as the new anticorruption czar, but it is not clear what her jurisdiction will be or how this office will interact with other public sector entities.

Meanwhile the majority of citizens remain excluded from the system, and little has been done to extend access to justice more broadly to the poor. The provisional and precarious nature of judgeships exacerbates the other inefficiencies of the system and makes it harder to achieve reform from within. Salaries and working conditions for judges and judicial employees also remain a sore point, as demonstrated in a prolonged strike by judicial workers in late 2007 and early 2008.

Policy Recommendations and Priorities

The need to reduce costs and other inefficiencies in the judicial system is widely recognized, and numerous reform proposals have been debated in recent years. External donors and lenders have also given judicial reform high priority, both in the 1990s (ironically) and since 2001. Proposals on the books range from mechanisms to improve judicial training, increase transparency, and increase sanctions on corruption to further initiatives to reduce caseloads directly by increasing the number of judges and courts.

There has been far less emphasis on efforts aimed at the broader sharing of benefits through reducing costs and increasing access for the low-income population, including individuals and small businesses. Proposals pending in this area include strengthening the justices of the peace and improving coordination between them and other levels of the system; providing better training for the judges and community leaders who exercise these functions; and including language, cultural, and gender understanding as part of that training. There is also an urgent need to install more basic institutions of justice in areas of high poverty, facilitate access to legal assistance and orientation for the most vulnerable, and expand initiatives such as the Centers for Free Legal Advice (Asistencia Legal Gratuita, or ALEGRA), which combine public defenders, legal consultants, and extra judicial conciliation services in one place. Expanding the commercial courts to include other jurisdictions beyond Lima, with judges versed in the needs and rights of small businesses as well as of larger firms, would also be an important step forward. However, in order to move from pilot efforts to broader systemic change, and to shift priorities to the most vulnerable sectors of society rather than the rich and powerful, considerably more political will is required than has been shown so far.

References

Alvarado, Betty, and Eduardo Morón. 2007. "Hacia un Presupuesto por Resultados: Afianzando la Transparencia y la Rendición de Cuentas en el Perú." Universidad del Pacífico.

Bhansali, Lisa L. 2007. "Justicia." In Marcelo M. Guigale, Vicente Fretes-Cibils, and John L. Newman, eds., *Perú: La Oportunidad de un País Diferente.* Washington: World Bank.

Bejar, R., and R. Montero. 2006. "Equidad y Financiamiento de la Educación Superior Universitaria Pública en el Peru: Análisis y Propuesta de Reforma." Universidad del Pacifico.

Benavides, M., and J. Rodríguez. 2006. "Políticas de Educación Básica 2006–2011." CIES, GRADE, Pontificia Universidad Católica del Perú.

Camacho, Luis, and Cynthia Sanborn. 2007. "Desempeño Institucional y Sostenibilidad Democrática: El Impacto de la Provisión Pública de Infraestructura sobre las Percepciones Políticas de la Ciudadanía." Universidad del Pacífico.

Campos, Milagros. 2008. "El Presidente y las Leyes en Camino." *Diario Correo,* February 13.

———. 2007a. "Reformas en el Congreso: La de los Asesores." *Diario Correo,* May 25.

———. 2007b. "El Congreso y las Políticas Públicas." *Diario Correo,* July 18.

Carey, John M. 2003. "Transparency Versus Collective Action: Fujimori's Legacy and the Peruvian Congress." *Comparative Political Studies* 36, no. 9: 983–1006.

Castro, J. F. 2006. "Política Fiscal y Gasto Social en el Perú: Cuánto Se Ha Avanzado y Qué Más Se Puede Hacer para Reducir la Vulnerabilidad de los Hogares." Documento de Discusion CIUP DD/06/05. Lima: Ministerio de Economía y Finanzas and Corporación Andina de Fomento.

Castro, J. F., and G. Yamada. 2006. "Evaluación de Estrategias de Desarrollo para Alcanzar los Objetivos del Milenio en América Latina: El Caso del Perú." Documento de Discusión CIUP DD/06/11. United Nations Development Program, World Bank, and Inter-American Development Bank.

Corrales, J. 2006. "Application of the Framework to Argentina's Reform of Primary and Secondary Education." Center for Global Development.

Cotlear, D., ed. 2006. *Un Nuevo Contrato Social para el Perú. ¿Cómo Lograr un País Más Educado, Saludable y Solidario?* Washington: World Bank.

Crabtree, J. 2006. "Partidos Políticos e Intermediación en el Peru." In *Construir Instituciones: Democracia, Desarrollo y Desigualdad en el Perú desde 1980,* pp. 34–50. Lima: Centro de Investigación de la Universidad del Pacífico and Red para el Desarrollo de las Ciencias Sociales.

Datt, G., and M. Ravallion. 1992. "Growth and Redistribution Components of Changes in Poverty Measures: A Decomposition with Applications to Brazil and India in the 1980s." The Living Standards Measurement Study. Washington: World Bank.

Eguiguren, Francisco. 2007. "Reforma Judicial y Reforma de la Constitución." *Peru21,* February 22.

Frieden, Jeffrey. 2007. "Peru in Latin America: Similarities and Differences, Causes and Effects." In Ricardo Hausmann, Eduardo Morón, and Francisco Rodriguez, eds., *The Peruvian Growth Puzzle.* Harvard University.

Goñi, Edwin, Humberto López, and Luis Servén. 2008. "Fiscal Redistribution and Income Inequality in Latin America." World Bank Policy Research Paper 4487. Washington: World Bank.

Hanushek, E., and L. Wöbmann. 2007. "The Role of Education Quality in Economic Growth." World Bank Policy Research Working Paper 4122. Washington: World Bank.

Hernández Breña, Wilson. 2004. "Implicancias entre la Insuficiencia Económica y la Demanda de Recursos." *Informativo Justicia Viva* no. 17. Lima.

Kakwani, N., and E. Pernia. 2000. "*What Is Pro-poor Growth?*" Manila: Asian Development Bank.

Karl, Terry. 1996. *¿Cuánta Democracia Acepta la Desigualdad?* Lima: Instituto de Estudios Peruanos, Materiales de Política, Cultura y Sociedad.

Keller, L. 2006. "La Ley de Partidos Políticos." Lima: Centro de Investigación de la Universidad del Pacífico.

Kenney, Charles. 2004. *Fujimori's Coup and the Breakdown of Democracy in Latin America.* Notre Dame University Press.

Llosa, Gonzalo, and Ugo Panizza. 2007. "Peru's Great Depression: A Perfect Storm?" In Ricardo Hausmann, Eduardo Morón, and Francisco Rodriguez, eds., *The Peruvian Growth Puzzle.* Harvard University.

Lucas, R. 1988. "On the Mechanics of Economic Development." *Journal of Monetary Economics* 22: 3–42.

McMillan, John, and Pablo Zoido. 2004. "How to Subvert Democracy: Montesinos in Peru." *Journal of Economic Perspectives* 18, no. 4 (Autumn): 69–92.

Mainwaring, S., and T. Scully. 1995. *Building Democratic Institutions.* Stanford University Press.

Ministerio de Educación. 2005. "IV Evaluación Nacional del Rendimiento Estudiantil—2004 Resultados." Lima.

Morón, Eduardo, and María Bernedo. 2007. "La Productividad de la Economía Peruana: 1950–2006." Centro de Investigación de la Universidad del Pacífico.

Morón, Eduardo, and Cynthia Sanborn. 2007. "Los Desafíos del Policymaking en el Perú: Actores, Instituciones y Reglas de Juego." Universidad del Pacífico.

Ortiz de Zevallos, G., H. Eyzaguirre, R. M. Palacios, and P. Pollarolo. 1999. "La Economía Política de las Reformas Institucionales en el Peru: Los Casos de Educación, Salud, y Pensiones." Working Paper R-348. Washington: Inter-American Development Bank.

Payne, M., D. Zovatto, F. Carrillo, et al. 2002. *Democracies in Development.* Washington: Inter-American Development Bank and International Institute for Democracy and Electoral Assistance.

Programa de las Naciones Unidas para el Desarrollo. 2005. *La Democracia en America Latina: Hacía una Democracia de Ciudadanos y Ciudadanas* (democracia.undp.org).

Rici, C. 2006. "Effect of the Electoral Threshold." *Peru Elections 2006* (weblog). University of British Columbia (weblogs.elearning.ubc.ca/peru/archives/025657.php).

Rodríguez, J. 2008. "La Educación Superior en el Perú." Pontificia Universidad Católica del Perú.

Rodrik, Dani. 1997. "Democracy and Economic Performance." Harvard University.

Saavedra, Jaime. 2000. "La Flexibilización del Mercado Laboral." In Roberto Abusada, Fritz DuBois, Eduardo Morón, and José Valderrama, eds., *La Reforma Incompleta.* Lima: Instituto Peruano de Economía y Universidad del Pacífico.

Sanborn, Cynthia. 1991. "The Democratic Left and the Persistence of Populism in Peru: 1975–1990." Ph.D. dissertation, Harvard University.

Sanborn, Cynthia, and Aldo Panfichi. 1996. "Fujimori y las Raíces del Neopopulismo." In Fernando Tuesta, ed., *Los Enigmas del Poder: Fujimori 1990–1996.* Lima: Fundación Friedrich Ebert.

Santiso, Carlos. 2004. "Legislatures and Budget Oversight in Latin America: Strengthening Public Finance Accountability in Emerging Economies." *OECD Journal on Budgeting* 4, no. 2: 47–76.

Santiso, Carlos, with Arturo Garcia Belgrano. 2004. "Politics of Budgeting in Peru: Legislative Budget Oversight and Public Finance Accountability in Presidential Systems." SAIS Working Paper WP/01/04. Johns Hopkins School of Advanced International Studies (January).

Schmidt, G. 2004. "Peru: The Politics of Surprise." Northern Illinois University.

Schmitter, P., and T. Karl. 1995 "¿Qué Es y Qué No Es Democracia?" In R. Grompone, ed., *Instituciones Políticas y Sociedad: Lecturas Introductorias.* Lima: Instituto de Estudios Peruanos.

Sen, Amartya. 1999. "Democracy as an Universal Value." *Journal of Democracy* 10, no. 3: 3–17.

Tanaka, Martín. 1998. "Los Espejismos de la Democracia: El Colapso del Sistema de Partidos en el Perú, 1980–1995, en Perspectiva Comparada." Lima: Instituto de Estudios Peruanos.

———. 2006. "La Reforma Política y el Nuevo Gobierno." *Argumentos* 1, no. 6: 4–6.

Távara, Francisco. 2007. "Los Juzgados Comerciales Registran Corrupción Cero." *El Peruano,* Lima (April 11).

Tuesta, Fernando. 1996. "El Impacto del Sistema Electoral sobre el Sistema Político Peruano." In F. Tuesta, ed., *Los Enigmas del Poder. Fujimori 1990–1996.* Lima: Fundación Friedrich Ebert.

———. 2005. *Representación Política: Las Reglas También Cuentan. Sistemas Electorales y Partidos Políticos.* Lima: Fundación Friedrich Ebert and Pontificia Universidad Católica del Perú.

Tuesta, Fernando, and Tatiana Mendieta. 2007. "Hecha la Ley ¿Hecha la Trampa?: Una Evaluación del Financiamiento de los Partidos Políticos." *Derecho-PUCP, Revista de la Facultad de Derecho de la Pontificia Universidad Católica del Perú* no. 59.

Ugarte, Mayen. 2000. "La Reforma del Estado: Alcances y Perspectivas." In Roberto Abusada, Fritz DuBois, Eduardo Morón, and José Valderrama, eds., *La Reforma Incompleta.* Lima: Instituto Peruano de Economía and Universidad del Pacífico.

Villavicencio, Alfredo. 2007a. "Reforma de la Justicia: Como el Ir y Venir de las Olas del Mar." *Ideele* no. 184 (December), p. 27.

———. 2007b. "Magistratura: Pocos Titulares y Muchos Precarios.", *Ideele* no. 184 (December), p. 28–29.

Webb, R., and S. Valencia. 2006. "Recursos Humanos." In M. Giugale, V. Fretes Cibilis, and J. Newman, eds., *Peru: La Oportunidad de un País Diferente.* Washington: World Bank.

Yamada, G., and J. F. Castro. 2007. "Poverty, Inequality and Social Policies in Perú: As Poor As It Gets." Documento de Discusion CIUP DD/07/06. Corporación Andina de Fomento and Harvard University Center for International Development.

Yamada, G., J. F. Castro, A. Beltrán, and M. De Cárdenas. 2007. "Educational Attainment, Growth and Poverty Reduction within the MDG Framework: Simulations and Costing for the Peruvian Case." PMMA Working Paper 2008–05. Quebec: Poverty and Economic Policy Research Network.

Contributors

REGIS BONELLI
ECOSTRAT Consultants and *Institute
  of Applied Economic Research*
Brazil

MAURICIO CÁRDENAS
Brookings Institution
United States

ARMANDO CASTELAR PINHEIRO
Institute of Applied Economic Research
Brazil

JUAN FRANCISCO CASTRO
Universidad del Pacifico
Peru

IRENE CLAVIJO
Fedesarrollo
Colombia

JORGE CORNICK
Eureka Comunicación and *Autoridad
  Reguladora de los Servicios Públicos*
Costa Rica

JAVIER CORRALES
Amherst College

SAMUEL DE ABREU PESSÔA
Getulio Vargas Foundation
Brazil

JOSÉ DE GREGORIO
Central Bank of Chile

AUGUSTO DE LA TORRE
World Bank

GERARDO ESQUIVEL
El Colegio de Mexico

FAUSTO HERNÁNDEZ-TRILLO
Centro de Investigación y Docencia
Económicas
Mexico

SIMON JOHNSON
Sloan School of Management,
Massachusetts Institute of
Technology

EDUARDO LORA
Inter-American Development Bank

EDUARDO MORÓN
Universidad del Pacífico
Peru

CARMEN PAGÉS
Inter-American Development Bank

LILIANA ROJAS-SUAREZ
Center for Global Development

NATALIA SALAZAR
Fedesarrollo
Colombia

CYNTHIA SANBORN
Universidad del Pacífico
Peru

ERNESTO STEIN
Inter-American Development Bank

ROBERTO STEINER
Fedesarrollo
Colombia

ALBERTO TREJOS
Instituto Centroamericano de
    Administración de Empresas
Costa Rica

KURT WEYLAND
University of Texas at Austin

JEROMIN ZETTELMEYER
International Monetary Fund

ABOUT THE EDITOR

LILIANA ROJAS-SUAREZ is a senior fellow at the Center for Global Development and chair of the Latin American Shadow Financial Regulatory Committee. She has previously served as managing director and chief economist for Latin America at Deutsche Bank and as the principal advisor in the Office of Chief Economist at the Inter-American Development Bank. From 1984 to 1994, she held various positions at the International Monetary Fund, most recently as deputy chief of the Capital Markets and Financial Studies Division of the Research Department. Rojas-Suarez has published widely in the areas of macroeconomic policy, international economics, and financial markets.

Index